thomson.com

changing the way the world learns

To get extra value from this book for no additional cost, go to:

http://www.thomson.com/wadsworth.html

thomson.com is the World Wide Web site for Wadsworth/ITP and is your direct source to dozens of on-line resources. *thomson.com* helps you find out about supplements, experiment with demonstration software, search for a job, and send e-mail to many of our authors. You can even preview new publications and exciting new technologies.

thomson.com: *It's where you'll find us in the future.*

Sense and Nonsense
about Crime
and Drugs

A Policy Guide

Fourth Edition

SAMUEL WALKER

University of Nebraska at Omaha

West/Wadsworth Publishing Company

I(T)P® An International Thomson Publishing Company

Belmont, CA • Albany, NY • Bonn • Boston • Cincinnati • Detroit • Johannesburg • London • Madrid
Melbourne • Mexico City • New York • Paris • San Francisco • Singapore • Tokyo • Toronto • Washington

Criminal Justice Editor: Sabra Horne
Assistant Editor: Claire Masson
Editorial Assistant: Jeff Kellner
Marketing Manager: Mike Dew
Senior Project Coordinator: Debby Kramer
Production: Merrill Peterson/Matrix Productions
Print Buyer: Karen Hunt
Permissions Editor: Peggy Meehan
Copy Editor: Laura Larson
Cartoonist: Steve Kline
Cover Designer: Sandra Kelch
Compositor: Thompson Type
Printer: Maple-Vail Book Manufacturing/Vail-Ballou
Cover Printer: Phoenix Color Corp

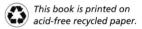
Printed in the United States of America
1 2 3 4 5 6 7 8 9 10

For more information, contact Wadsworth Publishing Company, 10 Davis Drive, Belmont, CA
94002, or electronically at http://www.thomson.com/wadsworth.html

International Thomson Publishing Europe
Berkshire House 168-173
High Holborn
London, WC1V 7AA, England

Thomas Nelson Australia
102 Dodds Street
South Melbourne 3205
Victoria, Australia

Nelson Canada
1120 Birchmount Road
Scarborough, Ontario
Canada M1K 5G4

International Thomson Publishing GmbH
Königswinterer Strasse 418
53227 Bonn, Germany

International Thomson Editores
Campos Eliseos 385, Piso 7
Col. Polanco
11560 México D.F. México

International Thomson Publishing Asia
221 Henderson Road
#05-10 Henderson Building
Singapore 0315

International Thomson Publishing Japan
Hirakawacho Kyowa Building, 3F
2-2-1 Hirakawacho
Chiyoda-ku, Tokyo 102, Japan

International Thomson Publishing
Southern Africa
Building 18, Constantia Park
240 Old Pretoria Road
Halfway House, 1685 South Africa

Library of Congress Cataloging-in-Publication Data

Walker, Samuel
    Sense and nonsense about crime and drugs : a policy guide / Samuel Walker — 4th ed.
    p.   cm. — (Contemporary issues in crime and justice series)
    Includes bibliographical references and index.
    ISBN   0-534-50867-7
    1. Criminal justice, Administration of—United States.   2. Crime prevention—United States.
3. Drug abuse and crime—United States.   4. Narcotics, Control of—United States.   I. Title.
II. Series.
HV9950.W35   1997
364.4'056'0973—dc21   97-28134

Contents

IV   REFORM: THE LIBERAL PRESCRIPTION   201

11   TREAT 'EM!   203

List of Propositions

1. Most current crime control proposals are nonsense.
2. Waging "war" is the wrong way to fight crime.
3. Both liberals and conservatives are guilty of peddling nonsense about crime.
4. Most crime control proposals rest on faith rather than on facts.
5. Most crime control ideas are based on false assumptions about how the criminal justice system works.
6. Adding more police officers will not reduce crime.
7. Limited and clearly focused police activities, directed toward specific problems, may be successful in reducing certain kinds of crime and disorder.
8. Faster response time will not produce more arrests or lower the crime rate.
9. More detective, or other changes in detective work, will not raise clearance rates or lower the crime rate.
10. Repeal or modification of the exclusionary rule will not help the police reduce serious crime.
11. Repeal or modification of the *Miranda* warning will not result in more convictions.
12. The death penalty does not deter crime.
13. Enforcement crackdowns will not deter drunk driving.
14. Deterrence-oriented policies that rely exclusively on the criminal justice system will not reduce crime.

15. Preventive detention is not a realistic strategy for reducing serious crime.
16. Speedy trials can reduce pretrial crime while preserving constitutional rights.
17. Selective incapacitation is not a realistic policy for reducing serious crime.
18. Gross incapacitation is not an effective strategy for reducing serious crime.
19. Mandatory sentencing is not an effective means of reducing serious crime.
20. "Three strikes and you're out laws" are a terrible crime policy.
21. Career criminal prosecution programs do not produce either higher conviction rates or lower crime rates.
22. Abolishing or limiting the insanity defense will have no impact on serious crime.
23. Abolishing plea bargaining will not reduce serious crime.
24. Limiting habeas corpus appeals of criminal convictions will have no effect on serious crime.
25. With the possible exception of domestic violence shelters, social service programs for crime victims will not reduce serious crime.
26. Victim recontact programs will not reduce crime.
27. Victim compensation programs may help crime victims but will not reduce serious crime.
28. Victim impact statements will not reduce serious crime.
29. Laws intended to get tough on crime will not help crime victims and may instead damage the justice system.
30. Attempts to ban all handguns, or certain kinds of guns, or bullets will not reduce serious crime.
31. Attempts to deny ownership of handguns to certain "bad" people are not likely to either limit ownership or reduce serious crime.
32. Bartley-Fox laws restricting the unauthorized carrying of handguns, if vigorously implemented, may help reduce gun violence.
33. Focused, proactive police programs to remove illegal guns from the streets may prove to be an effective way to reduce serious crime.
34. Trying to get tough on gun crimes, especially through mandatory sentences, will not reduce gun-related violence.
35. Diversion programs do not reduce serious crime.
36. Probation is an appropriate sanction for many offenders. Increased use of probation, however, is not likely to reduce serious crime.
37. Intensive probation supervision is not likely to reduce serious crime.
38. Intensive probation, electronic monitoring, boot camps, and other recent innovations will not reduce serious crime.
39. Changing or abolishing parole will not reduce serious crime.
40. Forms of restorative justice may prove to be an appropriate response to minor crimes by first-time offenders but are not likely to be an effective means of reducing serious crime.
41. Decriminalizing drunkenness, abortion, sex between consenting adults,

and gambling will have no impact on serious crime.

42. Eliminating discrimination from the system will result in a fairer system of justice but will not reduce crime.

43. Police crackdowns will not reduce drug use or serious crime associated with drugs.

44. Drug interdiction and eradication efforts are doomed to fail.

45. Tougher sentencing is not likely to reduce illegal drug use or crime associated with drugs.

46. No evidence indicates that drug education, including DARE, significantly reduces illegal drug use.

47. Drug treatment serves the needs of individuals who have decided to end their drug use. But treatment, as a primary strategy, will not reduce the nation's drug problem.

48. Legalization is a high-risk gamble that needs further discussion.

Foreword

E ver wonder why we seem to make so little progress in dealing with the
problem of crime? Sure enough, the latest statistics show that crime is
down nationally, especially so in some of our largest cities. Murder rates
are way down. This is very good news, of course, but some social scientists
warn that this is a mere respite in a long-term upward trend. Others warn that
we better watch out for "superpredators" who are beginning to arrive at the
crime-prone years. Whether or not you agree with them, it is undeniable that
America's crime rates, especially violent crime rates, are very high. Why do
we seem so incapable of dealing with crime?

The answer to this question is both complicated and simple. It is complicated in that some of our most cherished beliefs about crime and punishment
in the United States are incorrect. They are based upon bad evidence, wrong
facts, or just plain myths. The answer to our incompetence in the matter of
crime is also simple: we keep taking approaches that are non-sensical. These
are the profound and important conclusions of Professor Samuel Walker, presented in carefully documented and fascinatingly cogent detail in the chapters
of this, the fourth edition of *Sense and Nonsense about Crime and Drugs: A Policy
Guide.*

I am pleased to introduce this edition as the newest entry in Wadsworth's
Contemporary Issues in Crime and Justice Series. In many respects, this book
is a prototype of the purposes of this series. We seek to discuss topics that are
neglected by standard textbooks and to provide a more detailed treatment of
new and emerging issues in justice studies. Our aim is to help the student of

crime and justice have a richer and deeper understanding of the critical topics our authors present.

In this addition to the books in the series, Professor Walker ably provides a comprehensive review of the broad and varied approaches we now take to deal with crime. His suggestions are stunning. Most of what we now do about crime is mistaken—based upon false assumptions or repeating policy mistakes that research has demonstrated in the past to be ineffectual. One of the remarkable aspects of this book is the way in which it exposes the emptiness of ideological strategies about crime. "Get tough" strategies, fondly embraced by political conservatives, are not likely to get us very far, according to the evidence Walker presents. Yet the traditional liberal strategies of gun control, rehabilitation, and drug decriminalization are also not very promising as solutions to crime, either. In fact, it hardly matters what your politics are; in this remarkable book, Walker gives everyone something to think about and provides even-handed challenges to just about anyone's preconceived ideas about crime. The fact is, he argues, that there is not that much in the way of proven programs that can be done about criminal behavior.

It is not to say that "nothing works." To the contrary, sprinkled in among the seemingly endless list of policy failures is the hopeful review of programs that have worked and strategies that promise to work even better. Ironically, these strategies often have little ideological "purity." They work because they are based on what we know about crime and criminals. Walker makes the point that the search for effective crime policy is not a matter of ideology, but a matter of solid policy research, realistic expectations, and most of all, dealing with the social problems that lead to crime such as poverty, inequality, and family breakdown. The sad truth is that there is little the criminal justice system can do about these problems other than make them worse.

The fourth edition of this important book begins with the "good" news, that crime appears to be going down. It then analyzes this trend by uncovering its significance—does it mean we are finally getting smart about crime and developing good policies? Has the combination of community policing and get-tough punishment finally started to pay off? The answer, says, Walker, is "No."

The details about why our crime policy is so flawed—and about how the most recent evidence about current programs confirms the point made in earlier editions—is a compelling and disquieting narrative that is one of the most important books ever published for classroom use on crime and justice. I commend it to you, the student, in the hopes it will help you become wiser and more sophisticated as an advocate for change in criminal justice policy.

Todd Clear, Series Editor

Preface

The world continues to change. Nothing stands still. And so it is with the subject of crime in the United States. Extraordinary changes have occurred just since publication of the third edition of *Sense and Nonsense About Crime* in 1994—to say nothing of the changes since the first edition in the mid-1980s.

Beginning around 1992, the crime rate in the United States began to decline. It appears that this is not an aberration. Crime has been falling steadily for several years, and with particularly significant reductions in big cities such as New York. Something positive is happening with respect to crime in this country.

As I explain in Chapter 14, this situation presents us with a serious paradox. The basic argument of this book, from the first edition to the present one, is that popular crime control policies do not work. As the title of this book expresses it, they are nonsense. This is true for putting more police on the street, locking up more offenders, and implementing drug treatment and education programs. Yet, if they do not work, then how do we explain the reduction in crime? This is a serious question that demands an answer.

The purpose of this book is to explore the first half of that paradox: the ineffectiveness of most crime control policies. The first edition was written primarily as a response to the conservative crime control agenda that dominated public policy at the time. This conservative agenda stressed crime control through tougher law enforcement policies, including exciting new policy initiatives using the concepts of incapacitation, deterrence, and programs targeting career criminals. The book examined these proposals in light of what was then known about the administration of criminal justice. In the interests of fairness, I subjected liberal crime control policies to the same critical scrutiny. I found them equally lacking in empirical support.

By the time of the third edition, the wheel of the policy debate had changed in one significant respect. The conservative/liberal dichotomy that provided the framework for the first two editions was no longer as clearly defined as it was originally. Basically, the liberal perspective had collapsed, and most politicians who defined themselves as liberals had adopted most of the traditional conservative policy agenda: more police, more imprisonment, and so on. Meanwhile, some prominent conservatives had embraced the idea of legalizing drugs, a traditional liberal proposal. In short, the world of criminal justice policy has become more complex than it was when the first edition of this book appeared.

Finally, the state of knowledge about crime and criminal justice continues to advance. We know far more about what works and what does not than we did fifteen years ago when this book was originally conceived. I have attempted to incorporate this new knowledge with each edition. One consequence of the advancing state of knowledge is that many issues that once seemed simple are now ambiguous. With the advent of community policing, for example, it is no longer possible to say that police efforts have no effect on the communities they serve. The exact nature of those effects and their durability over time are matters of controversy, but we cannot simply declare that nothing works. Similarly, it is not necessarily true that all forms of mandatory sentencing are evaded by courtroom work groups. It appears that some mandatory provisions are not fully implemented, but many are.

The administration of justice is extremely complex. In this book I have attempted to capture some of this complexity while at the same time providing students with a clear sense of the general patterns of the administration of justice.

ACKNOWLEDGMENTS

This fourth edition represents a substantial revision of my understanding of crime and the administration of justice. I would like to give special acknowledgment to my colleagues in the Department of Criminal Justice at the University of Nebraska at Omaha for the atmosphere of collegiality that we have maintained. Whenever I have a question on a particular issue, I can always walk down the hall, engage someone in a conversation, and come away with a new insight or at least some useful suggestions on where I should look for the information I need.

I would also like to thank Steve Kline for his cartoons giving this edition a fresh look.

For their suggestions for revisions, based on the third edition, the publisher thanks: Allen Barrett, CSU Los Angeles; Paul Campbell, Wayne State College; Robert Hughes, University of Colorado, Colorado Springs; Steve Norland, University of Hartford; Gary Potter, Eastern Kentucky University; and Ralph Weisheit, Illinois State University.

Samuel Walker

PART I

❖

Thinking Clearly
About Crime

1

Crime and Policy:
A Complex Problem

"VICTORY" OR "TICKING TIME BOMB"?

Two sets of headlines in 1996 dramatized the complex problem of crime and crime policy in American society. One proclaimed "victory" in the war on crime. The other warned of a "ticking time bomb" of young people about to reach the high-crime teenage years.

The January 15, 1996, cover of *Time* magazine announced with great excitement, "Finally, We're Winning the War Against Crime."[1] The cover pictured William Bratton, then-commissioner of the New York City Police, who claimed that his "zero-tolerance" anticrime policies had produced a dramatic reduction in crime in that city. Murder was down 25 percent. Over a two-year period, the total number of reported felonies was down 27 percent.

Other cities reported similar good news. Murders were down 32 percent in Seattle between 1994 and 1995, 21 percent in San Diego, and 14 percent in New Orleans. Although there were a few exceptions (murders went up 56 percent in Minneapolis, for example), the overall trend was very encouraging. Further reductions were reported for 1996.

Other headlines, however, told a different and more ominous story. The murder rate among teenagers aged fourteen to seventeen rose 22 percent between 1990 and 1994, whereas the rate among adults twenty-five and over dropped 25 percent (Figure 1.1). Guns, moreover, played an increasing role in juvenile murders compared with adult homicides.[2]

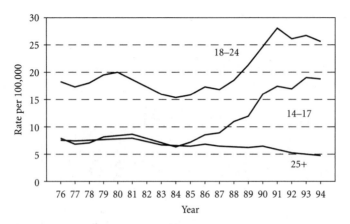

FIGURE 1.1 Homicide offending rate by age.

SOURCE: James Alan Fox, *Trends in Juvenile Violence* (Washington, D.C.: Bureau of Justice Statistics, 1996).

The future could be even worse. Because of changing birth rates, we may be facing a "ticking time bomb" of violent juvenile crime. The number of people between the ages of fourteen and seventeen is projected to grow by 20 percent between 1995 and 2005. Criminologist James Alan Fox argues, "There are actually two crime trends in America—one for the young, one for the mature—which are moving in opposite directions."[3]

THE SEARCH FOR ANSWERS

The conflicting headlines of 1996 dramatize the complex relationship between crime and crime policy. What caused the decline in serious crime in New York and other cities? Was it Commissioner Bratton's "zero-tolerance" policy? Or was it part of a general decline reflecting, as some criminologists believe, demographic trends and changes in the nature of drug markets? Some believe that the huge increase in the prison population has incapacitated many criminals and deterred others. Criminologist Lawrence W. Sherman, however, says that "it is very hard to say with any certainty" what caused this change. Michael Smith of the Vera Institute believes that it is may be a broader "cultural trend which is difficult to define."[4]

What has caused the upsurge in juvenile murder? The collapse of the family? And if so, what is responsible for that? A decline in the values of work and self-restraint, as many conservatives believe? Or is it the erosion of the economy of the inner cities? Is policing too tough, or not tough enough? Does our welfare system encourage a lack of personal responsibility, as conservatives argue, or does it contribute to family breakdown because it is so inadequate by European standards, as liberals argue?

These are difficult questions. Much controversy and conflicting evidence surround all of them. This book attempts to sort through the controversy by looking at the arguments and evidence. This book is about crime policy. It is a search for sensible answers to an urgent question: What can we do about serious crime? Our inquiry focuses on figuring out *what works.* Our agenda here is to review some of the major crime control proposals and evaluate their effectiveness in light of what we know about crime and justice.

Simplistic Solutions

One of the major obstacles in the search for sensible crime policies is the fact that there are many bad ideas. The crime problem has been so serious for so long that people grasp at any proposal that seems to offer a quick solution. Politicians readily oblige them, offering simplistic solutions that promise dramatic results. Over the last thirty years, we have had a series of "wars on crime," each one promising "victory."

One of the most popular new anticrime measures is the so-called "three-strikes" law, providing mandatory life prison sentences to persons convicted of a third felony. Most criminologists are horrified by the potential consequences of three-strikes laws, but their criticisms have not influenced public attitudes. In 1993 and 1994 alone, fifteen states passed some kind of three-strikes laws, and another twenty-two were considering them.[5]

New Jersey enacted the so-called "Megan's law" that required officials to notify local communities that a convicted sexual offender was relocating to their neighborhood.[6] Some politicians have proposed sending the military into Washington. State police were sent to help patrol both Camden, New Jersey, and Gary, Indiana, in 1995 because of the crime problem.[7]

Are these laws and policies likely to reduce crime? If they are not, then what does work? This book is a search for sensible and effective crime policies.

It is primarily an exercise in clear thinking. We will look carefully at the available evidence and expose the *nonsense* about crime and crime policy and identify crime policies that make *sense* because they are likely to reduce crime.

We will frame our discussion in terms of a series of propositions. Our first proposition is this:

PROPOSITION 1
Most current crime control proposals are nonsense.

UNDERSTANDING THE CRIME
PROBLEM IN THE UNITED STATES

Two Crime Problems

Crime in the United States is surrounded by myths. Public fear and concern about crime has been high for thirty years. Yet, during much of that period, serious crime has been decreasing. The National Criminal Victimization Survey (NCVS) data indicate that the victimization rate for personal crimes declined 26 percent between 1973 and 1992, robbery fell by 12 percent, and burglary dropped by 47 percent (Figure 1.2).[8]

Despite these declines, however, people do not feel safe. Gallup Polls in 1994, 1995, and 1996 consistently found that people regarded crime as "the most important problem facing the country." In other words, people still felt that crime was increasing despite the fact that it had been falling.[9]

A lot depends on who you are, however. The victimization rate for robbery in 1994 was 4.8 per 1,000 for white Americans and 14.0 for African Americans. The burglary rate was 78.6 per 1,000 for the poorest Americans (income of less than $7,500), compared with 40.9 for the wealthiest (income of $75,000 or more).[10]

Very poor neighborhoods have been overwhelmed by crime and drugs. For their residents, who some analysts call the "underclass," the quality of daily life is far worse than it ever was.[11] In many of these neighborhoods, the drug trade has almost completely taken over the streets, with open drug use and selling. One block in Brooklyn was described as an open "drug bazaar," where drugs occupied "the entire life of [the] neighborhood." Despite a steady stream of arrests, one police officer conceded that "the whole neighborhood is into it." Between May and August 1992, the police made 626 felony arrests for selling and 303 misdemeanor arrests for buying, and they issued 7,160 summons for other violations. The crackdown had no impact on the drug trade. The cop admitted that for every person arrested, "there is always a replacement."[12]

Four measures of violent crime

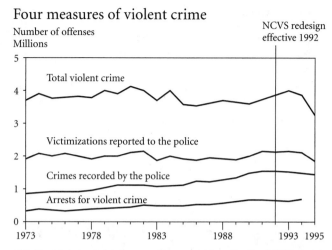

Note: The violent crimes included are rape, robbery, aggravated assault, and homicide. The vertical line at 1992 indicates that because of changes made to the victimization survey, data prior to 1992 are adjusted to make them comparable to data collected under the redesigned methodology. Data for 1995 are preliminary estimates.

Figure 1.2 Victimization rates, 1973–1992.

SOURCE: Bureau of Justice Statistics, *Highlights from 20 Years of Surveying Crime Victims* (Washington, D.C.: Government Printing Office, 1993).

What the Murder Data Tell

The data on homicide in the United States provide additional evidence about our two crime problems. The number of murders has fluctuated over the years. After peaking at 21,860 in 1980, it fell to 16,689 in 1984, rose to a new record of 26,250 in 1992, and then began dropping steadily, to 21,597 in 1995.[13] Aggregate data, however, obscure the very uneven distribution of murder in the United States. While the overall murder rate in 1992 was 10 per 100,000, it was 9.1 for white males and 67.5 for African American males. For white females it was only 2.8 but 13.1 for African American women.[14]

A map published by *Newsweek* dramatized the geographic aspect of our two crime problems. It indicated that virtually all of the murders in the city occurred in the poor African-American neighborhoods on the east side. Only a handful took place in the predominantly white Northwest sector. The risk of murder for a young African American male in D.C. was 1 in 400, compared with 1 in 7,000 for young white males—or 17.5 times greater![15]

Many observers believe that the drug crack, which arrived around 1985, had a particularly devastating effect on low-income neighborhoods and is responsible for the changing trends in murder. In Washington, D.C., the number of murders fell from 223 in 1981 to 147 in 1985, a 34 percent drop. Then, in an abrupt reversal, they soared to 482 in 1991. Other cities experienced similar declines and rises. Many observers attribute this pattern to drug gang wars battling for control of the local market.

Fear Versus Risk

The gap between public fear of crime and the real risk of victimization was dramatized by the celebrated Bernard Goetz case in 1984. Goetz, who is white, shot and wounded four young black men who he claimed tried to rob him of $5 in the New York City subway. The shooting generated enormous publicity. Some people saw him as a hero, the "subway vigilante" who finally did something about crime. This reaction revealed deep fear about crime on the New York subways. Yet, when Dennis Kenney tried to evaluate the impact of the Guardian Angels on crime in the subways, he found it impossible to do because the actual level of crime was so low. Only 9 of the 1,422 murders in 1984 occurred in the subways.[16] In short, the subways are actually relatively safe, but the environment (underground, dark, dirty, sleeping homeless people) evokes great fear.

The Goetz case also exposed the racial dimension of fear of crime. For many white Americans, the word *crime* means black crime. These fears were exploited in the 1988 presidential election campaign when Republican candidate George Bush ran a sensational television ad about Willie Horton, an African American imprisoned for murder, who raped a white woman while on release under a weekend furlough program. Yet, the failure rate of prisoners released on furloughs is very low. A 1990 survey found that in Florida only 31 of 96,745 released on furloughs "failed" in any way.[17] Moreover, about 90 percent of all rapes occur between people of the same race. In short, the Willie Horton advertisement presented a distorted picture of both the effectiveness of furlough programs and the racial aspects of violent crime.[18]

Two Drug Problems

Just as James Alan Fox believes that we have two crime problems, so Elliott Currie argues that we have two drug problems: one involving the majority of the population and the other concentrated in the inner cities.[19] The National Household Survey data indicates that use of illicit drugs dropped by more than half between 1979 and 1995, from 14.1 percent of the population to 5.8 percent. The decline in cocaine use was even greater.[20]

During the 1996 presidential election campaign, Republican candidate Bob Dole made a major issue of the fact that marijuana use among teenagers had doubled between 1992 and 1995. This increase, however, occurred in the context of a long, twenty-year decline and was limited to teenagers. Among older Americans, the steady downward trend continued.

Currie, however, argues that the National Household Survey fails to adequately assess some important components of the drug problem. Given the methodology, it is likely to undercount those people who are most at risk for serious drug abuse: adults who do not have stable employment or residence. Currie believes that the Drug Abuse Warning Network (DAWN) data provide a glimpse into the other part of the national drug problem.[21]

The DAWN survey uses data on hospital emergency room admissions in urban areas (489 hospitals participated in 1995). "Drug-related episodes" rose by 65 percent between 1978 and 1995. Cocaine-related episodes quadrupled between 1985 and 1989, declined for one year, and then increased significantly from 1991 to 1995.[22] Heroin-related episodes have also increased.

The DAWN data are supplemented by the data on AIDS. The fastest growing HIV-positive group in recent years has been very poor racial and ethnic minorities in the inner cities who contract the disease through needle drug use and/or through unprotected sex with people who are infected. In short, although drug use among the general population is down, serious drug *abuse* is up among the very poor, and among minorities in particular.[23]

As we search for sensible crime policies, we need to keep in mind which crime problem and which drug problem we are talking about. Many proposed policies are unrelated to the most serious parts of the crime problem. Some policies are justified in the name of serious crime but in practice affect less serious crimes.

The National Criminal Justice Commission, a private group that includes many leading criminologists, argues that the war on crime has been a case of "bait and switch."[24] (The term comes from the area of consumer fraud, where a retailer advertises a low-priced item and then claims that it is sold out and tries to sell a higher-priced item). According to the commission, the war on crime has promised to attack *violent* crime but has mainly resulted in the imprisonment of more *nonviolent* offenders. In California, for example, 73 percent of the increase in the prison population between 1980 and 1993 involved persons convicted of nonviolent crimes. As we examine different crime policies in the chapters ahead, we want to make sure that they have an impact on their intended target.

Crime Trends: Unraveling the Controversy

Much of the controversy over crime trends is due to the conflicting sources of data. We have two basic sources, and in large part because of their different methodologies, they present different pictures of the crime problem.

As we have already indicated, the National Crime Victimization Survey (NCVS) reports that serious crime has been declining for about twenty years (Figure 1.2). The FBI's Uniform Crime Reports (UCR) indicate a very different trend, however, with violent crime increasing 53 percent between 1975 and 1993.[25]

Which set of data are we to believe? In this book we will rely primarily on the NCVS. The UCR suffer from a number of serious problems. First, nearly two-thirds of all crimes (64 percent in 1994) are not reported to the police.[26] Second, the UCR system is not independently audited, and problems persist with how local police departments handle crime data. Police officers "unfound" many crimes, even though citizens claim they occurred.[27] Significant variations also arise in how departments record arrests.[28] For all of these reasons, the NCVS provides a more accurate estimate of crime in the United States, particularly with respect to crime trends.

THE WAR ON CRIME

The most important development in criminal justice over the past twenty-five years has been the so-called "war on crime." The number of people in prison has quintupled, from 196,429 in 1970 to 1.1 million by mid-1996. As a matter of national policy, the United States has been on an imprisonment orgy. The last twenty years represents a radical break with past policy. The incarceration rate went from 96 per 100,000 in 1970 to 350 per 100,000 in 1993. This compares with incarceration rates of 111 per 100,000 in Canada, 79 in Australia, and 42 in Japan (see Figure 1.3).[29]

The prisons are only part of the story. The national jail population more than doubled, rising from 153,394 in 1979 to 490,442 by 1994. The number of people on probation grew from 1,079,258 adults in 1976 to 2,811,611 in 1993, and the number of adults on parole soared from 156,194 to 671,470 in the same period. Thus, the total number of people "under correctional supervision" by the 1990s was about five million![30]

The imprisonment boom is the product of several forces. National attitudes about crime and criminals have become increasingly punitive, particularly with respect to drugs. These attitudes have been translated into laws and policies that include more drug arrests, more prison sentences for drug convictions, and longer prison sentences. The Clark Foundation report *Americans Behind Bars* concludes that "much of the growth in prison population has resulted from a doubling of the number of arrests for drug law violations and a tripling of the rate of incarceration for arrested drug offenders.[31] Mandatory minimum sentencing laws have resulted in more offenders going to prison and for longer terms.

The impact of the war on crime is one of the main themes of this book. What has this enormous increase in punitiveness done to American society? Has it contributed to the recent reduction in crime rates? Or has it made things worse and affected the upsurge in juvenile violence?

Conservatives such as John J. DiIulio and the Council on Crime in America argue that a punitive policy is necessary, morally justified, and (if used properly) effective. As the council puts it, prison is "socially beneficial and cost-effective." They believe that the recent decline in the crime rate is proof that punishment works and that if we are to deal effectively with the "ticking time bomb" of young offenders that lies in the immediate future, we need to be even tougher than we have been for the past twenty years.[32]

The War on Crime and the
African American Community

Other observers disagree. Elliott Currie, Jerome Miller, the Sentencing Project, the Clark Foundation, and the National Criminal Justice Commission believe that the war on crime has made things worse: that it has not deterred crime, that it is racially biased, and that it has contributed to the destruction of

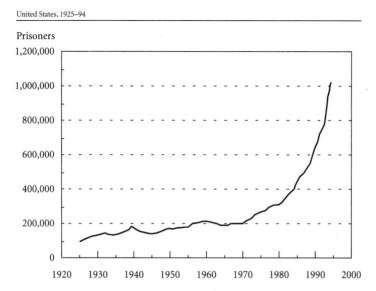

United States, 1925–94

Figure 1.3 Sentenced prisoners in state and federal institutions on December 31.

SOURCE: Bureau of Justice Statistics, *Sourcebook of Criminal Justice Statistics—1995* (Washington, D.C.: Government Printing Office, 1996), p. 554.

inner-city communities, and as a consequence it has increased the likelihood of juvenile violence.

Currie and others argue that the war on drugs has been waged primarily against young black men. Data compiled by the Sentencing Project support his contention (Figure 1.4). African Americans represent 13 percent of the population, 15 percent of all illicit drug users (according to the National Household survey), but 35 percent of all people arrested for drug offenses, 55 percent of those convicted, and 74 percent of those sentenced to prison for drug offenses.[33]

Jerome Miller characterizes the war on crime as a case of "search and destroy" directed at young African American men.[34] The National Center on Institutions and Alternatives, which he founded, estimates that on any given day, 42 percent of the young black men (ages eighteen to thirty-five) in Washington, D.C., are under the control of the justice system: either in prison or jail or on probation or parole. The figure for Baltimore was 56 percent. About 75 percent of the Washington black men were likely to be arrested before they reach age thirty-five.[35] A study by the California legislature painted a similar picture: one-sixth of the African American men over the age of sixteen are arrested every year. Many of these arrests are for drug offenses. Yet, the same study found that 92 percent of African American men arrested for drugs were subsequently released for lack of evidence. For whites the figure was only 64 percent.[36]

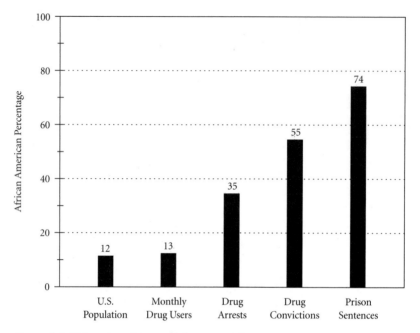

Figure 1.4 African Americans and drug possession.

SOURCE: Marc Mauer and Tracy Huling, *Young Black Americans and the Criminal Justice System: Five Years Later* (Washington, D.C.: The Sentencing Project, 1995), p. 12.

In short, a huge number of African American men are acquiring arrest records and experience the humiliation of arrest unnecessarily. By 1990, more black men were in prison than in college.

The disparate impact of the war on crime has had a profound impact on attitudes toward the justice system. One survey found that 80 percent of whites believed that O. J. Simpson was guilty of murdering his ex-wife Nicole Brown Simpson and her friend Ronald Goldman. But 80 percent of African Americans thought he was innocent.[37] The war on crime has contributed to deep distrust of the justice system among minorities.

Overloading the System

The war on crime has also overloaded the criminal justice system so that in some instances it cannot perform some of its basic functions. In Philadelphia, the police commissioner described the criminal courts as being "on the verge of collapse." The massive increase in arrests created a backlog of 12,129 cases, with the result many more defendants failed to make their scheduled court dates. The number of defendants who did not appear soared from 13,807 in January 1987 to a whopping 32,880 by July 1990. The system was incapable of tracking them down and bringing them into court. Law professor Gerald Caplan described it as "a kind of amnesty for some criminals."[38]

"Getting tough" has actually backfired in many states. As prisons become overcrowded, correctional officials are forced to release many offenders earlier than they normally would just to make room for the new arrivals. The percentage of sentences served in Texas dropped from about 30 to 35 percent during 1977–1980 to approximately 20 percent in 1990.[39] In Florida the average time served was cut in half—from 2 to 0.9 years—as a result of tougher sentencing practices, overcrowding, and early releases.[40] This process undermines the original intent of the tough sentencing law—to reduce crime through deterrence and incapacitation.[41]

A very basic lesson is apparent here. The justice system can only handle so much business. It does not "collapse" like a building. It keeps on going, but only through adjustments that are often undesirable. We will discuss these adjustments in more detail in Chapter 3.

Finally, the enormous costs of the war on crime has drained tax dollars from other social services, such as education, public health services, and the maintenance of the economic infrastructure of roads and bridges.[42] In California, for example, state expenditures for corrections were only half the amount spent on higher education in the early 1980s; by 1994, they were equal, at $3.8 billion. Prison budgets had risen dramatically, whereas the state colleges and universities had suffered drastic cuts.[43] If education has historically been an investment in the future of society, then the cuts in education to finance prison represent a *dis*investment in the future.

CRIME POLICY: A PLAGUE OF NONSENSE

Americans have trouble thinking clearly about crime. The result is a lot of crime control proposals that are nonsense. Why? What is the problem?

The main reason is that our society is overwhelmed by violent crime. Despite the substantial decline in recent years, we still have far more violent crime than any other industrialized country. We murder each other eight to twelve times as often as do people in Europe or Japan. In 1990 the American murder rate was 9.4 per 100,000, compared with only 1.3 for England and Wales. The American robbery rate was 257 per 100,000 but only 55 in West Germany and 47 in Ireland.[44]

The American crime problem is actually a problem of *violent* crime—murder and robbery, in particular. In a careful review of comparative crime rates, James Lynch points out that property crime rates in other industrialized countries are similar to, and in some cases higher than, those in the United States. The types of robbery also differ. Far more American robberies involve the use of a firearm. In this respect, they are more serious and instill more fear in their victims.[45]

Citing these data, James Q. Wilson joins James Alan Fox in arguing that we really have two crime problems in America.[46] Wilson sees a problem of property crime, in which the United States is not that different from other countries, and violent crime, in which we are very different. Elliott Currie, meanwhile, sees two distinct drug problems.

Crime pervades our daily lives like a plague, affecting the way we think, the way we act, the way we respond to one another. Fear of crime has a corrosive effect on interpersonal relations, making us wary of small acts of friendliness toward strangers. It distorts the political process, with politicians offering quick-fix solutions that offer no realistic hope of reducing crime. Fear and frustration about crime produce irrational thinking. Almost every year some new idea promises to reduce crime by 30 percent or 50 percent.

Even some of the most informed experts on criminal justice are overwhelmed by the problem. When Jerome Miller first sent the manuscript of his book *Search and Destroy* to the publisher, his editor wrote back that it was "too pessimistic," with no optimistic recommendations on how to solve the crime problem. Miller admitted that his editor was right; he did not "have many suggestions—and those I do have, aren't likely to be taken."[47] Many other people have had the same problem: an inability to formulate sensible, realistic proposals for reducing crime.

New examples of desperate, irrational proposals seem to appear almost every month. Chicago Alderman Edward Smith wanted to send the National Guard into his district, the Twenty-eighth Ward, because of the drug and crime problem. As someone explained to *Newsweek* magazine, "We need drastic measures."[48] But as William Geller pointed out, National Guard troops do not have arrest power, they are not trained as police officers (including training in criminal law, criminal procedure, and human relations), and they are not accountable to either the mayor or the city council.[49] And do we really want a permanent military occupation of our cities? The dollar cost would be matched by the cost to democracy.

Our response to the crime problem resembles the way many people deal with being overweight—by "binging." Just as people go on crash diets, lose weight, put it all back on, and then take up another diet fad a year later, so we tend to "binge" on crime control fads. Yesterday it was "selective incapacitation." Today it is "three strikes." And so it goes. Typically, everyone forgets yesterday's fad, without examining whether it really worked.

We need to make an important distinction on this issue. Many sensible proposals have been made for reducing the *harm* done by the criminal justice system. The Sentencing Project, the Edna McConnell Clark Foundation, and the National Criminal Justice Commission have all made proposals for reducing the harm done by our current sentencing practices. In *Malign Neglect,* Michael Tonry offers a specific proposal for reducing racial disparities in sentencing.[50] When we carefully look at these proposals, however, it is not clear that they will reduce *crime,* particularly serious crime. *Harm* reduction is one thing; *crime* reduction is something else.

The Futility of Waging "War" on Crime

Americans also love to declare "war" on crime. In the past thirty years we have had at least four wars on crime and three separate wars on drugs. President Lyndon Johnson declared the first war on crime in 1965. President Richard Nixon announced his war in 1969. President George Bush declared yet another war on drugs on September 5, 1989.[51]

War is the wrong way to think about crime for several reasons. It raises unrealistic expectations, promising a "victory." The effective control of crime, however, will not come quickly or easily. A final victory in the military sense will never be achieved. There will always be some crime. A sensible goal is to get it down to some tolerable level.[52]

The war metaphor is also wrong because it suggests that we are fighting a foreign enemy. The "us versus them" attitude encourages police officers to think that suspects do not have the rights of American citizens. Community policing, which emphasizes close working relations between police and citizens, is a far more appropriate approach for a democratic society. Finally, as we have already seen, the current war on crime has had a terrible effect on American society, particularly racial and ethnic minority communities.

This leads us to the following proposition:

> ## PROPOSITION 2
> ### Waging "war" is the wrong way to fight crime.

The truth is, we are not facing a foreign enemy. We are up against ourselves. We need to deal with our own social institutions, our own values, our own habits, and our own crime control policies. The weight loss problem offers a useful comparison. The solution does not lie in a miracle cure. Instead, it involves difficult long-term changes in your own behavior: eating less, eating less fattening food, and exercising more. By the same token, we will reduce crime when we make basic changes in all of our social policies that affect families, employment, and neighborhoods. There is no quick easy "miracle" cure for crime.

Traffic fatalities offer a good illustration of this point. Deaths went down in the 1980s. Some people think it was the result of the national crusade against drunk driving, which included tougher enforcement and mandatory sentences for convicted drunk drivers. Yet, as we will see in Chapter 6, the traffic fatality *rate* has been declining steadily since the 1920s.[53] This long-term trend is probably the result of a number of factors: safer cars, better roads, better driver education, the introduction of seat belts, and so on.[54] The criminal law, including tougher penalties, may have played some role in this process, but it is only part of the story.

In our search for sensible crime policies, we want to be on guard against people who claim too much for any single crime policy.

THE GROUND RULES

Our goal is to identify sensible and effective crime policies. Let us begin by establishing the ground rules for our inquiry. First, we will focus on crime control. We are concerned with policies that will reduce the level of serious crime. We will consider questions of justice and fairness as a basic constraint on crime policy. Effectiveness—defined as reduction in crime—is not the only criterion for a sensible crime control policy. We have limits to what we can do. A democratic society respects the rule of law and standards of justice and fairness, unlike totalitarian societies, which are based on the principle of un-limited government power. It might reduce crime if we just shot all robbers and drug dealers on sight. When an Islamic rebel group took power in Kabul, the capital of Afghanistan in 1996, it restored punishments such as stoning to death people guilty of adultery and cutting off the hands of thieves. One crim-inal was driven through the streets on a truck with an amputated hand and heavy weights holding his jaw open. Such practices, however, violate our stan-dards of decency and due process.

Second, we will focus primarily on the crimes of robbery and burglary. This limited focus helps impose discipline on our thinking. Too many people evade the hard questions about crime by changing the subject. Liberals often find it difficult to talk about robbery and burglary, changing the subject to victimless crimes such as gambling, marijuana use, and unconventional sexual behavior. Conservatives focus on celebrated cases (particularly mass murders or extremely vicious crimes) that have little to do with the routine felonies of robbery and burglary. We will discuss the celebrated case phenomenon in Chapter 2.

At several points along the way, we will consider other crimes to illustrate certain points. An entire section is devoted to drunk driving because this subject provides very useful insights into such issues as police crackdowns, sentencing reform, and deterrence. Domestic violence also illustrates some issues related to deterrence. Chapter 13 covers drugs, because it is impossible to talk about crime policy today without addressing the drug issue.

Third, this book concentrates on crimes committed by adults. Juvenile crime and delinquency are serious problems that warrant attention, but the world of juvenile justice is a special realm that deserves a separate critical inquiry.

The Question of Reasonable Goals

Our search for sensible and effective crime policies raises a difficult question of criteria. What do we mean by *effective*? Let us say we find a policy that would reduce crime by 5 percent without doing any serious harm. Is that a goal worth pursuing? A 5 percent reduction is not much, given the size of our crime problem. We would still be swamped by murder, robbery, rape, and drug abuse. It would be easy to dismiss that policy as hardly worth the effort.

The issue here is one of reasonable goals. In his discussion of gun crimes, Gary Kleck makes a persuasive case in favor of modest goals. We should not expect quick and dramatic changes. This creates unreasonable expectations and leads to disappointment and frustration. Kleck advises thinking in terms of modest goals that can be achieved.[55] In the long run, a sensible approach to crime will probably include a series of different policies, each one focusing on a different aspect of the larger problem, and each one producing a modest reduction in crime.

GUILTY: LIBERALS AND CONSERVATIVES

Nonsense about crime is politically nonpartisan. Over the years, both liberals and conservatives have been guilty of making extravagant promises about crime reduction. In 1967, the President's Crime Commission, representing a liberal perspective, promised "a significant reduction in crime" if its recommendations were "vigorously pursued."[56] In 1975, the conservative James Q. Wilson offered a program that he claimed would reduce serious crime by 30 percent.[57] The 1994 Violent Crime Control Act, supported by both liberals and conservatives, promises great reductions in crime. None of these promises are realistic. Consequently, my third proposition is as follows:

PROPOSITION 3
Both liberals and conservatives are guilty of peddling nonsense about crime.

Crime policies are guided by certain underlying assumptions. Liberals and conservatives begin with different assumptions about crime, the administration of justice, and human nature. To make sense of different crime control proposals, it is helpful to analyze the underlying assumptions of each side.

CRIME CONTROL THEOLOGY

A serious problem with the debate over crime policy is that faith usually triumphs over facts. Both liberals and conservatives begin with certain assumptions that are almost like religious beliefs. Too often, these assumptions are not supported by empirical evidence. We call this phenomenon *crime control theology.*[58]

Most conservatives, for example, believe the death penalty deters crime. This view persists despite the fact that no evidence conclusively supports it. Most liberals, meanwhile, believe that "treatment" works as a cure for crime and drug abuse. This opinion persists despite considerable evidence on the limited effectiveness of treatment programs.

In *Point Blank,* Gary Kleck points out how people switch sides on the deterrence question to suit their beliefs. Conservatives believe that the death penalty deters crime but then argue that the exclusionary rule will not deter police misconduct. Liberals switch sides in the opposite direction, arguing that the death penalty does not deter crime but that the exclusionary rule does work.[59]

Consequently, our next proposition is this:

PROPOSITION 4
Most crime control proposals rest on faith rather than on facts.

Conservative Theology

Crime control theologies represent idealized worlds that express people's highest hopes and deepest fears. Conservative crime control theology envisions a world of discipline and self-control in which people exercise self-restraint and subordinate their personal passions to the common good. It is a world of limits and clear rules about human behavior.

The problem, according to conservatives, is that criminals lack self-control. They succumb to their passions and break the rules. They kill because they cannot control their anger. They steal because they want something now and are unable to defer gratification. For conservatives, poverty is no excuse for crime. People remain poor because they lack the self-discipline to get an education, find a job, and steadily try to improve themselves.

Free will, rational choice, and moral responsibility reign supreme in conservative crime control theology. People are responsible for their own fate; they *choose* to commit crime. James Q. Wilson and Richard J. Herrnstein argue, "At any given moment, a person can choose between committing a crime and not committing it."[60] A good example of a policy based on rational choice theory is the "Just say no!" antidrug campaign. It assumes that we just have to persuade people to make the decision not to use drugs.

Rational choice theory holds that people weigh the relative risks and rewards of committing crime. If the risk of punishment is low or the punishments are relatively light, more people will tend to commit crime. If the chance of being caught and punished is high and the punishments are relatively severe, fewer people will choose to commit crime. Thus, the certainty and severity of punishment directly affects the crime rate.[61]

In conservative crime control theology, punishment has both a moral and a practical element. Because criminals choose to offend, they deserve punishment. They are morally responsible for their actions. Rules are the basis of a civil society, and rule breaking should be punished. This is called "retribution" or "desert." James Q. Wilson summed it up in a frequently quoted statement: "Wicked people exist. Nothing avails except to set them apart from innocent people."[62] Conservatives also believe that punishment shapes future behavior through the process of *deterrence*. Specific deterrence is directed at the individual offender, teaching him or her that bad actions have unpleasant consequences. General deterrence is directed at the general population, teaching by example.

Conservatives are somewhat contradictory about the role of government in controlling crime. James Q. Wilson and other conservatives attack liberal social welfare programs, arguing that government has little ability to affect human behavior and solve social programs. They argue that job training and family assistance programs have failed to eliminate poverty and that correctional treatment programs have not rehabilitated criminals.[63]

At the same time, however, conservatives clearly believe that *some* government programs shape human behavior and solve social problems. Their ideas about increasing the certainty and severity of prison sentences rest on the assumption that a change in government policy (in this case criminal sentencing) will affect people's behavior. As we will see shortly, liberals are also contradictory about the relationship among government policies, human behavior, and crime.

Underlying conservative crime control theology is an idealized image of the patriarchal family. Punishment resembles parental discipline. Minor misbehavior is greeted with a gentle warning, a second misstep earns a sterner reprimand, and serious wrongdoing receives a severe punishment. The point is to teach the wisdom of correct behavior by handing out progressively harsher sanctions and threatening even more unpleasant punishment if the behavior continues.

The real world of crime and justice, unfortunately, does not work like the family. It is filled with some very incorrigible children. Some are so deeply alienated from society that they do not respect the overall structure of authority. Punishment, in fact, may only distance them further. Some observers believe, for example, that arrest and imprisonment are such common experiences in some poor minority neighborhoods that they have lost whatever deterrent threat they might have once had.

John Braithwaite's provocative book *Crime, Shame, and Reintegration* offers a useful perspective on this problem. He describes the process of "reintegrative shaming" as being very much like the way a family handles someone who breaks the rules. But his theory also clearly indicates that informal sanctions work when close social bonds link the sanctioner and the sanctioned, where no great differences in values exist in the community—that is, when the relationship more closely resembles a family.[64]

This is the heart of the problem. The family analogy breaks down in the real world, because we have a highly fragmented society, characterized by great differences in wealth, race, religion, and lifestyles. Our society is anything but a tight-knit community with shared values. Braithewaite's theory, in fact, is a good explanation of why informal, family-style sanctions do not work in our society. His description of the conditions under which a system of reintegrative shaming can work is actually a very accurate description of a seventeenth-century New England village, where that approach to crime control was used very effectively.[65]

Conservatives explain the failure of punishment to work by focusing on problems in the criminal justice system. Punishment is not certain or severe enough. Too many loopholes allow criminals to beat the system: the exclusionary rule, the Miranda warning, the insanity defense, plea bargaining, and so on. The idea that many criminals "beat the system" and "get off easy" is an article of faith in conservative crime control theology. Close these loopholes, ensure certainty of punishment, and we can reduce crime. Longer prison terms and the death penalty, meanwhile, will increase the deterrent effect and reduce crime. We will take a close look at this idea several of the chapters ahead.

Liberal Crime Control Theology

Liberal crime control theology views crime in a social context. Criminal behavior is largely the result of social influences such as the family, the peer group, the neighborhood, economic opportunities, and discrimination.

Liberal crime policy seeks to alter these influences. Rehabilitation programs, for example, are designed to provide a structured set of influences that will shape the offender's behavior in a positive direction. Liberals favor community-based alternatives to imprisonment because they represent a healthier environment than prison. Supervised probation and parole are designed to provide positive external influences. Basic education and vocational training programs, meanwhile, are designed to equip the offender for success in life.

Liberals are as guilty of wishful thinking as are conservatives. A fundamental article of faith in liberal crime control theology is the belief that people's behavior can be reshaped through some kind of formal treatment program. The history of prison and correctional reform is the story of a continuing search for the Holy Grail of rehabilitation: a program that will truly reform offenders. The people who invented the prison in the nineteenth century thought it would do the job.[66] When it had obviously failed, reformers invented parole and the indeterminate sentence, advertising them as the magic keys to rehabilitation. When they did not solve the problem of crime, reformers came up with new variations (group counseling, intensive supervision, and so forth). None of these programs ever demonstrated that they were consistently effective.

If conservatives refuse to face the facts about the failure of punishment, liberals refuse to look at the sad history of the failure of rehabilitation. Faith continues to survive in the face of repeated failure.

It is also an article of faith among liberals that the United States is the most punitive country in the world. We do in fact lock up more people than any other country. Our current incarceration rate of 350 per 100,000 leads the world. James Lynch's research offers a valuable comparative perspective on this figure. Using arrests as a baseline, he notes that the probabilities of an offender going to prison are only slightly different in the United States, Canada, England, and West Germany. Our sentences, however, are much longer primarily because we have more serious crime than these other countries.[67]

If conservatives believe that most of our problems are the result of loopholes that let too many people off easy, liberals are guilty of blaming everything on overly harsh punishments.

Liberals are ambivalent on the question of individual responsibility. Although they emphasize the importance of social conditions in causing crime and reject the conservative preoccupation with individual responsibility, they cannot completely ignore the role of individual choice. Rehabilitation programs, in fact, are designed to influence individuals to make different (and better) choices. In the realm of the public policy debate, however, liberals tend to downplay the element of individual responsibility.

A Word About Rules

One way to distinguish between conservatives and liberals with respect to crime policy is their attitude toward *rules.* Everyone believes in rules and their application in a consistent fashion. This is what people mean when they refer to the "rule of law."

Conservatives and liberals mainly disagree over which set of rules to emphasize. In criminal justice, we have two basic sets: criminal law and criminal procedure. The substantive criminal law is a set of rules governing everyone's behavior. It defines certain behavior as criminal and specifies the penalty for breaking the rules. Criminal procedure, on the other hand, is a set of rules governing criminal justice officials. It tells them what they may not do (conduct unreasonable searches and seizures) and what they must do (bring the suspect before a magistrate without unnecessary delay).[68]

Conservatives emphasize the rules of the criminal law. Harming a person or taking someone else's property violates the basic standards of a decent society. Anyone who violates these rules should be punished. Liberals tend to emphasize the rules of criminal procedure. A free society is one that strictly limits the potentially awesome power of government officials.

One way to understand the difference between liberal and conservative attitudes toward rules is to recognize what each side sees as its worst nightmare. For conservatives, unchecked criminality leads to anarchy and the death of freedom. For liberals, unchecked government power leads to tyranny and the death of freedom. The difference is really a question of what represents the greatest threat to freedom.

Both sides are ambivalent about rule breaking. Conservatives tend to be willing to excuse violations of the rules of procedure to control crime. They will overlook the unreasonable search if it helps convict a criminal. Liberals, on the other hand, are more concerned about official rule breaking. They are willing to see a criminal suspect go free if a police officer or some other official has made a serious mistake. These differences are not absolute, of course. They are really matters of emphasis. Conservatives do not endorse gross abuses by the police, and liberals do not endorse crime.

The classic statement of the difference between conservatives and liberals on this issue is Herbert Packer's essay on the "two models of the criminal process."[69] Conservatives embrace the *crime control model,* which puts a high priority on the effective control of crime. To this end, they are willing to grant officials considerable leeway, not restricting them with a lot of rules. Liberals prefer the *due process model,* in which the highest priorities are fair treatment and the presumption of innocence. Formal rules (due process guarantees) are designed to achieve these goals.

Ideological Confusion: Switching Sides

The conservative/liberal dichotomy is a useful way to think about crime policy. It helps identify the basic assumptions that underlie different policies. In the last few years, however, this dichotomy is not quite as sharp as it was a few years ago. Strange things have been happening. Some conservatives have adopted traditional liberal policies, and many liberals have embraced traditional conservative ideas. Understanding the crime debate today requires sorting our way through this ideological confusion.

One major change involves the issue of legalizing drugs. Decriminalization has traditionally been a liberal proposal. They have argued that we should not criminalize behavior that does not harm others. Moreover, criminalizing a lot of behavior often tends to make things worse, by overloading the criminal justice system, encouraging corruption, and failing to respond effectively to what are really social and medical problems.

Surprisingly, many prominent conservatives endorse legalizing drugs. The most prominent is the writer and television talk show host William F. Buckley. We will examine the arguments in favor of drug legalization in Chapter 13. For the moment, it is important to note that some conservatives have switched sides and adopted a traditional liberal position.

Meanwhile, many liberals have adopted some conservative crime control proposals. The best example is President Bill Clinton. The 1994 Violent Crime Control Act, which he supported, calls for more police and longer prison sentences. In the 1996 presidential election campaign, political observers said that Clinton had moved to the right and embraced the traditional Republican position on crime.

In short, the ideological lineup on crime control policies has become very muddled. Nonetheless, it is still possible to identify a set of crime policies that, because of their underlying assumptions, can be classified as conservative and another set that can be classified as liberal. These categories will help us analyze the different policies we will consider in this book.

CONCLUSION

Crime is a serious problem in the United States, without doubt. Unfortunately, we do not have many good ideas about how to solve the crime problem. In this initial chapter, we have tried to sketch out some of the complexity of the U.S. crime problem. We have also indicated briefly why so many crime control policies are worthless. In the chapters that follow, we will develop these themes in more detail. The next two chapters take a closer look at how the criminal justice system actually works. Then we will turn our attention to specific crime control proposals. As we already indicated, our basic goal is to find some crime control policies that make sense, that are supported by persuasive evidence.

NOTES

1. "Finally, We're Winning the War Against Crime: Here's Why," *Time* (January 15, 1996).

2. James Alan Fox, *Trends in Juvenile Violence* (Washington, D.C.: Government Printing Office, 1996).

3. Ibid., "Executive Summary."

4. Quotes from Clifford Krauss, "Murder Rate Plunges in New York City," *New York Times* (July 8, 1995), pp. 1, 16.

5. Michael G. Turner, Jody L. Sundt, Brandon K. Applegate, and Francis T. Cullen, "'Three Strikes and You're Out' Legislation: A National Assessment," *Federal Probation* 59 (September 1995): 16–35.

6. Alexander D. Brooks, "Megan's Law: Constitutionality and Policy," *Criminal Justice Ethics* (Winter/Spring 1996): 56–66.

7. "Indiana's State Troopers Arrive to Help in Violence-Plagued Gary," *New York Times* (October 3, 1995), p. 22; Jennifer Preston, "New Jersey Troopers Return to Camden," *New York Times* (December 13, 1995), p. A13.

8. Bureau of Justice Statistics, *Criminal Victimization 1992* (Washington, D.C.: Government Printing Office, 1993).

9. Bureau of Justice Statistics, *Sourcebook of Criminal Justice Statistics—1995* (Washington, D.C.: Government Printing Office, 1996), p. 128.

10. Bureau of Justice Statistics, *Criminal Victimization 1994* (Washington, D.C.: Government Printing Office, 1996).

11. Elliott Currie, *Reckoning: Drugs, The Cities, and the American Future* (New York: Hill & Wang, 1992).

12. Mary B. Tabor, "The World of a Drug Bazaar," *New York Times* (October 1, 1992), pp. 1, 20; Mary B. Tabor, "Neighborhood Ruled by Drug Culture," *New York Times* (October 2, 1992), p. 18.

13. Federal Bureau of Investigation, *Crime in the United States* (Washington, D.C.: Government Printing Office, annual).

14. Bureau of the Census, *Statistical Abstract of the United States, 1995* (Washington, D.C.: Government Printing Office, 1995), p. 202.

15. "Murder Wave in the Capital," *Newsweek* (March 13, 1989), p. 17.

16. Dennis Jay Kenney, *Crime, Fear, and the New York Subways* (New York: Praeger, 1988).

17. Bureau of Justice Statistics, *Sourcebook of Criminal Justice Statistics—1991* (Washington, D.C.: Government Printing Office, 1992), p. 130.

18. David C. Anderson, *Crime and the Politics of Hysteria* (New York: Times Books, 1995).

19. Elliott Currie, *Reckoning*.

20. Department of Health and Human Services, *Preliminary Estimates From the 1995 National Household Survey on Drug Abuse,* Advance Report 18 (Washington, D.C.: Government Printing Office, 1996).

21. Currie, *Reckoning*.

22. Department of Health and Human Services, *Preliminary Estimates from the Drug Abuse Warning Network,* Advance Report 17 (Washington, D.C.: Government Printing Office, August 1996).

23. Bureau of the Census, *Statistical Abstract of the United States 1995,* p. 97.

24. Steven R. Donziger, ed., *The Real War on Crime: The Report of The National Criminal Justice Commission* (New York: HarperCollins, 1996), pp. 18–19.

25. Bureau of Justice Statistics, *Sourcebook of Criminal Justice Statistics—1994,* p. 305.

26. Bureau of Justice Statistics, *Criminal Victimization 1994.*

27. Donald Black, "The Production of Crime Rates," *The Manners and Customs of the Police* (New York: Academic Press, 1980), pp. 65–84.

28. Lawrence W. Sherman and Brian Glick, *The Quality of Police Arrest Statistics* (Washington, D.C.: The Police Foundation, 1984).

29. Marc Mauer, *Americans Behind Bars: One Year Later* (Washington, D.C.: Government Printing Office, 1992).

30. Bureau of Justice Statistics, *Sourcebook of Criminal Justice Statistics—1995,* pp. 544, 548, 594.

31. Edna McConnell Clark Foundation, *Americans Behind Bars* (New York: Edna McConnell Clark Foundation, 1994), p. 8.

32. Council on Crime in America, *The State of Violent Crime in America* (Washington, D.C.: Council on Crime in America, 1996).

33. Marc Mauer and Tracy Huling, *Young Black Americans and the Criminal Justice System: Five Years Later* (Washington, D.C.: The Sentencing Project, 1995).

34. Jerome G. Miller, *Search and Destroy: African American Males in the Criminal Justice System* (New York: Cambridge University Press, 1996).

35. National Center on Institutions and Alternatives, *Hobbling a Generation: African American Males in the District of Columbia's Criminal Justice System* (Alexandria, VA: National Center on Institutions and Alternatives, 1992); Miller, *Search and Destroy,* p. 7.

36. Miller, *Search and Destroy,* p. 8.

37. Donziger, ed., *The Real War on Crime,* pp. 169–170.

38. Michael de Courcy Hinds, "Philadelphia Justice System Overwhelmed," *New York Times* (August 15, 1990), pp. 1, 13.

39. Sheldon Ekland-Olson, "Crime and Incarceration: Some Comparative Findings from the 1980s," *Crime and Delinquency* 38 (July 1992): 392–416.

40. National Council on Crime and Delinquency, *The Consequences of Escalating the Use of Imprisonment: The Case of Florida* (San Francisco: NCCD, 1991).

41. The issue of the average time served is not completely clear. Currie argues that prison terms have declined: Currie, *Reckoning,* pp. 15–17. The decline appears to have been especially dramatic in Florida. National data are in Bureau of Justice Statistics, *Time Served in Prisons* (Washington, D.C.: Government Printing Office, 1984); Bureau of Justice Statistics, *National Corrections Reporting Program, 1988* (Washington, D.C.: Government Printing Office, 1992).

42. Edna McConnell Clark Foundation, *Americans Behind Bars.*

43. Vincent Schiraldi, "Corrections and Higher Ed Compete," *Overcrowded Times* (June 1994), p. 7; Stephen Gottfredson, "Fighting Crime at the Expense of College," *Chronicle of Higher Education* (January 20, 1995).

44. Ineke Haen Marshall, "How Exceptional Is the United States? Crime Trends in Europe and the US," *European Journal on Criminal Policy and Research* 4(2): 7–35.

45. James Lynch, "Crime in International Perspective," in James Q. Wilson and Joan Petersilia, eds., *Crime* (San Francisco: ICS Press, 1995), pp. 11–38.

46. James Q. Wilson, "Crime and Public Policy," in Wilson and Petersilia, eds., *Crime,* pp. 489–507.

47. Miller, *Search and Destroy,* p. 235.

48. "We Need Drastic Measures," *Newsweek* (March 13, 1989).

49. William Geller, "A Crime-Ridden Ward's Cry for Help," *Chicago Tribune* (May 16, 1990).

50. Michael Tonry, *Malign Neglect* (New York: Oxford University Press, 1995).

51. On the history of "wars" on crime, see Samuel Walker, *Popular Justice: A History of American Criminal Justice,* 2d ed. (New York: Oxford University Press, 1998).

52. Egon Bittner, "The Police and the 'War on Crime,'" in *The Functions of the Police in Modern Society* (Washington, D.C.: Government Printing Office, 1970), pp. 48–51.

53. National Safety Council, *Accident Facts 1992* (Washington, D.C.: National Safety Council, 1992), pp. 72–73.

54. James B. Jacobs, *Drunk Driving: An American Dilemma* (Chicago: University of Chicago Press, 1989).

55. Gary Kleck, *Point Blank: Guns and Violence in America* (New York: Aldine de Gruyter, 1991), pp. 432–433.

56. President's Commission on Law Enforcement and Administration of Justice, *The Challenge of Crime in a Free Society* (Washington, D.C.: Government Printing Office, 1967), p. vi.

57. James Q. Wilson, *Thinking About Crime* (New York: Basic Books, 1975).

58. George C. Thomas and David Edelman, "An Evaluation of Conservative Crime Control Theology," *Notre Dame Law Review* 63(2) (1988): 123–160.

59. Kleck, *Point Blank,* pp. 7, 13.

60. James Q. Wilson and Richard J. Herrnstein, *Crime and Human Nature: The Definitive Study of the Causes of Crime* (New York: Simon & Schuster, 1985), p. 44.

61. But everyone should read the article Wilson coauthored: James Q. Wilson and Allen Abrahamse, "Does Crime Pay?" *Justice Quarterly* 9 (September 1992): 359–377.

62. Wilson, *Thinking About Crime* [1975 ed.], p. 209.

63. Wilson, *Thinking About Crime*; Wilson and Herrnstein, *Crime and Human Nature.*

64. John Braithwaite, *Crime, Shame, and Reintegration* (New York: Cambridge University Press, 1989).

65. Lawrence M. Friedman, *Crime and Punishment in American History* (New York: Basic Books, 1993); Walker, *Popular Justice,* Chapter 1.

66. David Rothman, *The Discovery of the Asylum* (Boston: Little, Brown, 1971).

67. Lynch, "Crime in International Perspective."

68. On the subject of rules and discretion, see Samuel Walker, *Taming the System: The Control of Discretion in American Criminal Justice, 1950–1990* (New York: Oxford University Press, 1993).

69. Herbert L. Packer, "Two Models of the Criminal Process," in *The Limits of the Criminal Sanction* (Stanford, CA: Stanford University Press, 1968), Chapter 8.

2

Models of
Criminal Justice

The triumph of faith over facts requires a willful disregard of the realities of crime and criminal justice. Many people believe what they want to believe about how the justice system works. This problem is partly due to the fact the American criminal justice system is so complex. We actually have fifty-one separate criminal justice systems (fifty states plus the federal system). They include 17,358 separate state and local law enforcement agencies.[1] To get a sense of the bewildering variety of just the formal structure of different court systems, take a look at the Bureau of Justice Statistics (BJS) report *State Court Organization 1980*.[2] Both the criminal codes and the rules of criminal procedure vary in all of these systems.

The day-to-day administration of justice is even more complex than the formal machinery of the justice system. To the casual observer, things often seem chaotic. Many important decisions are made in informal, "low-visibility" settings, such as the hushed conference in front of the judge and the negotiated plea of guilty. Even many experts are mystified by some of the important features of our criminal justice system. We have only fairly recently begun to probe the hidden realms of police discretion and plea bargaining. There is a great controversy over the nature and extent of race discrimination in the system.[3] In this context, misunderstanding and myth prevail. Consequently, our next proposition is as follows:

PROPOSITION 5

Most crime control ideas are based on false assumptions about how the criminal justice system works.

Two attitudes dominate public thinking about the administration of criminal justice: the Old Idealism and the New Cynicism. Neither is very helpful in explaining how the system works.

The Old Idealism is the civics-book picture of justice; diligent and hardworking officials enforce the law as it is written in the statutes; a person who commits a crime is duly arrested and prosecuted for that offense; if convicted, he or she receives the prescribed punishment. It is an adversarial system of justice that determines the truth of guilt or innocence through a public contest between prosecution and defense, overseen by an impartial judge. Although inspiring, this version of the criminal process does not describe the reality of our justice system.

The New Cynicism is a mirror image of the Old Idealism. It portrays a chaotic criminal justice system in which there is neither law, order, nor justice. Police discretion is completely out of control, with officers arresting whomever they want. Prosecutors plea bargain wildly. Some guilty people get off, while others are railroaded into prison. Defense attorneys are in league with prosecutors, cutting deals to suit each other's needs.[4] Sentencing reflects the biases of judges. Parole boards grant or deny release without rational or scientific basis for their decisions.[5]

The New Cynicism comes in two versions. Conservative cynics see irrational decision making undermining effective crime control. Criminals are not punished for their crimes: either they are not arrested, they get their charges dropped, or they obtain early parole release. Crafty defense lawyers manipulate the rules of criminal procedure to beat the system. Liberal cynics, on the other hand, believe that the apparent chaos of the system produces systematic discrimination. The poor are punished while "respectable" offenders get off easy; African Americans and Hispanic Americans are the victims of systematic discrimination.

A major part of the challenge facing us is to find the truth about the justice system. It is undeniable that much criminal justice decision making *is* irrational. Many offenders *do* escape punishment: the risk of even being arrested for drunk driving, for example, is extremely low. There *is* racial discrimination in the system: the black person who murders a white person is far more likely to be sentenced to death than the white person who murders a black person.

But neither version of the New Cynicism adequately explains how the justice system handles most cases on a day-to-day basis. This is what we want to focus on. As we will explain in more detail later, our view is that some fairly consistent and predictable patterns are apparent in the administration of justice. Donald Black found predictable patterns in police arrest discretion.[6] One major study of plea bargaining found that about 80 percent of the

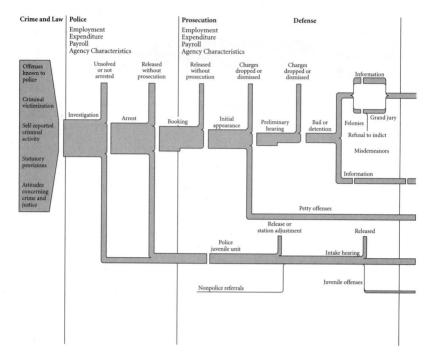

FIGURE 2.1 The Crime Commission's model of the criminal justice system.

SOURCE: President's Commission on Law Enforcement and Administration of Justice, *Task Force Report: Science and Technology* (Washington, D.C.: Government Printing Office, 1967), pp. 58–59.

outcomes were predictable if you knew the offense and the defendant's prior record.[7]

The problem is that the justice system is filled with paradoxes and inconsistencies. There is much truth in the comment that "[t]he problem is not that our system is too lenient, or too severe; sadly, it is both."[8] Norval Morris and Michael Tonry agree, pointing out that we simultaneously send too many people to prison and too many to meaningless forms of probation with little supervision. "We are both too lenient and too severe," they conclude.[9]

Policing offers a concrete example of the inconsistencies in the administration of justice. In the same city, in the same precinct, on the same night, within the space of an hour, a pair of police officers will both *over*enforce and *under*enforce the law: they will be overly aggressive toward some young black men on the street corner, and they will fail to make an arrest in a domestic violence incident a few blocks away.[10]

If we want to develop sensible crime policies, we have to sort our way through all of these complexities and identify the general patterns in how the vast majority of cases are handled in the justice system.

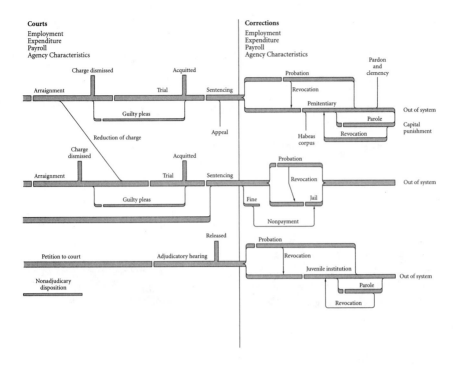

THE CRIME COMMISSION'S MODEL

To help us understand the administration of justice, social scientists have constructed models of the system. The first and most famous model (Figure 2.1) was developed thirty years ago by the President's Crime Commission (officially the President's Commission on Law Enforcement and the Administration of Justice).[11] It has been enormously influential, appearing in virtually every criminal justice textbook and shaping our thinking about criminal justice.

The Crime Commission's model popularized a "systems" approach to the administration of criminal justice. Until it appeared, people thought in terms of separate justice agencies that had little relationship to each other. Few people used the term criminal justice *system*. The systems model focuses attention on the flow of cases between agencies, the interrelationships between agencies (or "components"), and the pervasiveness of discretionary decision making in controlling the flow of cases.[12]

The Crime Commission's model was a great leap forward in our understanding of criminal justice. It accomplished exactly what models are designed to do: it provided a conceptual framework, or paradigm, that helped identify general patterns, define problems, and focus research and policy planning. For example, it focuses attention on discretion and the factors that influence decisions. It also emphasizes the dynamic relationship among components of the system and how decisions at one point (say, the prosecutor) affect decision's "upstream" (the police) and "downstream" (judges). The Crime Commission's model has its limitations, however. Based on the growing body of criminal justice research, we offer an alternative model.

THE CRIMINAL JUSTICE WEDDING CAKE

The major shortcoming of the Crime Commission's model is that it portrays a single justice system that handles all cases alike. Our alternative model is a four-layer wedding cake that focuses attention of important variations in how cases are handled (Figure 2.2). The wedding cake model was first developed by Lawrence Friedman and Robert V. Percival in *The Roots of Justice,* a history of criminal justice in Alameda County, California, between 1870 and 1910.[13] Additional support, based on contemporary evidence, is found in Michael and Don Gottfredson's *Decision Making in Criminal Justice.*[14]

The wedding cake model emphasizes two points. First, there are significant differences *between* types of cases, based on seriousness and other factors. Second, fairly consistent patterns of disposition exist *within* each category.

Celebrated Cases: The Top Layer

At the top of the wedding cake is a very small layer of "celebrated cases." These include exceptional and highly publicized crimes or controversies. The O. J. Simpson trial is, without a doubt, the all-time celebrated case. Because of Simpson's fame as an athlete and movie star, the viciousness of the crime, the money involved and high-powered legal defense team, and the volatile mix of race and sex, probably been no other case like this has appeared in American history.

Celebrated cases are different from other cases in several respects. First, they usually involve the full criminal process, including that rare event, the criminal trial. We get to see fundamental issues contested in public view: the sanity of the defendant; the admissibility of the evidence; the probity of the witnesses; and the competence of prosecutor, defense attorney, and judge. Trials are dramatic events, filled with suspense about the outcome.

Second, celebrated cases receive an enormous amount of publicity, usually because of the nature of the crime itself (typically something ghastly) or the fame of the people involved (as either victim or defendant). A few cases become celebrated because they result in landmark Supreme Court rulings. The *Miranda* case is an excellent example.

Because of all the publicity, celebrated cases have an enormous impact on public perceptions about criminal justice. People mistakenly assume that they are typical of all cases. This fosters the belief that people like Ernesto Miranda (whose case gave us the *Miranda* warning) are "beating the system" every day through "technicalities."

The O. J. Simpson trial offers an excellent example of how celebrated cases distort public perception. Simpson's acquittal led many people to conclude

FIGURE 2.2 The criminal justice wedding cake

that spouse murderers "beat the system" all the time. Even worse, it led many whites to believe that African American jurors will not convict an African American defendant. Both of these perceptions are grossly wrong.

In response to the Simpson trial outcome, the BJS analyzed its data on spouse murders from the seventy-five largest counties in the country for 1988. This included a total of 540 cases.[15] As Figure 2.3 indicates, very few accused murderers beat the system. In fact, only 2 percent of the husbands were acquitted. Wives were more likely to win acquittal (14 percent) because there were more likely to be mitigating circumstances, such as killing in self-defense. The system was tough on spouse murder defendants at every stage. Only 13 percent were not prosecuted. And of those who were convicted, 71 percent were sentenced to prison (81 percent of the husbands and 57 percent of the wives).

Unfortunately, the BJS data set does not include the racial composition of juries. Because the data come from the seventy-five largest urban counties in the country, however, it is a safe assumption that racial minorities were well

FIGURE 2.3 Spouse murder defendants.

SOURCE: Bureau of Justice Statistics, *Spouse Murder Defendants in Large Urban Counties* (Washington, D.C.: Government Printing Office, 1995).

represented. Thus, there is no truth to the idea that minority jurors refuse to convict minority defendants. The BJS data, in fact, found no difference in the conviction rates between whites and blacks: 81 percent of whites and 79 percent of blacks were convicted.

The great value of the BJS data set is that it reflects the routine, day-in, day-out administration of justice. It gives us a far more accurate picture than the headlines from the celebrated O. J. Simpson case. To understand how routine robberies and burglaries are handled, we need to turn our attention to the second and third layers of the wedding cake.

Serious Felonies: The Second and Third Layers

In their original version of the wedding cake, Friedman and Percival put all felony cases in one layer. The Gottfredsons made an extremely important refinement by dividing felonies into two categories, based on seriousness.[16] In our wedding cake, the more serious felonies go into the second layer and the less serious felonies go into the third.

A large body of research leads us to conclude that criminal justice officials consistently classify cases on the basis of three factors that define seriousness: (1) the nature of the crime, (2) the suspect's prior record, and (3) the relationship between the victim and the offender. In a study of violent felony cases in Detroit, Spohn and Cederblom identified five different factors that distinguish the more serious from the less serious cases: (1) the seriousness of the charge, (2) the defendant's prior record, (3) whether the victim and the offender were strangers, (4) whether the victim was injured, and (5) whether the offender used a gun.[17]

This classification process is informal; there is no actual checklist of factors (although some prosecutor's offices have formal limits on plea-bargaining certain kinds of cases, such as those that involve drugs, weapons, or rape).[18]

Essentially, officials ask themselves, "How much is this case worth?"[19] The everyday language of police and prosecutors express their judgments about the relative "worth" of cases. They refer to "heavy" cases and "real" crimes as opposed to the "garbage" or "bullshit" cases.[20] A study of California probation officers found that they used the same definitions of "heavy-duty" and "lightweight" cases that judges and prosecutors used.[21]

These judgments about seriousness are shared by all the members of the courtroom work group. We will explain the work group in more detail in Chapter 3. In brief, criminal justice officials work together day in and day out. To get their work done, they develop shared understandings about how things should be done. This approach has two important consequences. First, it means that individual discretion is controlled informally. Second, it produces a high degree of consistency *within* each layer of the wedding cake.

The shared definition of seriousness facilitates rapid disposition of a high volume of cases. Prosecutors and defense attorneys do not spend a lot of time arguing over particular cases. (We will discuss this in more detail in Chapter 8.) Actually, the idea of plea "bargaining" is misleading. The criminal court is not a Middle Eastern bazaar, where people haggle the price of each item. Instead, as Malcolm Feeley argues, it is a modern supermarket, with set prices and high volume.[22] The "fixed prices" reflect the shared assumptions about how much cases are "worth."

Robbery illustrates how officials distribute cases between the second and third layers. Because robbery is generally considered a very serious crime, most such cases end up in the second layer. About one-third of all robberies, however, are between acquaintances. These are usually private disputes: a disagreement over borrowed money or tools where the "offender" takes back his or her property by force.[23] These cases tend to end up in the third layer. If the offender has a long prior record of arrests and convictions, however, the case might remain in the second layer.

The Vera Institute's study of felony arrests in New York City illustrates the tremendous impact of the relationship between the offender and the victim.[24] Figure 2.4 indicates that 88 percent of the stranger robberies resulted in conviction. Moreover, prosecutors were not lenient in plea bargaining: 77 percent of those convictions (68 percent of the original arrests) were on felony charges. Nearly three-quarters (74 percent) of those convicted were incarcerated, and half of them did a year or more. This is hardly the picture of a system "soft" on crime.

The prior-relationship robberies are a completely different story. Only about a third (37 percent) of the suspects were convicted, and only 13 percent of them (5 percent of the number originally arrested) were convicted on felony charges. Slightly more than half (56 percent) of those convicted were incarcerated, but none did a year or more.

The powerful effect of prior relationships is also evident in rape cases. About half of the sexual assaults in the Vera Institute study were committed by men who know the victim. Sixty percent of these cases were dismissed; another 20 percent ended in a guilty plea with only minor punishment. All of

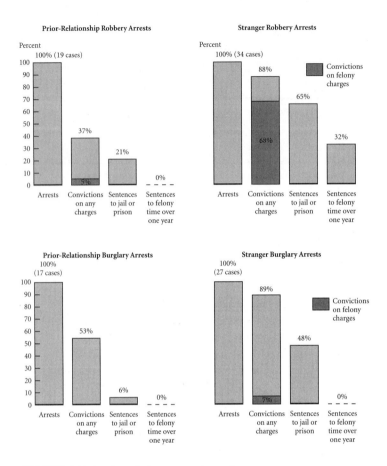

FIGURE 2.4 Outcomes of stranger and nonstranger robberies and burglaries, New York City.

SOURCE: Vera Institute, *Felony Arrests*, rev. ed. (New York: Longman, 1981), pp. 68, 86. Reprinted by permission.

the stranger-rape cases, however, went to trial. Three-quarters of these resulted in conviction and imprisonment, and two-thirds of the prison terms exceeded twenty-five years.[25]

The most important point that emerges from this analysis is that the criminal justice system is very tough on second-layer felonies. Offenders who have committed a serious crime, against a stranger, and have a long prior record are very likely to be (1) prosecuted on the top charge, (2) convicted, and (3) given a relatively severe sentence (usually prison). And as Spohn and Cederblom found, the use of a weapon and/or injury to the victim only increases the severity of the disposition.

The third layer is a different story altogether. The less serious cases are regularly dismissed, defendants are often allowed to plead guilty to lesser offenses, and if convicted they are placed on probation. Outcomes are less predictable in the third layer because less consensus prevails about seriousness and the appropriate response than in the second layer.

In their classic study of the jury, Harry Kalven and Hans Zeisel explain this lack of consensus in terms of a "liberation" hypothesis. Under certain circumstances, they argue, jurors are "liberated" from normal constraints.[26] Applying this hypothesis to the wedding cake, we can say that in the third layer the lack of consensus about the seriousness of the crime or the offender's prior record liberates prosecutors and judges from the usual definition of seriousness. This allows them to base their decision on other factors. In some instances, the defendant's race then becomes a factor.

Spohn and Cederblom explored the liberation hypothesis in a study of 4,655 violent felony cases in Detroit from 1976 to 1978.[27] They found that African Americans were more likely to be incarcerated. But this was true only in the less serious crimes: in assaults rather than more serious felonies, in acquaintance crimes, in cases in which there were no prior violent felony convictions or no gun was involved. The outcomes in the more serious crimes (that is, the second-layer cases) appeared more consistent, and whites and African Americans were treated equally harshly. In the less serious cases (that is, third-layer), there was less consensus about how much they were "worth," which allowed extralegal factors such as race to come into play.

We might note that crime *victims* make the same distinctions about seriousness as do criminal justice officials. The National Criminal Victimization Survey (NCVS) consistently finds that victims report the more serious crimes at a higher rate than less serious ones. In 1993, for example, victims reported 56.1 percent of all robberies but only 25.6 percent of all thefts. Moreover, they reported 67.6 percent of completed robberies but only 36.3 percent of attempted robberies. The higher the value of the stolen property, the greater the likelihood that the victim would report the crime. Victims reported 87.2 percent of burglaries in which the value was $1,000 or more but only 24.6 percent of those in which the value was between $50 and $99.[28]

Prior Relationship: A Policy Dilemma

The role of the prior relationship between victim and offender presents a major policy dilemma. At issue is whether it is legitimate to use it as a factor for decision making.

In the area of domestic violence, research has found that police traditionally have taken into account the nature of the relationship. The more intimate the relationship, the less likely the police are to make an arrest.[29] Thus, they are less likely to arrest the abusive husband than the abusive boyfriend or lover. In response to protests from women's groups, many police departments have adopted mandatory arrest or arrest-preferred policies. These either require an arrest in a felonious domestic assault or instruct police officers that arrest is the preferred disposition. The intent is to ensure equal enforcement of the law and to eliminate discrimination based on marital status.

Along the same lines, Susan Estrich argues that all sexual assaults should be prosecuted with equal vigor. Rapes between acquaintances should not be treated less seriously than stranger rapes. Estrich describes her conversation with a local prosecutor who explained that he used the prior-relationship criterion in *all* criminal cases, not just rape. He was accurately describing how officials generally handle criminal cases.[30]

What would happen if we did eliminate prior relationship as a decision-making factor in all criminal cases? At the arrest stage, it would produce more domestic violence arrests. (In fact, some evidence suggests that the police have been making more domestic violence arrests in recent years. The FBI's arrest data indicate that aggravated assault arrests have been increasing, compared with other felony arrests.[31]) At the prosecution stage, it would move a large number of cases from the third to the second layer of the wedding cake. This would, in turn, result in more offenders being sentenced to prison.

This presents us with a policy dilemma. Eliminating prior relationship as a decision-making factor would produce greater equality in the administration of justice—a desirable outcome. At the same time, however, it would increase the overall punitiveness of the justice system. Is that a desirable result?

A general lesson can be learned here. Significant changes in criminal justice policy often involve major trade-offs. The gains on one side of the equation need to be considered in light of the consequences on the other side.

Hard or Soft on Crime? Unraveling the Paradox

Is the criminal justice system hard or soft on crime? Our wedding cake helps resolve the paradox noted by Zimring, Morris, and Tonry. The system is both harsh and lenient. A lot depends on the seriousness of the case. It is very hard on second-layer cases, such as robberies by people with long prior records. But it is relatively soft on, for example, an assault by someone with no prior record. It is hard on stranger rapes but lenient on acquaintance assaults.

Additional support for the distinction between the second and third layers of the wedding cake is found in some career criminal prosecution programs. We will look at these in detail in Chapter 8. These programs are designed to concentrate prosecutorial resources on a special class of cases involving career criminals to make sure they are convicted and sentenced to prison. The San Diego Major Violator Unit succeeded in convicting 91.5 percent of the career criminals it handled. But 89.5 percent of the career criminals were being convicted before the program began. Under the program, 100 percent of the convicted career criminals were incarcerated, but the rate was 95.3 percent beforehand.[32] In short, criminals deemed "serious" by commonsense criteria were already being taken very seriously. As Diana Gordon, former director of the National Council on Crime and Delinquency, puts it, "Being tough doesn't work because being lenient is not the source of the problem."[33]

The idea that our criminal justice system is already fairly tough on serious crime comes as a surprise to many people, partly because the usual aggregation of crime statistics into gross categories obscures the important distinctions we have identified. Aggregate data give the *appearance* of softness because relatively few cases end up in the second layer. Violent crimes represent only 10 percent of all felonies reported to the police. Larceny, the least serious felony, accounts for 54 percent of the total.[34] The wedding cake model allows us to focus on how the system responds to the most serious crimes, those in the second layer.

The Lower Depths: The Fourth Layer

The fourth layer of the wedding cake is a world unto itself. The lower criminal courts handle all of the misdemeanors in most jurisdictions. The volume of cases is staggering, far outnumbering felonies. The eight Part I index crimes account for only 20 percent of the 14 million arrests in 1993. About half of the Part II arrests involve "public order" offenses: disorderly conduct, breach of the peace, drunkenness, and so on. In fact, the largest arrest category in 1993 was "All other offenses (except traffic)," with a total of 3.5 million.[35]

Under the criterion of seriousness, these cases are not considered to be "worth" much at all. Few of the defendants are regarded as real threats to public safety.

Because of the huge volume of cases and their relative lack of seriousness, relatively little concern is shown for the formalities of the felony process. In an excellent study of the lower courts of New Haven, Connecticut, Malcolm Feeley concludes that these institutions remain virtually untouched by the due process revolution.[36] To enter these courts is to step back in time eighty years. None of the defendants in the 1,640 cases he examined insisted on a jury trial. Half never had an attorney. Even for those that did, the lawyer's contribution was minimal. Even more shocking by our standards of due process, defendants were arraigned en masse, in assembly-line fashion. Sentences were extremely light. Half of the defendants received a fine of $50 or less, and only 4.9 percent were sentenced to jail.

Feeley concludes that the "process is the punishment": simply being brought into the lower courts is punishment enough. Insisting on your "rights" only increases the "punishment." A private attorney, for example, would charge $200 to handle the case (these figures represent 1970s standards). This is four times the fine if you simply copped a plea at the earliest possible moment. Moreover, because most defendants in the lower courts are hourly wage earners rather than salaried professionals, the lost wages involved in fighting a case would generally exceed the potential fine. (Each case in Feeley's study averaged three court appearances. Fighting the case would only increase the number and length of court dates.)

The closer we look, however, the more complicated the picture becomes. A study of the Philadelphia lower courts offers a different view and illustrates the hazards of generalizing about American criminal justice. Stephen J. Schulhofer found that in Philadelphia's two lower courts—Municipal Court and the Court of Common Pleas—about half (48 percent) of all cases went to trial, virtually all defendants had legal counsel, and the punishments meted out to the guilty were relatively significant. Nearly a quarter (22 percent) of the convicted offenders received a jail sentence, and 17.4 percent received fines (which ranged as high as several hundred dollars). Schulhofer argues that Feeley overstated the "process" costs of contesting a case in the lower courts. The price of the likely penalty, at least in Philadelphia, makes the case worth fighting. The main reason appears to be that penalties are significantly stiffer in Philadelphia than in New Haven.[37]

We do not need to resolve the debate between Feeley and Schulhofer here. The basic points are, first, that the lower courts are very different from the upper courts and, second, that there are significant differences between courts in different jurisdictions.

CONCLUSION

Our wedding cake model of the criminal justice system is designed to help us make sense of the administration of justice in action. As we go along, the most important thing to keep in mind is that we should not be distracted by celebrated cases. They make great stories for the tabloids, but they interfere with our understanding of routine operations in criminal justice. In particular, we want to be very skeptical of any policies that are based on celebrated cases. And because we are primarily concerned with the control of serious crime—robbery and burglary in particular—we need to keep our eyes focused on the second layer of the wedding cake.

NOTES

1. Bureau of Justice Statistics, *Census of State and Local Law Enforcement Agencies, 1992* (Washington, D.C.: Government Printing Office, 1993).

2. Bureau of Justice Statistics, *State Court Organization 1980* (Washington, D.C.: Government Printing Office, 1982).

3. Samuel Walker, Cassia Spohn, and Miriam DeLone, *The Color of Justice: Race, Ethnicity, and Crime in America* (Belmont, CA: Wadsworth, 1996).

4. This interpretation is vividly captured in "The Practice of Law as a Confidence Game," in Abraham Blumberg, *Criminal Justice,* 2d ed. (New York: New Viewpoints, 1979), pp. 242–243.

5. See American Friends Service Committee, *Struggle for Justice* (New York: Hill & Wang, 1971).

6. Donald Black, *The Manners and Customs of the Police* (New York: Academic Press, 1980).

7. Peter F. Nardulli, James Eisenstein, and Roy B. Flemming, *The Tenor of Justice: Criminal Courts and the Guilty Plea Process*

(Urbana: University of Illinois Press, 1988).

8. Franklin Zimring, Shelia O'Malley, and Joel Eigen, "Punishing Homicide in Philadelphia: Perspectives on the Death Penalty," *University of Chicago Law Review* 43 (Winter 1976): 252.

9. Norval Morris and Michael H. Tonry, *Between Prison and Probation: Intermediate Punishments in a Rational Sentencing System* (New York: Oxford University Press, 1990), p. 3.

10. Walker et al., *The Color of Justice,* Chapter 4.

11. President's Commission on Law Enforcement and Administration of Justice, *Task Force Report: Science and Technology* (Washington, D.C.: Government Printing Office, 1967), pp. 58–59.

12. On the origins of the systems perspective, see Samuel Walker, "Origins of the Contemporary Criminal Justice Paradigm: The American Bar Foundation Survey, 1953–1969," *Justice Quarterly* 9 (March 1992): 201–229.

13. Lawrence M. Friedman and Robert V. Percival, *The Roots of Justice: Crime and Punishment in Alameda County, California, 1870–1910* (Chapel Hill: University of North Carolina Press, 1981).

14. Michael R. Gottfredson and Don M. Gottfredson, *Decision Making in Criminal Justice: Toward the Rational Exercise of Discretion,* 2d ed. (New York: Plenum, 1988).

15. Bureau of Justice Statistics, *Spouse Murder Defendants in Large Urban Counties* (Washington, D.C.: Government Printing Office, 1995).

16. Gottfredson and Gottfredson, *Decision Making in Criminal Justice.*

17. Cassia Spohn and Jerry Cederblom, "Race Disparities in Sentencing: A Test of the Liberation Hypothesis," *Justice Quarterly* 8 (September 1991): 306.

18. William F. McDonald, *Plea Bargaining: Critical Issues and Common Practices* (Washington, D.C.: Government Printing Office, 1985).

19. Lynn Mather, "Some Determinants of the Method of Case Disposition: Decision Making by Public Defenders in Los Angeles," *Law and Society Review* 8 (Winter 1974): 187–216.

20. David Sudnow, "Normal Crimes: Sociological Features of the Penal Code in a Public Defender Office," *Social Problems* 12 (Winter 1965): 255–276.

21. John Rosecrance, "Maintaining the Myth of Individualized Justice: Probation Presentence Reports," *Justice Quarterly* 5 (June 1988): 235–256.

22. Malcolm M. Feeley, "Perspectives on Plea Bargaining," *Law and Society Review* 13 (Winter 1979): 199.

23. Donald Black, *Toward a General Theory of Social Control,* vol. 2 (Orlando, FL: Academic Press, 1984), pp. 1–28.

24. Vera Institute, *Felony Arrests,* rev. ed. (New York: Longman, 1981).

25. Ibid., pp. 42–43.

26. Harry Kalven, Jr., and Hans Zeisel, *The American Jury* (Boston: Little, Brown, 1966), pp. 164–166.

27. Spohn and Cederblom, "Race and Disparities in Sentencing."

28. Bureau of Justice Statistics, *Criminal Victimization in the United States, 1993* (Washington, D.C.: Government Printing Office, 1996).

29. Black, *The Manners and Customs of the Police.*

30. Susan Estrich, *Real Rape* (Cambridge, MA: Harvard University Press, 1987).

31. Bureau of Justice Statistics, *Sourcebook of Criminal Justice Statistics—1994* (Washington, D.C.: Government Printing Office, 1995), p. 375.

32. Eleanor Chelimsky and Judith Dahmann, *National Evaluation of the Career Criminal Program: Final Report* (MacLean, VA: MITRE, 1979).

33. Diana R. Gordon, *Towards Realistic Reform: A Commentary on Proposals for Change in New York City's Criminal Justice System* (Hackensack, NJ: National Council on Crime and Delinquency, 1981), p. 16.

34. Federal Bureau of Investigation, *Crime in the United States, 1994* (Washington, D.C.: Government Printing Office, 1995).

35. Federal Bureau of Investigation, *Crime in the United States, 1993.*

36. Malcolm M. Feeley, *The Process Is the Punishment* (New York: Russell Sage Foundation, 1979).

37. Stephen J. Schulhofer, "No Job Too Small: Justice Without Bargaining in the Lower Criminal Courts," *American Bar Foundation Research Journal* (Summer 1985): 519–598.

3

The Going Rate

EVALUATING THE SYSTEM

We now turn our attention to the question of how the criminal justice system works on a day-to-day basis. How effectively does it control crime? How successful is it in catching, prosecuting, and punishing dangerous criminals? Is the system fair? Is there a pattern of racial discrimination?

There is a lot of controversy over these basic questions. In a book subtitled *The Collapse of Criminal Justice,* Judge Harold Rothwax bluntly declares, "The long arm of the law is somewhat fractured these days."[1] He goes on to describe case after case of criminals not being punished. Other experts take a very different view. Jerome G. Miller argues in *Search and Destroy* that the system is "highly influenced by race," that there is systematic discrimination against African Americans, and that the criminal process "is an alienating and socially destabilizing exercise that usually creates more problems than it solves."[2]

Where does the truth lie? Is the system too weak or too harsh? Evaluating the performance of our criminal justice system is a difficult task. On some questions we do not have good data. Even where reasonably good data are available, experts disagree over what they mean. Is a three-year prison sentence for burglary "tough" or "lenient"? People disagree sharply over that question. Is there systematic racial discrimination in sentencing? Some experts say yes, others say no.[3] Judgments about the criminal justice system reflect our social and political values.

The debate is complicated by the fact that we have fifty-one separate criminal justice systems. Each one has its own distinct local legal culture, with slightly different traditions about how cases are handled. The Bureau of Justice Statistics (BJS) report *The Prosecution of Felony Arrests* illustrates these differences. In Los Angeles, 36 percent of all arrests are rejected by the prosecutor, compared with only 18 percent in Washington, D.C. In Portland, Oregon, 10 percent of all cases go to trial, compared with a national average of 3 percent. In Rhode Island, 43 percent of the cases that go to trial result in acquittal, compared with only 15 percent in Seattle.[4] Offenders convicted of a violent felony serve an average of 34 months in jail and prison in Illinois but 59 months in Pennsylvania; the national average is 54 months.[5]

Despite the local variations, we can identify some general features of the criminal process in this country. There is a "going rate" for crime.[6] A fairly standard outcome for about 80 percent of all cases occurs in every jurisdiction. If you know the offense and the defendant's prior criminal record, you can probably predict the outcome of the case. In their study of plea bargaining in nine different local courts, Nardulli, Eisenstein, and Flemming found that "bargaining" had little real impact on the general patterns. As they put it, "the process of what to do with the culpable is so routinized that manipulation [as in plea bargaining] plays only a minor part in the process."[7]

The going rate can change, however. Change can be the result of two factors. The first is a conscious change in *policy*. The tremendous increase in the prison population and the incarceration rate (see Chapter 1) over the past twenty years represents a major change in the going rate as a result of deliberate changes in sentencing policy. A second kind of change is the result of *unplanned* developments. The impact of the post–World War II baby boom on crime was not planned by anyone. A significant increase in the workload of the justice system, meanwhile, produces adaptations. Arrests for "public order" offenses, for example, declined significantly between the 1960s and 1980s.[8] Some analysts believe that as serious crime increased, police simply shifted their priorities and gave less attention to relatively minor crimes.

THE FUNNEL

In our search for the going rate, a good place to begin is the President's Crime Commission's analysis of the flow of cases through the system (Figure 3.1). These data are from the 1960s, but they are still relevant in terms of some general patterns in the administration of justice. The Crime Commission concluded that only 1 percent of all criminals go to prison. Only 63,000 offenders were sentenced to prison, despite about 6 million reported and unreported crimes. Many people cite this 1 percent figure as evidence of the weakness of the system.

Charles Silberman argues that the Crime Commission's analysis is "grossly misleading."[9] Reanalyzing the same data, he offers a very different picture (Figure 3.2). He attacks the idea that 75 percent of cases are "lost" between arrest and the felony complaint stage. About 260,000 (35.7 percent) of the original 727,000 arrests involve juveniles whose cases are transferred to juvenile court. What happens to those juveniles is, of course, extremely important. To remain consistent with our ground rules, however, we will concentrate on the adults. For the most recent data on juveniles, consult the BJS report, *Offenders in Juvenile Court, 1993.*[10]

Subtracting the juveniles leaves 467,000 adult arrests. Silberman argues that this is the proper baseline for assessing the performance of the adult criminal justice system. About 27 percent of these arrests (128,000) are dismissed, leaving 339,000 prosecuted adults. A prosecution rate of 73 percent is hardly a sign of softness on crime. Then, about half (48 percent) of these defendants plead guilty to a misdemeanor. These cases are not "lost"; the defendants are convicted and acquire a criminal record. We might disagree about severity of punishment, but the fact is that they are convicted.

This leaves 177,000 adult felony complaints. Of these, 90 percent are convicted: 130,000 by a guilty plea and 30,000 by trial. This is an extremely impressive conviction rate. When we combine the 177,000 felony convictions with the 162,000 misdemeanor convictions, we have a total of 332,000 adults convicted. This represents 69 percent of the adults arrested and 95 percent of those prosecuted. This is a picture of a fairly tough criminal justice system.

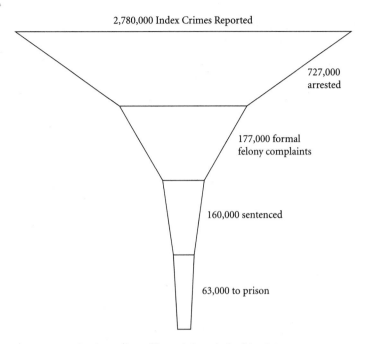

FIGURE 3.1 The funneling effect of the criminal justice system.

SOURCE: President's Commission on Law Enforcement and Administration of Justice, *Task Force Report: Science and Technology* (Washington, D.C.: Government Printing Office), p. 61.

The Crime Commission and Silberman both used 1960s data. Have things changed in the past thirty years? The best data on the flow of cases are in the BJS report *The Prosecution of Felony Arrests.* As Figure 3.3 indicates, nearly half (45 percent) of all felony arrests are rejected, dismissed, diverted, or referred. Of those cases that are prosecuted, however, 95 percent are settled with a guilty plea. Of the very few that go to trial, about two-thirds are convicted. In short, the conviction rate of adult felons whose cases are prosecuted remains extremely high.

The BJS data also indicate that almost 60 percent of convicted felons are sentenced to some form of incarceration. These figures do not represent a system that is soft on crime.

The criminal justice system got even tougher on crime during the 1980s. The percentage of all cases prosecuted increased from 49 percent in 1981 to 55 percent in 1988. The percentage of those convicted who were sentenced to some form of incarceration increased from 50 percent to 59 percent.[11] In the federal system, the percentage of convicted offenders sent to prison increased from 52 to 60 percent just between 1986 and 1990.[12] Meanwhile, the average amount of time served in prison (including jail time) by persons convicted of a violent crime increased from 46 to 54 months just between 1992 and 1994.[13] Although each of these changes represent relatively small percentage increases, the cumulative effect is enormous.

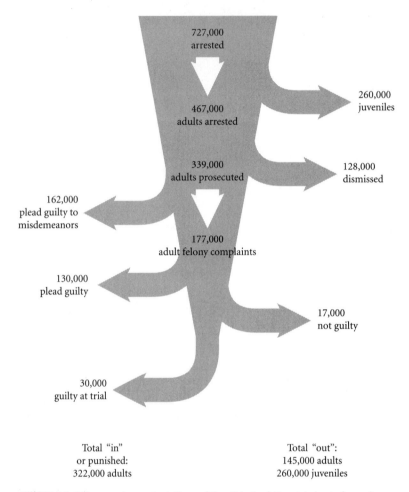

FIGURE 3.2 Silberman's recalculation of the Criminal Commission's funnel.

SOURCE: Charles Silberman, *Criminal Violence, Criminal Justice* (New York: Random House, 1978), pp. 257–261.

We can refine the analysis even further by applying the wedding-cake model. The BJS report on *The Prosecution of Felony Arrests* tracks the disposition of particular offenses. In Seattle, 75 percent of all robbery arrests and 73 percent of all burglary arrests result in a conviction. The rates are much lower for the less serious crimes such as aggravated assault (56 percent) and stolen property (43 percent). In San Diego, 66 percent of all robbery arrests and 77 percent of all burglary arrests result in a conviction.[14]

These data confirm the point we made in Chapter 2: the seriousness of the offense is a major factor in the disposition of felony cases, and the more serious crimes are treated more harshly. A conviction rate of over 70 percent of all arrests represents a system that is very tough on crime.

FIGURE 3.3 Typical outcome of 100 felony arrests brought by the police for prosecution.

SOURCE: Bureau of Justice Statistics, *The Prosecution of Felony Arrests, 1988* (Washington, D.C.: Government Printing Office, 1992).

At the same time, however, the 42 percent conviction rate for rape in Seattle is very low for such a serious crime. A major part of the explanation includes the problems associated with the handling of rape cases: the reluctance of some victims to pursue the case because of embarrassment and trauma, possible bias or insensitivity on the part of police and prosecutors, the standard of proof required, and the difficult question of possible consent.[15]

Rejections and Dismissals: Loophole?

The attrition of cases between arrest and indictment is clearly a weak point in the system. It is important to take a closer look at the 45 percent of the adult felony arrests that do not result in an indictment.

Cases drop out of the system after arrest in one of three different ways. The first is not reflected in the BJS data. Some arrests are dismissed by the police themselves. Often, an officer makes an arrest, but a supervisor refuses to sign off on it and the suspect is released. Joan Petersilia found that about 11 percent of all arrests in California were dropped this way.[16] The Police Foundation found that many of these arrests are not officially recorded by police departments.[17] Second, prosecutors reject or refuse to accept some cases. Typically, they conclude that there is not sufficient evidence to prosecute the suspect. Third, some cases are dismissed later by the prosecutor or a judge.

Even though the person was legally arrested and experienced the psychological pain of arrest, it does not show up in the official arrest statistics.

Table 3.1 presents the BJS data on the reasons for rejections and dismissals in New York and San Diego. Evidence problems—either insufficient evidence or lack of any evidence—account for most of the rejections by prosecutors: 61 percent in New York and 51 percent in San Diego. Witness problems are the second most important reason: 18 percent of the rejections in New York and 19 percent in San Diego. For most crimes against persons (robbery, rape, assault), the testimony of the victim or a witness is the primary evidence. These data indicate that evidence and witness problems account for about 70 to 80 percent of all rejections.

Evidence and witness problems are also important factors in the dismissal of cases, accounting for 33 percent of the dismissals in New York City and 20 percent in San Diego.

The lack of evidence or witnesses is a legitimate reason for dropping a case. A prosecutor cannot win a case without them. Dismissing cases for these reasons does not mean that the system is soft on crime. Officials are simply doing what circumstances force them to do. In short, rejections and dismissals are not a "loophole."

A closer look reveals that the term *dismissal* is misleading. Many of these cases are not really "lost." In San Diego, for example, almost half of the "dismissals" were diverted (11 percent), referred for other prosecution (27 percent), or covered by another case (10 percent). In other words, the defendant experienced some kind of sanction at the hands of the criminal justice system, through either prosecution on a lesser charge or involuntary treatment in a diversion program.

The BJS data clearly indicate that due process problems—illegal searches or confessions—are not a major cause of rejections and dismissals. They accounted for only 15 percent of the rejections and none of the dismissals in San Diego. Equally important, due process problems arose primarily in drug and weapons cases. They accounted for only 1 percent of the rejections of robbery cases and 8 percent of the burglary rejections. In short, thousands of criminals are not "beating the system" through legal "technicalities." Judge Harold Rothwax's attack on the rights of criminal suspects in his book *Guilty* is an excellent example of using only "celebrated cases" and ignoring the general patterns in the administration of justice.[18]

One unresolved question remains, however. The BJS data indicate that many cases are dismissed in the "interest of justice." What exactly does this mean? It may mean that the offense was not that serious, or that the victim and offender know each other, or that some form of private settlement has been worked out. Until more detailed research is done on this question, we do not know whether these dismissals are appropriate or whether they represent a covert pattern of bias in the system.

The decision to reject or dismiss a case is a highly discretionary one. Most of these decisions are made very quietly, and the prosecutor does not really have to account to anyone for them. An important question is whether a pattern of racial and ethnic bias is apparent in these decisions. Cassie Spohn and her colleagues found that women and white defendants were more likely to have their cases rejected than males and minorities. The racial and ethnic disparities were strongest at the rejection stage only. This may be due to the fact that the decision to reject is much less visible than the decision to dismiss. Once a case has been accepted for prosecution, it becomes known to a wider range of people, and this visibility may act as a constraint on prosecutors and judges.[19]

Joan Petersilia's analysis of racial disparities found that black defendants were more likely to have their cases rejected and dismissed than whites. This apparent favored treatment, however, may be a result of discrimination at the arrest stage. Some research suggests that police arrest African Americans on weaker evidence than whites. When these weak evidence cases reach the prosecutor, they are then more likely to be dismissed or rejected. In short, discrimination takes place, but at an earlier point than found by Spohn and her colleagues.[20]

From Indictment to Punishment

Once the weak cases have been weeded out, the criminal justice system becomes extremely punitive. Figure 3.3 indicates that almost all of those indicted are convicted; only one of fifty-five was acquitted at trial. Moreover, the majority of those convicted are incarcerated, in either prison or jail. Persons convicted of violent crimes are even more likely to be incarcerated: 70 percent for all violent crimes, 82 percent of those convicted of robbery, and 87 percent of those convicted of rape.[21]

It is important to note that the term *incarcerated* includes people sent to prison and jail. Many people conclude that the system is soft on crime because they look only at the data on felons sent to prison. In practice, however, there are many "split sentences," involving a jail term followed by probation. Only 30 percent of all convicted felons get "straight probation;" 45 percent go to prison and 25 percent go to jail. Only 19 percent of those convicted of a violent felony get "straight probation."[22]

The category of *time served* is also important in trying to assess the going rate. The sentence pronounced by the judge does represent how much time the offender will serve. Most offenders sentenced to prison are released early, as a result of good-time reductions and parole. According to the National Corrections Reporting Program, only about 11 percent of all prisoners "max out," or serve their entire sentence.[23] The amount of actual time served, then, is the true indicator of the going rate for crime. In 1992 offenders in state

Table 3.1 Why felony arrests are declined for prosecution

Manhattan, New York 1988

Most serious charge		Arrests declined due to:						
	Diversion	Other prosecution	Evidence	Witness	Due process	Interest of justice	Covered by other case	Other
Percentage of declinations	0%	3%	61%	18%	2%	10%	0%	6%
Murder and manslaughter	0	0	75	25	0	0	0	0
Rape	0	0	30	40	0	30	0	0
Robbery	0	8	63	22	0	3	0	4
Aggravated assault	0	3	33	40	0	13	0	11
Burglary	0	0	79	21	0	0	0	0

San Diego, California 1988

Most serious charge		Arrests declined due to:						
	Diversion	Other prosecution	Evidence	Witness	Due process	Interest of justice	Covered by other case	Other
Percentage of declinations	0%	0%	51%	19%	13%	11%	3%	4%
Murder and manslaughter	0	0	50	3	0	30	0	17
Rape	0	0	30	60	0	8	1	2
Robbery	0	0	49	36	1	6	0	7
Aggravated assault	0	0	39	46	2	9	1	3
Burglary	0	0	59	15	8	8	5	5

Table 3.1 continued Why cases are dismissed after filing or indictment

Manhattan, New York 1988

Most serious charge		Cases dismissed due to:						
	Diversion	Other prosecution	Evidence	Witness	Due process	Interest of justice	Covered by other case	Other
Percentage of declinations	0%	0%	19%	14%	0%	10%	6%	51%
Murder and manslaughter	11	1	17	15	0	2	14	39
Rape	0	0	13	33	0	4	3	47
Robery	0	0	18	21	0	4	4	53
Aggravated assault	1	0	10	26	0	13	3	48
Burglary	0	0	15	11	0	13	6	54

San Diego, California 1988

Most serious charge		Cases dismissed due to:						
	Diversion	Other prosecution	Evidence	Witness	Due process	Interest of justice	Covered by other case	Other
Percentage of declinations	11%	27%	14%	6%	0%	7%	10%	25%
Murder and manslaughter	0	20	20	0	0	30	0	30
Rape	0	4	22	22	0	31	4	18
Robbery	0	17	27	27	1	4	3	22
Aggravated assault	2	26	21	17	0	5	5	23
Burglary	2	25	12	10	0	6	13	32

SOURCE: Bureau of Justice Statistics, *The Prosecution of Felony Arrests, 1988* (Washington, D.C.: Government Printing Office, 1992).

prisons served an average of seventy-one months for murder, sixty-five months for rape, and forty-four months for robbery.[24]

An International Perspective on the Going Rate

How does the going rate for crime in the United States compare with other countries? One of the standard liberal criticisms is that our criminal justice system is far more punitive than that of any other country. Conservatives, meanwhile, argue that we are too lenient and fail to punish criminals. James Lynch's careful analysis of comparative data suggests that both liberals and conservatives are clinging to their favorite myths on this question.[25]

On the one hand, we do lock up a lot of people. We already have the highest incarceration rate in the world (350 per 100,000), and current sentencing trends suggest that this will continue.[26] And as our previous discussion indicates, we are fairly tough on those offenders we manage to arrest. From this perspective, it is hard to say that we are soft on crime.

At the same time, however, our high incarceration rate is mainly the result of our high rates of violent crime. The American murder rate is four times higher than Canada and ten times higher than England and West Germany. Our robbery rate is five times higher than England and West Germany. Violent crimes, moreover, are more likely to result in prison sentences. Furthermore, armed robbery is even more likely to result in a prison sentence than unarmed robbery. Lynch points out that a far higher proportion of robberies in the United States are armed than in other countries. In other words, we have a high incarceration rate in large part because we have such high rates of those crimes that typically send an offender to prison.[27]

The relevant question becomes, Is the going rate for particular crimes significantly higher in the United States than it is in other countries? Lynch estimated the chances of going to prison for a person arrested for murder, robbery, burglary, and larceny/theft in the United States, England, Canada, and West Germany. He found that a robber's chance of going to prison was 36 percent in the United States, 41 percent in Canada, and 39 percent in the United Kingdom. The odds were lower only in West Germany. The odds of going to prison were also roughly the same for murder, burglary, and larceny in the three English-speaking countries. In terms of the tendency to send convicted offenders to prison, then, the United States is not that much more punitive than other countries.[28]

In terms of time served, however, the United States is significantly more punitive, especially for property crimes. Lynch found that average number of months served in prison for murder in the United States (50.5) was slightly higher than in England and Wales (43) but lower than in Canada (57). (Because of different methodologies, these estimates for the United States vary slightly from the ones cited earlier in this section.) Average time served for robbery was somewhat higher in the United States and substantially higher for both burglary and theft. Burglars in the United States, for example, serve an average of 16.06 months, compared with 5.23 in Canada and 6.72 in England

and Wales. The gap was even greater for theft. Convicted thieves in America serve an average of 12 months, compared with only 2 in Canada and 4.65 in England and Wales.

Lynch's comparative research highlights the fact that the going rate consists of two components. The first is the tendency to send offenders to prison. On this point, the American going rate is very similar to other industrialized countries. The second is the amount of prison time actually served. Here, the United States is more punitive—but primarily for property and not violent crimes.

Lynch did not study drug offenses, but the United States is likely comparatively very punitive, in terms of both incarceration and length of sentences.

THE COURTROOM WORK GROUP

The going rate is established and maintained by the people who operate the criminal justice system. It is important to remember that "the system" is not some impersonal entity. It is a process carried out by people making series of discretionary decisions.[29] A police officer decides to make an arrest; a prosecutor rejects a case; a judge sentences an offender to prison, and so on. To understand how the system works, we need to examine the factors that influence these decisions.

Prosecutors, defense attorneys, judges, and to some extent police officers comprise the *courtroom work group.* In perhaps the best study of this phenomenon, Nardulli, Eisenstein, and Flemming characterize local courthouses as "communities." "After spending an enormous number of hours in various county courts," they write, "we became convinced that the concept of a courthouse community can be an immensely useful too in trying to understand them."[30]

The decisions of individual officials are heavily influenced by the bureaucratic setting in which they work. Even though a police officer has enormous discretion to make an arrest, he or she will usually have to have a supervisor sign off on it. A prosecutor will examine the arrest report, and a defense attorney may challenge the arrest or the accompanying search. A judge will rule on a number of issues. The actions of these other officials act as a major constraint on the police officer's actions.

Working together day in and day out, members of the courtroom work group reach a general consensus about how different kinds of cases should be handled. This involves a shared understanding about how much cases are "worth." There are "heavy" cases (that is, serious violent crimes) and "garbage" cases (relatively minor theft).

This shared understanding allows them to work together smoothly and efficiently, moving cases along quickly. Conflict between prosecution and defense is the exception rather than the rule. Although in theory we have an *adversarial* process, with truth determined through conflict between prosecution and defense, the reality is that an *administrative* system is in effect, with a high degree of consensus and cooperation. Experts on plea bargaining describe the process as a "supermarket": set prices and a high volume of business.[31] (We will discuss this in more detail in Chapter 8.)

Frederic Suffett's study of bail setting offers an excellent illustration of consensus and cooperation in the courtroom work group. Only 3 percent of the cases he examined involve any conflict over the bail decision; some disagreement arose in another 9 percent.[32] Over the years, the members of this work group had developed a shared understanding about how much bail to set for different kinds of cases—in other words, how much each case was worth.

In her study of plea bargaining, Alissa Pollitz Worden found a high degree of judicial agreement with prosecutorial sentence recommendations. She speculates that going rates "may be so predictable that a prosecutor need not make a formal recommendation in order to ensure that a sentence bargain will be honored by the court."[33]

Another example is John Rosecrance's study of presentence investigation (PSI) reports by probation officers. In theory, the PSI is an independent evaluation of a convicted offender's social history, taking into account criminal record, employment history, family status, and so on. Yet, Rosecrance found that probation officers (POs) classified offenders very quickly on the basis of their offense and prior record. Even more important, they based their recommendations on what they thought judges and prosecutors wanted. The California POs he studied were in regular contact with prosecutors and discussed their cases with them. They rarely challenged plea agreements, which often included an understanding about the sentence. As one PO put it, "It's stupid to try and bust a deal. . . . Who needs the hassle? . . . Everyone, including the defendant, has already agreed."[34]

Nardulli, Eisenstein, and Flemming add the important point that courtroom work groups vary from jurisdiction to jurisdiction. Each "community" has its own "distinctive character." Typically, one person plays "a dominant role," "by virtue of personality, professional skills (or reputation), political power, longevity, or some other attribute."[35]

These variations help explain the different going rates they found in nine counties. Kalamazoo and Oakland Counties, Michigan, were least likely to grant felons probation, whereas Montgomery County, Pennsylvania, and Du-Page and St. Clair Counties, Illinois, granted probation to most offenders.[36]

The Limits of Reform

The courtroom work group has enormous power to limit, frustrate, or even block reforms in the administration of justice. A state legislature might pass a new law, or the Supreme Court might issue a "landmark" ruling, but that does not guarantee that anything will really change. A few examples illustrate the point.

- The Supreme Court ruled in 1967 that defendants in juvenile court have a constitutional right to an attorney (*In re Gault*). Barry Feld, however, found that only half (47.7 percent) of the kids in Minnesota juvenile courts in 1984 actually had legal counsel. State officials simply did not comply with the law.[37]

■ Congress passed a "speedy trial" law in 1974, and several states enacted similar laws. Malcolm Feeley, however, found that these laws had almost no effect on the flow of cases. All members of the courtroom work group—judges, prosecutors, and defense attorneys—had their own reasons for delaying cases. The laws permit exceptions to the requirement and officials take advantage of them. As one judge explained, "Our court has figured out ways to deal with the [speedy trial] act that don't cause us to change our practices at all."[38]

■ A study of the new "three strikes and you're out" laws found that, with the exception of California, prosecutors in most states were simply not using the law. Wisconsin had used it only once in a year and a half, whereas five other states had not used it at all.[39]

We should not be completely cynical about the prospects for change. Some reforms are implemented. A few examples illustrate the point.

■ The "defense of life" rule was designed to reduce police use of deadly force. The number of persons shot and killed by the police fell from 559 in 1975 to 300 in 1987.[40]

■ The Minnesota Sentencing Guidelines enacted in 1980 had the explicit goal of limiting the use of imprisonment. To a great extent this has worked, and Minnesota has maintained the lowest incarceration rate of any state (with the possible exception of South Dakota).[41]

■ The federal sentencing guidelines were explicitly designed to increase punishment for serious crimes. They have achieved this goal. The number of federal prisoners increased from 32,695 in 1985 to 99,466 by 1995.[42]

The Dynamics of Reform

Which reforms work and which ones fail? A lot depends on the nature of the reform itself. Some experts believe that modest reforms, which require only slight changes in how the courtroom work group operates, are more likely to succeed than sweeping changes. Raymond T. Nimmer argues that "the probability of system change is inversely related to the degree of change sought by a reform."[43] Eisenstein, Flemming, and Nardulli agree, concluding that "the more radical a proposed change the less likely is its adoption."[44]

In their study of rape law reform, on the other hand, Cassia Spohn and Julie Horney found significant changes in only one of six jurisdictions. They speculate that the new Michigan rape law was so comprehensive that it forced changes in the attitudes and behavior of courtroom work group officials, whereas the minor reforms in the other five jurisdictions had little impact.[45]

In the conclusion of their study of courts and their communities, Eisenstein, Flemming, and Nardulli offer some other sobering conclusions about the possibilities for reform. On the one hand, changes mandated from outside the courtroom work groups face serious obstacles. They agree with Feeley that work groups have enormous ability to resist change. At the same time, however, change initiated from within, by the work group itself, also faces major obstacles. Efforts by judges to speed up trials may be blocked by prosecution and defense attorneys.[46]

In short, *some* things work. We should not assume that "nothing works" or that "everything works." The important point here is that the power of the courtroom work group to frustrate reform is extremely relevant to our search for sensible and effective crime policies. Even if we find a good policy, officials could not implement it.

Criminal Justice Thermodynamics

The systems perspective on the administration of justice helps us see how changes in one part of the system affect decisions in other parts. Malcolm Feeley suggests that a major change may set off a "chain reaction throughout the entire system," forcing other officials to adapt and in some cases creating new and unanticipated problems.[47] We explain this chain reaction effect in terms of "criminal justice thermodynamics." You may remember from a physics class that the law of thermodynamics says that every action has an equal and opposite reaction. The justice system works in much the same way: actions produce reactions.

Our law of criminal justice thermodynamics states:

■ *An increase in the severity of the penalty will result in less frequent application of that penalty.*

Our law has an important corollary:

■ *The less often a severe penalty is applied, the more arbitrary will be the occasions when it is applied.*

The death penalty is an excellent example of the law of thermodynamics. Because it is the ultimate penalty, it exerts enormous pressure on the courtroom work group. Many devices are used to evade its application (plea bargaining to a second-degree murder charge, demanding a jury trial, using the insanity defense, appealing on every potential issue, requesting pardon or commutation, and so forth). Thus, the action of the prosecutor in filing first-degree murder charges (making the case eligible for the death penalty) causes a reaction by the defense.

Because the death penalty is rarely used, its application is very arbitrary. In the landmark case of *Furman v. Georgia* (1972), the Supreme Court characterized the application of the death penalty as being so rare that it is "freakish" and akin to being "struck by lightning."[48]

Another example involves the new "three strikes and you're out" laws. These laws represent a dramatic increase in the severity of the punishment: typically, life in prison for conviction on a third felony (or in some states, third violent felony). A study by the Campaign for an Effective Crime Policy, however, found that the laws were not being used in most states. In at least three

BOX 1

Let us say we wanted to improve the overall crime control effectiveness of the criminal justice system. Where is the best place to start?

The table presented here provides an overview of the administration of justice including reported and unreported crime. Let us begin with 1,000 actual felonies. The NCVS tells us that only 360 will be reported to the police. The FBI tells us that only 21 percent of those cases, or seventy-six, will be cleared by arrest. The BJS data tell us that 45 percent (thirty-four) of those cases will not be prosecuted. That leaves forty-two adult felony indictments. Almost all of them will be convicted, and most will serve some time in prison or jail.

1,000	Actual felonies
360	Reported to police (36 percent reporting rate)
76	Arrests (21 percent clearance rate)
42	Felony indictments (55 percent prosecution rate)
41	Convicted
23	Incarcerated

It is obvious that the weakest point in the system is the failure of victims to report crimes. Some people might assume that if more crimes were reported, there would be more arrests (assuming a stable clearance rate of 21 percent), more convictions, and so on. This analysis might suggest that raising the reporting rate would increase the overall effectiveness of the system.

But would it? We need to consider the impact "downstream" of a higher reporting rate. First, the police would have more work, which would leave them with less time for other responsibilities. Second, it is not necessarily true that the clearance rate would remain the same. It might fall if it happened that people were reporting more crimes where there were no good leads (as in larcenies where there was no witness). Third, if the number of arrests did increase substantially, the jails would be more crowded, prosecutors and defense attorneys would have much heavier caseloads, court dockets might become more backlogged, and so on. In short, an increase in the reporting rate might create more problems than it solved. The justice system might become less rather than more efficient, and the result would not necessarily be more offenders convicted and sentenced to prison. This exercise offers another illustration of the thermodynamics of the criminal justice system and the "billiard ball effect" of a major change "upstream."

states they had not been used at all. The laws disrupted the going rate so much that local prosecutors simply did not use them.[49]

The new "three strikes" law was being used extensively in California, and the impact illustrates a "billiard ball effect" on the rest of the criminal justice system. More defendants were refusing to plead guilty and demanding trials. The backlog of defendants waiting jury trials immediately increased from 480 to 700 in the first ten months. This produced overcrowding in county jails, with additional costs to taxpayers. The county auditor in Los Angeles reported that the law had cost the county $169 million in extra costs in less than two years. And as a result of overcrowding, more convicted offenders were being released to make room for those awaiting trials.[50]

Pamala L. Griset's study of correctional practices in New York illustrates how an increase in severity can produce adaptations that, in many respects, undermine the original intent of getting tougher with criminals. New York adopted a series of mandatory sentencing laws in 1973 and 1978, followed by several early release programs in 1987 and 1989. The result was an "odd mix" of indeterminate and mandatory sentencing policies. The prison population began to increase, but because of financial constraints, the state did not build all of the planned new prisons.[51]

The three new early release programs—shock incarceration, "earned eligibility" for parole, and CASAT (Comprehensive Alcohol and Substance Abuse Treatment)—gave correctional officials enormous discretion over offenders' eligibility for early release. They began using these programs to reduce prison populations. Under earned eligibility, inmates gained a "presumption of release" for merely participating in a treatment, educational, or work program. Thus, they received a reward for what in the past had been considered minimal good conduct. The net effect was to release them early and to undercut the intent of mandatory minimum sentencing laws. Meanwhile, many offenders released under work release programs were allowed to live at home and report in twice a week. Over one-third of the participants in this "day reporting" program had been convicted of violent crimes. Here, also, correctional officials gained a vast amount of hidden discretion and used it to undercut the supposedly "tough" sentencing laws.

HOW MANY MISTAKES?

The fact that the administration of justice is a human process introduces the possibility of human error. How often does the courtroom work group make a mistake and convict an innocent person? Every year, a few spectacular examples come to light. The relevant question is, How often do such mistakes happen? What is the error rate? Are there just a few "celebrated cases," or do miscarriages of justice happen all the time?

C. Ronald Huff and his colleagues undertook an ingenious effort to estimate the number of wrongful convictions. They surveyed 229 Ohio criminal justice officials (judges, prosecutors, public defenders, police), along with attorneys general from all states, and asked for *their* estimate of the frequency of wrongful convictions. After eliminating the extremely high and low estimates (about 6 percent believed that mistakes never happen), they concluded that errors occur in slightly less than 1 percent of all felony cases.[52]

What are we to make of this estimate? From one perspective, an error rate of less than 1 percent is very good. We should all be so successful in whatever we do. It compares very favorably with the false positive and false negative rates we will encounter with the prediction problem in Chapter 4. But Huff and his associates projected this error rate to the national level and estimated 5,729 wrongful convictions in 1981 (one-half of 1 percent of the total of 1,145,780 convictions). Six thousand innocent people convicted of a felony every year is a shocking fact to contemplate.

A second estimate of mistakes in the administration of justice was Hugo Bedeau and Michael Radelet's study of the death penalty. They estimated that for every twenty persons executed in this country since 1900, at least one innocent person was convicted of a capital crime. They found a total of 343 persons mistakenly convicted of capital crimes; 25 were actually executed, while many of the others served prison terms of up to twenty-five years.[53]

CONCLUSION

A going rate for crime exists in the United States. If you are convicted of a certain crime and have a certain prior record, it is possible to predict the outcome of your case with a high degree of accuracy. The going rate does vary between jurisdictions but is fairly stable within each one. It is established and maintained by the members of the courtroom work group, the members of which work together daily.

The concept of the going rate is extremely important for our search for sensible and effective crime policies for two reasons. First, many proposed policies are based on mistaken assumptions about how the system works. They do not take into account the fact that the administration of justice is very stable, consistent, and predictable and that it is relatively tough on those offenders who are caught and prosecuted. Second, many proposed reforms would have trouble being implemented. The going rate is determined by the courtroom work group, which has tremendous power to adapt and either ignore or evade the intent of a new law or policy. Simply passing a new law does not necessarily mean that the intended changes will occur.

NOTES

1. Judge Harold J. Rothwax, *Guilty: The Collapse of Criminal Justice* (New York: Random House, 1996), p. 25.

2. Jerome G. Miller, *Search and Destroy: African-American Males in the Criminal Justice System* (Cambridge: Cambridge University Press, 1996), p. xii.

3. Samuel Walker, Cassia Spohn, and Miriam DeLone, *The Color of Justice: Race, Ethnicity, and Crime in America* (Belmont, CA: Wadsworth, 1996).

4. Bureau of Justice Statistics, *The Prosecution of Felony Arrests, 1988* (Washington, D.C.: Government Printing Office, 1992), Table 2.

5. Bureau of Justice Statistics, *Violent Offenders in State Prison: Sentences and Time Served* (Washington, D.C.: Government Printing Office, 1995).

6. An excellent discussion of the going rate is in James Eisenstein, Roy B. Flemming, and Peter F. Nardulli, *The Contours of Justice: Communities and Their Courts*

(Boston: Little, Brown, 1988), and Peter
F. Nardulli, Roy B. Flemming, and James
Eisenstein, *The Tenor of Justice* (Urbana:
University of Illinois Press, 1988).

7. Nardulli et al., *The Tenor of Justice,*
p. 246.

8. Federal Bureau of Investigation, *Crime
in the United States* (Washington, D.C.:
Government Printing Office, annual).

9. Charles Silberman, *Criminal Violence,
Criminal Justice* (New York: Random
House, 1978), p. 258.

10. Office of Juvenile Justice and Delinquency Prevention, *Offenders in Juvenile
Court, 1993* (Washington, D.C.: Government Printing Office, 1996).

11. Bureau of Justice Statistics, *The Prosecution of Felony Arrests, 1981* (Washington,
D.C.: Government Printing Office, 1986);
Bureau of Justice Statistics, *The Prosecution
of Felony Arrests, 1988.*

12. Bureau of Justice Statistics, *Federal
Sentencing in Transition, 1986–1990*
(Washington, D.C.: Government Printing
Office, 1992).

13. Bureau of Justice Statistics, *Violent
Offenders in State Prison: Sentences and Time
Served,* Table 3.

14. Bureau of Justice Statistics, *The Prosecution of Felony Arrests, 1981.*

15. Cassia Spohn and Julie Horney, *Rape
Law Reform: A Grassroots Revolution and Its
Impact* (New York: Plenum, 1992).

16. Joan Petersilia, *Racial Disparities in the
Criminal Justice System* (Santa Monica, CA:
Rand, 1983), p. 21.

17. Lawrence W. Sherman and Barry
Glick, *The Quality of Police Arrest Statistics*
(Washington, D.C.: The Police Founda-
tion, 1984).

18. Rothwax, *Guilty: The Collapse of
Criminal Justice.*

19. Cassia Spohn, John Gruhl, and Susan
Welch, "The Impact of the Ethnicity and
Gender of Defendants on the Decision to
Reject or Dismiss Felony Charges," *Crim-
inology* 25(1) (1987): 175–191.

20. Petersilia, *Racial Disparities in the
Criminal Justice System,* pp. 20–30.

21. Bureau of Justice Statistics, *Felony
Sentences in the United States, 1992* (Wash-

ington, D.C.: Government Printing Office, 1996), Table 4.

22. Ibid.

23. Bureau of Justice Statistics, *National
Corrections Reporting Program, 1992* (Washington, D.C.: Government Printing Office, 1994), p. 35.

24. Bureau of Justice Statistics, *Prison
Sentences and Time Served for Violence*
(Washington, D.C.: Government Printing
Office, 1995).

25. James Lynch, "Crime in International
Perspective," in James Q. Wilson and Joan
Petersilia, eds., *Crime* (San Francisco: ICS
Press, 1995), pp. 11–38.

26. Marc Mauer, *Americans Behind Bars: A
Comparison of International Rates of Incarcera-
tion* (Washington, D.C.: The Sentencing
Project, 1991).

27. Lynch, "Crime in International Perspective." Considerable controversy prevails over these comparative crime rates.
In particular, many observers question the
findings of the International Crime Survey
(ICS) that U.S. violent crime rates are not
that much higher than those of other
countries: Jan van Dijk, P. Mayhew, and
M. Killias, *Experiences of Crime Across the
World* (Boston: Klewer, 1990).

28. Lynch, "Crime in International Perspective."

29. Samuel Walker, *Taming the System:
The Control of Discretion in Criminal Justice,
1950–1990* (New York: Oxford University Press, 1993); Michael R. Gottfredson
and Don M. Gottfredson, *Decision Making
in Criminal Justice,* 2d ed. (New York:
Plenum, 1988).

30. Nardulli et al., *The Tenor of Justice,*
p. 39.

31. Malcolm Feeley, "Perspectives on
Plea Bargaining," *Law and Society Review*
13 (Winter 1979): 199.

32. Frederick Suffett, "Bail-Setting: A
Study in Courtroom Interaction," *Crime
and Delinquency* 12 (1966): 318–331.

33. Alissa Pollitz Worden, "The Judge's
Role in Plea Bargaining: An Analysis of
Judges' Agreement with Prosecutors'
Sentencing Recommendations," *Justice
Quarterly* 12 (June 1995): 273.

34. John Rosecrance, "Maintaining the Myth of Individualized Justice: Probation Presentence Reports," *Justice Quarterly* 5 (June 1988): 235–256.

35. Nardulli et al., *The Tenor of Justice,* p. 41.

36. Ibid., pp. 279–280.

37. Barry C. Feld, *Justice for Children: The Right to Counsel and the Juvenile Courts* (Boston: Northeastern University Press, 1993), p. 55.

38. Malcolm Feeley, *Court Reform on Trial* (New York: Basic Books, 1983), p. 173.

39. Campaign for an Effective Crime Policy, *The Impact of "Three Strikes and You're Out Laws: What Have We Learned?* (Washington, D.C.: Campaign for an Effective Crime Policy, 1996).

40. William A. Geller and Michael S. Scott, *Deadly Force: What We Know* (Washington, D.C.: Police Executive Research Forum, 1992), p. 503.

41. Terance D. Miethe and Charles A. Moore, *Sentencing Guidelines: Their Effect in Minnesota* (Washington, D.C.: Government Printing Office, 1989). Bureau of Justice Statistics, *Sourcebook of Criminal Justice Statistics—1994* (Washington, D.C.: Government Printing Office, 1995), p. 541.

42. Department of Justice, *State and Federal Prisons: Report,* press release (December 3, 1995).

43. Raymond T. Nimmer, *The Nature of System Change* (Chicago: American Bar Foundation, 1978), p. 181.

44. Eisenstein et al., *The Contours of Justice,* p. 294.

45. Cassia Spohn and Julie Horney, *Rape Law Reform: A Grassroots Revolution and Its Impact* (New York: Plenum, 1992), pp. 171–173.

46. Ibid., pp. 291–305.

47. Feeley, *Court Reform on Trial,* p. 184.

48. *Furman v. Georgia,* 408 U.S. 238 (1972); Raymond Paternoster, *Capital Punishment in America* (Lexington, MA: Lexington Books, 1991).

49. Campaign for an Effective Crime Policy, *The Impact of "Three Strikes and You're Out" Laws.*

50. William Claiborne, "'Three Strikes' Tough on Courts Too," *Washington Post* (March 8, 1995), pp. 1, 14; Fox Butterfield, "Tough Law on Sentences in Criticized," *New York Times* (March 8, 1996), p. A8.

51. Pamala L. Griset, "The Politics and Economics of Increased Correctional Discretion over Time Served: A New York Case Study," *Justice Quarterly* 12 (June 1995): 307–323.

52. C. Ronald Huff, Arye Rattner, and Edward Sagarin, "Guilty Until Proven Innocent: Wrongful Convictions and Public Policy," *Crime and Delinquency* 32 (October 1986): 518–544; C. Ronald Huff, Arye Rattner, and Edward Sagarin, *Convicted but Innocent* (Beverly Hills, CA: Sage, 1996).

53. Hugo Adam Bedeau and Michael L. Radelet, "Miscarriages of Justice in Potentially Capital Cases," *Stanford Law Review* 40 (November 1987): 21–179.

4

The Career Criminal

The career criminal has been a major focus of crime control policy for twenty-five years. Several important crime control policies—preventive detention, major-offender prosecution programs, selective incapacitation—are aimed at the so-called career criminal. Anticrime rhetoric has always conjured up images of "hard-core" criminals, "repeaters," or "chronic recidivists." In the past, these terms were based largely on myth and stereotypes. We are indebted to Marvin Wolfgang and his associates for giving us a detailed profile of these people. Their landmark study, *Delinquency in a Birth Cohort*, one of the most important pieces of criminal justice research in the last twenty-five years, has had a profound influence on thinking about crime policy.[1]

WOLFGANG'S BIRTH COHORT

Wolfgang's birth cohort traced the careers of all the males born in Philadelphia in 1945 through their eighteenth birthday in 1963. Using official records, such as police and school records, the study reconstructed the criminal careers of a sample of 9,945 juveniles. The principal finding was that a small percentage of delinquents are responsible for a majority of all crimes and for about two-thirds of all violent crimes.

As Table 4.1 indicates, 35 percent of the cohort had at least one *officially recorded contact* with the police. Of that group, 46 percent had no more con-

Table 4.1 Wolfgang's birth cohort

	Number	Percentage of original sample	Total Criminal offenses	Percentage of total offenses
Original sample	9,945			
Delinquents	3,475	34.9%	10,214	
One officially recorded contact with police	1,613	16.2	1,613	15.8%
Two to four contacts	1,235	12.4	3,296	32.3
Five or more contacts	627	6.3	5,305	51.9

SOURCE: Marvin Wolfgang, Robert M. Figlio, and Thorsten Sellin, *Delinquency in a Birth Cohort* (Chicago: University of Chicago Press, 1972).

tacts. Wolfgang labeled them "one-time offenders." He divided the remaining 1,862 juveniles into two groups. The 1,235 with two, three, or four contacts were labeled the "non-chronic recidivists." The remaining 627 with five or more contacts were the "chronic delinquents." They represented 6 percent of the original cohort and 18 percent of the 3,475 delinquents. These 627 are the so-called career criminals.

Several comments about Wolfgang's data are in order. Most important, he measured delinquency in terms of officially recorded police contacts. Obviously, many delinquents were never caught, and the actual prevalence of criminal behavior was higher than 35 percent. Also, many of the "one-time delinquents" committed other illegal acts but were never caught. And, finally, some "non-chronic delinquents" committed more than four crimes.

Despite this limitation, however, the cohort study highlighted a general pattern: most delinquents stop committing illegal acts at some point, and most of them stop relatively early. We do not know what makes them stop. It may be because they "matured out," or their contact with the police deterred them from further delinquency, or they were sentenced to some treatment program that worked. All we know for sure is that most eventually stop.

The amount of undetected criminality is an important question. Frank Dunford and Delbert Elliot tried to measure this through self-report interviews. Of 242 delinquents they defined as "career offenders" (either three index offenses in any two consecutive years or twelve delinquent acts in two consecutive years), 86 percent were never arrested. Twelve percent had between one and four arrests, while only 2 percent of the total had five or more.[2] These data reinforce the point we made in Chapter 3—that the risk of arrest is fairly low and that the unlikelihood of arrest is the weakest part of the entire criminal justice system.

The significance of Wolfgang's 627 "chronic recidivists" is dramatized when we see that they were responsible for more than half (52 percent) of all the crimes committed by the entire cohort. This amount included 63 percent of all the index crimes committed by the cohort and 71 percent of the murders, 73 percent of the rapes, and 82 percent of all the robberies. The onetime offenders committed only 16 percent of the total; and the nonchronic recidivists, the remaining 32 percent.

The policy implications of these data are obvious: if we could identify and control that 6 percent, we could achieve a major reduction in serious crime. This idea generated much excitement among policy makers. Moreover, it does not make any difference what your basic crime policy perspective is. If you are a liberal who believes in rehabilitation, then identifying and treating that 6 percent will achieve a huge reduction in crime. If you are conservative, you will get the same results by incapacitating that same 6 percent.

OTHER COHORT STUDIES

Wolfgang's original findings have been confirmed by other cohort studies. He and his associates conducted a follow-up study of males and females born in Philadelphia in 1958. This was a larger cohort (28,338 subjects) and more representative in terms of race and sex. Following their criminal careers between 1968 and 1974 (age ten to eighteen), they found a similar pattern in criminal behavior: 33 percent had at least one recorded contact with the police, whereas the chronic recidivists represented 7.5 percent of the total cohort (compared with 6 percent in the original study).[3]

The 1958 cohort did commit more crimes. Remember, this study covered the late 1960s when the crime rate soared. The murder rate was three times higher and the robbery rate five times higher than for the 1945 cohort. Thus, about the same percentage of cohort members became delinquent, but those who did committed more crimes and far more serious ones.

Some people might question whether Philadelphia is representative of the rest of the country. Lyle Shannon studied three cohorts in Racine, Wisconsin, tracing the careers of 6,127 persons born in 1942, 1949, and 1955. Unlike Wolfgang, he followed his subjects into adulthood. Members of the 1942 cohort were thirty-three years old when the study ended.[4]

Shannon found that most of his subjects had at least one contact with the police: 68 percent of the 1942 group, 69 percent of the 1949 cohort, and 59 percent of the 1955 cohort (but the members of this last cohort were only twenty-two years old when the data collection ended, so it missed part of their high-crime years). These figures may seem frightening until we learn that most of the arrests were for relatively minor crimes. Part I index crimes represented only 12.7 percent of all the arrests for the 1942 cohort and 15.9 percent and 24.6 percent for the other two cohorts, respectively. These data confirm what criminologists have long known: that most males in this country break the law at some point in their lives but that most of the law breaking involves minor crimes such as vandalism.

The career criminal patterns in Racine resembled those in Philadelphia. Shannon found that 9.5 percent of the 1942 cohort had 51 percent of the police contacts, 8 percent of the 1949 group had 50.8 percent of the contacts, and 5.8 percent of the 1955 group had 50.8 percent of that group's police contacts. Looking at felony arrests only, he found that people with four or more contacts represented 0.6 percent of the 1942 cohort but accounted for 27.1 percent of the felony arrests. For the 1949 group, 1.7 percent of the cohort had four or more contacts and were responsible for 44.1 percent of the felony contacts; for the 1955 group, 3.5 percent of the cohort had four or more and accounted for 63.8 percent of the felony contacts.

The fact that the Racine findings parallel those from Philadelphia is fairly significant. Racine is a relatively small Midwestern community, with a population of only 71,000 in 1950 and 95,000 in 1970. Racial minorities constituted only 11 percent of the population in 1970. Philadelphia in 1970 was the third largest city in the country with a minority population of 33.6 percent. The Racine study suggests that Wolfgang's most important finding holds true for other communities. Additional support is found in David Farrington's study of young men in London. He found that 6 percent of his sample accounted for 49 percent of all the criminal convictions in the cohort.[5]

In short, a near-universal pattern seems to exist in which a small group of offenders account for a very high proportion of all the crimes committed by their cohort.

Before going any further, it is useful to clarify some of the terminology used in career criminal research.[6] First, we can distinguish *criminal careers* from *career criminals*. Every offender has a criminal career. Some have short ones; others have long ones. Everyone who goes to school has an academic career. If you drop this and every other course tomorrow and never return to school, you have an academic career—a very short one. The kid who commits one act of minor vandalism has a criminal career—a short one. The career criminal is the person with a long criminal career.

Another basic issue is the *prevalence* of criminality. We define this in terms of *participation*, which distinguishes between those who commit at least one crime and those who do not commit any. To identify the real career criminals, we need to know the *frequency* of offending—that is, the rate at which active criminals commit crimes. Determining the *seriousness* of offending is also important, because we want to identify those who commit the more serious crimes. The beginning of a criminal career is referred to as the *onset*. Do career criminals begin earlier than the one-time offenders? If they do, we might be able to spot them that way. *Persistence* refers to continuing criminal activity and *desistance* to stopping. The amount of time between onset and desistance is the *career length*.

FROM RESEARCH TO POLICY

Wolfgang's original birth cohort study generated an enormous amount of excitement, stimulating research and influencing public policy. The study was published at a politically opportune moment. By 1972, crime rates had been rising dramatically for a decade. The public was disillusioned with the liberal rehabilitation-oriented policies of the 1960s. They were ready for programs that promised to "get tough" with hard-core criminals.[7] Wolfgang's data suggested that it might be possible to identify that small group.

This book examines some of the specific policies inspired by the career criminal research. They include police programs that target suspected career criminals for intensive surveillance (Chapter 5), pretrial detention of "dangerous" offenders (Chapter 7), career criminal prosecution programs (Chapter 8), and selective incapacitation for repeat offenders (Chapter 7). Many of the treatment-oriented crime control policies proposed by liberals are also designed to deal with particular classes of offenders. Intensive probation programs (Chapter 11) are designed for "high-risk" offenders, whereas boot camps are designed for special categories of offenders.

The data in Table 4.1 make it look simple: spot the chronic recidivists, and either treat or punish them accordingly. There is only one problem, however. Nothing is simple in the real world of criminal justice. Ideas that sound good in theory do not necessarily work out in practice. Let us look at some of the problems that arise when we try to translate Wolfgang's birth cohort research into crime control policy.

As is so often the case with path-breaking research, *Delinquency in a Birth Cohort* raised more questions than it answered. Identifying that 6 percent was a major breakthrough, but it was only the beginning. Criminologists have devoted an enormous amount of time and energy to answering some basic questions. Exactly who are the career criminals? How can we identify them? How much crime does each one commit? What kinds of crime do they commit? How long do they stay active as criminals? When do they start their careers in crime? When do they stop? Why do they stop?

These questions are fundamental to any program targeting career criminals. The point is to control them *and only them*. It is a waste of time and money to imprison onetime offenders who do not repeat. Traditionally, criminal justice officials believed that they could identify the repeat offenders or the truly dangerous criminals. Judges denied bail to defendants they "knew" were dangerous. Judges granted some convicted offenders probation because they "knew" they were not going to commit more crimes. Most of these decisions were based on hunch, guesswork, or just plain bias. At best, they relied on the seriousness of the immediate offense and the offender's prior record.

This process is illustrated by the famous story about how one Supreme Court justice defined pornography. In the *Jacobellis* case (1964), Justice Potter Stewart admitted that he could not define "hard-core pornography" but said "I know it when I see it."[8] Many criminal justice officials believe they know a career criminal when they see one.

In the real world of criminal justice, career criminal programs run into two serious problems. The first is identifying the career criminal. We call this the prediction problem. The second is accurately estimating how much crime these career criminals actually do—and thus how much crime we will prevent by either imprisoning or treating them. Let us look at both of these problems in detail.

THE PREDICTION PROBLEM

We can use three basic methods for predicting criminal behavior. The first is an *actuarial* approach that relies on patterns of behavior among individuals with similar characteristics. Insurance companies use this method. The data indicate that young drivers have more accidents than middle-age drivers and that young men have much worse records than young women. Thus, they charge higher insurance rates for young people.

A second approach uses the *prior history* of the individual. You flunked the first test in this course; therefore, we predict that you will flunk the next one. As we learned in Chapter 3, criminal justice officials typically use prior criminal record to assess offenders. Sentencing guidelines build prior record into the matrix, assigning more points for each offense.

A third approach is *clinical evaluation*. Here, predictions about future behavior are based on the assessments of trained experts. A psychologist or social worker, for example, might conduct a personal interview, review the individual's social history (family, employment record, and so forth), and possibly administer a psychological test. Presentence investigations by probation officers are an example of clinical evaluations.

The question is, Can these techniques be used to successfully predict future criminal behavior? A good test was conducted on behalf of the National Council on Crime and Delinquency (NCCD) by Ernst A. Wenk, James O. Robison, and Gerald W. Smith. The results were not reassuring.

Wenk and his colleagues began with a sample of 4,146 youths committed to the California Youth Authority. Of this group, 104 subsequently became "violent recidivists." Wenk and his colleagues sought to develop a prediction instrument that would have identified these 104 individuals if it had been used in advance. Their instrument involved a combination of prior record and clinical assessment, using each juvenile's prior criminal record, history of violence and substance abuse, among other factors. Clinical assessments were based on psychological tests and interviews.[9]

Table 4.2 indicates the results. As is obvious, the method successfully identified only half (52) of the 104 who subsequently committed a violent act. This group is referred to as the "true positives." They were correctly and positively identified as likely to commit a violent act. The other fifty-two slipped through the net, however. We call them the "false negatives." They were falsely (or incorrectly) predicted not to be violent. From this perspective, the prediction instrument was only 50 percent accurate; it missed half of those who actually became violent.

There is an additional problem, however. As Table 4.2 indicates, 404 people were incorrectly predicted as likely to become violent. These are referred to as the "false positives." What this means is that the method used by Wenk and his associates incorrectly identified about eight people for every one who was successfully identified as likely to become violent. From this perspective, the prediction instrument is accurate only about 12 percent of the time (52 out of the total of 456 predicted to be violent). To translate this into real-world terms, it would mean imprisoning eight nonrecidivists for every violent recidivist correctly identified. Obviously, the costs in terms of dollars and unnecessary deprivation of liberty would be enormous.

The Wenk study reveals the difficulty in predicting human behavior. Even with the extensive data available to them, the study's method produced large number of both false positives and false negatives. Even though many people think they "know" career criminals "when they see one," in fact it is very difficult to predict future behavior accurately.

One way of illustrating this problem is to apply it to Wolfgang's birth cohort. If juvenile court officials used the same prediction instrument to identify the 627 chronic recidivists, they would first miss half of them (313) and, second, would needlessly lock up 2,500 juveniles who would not have become chronic recidivists.

Table 4.2 Number of youths predicted to be violent and nonviolent who proved to be violent and nonviolent, California, 1972

	Predicted violent	**Predicted nonviolent**
Actual violent	True positives: Violent persons correctly identified as violent and incarcerated 52	False negatives: Violent persons incorrectly identified as nonviolent and not incarcerated 52
Actual nonviolent	False positives: Nonviolent persons incorrectly identified as violent and needlessly incarcerated 404	True negatives: Nonviolent persons correctly identified as nonviolent 3,638

SOURCE: Ernst A. Wenk, James O. Robison, and Gerald W. Smith, "Can Violence Be Predicted?" *Crime and Delinquency,* 18 (October 1972): 393–402.

The Rand Selective Incapacitation Study

A second exercise in prediction was conducted by the Rand Corporation in its report *Selective Incapacitation.*[10] For this they used the Rand Inmate Survey (RIS), which involved self-report interviews with prison inmates in California, Texas, and Michigan. The survey asked inmates how many crimes they had committed between arrests.

Rand then used the actuarial method of prediction. It correlated the self-reported criminal activity with the social histories of the 2,190 inmates. This identified thirteen characteristics that were correlated with high rates of criminal activity. Only those characteristics that were legally relevant and appropriate were used. An offender's race is not a legally appropriate factor, for example. Rand then used this data to develop a seven-point prediction scale (Table 4.3). Offenders with four or more points were then predicted to be high-rate offenders; those with two to three points were predicted to be medium rate, and those with only one or no points were low-rate offenders.

In the next stage, Rand retrospectively correlated the prediction scores with inmates' actual reported criminal activity. The results appear in Table 4.4. The prediction device was correct only 51 percent of the time. This represents the combination of the predicted low-risk offenders who proved to be low risks (14 percent), the predicted medium risks who proved to be medium risks (22 percent), and the predicted high risks who actually proved to be high risks (15 percent). A 51 percent accuracy rate is not very good. You could do as well flipping a coin.

At the same time, the prediction device was *grossly* wrong in 7 percent of the cases: the 4 percent who were predicted to be high risks but who turned out to be low risks (false positives) and the 3 percent who were predicted to be low risks but proved to be high risks (false negatives). The prediction device was only *moderately* wrong in the remaining 42 percent of the cases.

Table 4.3 Seven-point scale of factors affecting prediction of offense rates

1. Prior conviction for the instant offense type
2. Incarcerated more than 50 percent of preceding two years
3. Conviction before age sixteen
4. Served time in a state juvenile facility
5. Drug use in preceding two years
6. Drug use as a juvenile
7. Employed less than 50 percent of the preceding two years

SOURCE: Peter W. Greenwood, *Selective Incapacitation* (Santa Monica, CA: Rand, 1982), p. 50.

Table 4.4 Predicted versus self-reported offense ratio for robbery and burglary

		Self-reported offense rates (%)			
Score on prediction scale		Low	Medium	High	Total
Low	(0–1)	14	10	3	27
Medium	(2–3)	12	22	10	44
High	(4–7)	4	10	15	29
Total		30	42	28	100

SOURCE: Peter W. Greenwood, *Selective Incapacitation* (Santa Monica, CA: Rand, 1982), p. 59.

We can hardly expect any system to be perfect. The relevant question is whether the Rand prediction device is *better* than existing sentencing practices. If it leads to a substantial improvement, even though less than perfect, the device would be useful. Peter Greenwood took his sample of offenders and categorized them as low, medium, or high risks according to the sentences they had actually received. These sentences were "correct" 42 percent of the time. That is, in 42 percent of the cases, the sentencing judges had correctly identified the high-rate offenders and sentenced them to long prison terms and correctly identified low-rate offenders and sentenced them to short terms. Meanwhile, the judges were grossly wrong 12 percent of the time. In short, the extremely sophisticated Rand prediction device was only slightly better than what judges had in fact already done with these offenders (51 percent versus 42 percent).

Several years later, Rand researchers made another attempt at predicting career criminals. They used two samples. One included 2,700 men who had been committed to the California Youth Authority (CYA) as juveniles between 1966 and 1971. The second group included 200 Rand Inmate Survey (RIS) inmates who had been incarcerated for either burglary or robbery and had been released at least two years before the new study. Rand used the original seven-point prediction scale for the RIS group and a modified five-point scale for the CYA group.[11]

The results of this study are expressed in the subtitle of the Rand report: *Why the High Rate Offenders Are Hard to Predict.* The authors concluded that "high rate offenders cannot be accurately identified, either prospectively or retrospectively, on the basis of their arrest rates alone."[12] They conceded that the earlier Rand conclusions about the ability to identify high-rate offenders and reduce crime by selectively incapacitating them were "overly optimistic."[13]

HOW MUCH CRIME DO THEY DO?

The second problem in translating career criminal research into policy involves estimating how many crimes the average high-rate offender commits. The estimate has important practical ramifications. Let us assume we want to lock up all armed robbers for a minimum of five years. How many crimes will we prevent? How much additional crime prevention will we achieve if we lock them all up for ten years?

The Rand Inmate Survey (RIS) attempted to estimate annual offending rates through interviews with inmates in three states: Michigan, Texas, and California. The RIS was one of the most influential studies, and its findings have been widely used. The self-report method was a major advance because official records on criminal activity do not provide a complete picture of what criminals actually do. Many crimes are not reported, and obviously, most crimes do not result in an arrest.

The RIS estimated high rates of criminal activity, but with some important variations. California robbers averaged fifty-three robberies per year, compared with seventy-seven for Michigan robbers but only nine a year for those in Texas. The RIS also found that criminals do not specialize in one type of crime. California robbers also averaged 90 burglaries, 163 thefts or frauds, and 646 drug offenses each year. Texas robbers, meanwhile, averaged twenty-four burglaries and ninety-eight thefts each year.[14]

Why were the rates so much higher for Michigan and California compared with those for Texas? The best explanation is that Texas judges send more robbers to prison. As a result, the Texas sample includes a higher proportion of low-rate offenders than Michigan and California. California judges were incarcerating only the worst robbers, with the result that the inmates had much higher annual crime rates.

The difference may seem like a minor technical point, but it has tremendous practical consequences. We need a precise estimate of the annual offending rate to calculate the amount of crime reduction we will get. The annual offending rate is expressed as *lambda.* If the lambda is large, then we can expect a substantial reduction in crime for every career criminal who is imprisoned or rehabilitated. But if the lambda is low (that is, if the average career criminal commits relatively few crimes each year), then the payoff will be much lower.

Estimates of lambda by respected scholars vary enormously. Alfred Blumstein and Jacqueline Cohen estimated that adult arrestees committed an annual average of 3.4 robberies and 5.7 burglaries in Washington and 4.7 robberies and 5.3 burglaries in Detroit. The National Youth Survey estimated that active offenders committed an average of 8.4 robberies and 7.1 burglaries per year.[15] At the other end of the scale, Edwin W. Zedlewski, in *Making Confinement Decisions*, used an estimate of 187 felonies per year.[16] The practical implications of these different estimates is obvious. If we accept Zedlewski's figure, we could expect a great reduction in crime. But if we accept Blumstein and Cohen's figure, we will get a much smaller payoff for locking up each offender. When we discuss incapacitation as sentencing policy in Chapter 7, we will take a critical look at Zedlewski's use of his 187 figure.

A major part of the problem here is the concept of *average* offending rates. The RIS data clearly indicate that there is no such thing as an "average" career criminal. The median annual robbery rate for the RIS inmates was five per year. The top 10 percent, however, averaged eighty-seven robberies per year.[17] It is important to remember that the RIS inmates are a pretty select group: they got caught and were sent to prison because judges regarded them as dangerous offenders. The top 10 percent of the RIS sample, then, are the worst of the worst.

From a practical standpoint, to get some real payoff in terms of crime reduction, it is necessary to identify this small group from among all the other "serious" offenders. Say, for example, that you wanted to send most robbers (five per year) to five-year prison terms and give the really high-rate robbers (eighty-seven per year) fifteen years. You would have to make very precise predictions.

We will examine this subject again in Chapter 7 when we discuss incapacitation as a crime control strategy. It is worth pointing out, however, that despite all the initial excitement about the possibilities of applying career criminal research through selective incapacitation, we have in practice abandoned that goal and adopted a policy of gross incapacitation. The prison population has soared because we are locking up lots of people without making fine distinctions.

CONCLUSION

The subject of career criminals is an excellent example of the difficulties of translating research into policy. No one seriously questions Wolfgang's original finding about the fact that a small group of offenders are responsible for a huge percentage of all crime. Subsequent research has tended to confirm it. Nor does anyone serious question the argument that we could make a substantial reduction in crime *if* we could correctly identify those people and keep them from committing more crime.

The key word here, of course, is *if.* Research on the prediction problem indicates that it is difficult, if not impossible, to precisely identify in advance the small group of high-rate offenders. This difficulty is compounded by the fact that estimates conflict on how much crime these high-rate offenders actually do. If the averages are in fact low, we will not get that much payoff in terms of crime reduction.

The problems we have identified here have a direct impact on many of the crime control policies we will examine in the chapters ahead. As we mentioned earlier, the administration of justice consists of a series of discretionary decision points. Many of those decisions involve predictions about who is and who is not dangerous.

NOTES

1. Marvin Wolfgang, Robert M. Figlio, and Thorsten Sellin, *Delinquency in a Birth Cohort* (Chicago: University of Chicago Press, 1972).

2. F. W. Dunford and D. S. Elliott, "Identifying Career Offenders Using Self-Reported Data," *Journal of Research in Crime and Delinquency* 21 (1984): 57–86.

3. Paul E. Tracy, Marvin E. Wolfgang, and Robert M. Figlio, *Delinquency in Two Birth Cohorts* (Chicago: University of Chicago Press, 1985).

4. Lyle W. Shannon, Judith L. McKim, James P. Curry, and Lawrence J. Haffner, *Criminal Career Continuity: Its Social Context* (New York: Human Sciences Press, 1988).

5. The findings of all the longitudinal studies are reviewed in David P. Farrington, Lloyd E. Ohlin, and James Q. Wilson, *Understanding and Controlling Crime: Toward a New Research Strategy* (New York: Springer, 1986); see especially pp. 50–52.

6. Alfred Blumstein, Jacqueline Cohen, Jeffrey Roth, and Christy A. Visher, eds., *Criminal Careers and "Career Criminals"* (Washington, D.C.: National Academy Press, 1986).

7. Samuel Walker, *Popular Justice: A History of American Criminal Justice*, 2d ed. (New York: Oxford University Press, 1997).

8. *Jacobellis v. Ohio*, 378 U.S. 184, 197 (1964).

9. Ernest A. Wenk, James O. Robison, and Gerald W. Smith, "Can Violence Be Predicted?" *Crime and Delinquency* 18 (October 1972): 339–402.

10. Peter W. Greenwood and Allan Abrahamse, *Selective Incapacitation* (Santa Monica, CA: Rand, 1982).

11. Peter W. Greenwood and Susan Turner, *Selective Incapacitation Revisited: Why the High-Rate Offenders Are Hard to Predict* (Santa Monica, CA: Rand, 1987).

12. Ibid., p. x.

13. Ibid., p. 49.

14. The data are in Greenwood and Abrahamse, *Selective Incapacitation*. The original report is Joan Petersilia, Peter W. Greenwood, and Marvin Lavin, *Criminal Careers of Habitual Felons* (Santa Monica, CA: Rand, 1977).

15. Alfred Blumstein and Jacqueline Cohen, "Estimating Individual Crime Rates from Arrest Records," *Journal of Criminal Law and Criminology* 70 (1979): 561–585; Blumstein et al., *Criminal Careers and "Career Criminals."*

16. Edwin W. Zedlewski, *Making Confinement Decisions* (Washington, D.C.: Government Printing Office, 1987).

17. Petersilia et al., *Criminal Careers of Habitual Felons.*

"Get Tough": The Conservative Attack on Crime

Conservatives argue that we can reduce serious crime if we just "get tough" with criminals. Their crime control agenda, which has not changed in thirty years, includes the following items.

First, we would reduce crime if we would just unleash the cops and give them more power and resources. We will look at several strategies for unleashing the cops in Chapter 5.

Second, we should (and can) deter crime through swifter, more certain and more severe punishments. We will take a close look at the theory of deterrence and some deterrence-oriented programs in Chapter 6.

Third, we should lock up more criminals by sending more to prison and for longer prison terms. This represents a strategy of incapacitation. We will look as several incapacitation programs in Chapter 7.

Fourth, conservatives believe that too many criminals "get off" through loopholes in the criminal justice system. We will examine four proposals designed to close loopholes in Chapter 8.

The 1994 Violent Crime Control Act incorporated much of the conservative agenda. It authorized $9 billion to hire 100,000 additional police officers, extended the death penalty to sixty different federal crimes, provided mandatory imprisonment for certain crimes, increased the penalties for certain drug offenses and other crimes, and offered financial assistance to states where persons convicted of violent crimes serve at least 85 percent of their prison terms.

The fact that President Bill Clinton sponsored and signed this law indicates the extent to which many liberals have adopted the conservative crime control agenda. Now let us take a look at these and other conservative crime control policies.

Unleash the Cops!

Conservatives believe we can reduce crime if we just unleash the cops. Give them more resources and powers, this argument goes, and the police will deter more crime and arrest more criminals. Two basic strategies are proposed for accomplishing this: hiring more police officers and removing the procedural restraints on obtaining evidence and confessions. Let us look at these and some other proposals to see whether they are likely to reduce crime.

MORE COPS

The 1994 Violent Crime Control and Law Enforcement Act authorized $9 billion to support the hiring of 100,000 additional police officers. The underlying idea is a popular one: reduce crime by putting more cops on the street. When the National Crime Survey asked people what improvement in policing they would like, both whites and African Americans said they wanted more police.[1] The fact that President Bill Clinton enthusiastically supported this idea is a good example of how many liberals have adopted traditional conservative crime control ideas in recent years.[2]

Putting more cops on the street has a certain commonsense logic to it: if police patrol prevents crime, then more police will reduce crime even further. Let us see whether this idea works.

**Table 5.1 Police-population ratios,
selected major cities, 1993**

City	Sworn officers per 1,000 citizens
District of Columbia	7.0
Newark, NJ	4.0
Detroit, MI	3.8
New York, NY	3.8
Philadelphia, PA	3.8
Houston, TX	2.8
Dallas, TX	2.8
Los Angeles, CA	2.2
San Diego, CA	1.7
San Jose, CA	1.6

SOURCE: Bureau of Justice Statistics, *Law Enforcement Management and Administrative Statistics, 1993* (Washington, D.C.: Government Printing Office, 1995).

The Police and Crime

A lot of mythology exists about police and crime. Simply hiring more police officers does not necessarily mean that more patrol officers will be on the street or that they will be more effective in fighting crime.

The standard measure of the level of police protection is the police-population ratio: the number of officers per 1,000 people.[3] Table 5.1 indicates that police-population ratios vary enormously. For instance, the fact that Washington, D.C., has three times as much police protection as Los Angeles and almost four and a half times as much as San Jose hardly makes it a safer city.

The police-population ratio is a virtually meaningless figure because it does not tell us how police departments *use* their officers. If a department does not get those officers out on the street, or if it uses inefficient two-officer patrols, additional officers will not have any real impact. Table 5.2 illustrates the point by comparing two hypothetical police departments, one that is very efficiently operated and one that is not. Both are in cities with populations of 500,000. One has 900 sworn officers, the other 600. The department with 900 officers, however, assigns a lower percentage to patrol. Many officers are probably assigned to desk jobs. The department also does not assign its patrol officers according to a rational workload formula, leaving the busy evening shift understaffed. Finally, it employs two-officer patrol units, which are much less efficient than one-officer units. The net result is that the city with the higher police-population ratio actually has fewer patrol units on the street during the high-crime evening shift. The citizens are paying more for police protection but getting less.

Table 5.2 Deployment of patrol officers in two hypothetical cities

	City X	City Y
Population	500,000	500,000
Sworn officers	900	600
Percentage of officers assigned to patrol	50	70
Officers assigned to patrol	450	420
Percentage of patrol officers assigned to 4 P.M.–12 A.M. shift	33	50
Patrol officers, 4 P.M.–12 A.M. shift	148	210
One-officer patrols	20	190
Two-officer patrols	64	10
Total patrols, 4 P.M.–12 A.M.	84	200

Even more important, the data in Table 5.2 do not address the question of what officers actually *do* when they are on the street.[4] A department may actually put a lot of officers on patrol, but if they do little real work, such as stopping and questioning suspects, the public will not get much in the way of actual crime fighting. We will look at some focused police activities shortly.

In short, simply adding more police to an already inefficient department is throwing money—or cops, in this case—at the problem. Conservatives are fond of attacking liberals for throwing money at social problems. This criticism applies to the idea of hiring more police.

The Lessons of Kansas City

Even if a police department succeeds in increasing the number of patrol officers, no evidence indicates that this reduces criminal activity. The idea that a visible police presence deters crime has been the core principle of modern policing since Robert Peel created the London Metropolitan Police in 1829. For nearly 150 years everyone accepted this idea on faith, without any scientific evidence to back it up. Finally, in the early 1970s, this traditional assumption was tested in the Kansas City Preventive Patrol Experiment, one of the most important events in police history.[5]

The experiment divided the South Patrol District into three groups of patrol beats. *Proactive* beats received two or three times the normal level of patrol. *Reactive* beats received no routine patrol. Police cars entered those areas only in response to a citizen's request. They handled the call and then left the beat area. *Control* beats kept the normal level of patrol. Using a victimization survey, the experiment examined the effect of different levels of patrol on criminal activity and citizen perceptions of police protection. Unlike in earlier experiments, they controlled for other variables that might affect the level of criminal activity: temporary or random changes in criminal activity,

The mayor wanted a more visible police presence.

unreported crime, the possible displacement of crime into neighboring areas, and the reactions of both police officers and citizens to changes in police activity.

The experiment found that the level of patrol activity had no effect on either crime or public perceptions. Crime did not increase in the reactive beats and did not decline in the proactive beats. Perhaps even more surprising, the public did not seem to notice the differences in the level of patrol activity. Fear of crime did not go up in the reactive beats where there was less patrol and did not go down in the proactive beats where there was more patrol.[6]

It is important to emphasize that the experiment did *not* prove that patrol has absolutely no effect on crime. No beats ever had no police presence whatsoever for any extended period of time. Patrol cars entered the reactive beats to handle calls, while officers in other units (for example, juvenile) entered these beats to handle their own assignments. Law-abiding citizens and potential criminals alike saw a marked police car and assumed that the police were patrolling the area. This phenomenon has been described as the "phantom effect": even if there are no police around, patrol works if people believe they are.

Most important for our purposes, the experiment confirmed the fact that *more* police patrol does not *reduce* the criminal activity. The Newark Foot Patrol Experiment also found that additional foot patrol had no effect on the crime rate, although it did reduce citizen fear of crime.[7]

Patrol has such a limited impact for several reasons. First, patrol is spread very thin even in the best of circumstances. A patrol car actually passes each point in its assigned beat very few times in any seven-day period. Doubling the number of patrol units still leaves a very thin layer of coverage.[8]

Second, many crimes are inherently not "suppressible" by patrol. The majority of murders and assaults, and about half of all rapes, occur between people who know each other. They usually occur indoors and in the heat of passion. The amount of patrol out on the street is not going to have any effect on these crimes. Robbery, burglary, and auto theft, which occur outside, are at least theoretically "suppressible" through patrol.[9]

A third limitation involves the concept of deterrence. Deterrence theory assumes that the threat of apprehension is *communicated* to its target audience, is *perceived* as a threat, and that people make *rational decisions* on the basis of that information.[10]

Several factors limit the deterrent effect of police patrol. First, as we have already pointed out, patrol is spread so thin that it does not communicate a threat to potential criminals; adding more patrol officers does not increase the perception of a police presence. Second, many criminals do not perceive police patrol or the possibility of arrest as a threat. Many believe that they will not be caught; other experienced criminals, on the other hand, are fatalistic and assume that sooner or later they will be caught. In either case, offenders are not making rational calculations about the risk of arrest and punishment. Analyzing the Rand Inmate Survey (RIS), James Q. Wilson and Alan Abrahamse found that most inmates were fatalistic and thought there was a good chance they would be arrested, convicted, or even injured as a result of doing crime.[11]

Our conclusion, then, is as follows:

PROPOSITION 6
Adding more police officers will not reduce crime.

What benefit are we likely to get from the 100,000 new police officers under the 1994 Violent Crime Control Act? If police departments simply use them in a traditional way, we will not get much. If they are used in creative ways, however, there might be some payoff. Let us take a look at some of these possibilities.

Focused Police Patrol Activities

Crackdowns A traditional form of focused police activity is the "crackdown:" a short burst of intensive law enforcement.[12] Most police crackdowns are crude and unsophisticated. Under Operation Hammer, for example, the Los Angeles Police Department made nearly 1,000 arrests of suspected drug gang members in a single weekend. Most of those arrested were quickly released, usually because of insufficient evidence, and no evidence indicated any reduction in either drug trafficking or gang activity.[13] Crackdowns of this sort are really media events, designed to convince the public that the police are "doing something" about crime.

The most well-known antidrug crackdown was Operation Pressure Point (OPP) in New York City. In the early 1980s, the police targeted an open drug market on the city's lower East Side that had been described as a "drug buyer's paradise." Under OPP an additional 240 officers flooded the area, dispersing crowds, stopping and questioning suspected drug buyers and sellers, writing traffic tickets, and making a high volume of arrests (more than 2,000 in the first month alone). Also, the police department ended its Desk Appearance Ticket (DAT) policy, which allowed persons charged with misdemeanors to be released immediately, and the U.S. attorney's office agreed to process many of the drug arrests in federal court where the defendants would face harsher sentences.[14]

Although an evaluation of Operation Pressure Point claimed that it effectively reduced the level of drug trafficking in the neighborhood, it left a number of important questions unanswered. It did not control for the possible displacement of drug trafficking into other neighborhoods. Moreover, drug dealers adapted to the crackdown with more sophisticated techniques, such as using lookouts and steerers to insulate the actual dealers from the police. The cost effectiveness of the arrests was not evaluated. Finally, the evaluation mentioned but did not discuss in detail the implications of the police misconduct that the program encouraged. Officers disrupted drug dealing by harassing potential buyers and scaring them off.[15]

Perhaps even more significant, the drug problem in the city as a whole only got worse after Operation Pressure Point. With the arrival of crack in the mid-1980s, entire neighborhoods were overtaken by open drug dealing. Police officers in those neighborhoods have conceded that large numbers of arrests do little good. As one put it, for every person arrested "there is always a replacement."[16]

Hot Spots A more sophisticated focused police activity involves targeting "hot spots." Lawrence W. Sherman's analysis of 911 calls in Minneapolis found the astonishing fact that 5 percent of the addresses in the city accounted for 64 percent of all 911 calls. A very few places, which he labeled "hot spots," were consuming the vast majority of police time and effort.[17]

Sherman and his colleagues then devised an experiment with intensive, focused police patrol of hot spots. Fifty-five hot spots received additional police patrol and were matched with a control group of fifty-five hot spots. The increased police patrol presence involved a "crackdown-backoff" pattern. Patrol cars would be in the target area for a short time, leave, and return again later. The experiment found that increased police presence had a "modest" deterrent effect, producing fewer calls for crime and lower rates of observed crime and disorder.[18] Christopher Koper's analysis of the data, moreover, indicated that the optimum "dosage" was between eleven and fifteen minutes of patrol presence. Longer police presence brought diminishing returns.[19]

Community Policing or "Problem-Oriented" Policing A number of community policing or "problem-oriented" policing experiments also involve focused police activity. Community policing is an alternative to the traditional crime-attack strategy of policing, emphasizing closer working relations with neighborhood residents, more decision-making authority for rank-and-file officers, and programs that target specific problems in the area. It often incorporates Herman Goldstein's concept of "problem-oriented" policing under which the police identify and focus on particular kinds of crime and disorder.[20]

The SMART program in Oakland involved a combination of problem-oriented policing and hot spots. The police participated in a multiagency task force targeting drug hot spots. In addition to increased police activity (more patrol, field interrogations, arrests), SMART mobilized officials from the Oakland housing, fire, and public works departments to enforce local building codes and clean up the physical appearance of the neighborhood. A training program for landlords was designed to help them screen prospective tenants and evict existing tenants for rules violations. Lorraine Green's evaluation of SMART found that it reduced the level of drug activity and, instead of displacing crime to nearby areas, actually had a "diffusion" effect leading to improvements in surrounding areas.[21]

In Chapter 10, we will look at another focused police activity, the Kansas City Gun Experiment, designed to reduce the number of handguns in high-crime areas.

Does Policing Make Any Difference at All?

It appears that some of the recent innovations in policing, involving limited and clearly focused police activities, may be successful in reducing crime and disorder. It is important to point out, however, that these programs do not necessarily require *more* police officers. They rely on different approaches to police work. This leads us to a new proposition:

PROPOSITION 7

Limited and clearly focused police activities, directed toward specific problems, may be successful in reducing certain kinds of crime and disorder.

The important point here is not to claim too much for some of these recent innovations. The impact of the police on crime is still a matter of great controversy. In the mid-1990s, serious crime has begun to fall. The decline is particularly dramatic in New York City. In 1996 the number of murders in New York fell to the lowest level since 1968. Major felonies fell 16 percent, marking the sixth straight year of decline. Similar reductions in serious crime have occurred in other big cities.[22]

What is responsible for this significant drop in crime? Many people are trying to claim credit. Former New York City Police Commissioner William Bratton claims that it is the result of his "zero-tolerance" policy regarding minor quality-of-life issues. The police have been aggressive in making arrests for minor crimes such as urinating in the street.[23] George Kelling sees the zero-tolerance policy as an application of "broken windows" theory. According to this theory, if the police concentrate on small quality of life issues, the improvement in the quality of life will indirectly lower the rate of serious crime.[24]

This interpretation has a number of problems as it applies to New York City, however. First, many cities have experienced reductions in crime, so the crime trends in New York City may not be the result of its zero-tolerance policy. Second, crime began to decline before Bratton became police commissioner. Some criminologists believe that it may be due to the aging of the population, with fewer people in the high-crime age group of fourteen to twenty-four. Also, a number of observers believe it is the result of the "maturing" of the drug markets. Much of the increase in the 1980s was a direct result of the advent of crack around 1985. It may be that the destabilizing effects of this epidemic are passing. In it important to point out that in New York City, Washington, D.C., and other cities, murder rates were falling in the early 1980s. It is possible that we are now returning to the trend that crack interrupted. Other social changes could also be contributing to these changes.[25]

In short, there is no easy answer to the question about the impact of the police on crime. In the search for sensible and effective crime policies, we should avoid the clichés on both sides. We should reject simplistic claims that the police reduce crime, and we should also reject the idea that "nothing works."

FASTER RESPONSE TIME

Many people believe that we could reduce crime if the police got to crime scenes faster. This idea has a basic, commonsense logic to it: the faster the police get there, the greater the likelihood they will arrest the offender. More arrests, meanwhile, will deter or incapacitate more criminals and lower the crime rate. Let us take a look at this idea.

Faster response time will not produce more arrests because the police are called to very few crimes in progress. At most only about 30 percent of all patrol dispatches involve criminal activity. Some studies put the figure as low as 17 percent. Moreover, about 75 percent of these crime-related calls involve "cold" crimes: typically, a burglary that occurred many hours earlier. The offender is long gone, and it makes no difference whether the police get there in three minutes or three hours.[26]

The remaining 25 percent of crime-related calls are "involvement" crimes, meaning a confrontation exists between the victim and a suspect. Response time rarely makes a difference in these crimes, either. In many cases the victim and offender are acquaintances. The victim can identify the suspect no matter when the police arrive. Also, victims usually do not call the police immediately. Traumatized and confused, they often try to compose themselves, decide whether to even call the police and often call a friend or family member first. This delay in calling the police renders the police travel time irrelevant in terms of catching the offender. Faster police response might make a difference in a very small number of crime calls: about 3 percent, according to a study by the Police Executive Research Forum. Commercial robberies are the best example. If someone calls the police while the crime is in progress, a very quick response time might improve the chances of catching the offender at the scene. But these kinds of crime are rare events.[27]

This leads to our next proposition:

PROPOSITION 8
Faster response time will not produce more arrests or lower the crime rate.

MORE DETECTIVES

As we have already pointed out, arrest is the weakest point in the criminal justice system. The police clear only about 21 percent of all Index crimes. Some people believe that we could increase the clearance rate if we just had more detectives or made other improvements in detective work. Let us take a look at this idea.

Myths and Realities of Detective Work

Some of the most durable myths about policing surround detectives. Movies and television cop shows portray criminal investigation as fast-paced, exciting, and dangerous work, with frequent shootings, car chases, and confrontations with dangerous criminals. In the classic television show from the 1950s, *Dragnet*, Sgt. Jack Webb always caught the offender. This media image of the police as "crime fighters" is pure mythology.

The reality of criminal investigation is very different from the media myth. It is generally boring, unglamorous, and highly unproductive. Instead of kicking in doors, ducking bullets, and wrestling with dangerous sociopaths, detectives spend most of their time writing reports. The Rand study of criminal investigation found that the typical case gets an average of about four hours' work, and most of that involves paperwork.[28]

Most of the crimes that are cleared are readily solved. The victim or a witness either knows the offender or can provide a good lead to the first police officer who arrives on the scene.[29] In many acquaintance crimes, the offender is still there when the police arrive, so that no real "detective" work is required. This explains why between 60 and 80 percent of all arrests are made by patrol officers instead of detectives.[30]

The importance of having a good lead at the very beginning was documented by the President's Crime Commission in a study of 1,905 cases handled by the Los Angeles police (Figure 5.1). The police cleared 86 percent of the 349 cases in which a suspect was immediately identified by the victim or witness. But they cleared only 12 percent of the remaining 1,556 cases in which no suspect was immediately identified.[31]

The key to solving crimes and making arrests, in short, is information about a suspect. Where no good information to work with is available at the very beginning of a case, the chances of clearing the crime are very limited. In other words, the chances of solving a crime depend primarily on the circumstances of the crime rather than the number of police officers or the amount of detective work. Increasing the number of detectives is not going to help. Having twice as many detectives, or spending twice as much time on a case, is not going to overcome the lack of any good leads. Detectives always complain about being overworked, and it is true that they are swamped with cases. Information, not time however, is the critical factor.[32]

We should not be distracted by celebrated cases. Every now and then detectives do solve a crime—often a high-profile murder or robbery—as a result of extensive detective work. But these are rare events and not typical of most cases. The famous "Unabomber" case is a good example of how crimes are solved. A nationwide manhunt by the FBI produced nothing for twenty years. A suspect was finally identified when his own brother, who had access to the suspect's writings and recognized a similarity to the Unabomber's manifesto, tipped off the FBI.

For the same reasons, better training for detectives is not likely to increase the clearance rate. Even the smartest and best-trained detective is not likely to solve a "cold" crime for which there are no leads. The Rand study of criminal investigation found that the quality of training made little difference in clearance rates between departments.[33] Training is not completely irrelevant. An incompetent detective can easily lose a case by bungling the interrogation or mishandling the evidence. Skill does make a difference and training can improve skills. But this assumes that there is some evidence to begin with.

A Word About Fingerprints   A lot of mythology surrounds fingerprints. The FBI has elevated fingerprints to near-mythical status. The Bureau now has nearly 200 million prints on file, and thousands of new sets arrive every day. (In the 1930s, the FBI launched an abortive campaign to fingerprint the entire population). The mystique of fingerprints was designed to project an image of the bureau as an incredibly efficient agency—efficient because it was backed by the massive weight of "science."

In reality, fingerprints are rarely the critical factor in solving crimes. It is extremely difficult to get usable prints from a crime scene. The New York City police obtain useful prints in only about 10 percent of all burglaries. And in only 3 percent of those cases did the prints help with the arrest. In Long

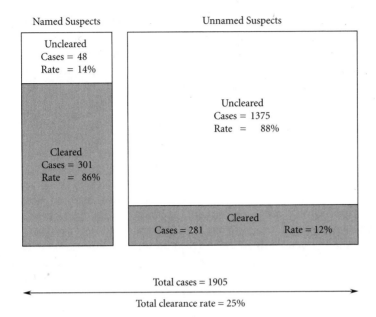

FIGURE 5.1 Clearance of crimes with names and unnamed suspects, Los Angeles Police Department, 1966.

SOURCE: President's Police Commission on Law Enforcement and Administration of Justice, *Task Force Report: Science and Technology* (Washington, D.C.: Government Printing Office, 1967), p. 8.

Beach, California, a suspect was identified through fingerprints in only 1.5 percent of all cases.[34]

Targeting Career Criminals

One of the hot new ideas in the 1980s called for the police to target a small number of suspected career criminals. Like selective incapacitation and major-offender prosecution programs, these programs are based on Wolfgang's birth cohort study, which we examined in Chapter 4. The assumption is that if detectives succeeded in arresting this small group of high-rate offenders, a significant reduction in crime will follow.

The Repeat Offender Project (ROP, pronounced "rope") in the Washington, D.C., police department involved a special unit of sixty officers targeting suspects they believed were committing five or more Index crimes a week. The list of suspects was developed by cross-indexing information from other units in the department, such as Investigation Services, the Career Criminal Unit, the Warrant Squad, the Court Liaison Division, the district commanders, and the Youth Division. ROP officers surveilled these suspects to arrest them for felonies.[35]

An evaluation of Washington's ROP program revealed mixed results. Around-the-clock surveillance of suspects quickly proved to be "time-consuming, frustrating, and unproductive." ROP officers got bored waiting and watching. As a result, ROP shifted its emphasis to suspects with arrest warrants on file. Eventually, half of the unit's time was devoted to this activity. In this respect, then, ROP essentially became an intensified warrant enforcement unit. Like many other supposed innovations, it called for officers to do what they always said they were doing.

The ROP unit officers succeeded in arresting 58 percent of their targeted group, significantly more than the 8 percent arrested among a control group of potential suspects. Nonetheless, the overall arrest productivity of ROP officers was less than that of a comparison group of officers. The sixty-two ROP officers produced sixty-six convictions by the end of the first year, or a little more than one per officer. Whether this is money well spent is a good question. Even more disturbing is the 37.2 percent conviction rate for ROP arrests (66 of 177). This seems to defy the basic rationale of career-criminal programs that supposedly target people who are believed to be active, high-rate offenders. You would expect a high conviction rate for these suspects. Given the cost of the program, and the reduction of nonarrest activities (such as order maintenance) by ROP officers, the evaluation raised serious questions about the cost-effectiveness of the program.[36]

PROPOSITION 9

More detectives, or other changes in detective work, will not raise clearance rates or lower the crime rate.

Arrest is the weakest point in the criminal justice system. Unfortunately, there does not appear to be any way to increase the clearance rate significantly. The ability of the police to solve crimes is primarily determined by the nature to individual crimes, and in particular whether there is a good lead about a suspect.

ELIMINATE THE "TECHNICALITIES"

Conservatives firmly believe that the courts have "handcuffed" the police with procedural rules that limit their power to investigate and solve crimes. According to this view, these "technicalities" of criminal procedure allow streetwise criminals to "beat the system" and avoid punishment. In a sweeping indictment of the criminal justice system, Judge Harold Rothwax of New York argues that the system is geared for "anything but the truth." Procedural rules designed to ensure "fairness" undermine the search for truth about guilt or innocence, with the result that "criminals go free."[37]

Conservatives direct their fire at the Supreme Court, particularly the Warren Court (1954–1968), which issued a series of decisions protecting the rights of suspects and limiting the powers of the police. The two most famous decisions, *Mapp* (1961) and *Miranda* (1966), coincided with the great increase in crime between the early 1960s and early 1970s. Consequently, many people blame the Court for our high rates of crime.[38]

Repeal the Exclusionary Rule

The Supreme Court established the exclusionary rule in the 1961 *Mapp v. Ohio* decision. The Court held that "all evidence obtained by searches and seizures in violation of the Constitution is, by that same authority, inadmissible in a state court."[39] Prosecutors cannot use evidence obtained in violation of the Fourth Amendment's guarantee of "the right of the people to be secure in their persons, houses, papers, and effects, against unreasonable searches and seizures." Evidence obtained illegally is "excluded" or inadmissible in court.

Mapp produced a storm of controversy that has continued for over thirty-five years. Critics charge that the exclusionary rule has limited the ability of the police to gather evidence necessary to convict criminals. Actually, the exclusionary rule was nothing new in 1961. The Supreme Court had applied it to federal proceedings in 1914 (*Weeks v. United States*). By 1961, it was already in effect in more than half of the states, mainly through decisions by state supreme courts. *Mapp* simply applied the exclusionary rule to all the states.

The exclusionary rule has three basic purposes: to protect the rights of individuals against police misconduct, to maintain the integrity of the judiciary, and to deter the police from misconduct. The rule has always evoked far more outrage than the equally famous *Miranda* warning. *Miranda* excludes confessions that have been obtained improperly. Even many law-and-order advocates concede that a coerced confession is wrong. But the *Mapp* exclusionary rule applies to physical evidence that speaks for itself, no matter how it was obtained. Therefore, they believe it should be allowed as evidence.

The Exclusionary Rule and Crime Fighting

Several studies indicate that the exclusionary rule has virtually no impact on the crime-fighting capacity of the police. James J. Fyfe argues that the impact is "minuscule" and "infinitesimal."[40] Very few cases are "lost" because the evidence is excluded as a result of an improper search. Drug cases are the only area where the rule has any noticeable impact, and even there the effect is fairly small. Take another look at the data in Table 3.1 in Chapter 3. It indicates that due process problems account for a very small percentage of all rejections and dismissals, and not all of those due process problems involve the exclusionary rule.

When we consider the realities of police work, we can understand why the exclusionary rule has such a limited impact. As we pointed out earlier, the police solve crimes when they immediately obtain a good lead about a suspect, from either the victim or a witness. Physical evidence, independent of some other kind of identification of the suspect, is rarely the primary factor in making an arrest and convicting an offender.

The limited impact of the exclusionary rule is mainly confined to drug possession, weapons possession, and gambling cases. It is not hard to see why.

The most important element of a drug possession case is whether the defendant actually had the drugs and how the police obtained the evidence. Robbery cases, on the other hand, are more likely to depend on eyewitness identification of the suspect. Physical evidence is rarely the crucial factor.

Once in court, few defendants try to use the exclusionary rule, and even fewer succeed. Procedurally, the defense attorney asks the court to exclude or suppress the evidence. Judges have the discretion to grant or deny the motion. Peter F. Nardulli found that motions to suppress physical evidence were made in fewer than 5 percent of all cases and were successful in only 0.69 percent of the total. A General Accounting Office (GAO) study of the federal courts found that motions to suppress evidence were filed in only 11 percent of all cases and that between 80 and 90 percent were denied. Finally, a study of search warrants by the National Center for State Courts showed that only 5 percent of all motions to suppress were successful.[41]

Defense lawyers file motions to suppress evidence because they have a professional obligation to represent their clients' interests. Not filing such motions might raise questions about their competence. Most of the time, however, they are just going through the motions, if you will pardon the expression. They are not the "crafty" lawyers of popular folklore. Most felony cases are handled by public defenders who are conscientious but extremely overworked. They have little time to devote to any one case, and in some jurisdictions they meet their clients only moments before entering the courtroom.

Even when a motion to exclude evidence succeeds, the defendant will not necessarily go free. He or she can still be convicted on other evidence. If an appeals court overturns a conviction under the exclusionary rule, the prosecutor can refile charges on the basis of the remaining evidence. A study of search warrant cases found that twelve of the seventeen defendants (70 percent) who succeeded in having evidence suppressed were subsequently convicted on other charges.[42]

Judges vary greatly in their willingness to invoke the exclusionary rule. Sheldon Krantz and his colleagues found in his study of Boston that one judge granted 45.4 percent of the motions to suppress, whereas another granted only 22.2 percent. Three judges denied all of motions presented to them. Motions to suppress were successful in only 2 percent of all the gambling and drug cases that Krantz et al. studied.[43]

A controversial 1982 study by the National Institute of Justice produced a much higher estimate of the rule's impact. It found that in 520,993 felony arrests in California between 1976 and 1979 prosecutors rejected a total of 86,033 cases for various reasons. Illegally obtained evidence accounted for 4,130 of those rejections. The Justice Department claimed that the 4,130 represented 4.8 percent of the 86,033 rejections.[44] In a pair of stinging critiques, Thomas Y. Davies and James J. Fyfe argued that it was more accurate to consider the 4,130 rejections as a percentage of the original 520,993 cases. This produces a rejection rate of only 0.8 percent (a figure that is very close to some of the other studies).[45]

In short, the exclusionary rule does not let "thousands" of dangerous criminals loose on the streets, and it has almost no effect on violent crime. Judge
Rothwax and other critics of the exclusionary rule are guilty of reacting to a
few celebrated cases. Yes, some convictions are overturned, and some of those
defendants who are factually guilty are released, but these are rare events.

Our position, therefore, is this:

PROPOSITION 10

**Repeal or modification of the exclusionary rule will not help
the police reduce serious crime.**

The Positive Impact of the Exclusionary Rule

Far from impairing police work, the exclusionary rule has played a major role
in improving the professionalism of police work. Myron Orfield's study of
narcotics officers in Chicago found that the exclusionary rule produced a
number of significant reforms. The Chicago police and the Illinois state's attorney office developed a closer working relationship, the state attorney scru-
tinized applications for warrants more closely, and the police department
improved its own training and supervision. The result was better police work.
Interviews with Chicago narcotics detectives found that they supported the
rule and were very concerned that weakening it would open the door to police abuse. Officers said that the experience of having evidence excluded in
court was a valuable learning experience—the best on-the-job training they
ever got.[46]

Response to the exclusionary rule depends on the professionalism of a police department. Craig Uchida and Tim Bynum studied the impact of the
Leon decision in seven jurisdictions. Like the earlier studies, they found that
the overall impact of the exclusionary rule was "slight." Less than one percent
(0.9) of all motions to suppress evidence obtained by search warrants were
successful. In three of the seven jurisdictions, no motions to suppress evidence
were successful. Those sites had a high degree of cooperation between police
and prosecutors that included training of police officers and supervision of
warrants. In "River City," however, the police were less professional and had
an antagonistic relationship with prosecutors. Motions to suppress were filed
in 57 percent of all cases, and 14 percent of them were successful.[47]

Many thoughtful law enforcement executives now accept and even wel-
come the rule. Former FBI Director William Sessions said that "protections
that are afforded by the exclusionary rule are extremely important to fair play
and the proper carrying out of the law enforcement responsibility."[48] Because
of the rule, law-abiding citizens do not have to fear overzealous and intrusive
action by a cop, and so the police enjoy greater public respect.

Instead of abolishing the exclusionary rule altogether, some critics propose
modifying it to permit "good-faith" searches: cases in which the officer made

an honest mistake (as in getting a number wrong on a street address). The Supreme Court adopted the good faith exception in *United States v. Leon* (1984), ruling that evidence could be admitted if it were obtained under a valid search warrant even though it was later found that there was not probable cause to issue the warrant.[49]

The good-faith exception, however, presents several problems. First, it complicates rather than simplifies search-and-seizure cases by opening the door to appeals based on whether the search was in good or bad faith and whether the officer made an honest mistake or a deliberate one. Fyfe argues that this makes the judge's job even harder. Second, the good-faith exception encourages police incompetence. It gives officers an incentive to claim that they made a minor mistake instead of prodding them to do a professional job in the first place. One of the main effects of the exclusionary rule has been to stimulate police professionalism.[50]

Finally, and most important in terms of crime fighting, the good-faith search is not going to significantly increase the number of convictions because few convictions are being "lost" owing to the exclusionary rule's existence.

Abolish *Miranda*

The *Miranda* warning is the second major "technicality" that conservatives believe "handcuffs" the police. The 1966 *Miranda v. Arizona* decision held that, to ensure a suspect's Fifth Amendment protection against self-incrimination, the police must advise a criminal suspect of certain rights: Prior to any questioning, the person must be warned that he has a right to remain silent, that any statement he does make may be used against him, and that he has a right to the presence of an attorney, either retained or appointed.[51]

Conservatives have been angry about *Miranda* ever since. In the original decision, Justice Byron White dissented on the grounds that it "return[s] a killer, a rapist or other criminal to the streets and to the environment which produced him, to repeat his crime whenever it pleases him." Other opponents have repeated this criticism for thirty years.[52]

Thirty years later, the *Miranda* warning is the most widely known and probably most misunderstood element of police procedure. Hollywood and television writers love it. The warning adds a special dramatic complication to the plot. In one movie, a narcotics detective wrestles the suspect to the ground with one arm while reading from the *Miranda* warning card he holds in the other hand. Get it? The police have one hand tied behind their backs. Because movies and TV shows have included the rule so often, most kids on the street know about it. A 1991 public opinion poll on the two-hundredth anniversary of the Bill of Rights found that while only 10 percent knew why it was originally adopted, 80 percent knew about their right to remain silent if arrested.[53]

Miranda in Operation

Does the *Miranda* warning really handcuff the police? Let us look at it in operation. First, let us clear up a few myths about the decision. The *Miranda* warning does not have to be given at the moment of arrest but only before questioning. If a suspect blurts out a confession ("Why did I do it?"), the confession is admissible. Also, a suspect can waive his or her rights by agreeing to talk and agreeing to talk without a lawyer. In fact, many suspects do waive their rights.

Paul G. Cassell, a strong critic of *Miranda*, properly raises the question of how we should measure the impact (or the "cost") of *Miranda*. He makes a persuasive argument that we should not look at the number of convictions overturned because of a *Miranda* violation but the number of confessions the police do not get. Surveying all of the studies done to date, he estimates that the rate of confessions has declined by 16 percent because of *Miranda*. But that is not the whole story, because some offenders are convicted even without a confession. He estimates that confessions are needed in about 24 percent of all cases. Thus, the net effect is that *Miranda* results in a "loss" of convictions in 3.8 percent of all cases (16 percent of 24 percent = 3.8 percent). Despite Professor Cassell's own claims, this is not a very significant impact.[54]

The best study of *Miranda* in operation is Richard Leo's "Inside the Interrogation Room," in which he directly observed a total of 182 police interrogations in a major urban department. He found that seventy-eight of the suspects waived their *Miranda* rights and cooperated with the police. (Cassell found that 84 percent of the suspects in Salt Lake waived their *Miranda* rights).[55] As a result, two-thirds (64 percent) made a full confession, a partial confession, or some incriminating statement. What tactics did the police use to get them to cooperate? In over 80 percent of the cases, the police either confronted them with evidence of their guilt or appealed to their self-interest (it will help you if you talk), or both.[56]

In short, the *Miranda* warning was no barrier to successful police work. In the vast majority of the cases, the police got suspects to waive their rights, to confess or make an incriminating statement, and they did through lawful means. (It should be noted that in 30 percent of the cases, the police lied by confronting the suspects with false information about their guilt, as in falsely telling them that their partner had confessed).

Why do suspects waive their rights and confess? Why do only about 20 percent of suspects take advantage of their right to remain silent? The first point is that the police do not arrest very many suspects. They only clear about 26 percent of all robberies and 14 percent of all burglaries. Thus, they usually have some evidence against the few suspects they do arrest. This leaves a small group of cases in which there is reasonably strong evidence. And as Leo discovered, detectives confront 85 percent of all suspects with evidence of their guilt. The suspects in these remaining cases have powerful incentives to cooperate and confess. They know that they committed the crime, and they realize that the police have some fairly good evidence against them. A lot of them feel guilty about it. Leo found that detectives appealed to suspects' conscience in 23 percent of all cases. Some hope to get a better deal in a plea bargaining. The detectives in Leo's study appealed to the suspects' self-interest in 88 percent of the cases.[57]

The image of the tough streetwise criminal who is skilled at manipulating the rules is another myth. Some suspects do invoke their *Miranda* rights, but the majority cooperate with the police. Felony suspects are typically young, poorly educated, and in many instances functionally illiterate. Most failed to learn how to manipulate the public school bureaucracy to their advantage, and they are not much more successful in the criminal justice system. The typical robber or burglar is so disorganized and impulsive that he does not even plan his crimes very well. The Rand Inmate Survey found that 40 percent of the juvenile robbers and 25 percent of the adults had not even intended to rob anyone when they left home. As one kid put it, "It was just a sudden thing. I didn't really mean to do it. I didn't plan nothing; it just happened." Among the adult "career criminals," only 40 percent bothered to visit the sites of their crimes in advance, and as few as 22 percent made an effort to check on police patrol in the area.[58]

In custody, young offenders may strike a tough pose, but it is usually nothing more than that—a pose, an act. A skilled, professional detective can get most suspects to talk.

Modifying *Miranda*

In 1984 the Supreme Court finally accepted the conservative argument and created a "public safety" exception to the *Miranda* warning. In *New York v. Quarles*, the Court held that when the safety of an officer or a citizen is threatened, as by the presence of a gun, the officer may ask questions before advising a suspect of his or her rights.[59] The decision represents a major victory in the conservatives' thirty-year campaign to reverse the rules laid down by the Warren Court. Given the limited impact of the *Miranda* warning on confessions, however, it is hard to imagine that this limited exception would result many more arrests or any significant crime reduction.

Consequently, our conclusion is as follows:

> ### PROPOSITION 11
> **Repeal or modification of the *Miranda* warning
> will not result in more convictions.**

CONCLUSION

The police are the front line of the criminal justice system. Patrol is the primary strategy for preventing crime, and arrest is "gatekeeping" point for all criminal cases. Many people believe we could reduce crime significantly if we would just "unleash" the cops: give them more resources and more powers. We have found that these ideas are not likely to reduce crime. The only promising strategies involve some of the new focused police programs, such as "hot spots" and some community policing programs.

NOTES

1. *Department of Justice, The Police and Public Opinion* (Washington, D.C.: Government Printing Office, 1977).

2. Bill Clinton and Al Gore, *Putting People First* (New York: Times Books, 1992), p. 72.

3. Police-population ratios are regularly published in Federal Bureau of Investigation, *Crime in the United States* (Washington, D.C.: Government Printing Office, annual), and Bureau of Justice Statistics, *Law Enforcement Management and Administrative Statistics, 1993* (Washington, D.C.: Government Printing Office, 1995).

4. Lawrence W. Sherman and David Weisburd, "General Deterrent Effects of Police Patrol in Crime 'Hot Spots': A Randomized Controlled Trial," *Justice Quarterly* 12 (December 1995): 625–648.

5. George L. Kelling, Tony Pate, Duane Diekman, and Charles E. Brown, *The Kansas City Preventive Patrol Experiment: A Summary Report* (Washington, D.C.: The Police Foundation, 1974).

6. Ibid.

7. The Police Foundation, *The Newark Foot Patrol Experiment* (Washington, D.C.: The Police Foundation, 1981).

8. This and other points are discussed in Sherman and Weisburd, "General Deterrent Effects of Police Patrol in Crime 'Hot Spots.'"

9. Wesley G. Skogan and George E. Antunes, "Information, Apprehension, and Deterrence: Exploring the Limits of Police Productivity," *Journal of Criminal Justice* 7 (Fall 1979): 228–229.

10. Franklin E. Zimring and Gordon J. Hawkins, *Deterrence: The Legal Threat in Crime Control* (Chicago: University of Chicago Press, 1973).

11. James Q. Wilson and Alan Abrahamse, "Does Crime Pay?" *Justice Quarterly* 9 (September 1992): 372–373.

12. Lawrence W. Sherman, "Police Crackdowns," in Michael Tonry and Norval Morris, eds., *Crime and Justice: An Annual Review of Research*, vol. 12 (Chicago: University of Chicago Press, 1990), pp. 1–48.

13. Jerome Skolnick and James J. Fyfe, *Above the Law* (New York: Free Press, 1993).

14. Lynn Zimmer, "Proactive Policing Against Street-Level Drug Trafficking," *American Journal of Police* 9(1) (1990): 43–74.

15. Ibid.

16. "The World of the Drug Bazaar," *New York Times* (October 1, 1992); "Neighborhood Ruled by Drug Culture," *New York Times* (October 2, 1992).

17. Lawrence W. Sherman, Patrick R. Gartin, and Michael E. Buerger, "Hot Spots of Predatory Crime: Routine Activities and the Criminology of Place," *Criminology* 27(2) (1989): 27–55.

18. Lawrence W. Sherman and David Weisburd, "General Deterrent Effects of Police Patrol in Crime 'Hot Spots': A Randomized, Controlled Trial," *Justice Quarterly* 12 (December 1995): 625–648.

19. Christopher S. Koper, "Just Enough Police Presence: Reducing Crime and Disorderly Behavior by Optimizing Patrol Time in Crime Hot Spots," *Justice Quarterly* 12 (December 1995): 649–672.

20. Herman Goldstein, *Problem-Oriented Policing* (New York: McGraw-Hill, 1990).

21. Lorraine Green, "Cleaning Up Drug Hot Spots in Oakland, California: The Displacement and Diffusion Effects," *Justice Quarterly* 12 (December 1995): 737–754.

22. "Crime Rate Drops in New York City," *New York Times* (December 20, 1996).

23. "Finally, We're Winning the War Against Crime," *Time* (January 15, 1996).

24. George Kelling and Catherine M. Coles, *Fixing Broken Windows* (New York: Martin Kessler Books, 1996).

25. "Barrooms' Decline Underlies Drip in Adult Killings, Police Say," *New York Times* (August 19, 1996).

26. William Spelman and Dale K. Brown, *Calling the Police: Citizen Reporting of Serious Crime* (Washington, D.C.: Government Printing Office, 1984).

27. Ibid.

28. Peter Greenwood, *The Criminal Investigation Process* (Santa Monica, CA: Rand, 1975).

29. Skogan and Antunes, "Information, Apprehension, and Deterrence."

30. Albert J. Reiss, *The Police and the Public* (New Haven, CT: Yale University Press, 1971), p. 104.

31. President's Commission on Law Enforcement and Administration of Justice, *Task Force Report: Science and Technology* (Washington, D.C.: Government Printing Office, 1967), p. 8.

32. John E. Eck, *Solving Crimes: The Investigation of Burglary and Robbery* (Washington, D.C.: Police Executive Research Forum, 1983).

33. Greenwood, *The Criminal Investigation Process.*

34. Joan Petersilia, "Processing Latent Fingerprints—What Are the Payoffs?" *Journal of Police Science and Administration* 6 (June 1978): 157–167.

35. Susan E. Martin and Lawrence W. Sherman, "Selective Apprehension: A Police Strategy for Repeat Offenders," *Criminology* 24 (February 1986): 155–173; Susan E. Martin, "Policing Career Criminals: An Examination of an Innovative Crime Control Program," *Journal of Criminal Law and Criminology* 77 (Winter 1986): 1159–1182.

36. Ibid.

37. Harold J. Rothwax, *Guilty: The Collapse of Criminal Justice* (New York: Random House, 1996), p. 15.

38. Samuel Walker, *Popular Justice: A History of American Criminal Justice*, 2d ed. (New York: Oxford University Press, 1998).

39. *Mapp v. Ohio*, 367 U.S. 643 (1961).

40. James J. Fyfe, "The NIJ Study of the Exclusionary Rule," *Criminal Law Bulletin* 19 (May–June 1983): 253–260.

41. Peter F. Nardulli, "The Societal Costs of the Exclusionary Rule: An Empirical Assessment," *American Bar Foundation Research Journal* 1983 (Summer 1983): 585–690; Comptroller General of the United States, *Impact of the Exclusionary Rule on Federal Criminal Prosecutions*, Report #GGD-79-45 (April 19, 1979); National Center for State Courts, *The Search Warrant Process* (Williamsburg, VA: National Center for State Courts, 1986).

42. National Center for State Courts, *The Search Warrant Process.*

43. Sheldon Krantz, Bernard Gilman, Charles G. Benda, Carol Rogoff Hallstrom, and Gail J. Nadworny, *Police Policymaking* (Lexington, MA: Lexington Books, 1979), pp. 189–192.

44. National Institute of Justice, *The Effects of the Exclusionary Rule: A Study in California* (Washington, D.C.: Government Printing Office, 1982).

45. Fyfe, "The NIJ Study of the Exclusionary Rule"; Thomas Y. Davies, "A Hard Look at What We Know (And Still Need to Learn) About the 'Costs' of the Exclusionary Rule: The NIJ Study and Other Studies of 'Lost' Arrests," *American Bar Foundation Research Journal* 1983 (Summer 1983): 611–690.

46. Myron W. Orfield, Jr., "The Exclusionary Rule and Deterrence: An Empirical Study of Chicago Narcotics Officers," *University of Chicago Law Review* 54 (Summer 1987): 1016–1055.

47. Craig Uchida and Tim Bynum, "Search Warrants, Motions to Suppress and 'Lost Cases': The Effects of the Exclusionary Rule in Seven Jurisdictions," *Journal of Criminal Law and Criminology* 81 (Winter 1991): 1034–1066.

48. Sessions quoted in *New York Times* (November 5, 1987).

49. *United States v. Leon*, 468 U.S. 897 (1984).

50. James J. Fyfe, "In Search of the 'Bad Faith' Search," *Criminal Law Bulletin* 18 (May–June 1982): 260–264.

51. *Miranda v. Arizona*, 384 U.S. 436 (1966).

52. The best overview is Richard Leo, "The Impact of *Miranda* Revisited," *Journal of Criminal Law and Criminology* 86(3) (1996): 621–692.

53. "Poll Finds Only 33% Can Identify Bill of Rights," *New York Times* (December 15, 1991).

54. Paul G. Cassell and Bret S. Hayman, "Police Interrogation in the 1990s: An Empirical Study of the Effects of Miranda," *UCLA Law Review* 43 (February 1996): 860.

55. Paul G. Cassell, "Miranda's Social Costs: An Empirical Reassessment," *Northwestern University Law Review* 90 (Winter 1996): 387–499.

56. Richard A. Leo, "Inside the Interrogation Room," *Journal of Criminal Law and Criminology* 86(2) (1996): 266–303.

57. Ibid.

58. Joan Petersilia, Peter W. Greenwood, and Martin Lavin, *The Criminal Careers of Habitual Felons* (Washington, D.C.: Government Printing Office, 1978).

59. *New York v. Quarles*, 467 U.S. 649 (1984).

6

Deter the Criminals

Determinism is an article of faith among conservatives: punishment deters crime; swifter, more certain, and more severe punishments will reduce crime even further. In this chapter we will look at deterrence in theory and practice. We are going to violate our own ground rules and discuss some issues that fall outside the scope of our inquiry: the death penalty, drunk driving crackdowns, and domestic violence. They are not directly related to robbery and burglary, but they offer some important evidence about deterrence.

DETERRENCE THEORY

The theory of deterrence has a fairly simple, intuitive appeal. People want to avoid unpleasant experiences; if we make the punishment for crime more unpleasant, fewer people will commit crime. The basic theory is simple, but in actual practice it is very complex, resting on a number of related assumptions that may not be valid in the real world of the criminal justice.[1]

Several examples of deterrence-oriented policies can be found in criminal justice. Traditional police patrol is based on the idea that a visible police presence deters crime. Yet, as we learned in the previous chapter, there are serious limits to how well it works in practice. Simply adding more patrol officers does not automatically reduce the crime rate.

Another even more controversial example involves the death penalty. Advocates of capital punishment believe it deters crime. They cite the trends in the 1960s when executions ended and the violent crime rate soared. Later in this chapter we will examine this argument. Along the same lines, David P. Farrington and Patrick A. Langan argue that crime increased in England in the 1980s as the level of imprisonment declined. During the same period, crime in the United States declined as imprisonment soared.[2] Advocates of imprisonment believe this situation reflects the combined effects of deterrence and incapacitation. The relationship between punishment and crime rates is extremely complex, however, and not everyone accepts this argument.

Assumptions Underlying Deterrence

The theory of deterrence involves a number of basic assumptions. Most important, it assumes that people are *rational actors* who weigh the relative costs and benefits of potential actions and then make conscious decisions about the best course of action. It further assumes that we can influence people's behavior by altering the perceived costs and benefits. Thus, if we make punishment more certain and/or more severe, we will influence them not to commit crime.

Deterrence theory assumes the existence of an information loop involving potential offenders' knowledge and perception of the potential punishment. First, offenders have to be *aware* of the penalty for particular crimes (for example, mandatory jail term for a first-offense drunk driving conviction). Second, they have to *perceive* the consequences as *unpleasant* and therefore something to be avoided. Third, they have to *believe* a real *risk* of arrest, conviction, and punishment is present. As Scott Decker and his colleagues point out, "Deterrence is essentially a psychological process that involves the balancing of personally held beliefs about possible punishment and anticipated gain."[3] Certainty and swiftness of punishment are regarded as essential to this process in order to heighten the connection between the crime and its consequences.

Deterrence can be of two types, depending on the target audience. *Specific* deterrence is directed at the individual offender. The punishment is intended to teach that person right and wrong, that criminal activity leads to unpleasant consequences. *General* deterrence is directed at the society as a whole. Punishing a few criminals is designed to communicate a message to the larger audience.[4]

With respect to designing crime policies, an important distinction must also be made between *absolute* and *marginal* deterrence. The idea of absolute deterrence posits that a particular punishment deters crime (or a particular crime) completely. Marginal deterrence holds that a relatively more severe penalty will produce *some* reduction in crime.[5] No one realistically expects any punishment to eliminate crime completely. Therefore, in this book we are really concerned with policy that will make some marginal but significant reduction in crime.

After being out of favor among criminologists for decades, deterrence theory enjoyed a tremendous revival in the 1980s. The revival was not confined to criminal justice policy. Ronald L. Akers points out that the underlying theory of rational choice became a "hot topic" in many of the social sciences in the 1980s.[6] It was especially influential in economic theory and many aspects of social policy. Conservative policy on welfare reform, for example, rests on the belief that traditional welfare programs provide too few incentives for finding employment. Cutting welfare benefits and putting a cap on the number of years of welfare eligibility, conservatives argue, will give people an incentive to find employment and get off welfare.[7]

We should also point out that on certain issues, many liberals also believe in deterrence. They believe, for example, that the exclusionary rule deters police misconduct and that gun control laws with stiff penalties will deter illegal gun ownership.[8]

THE RISK OF CRIME:
SOME PRELIMINARY EVIDENCE

Because deterrence theory rests on the actual and perceived risk of crime, it is useful to review what we learned in Chapters 2 and 3 about the administration of justice. Only 37 percent of all Index crimes are reported to the police, and the police clear only 21 percent of those crimes. Thus, only 8 percent of all Index crimes result in arrest. Since about half of all felony arrests are dismissed, only 4 percent of all crimes are prosecuted. In short, the overall risk of punishment (defined as conviction) is extremely low. This creates a serious problem for deterrence theory. Moreover, as we learned in the previous chapter, the prospects for increasing the number of arrests are not very good.

The risks are somewhat higher for particular crimes. Virtually all murders are reported, and the police clear about 68 percent of them. A Justice Department report found that 87 percent of all husbands tried for murdering their wives are convicted, and 81 percent of them are sentenced to prison.[9] Meanwhile, about 54 percent of all robberies are reported, and the police clear about 26 percent of them. This yields an overall apprehension risk of 14 percent, which is significantly higher than the rate for all Index crimes.

Looking at the risks of crime from the perspective of individual offenders, particularly career criminals, creates some additional problems for deterrence theory. The Rand Inmate Survey (RIS) found that offenders were extremely fatalistic about their chances of being arrested and punished. Unfortunately, neither the perceived risk nor the actual experience of imprisonment seems to deter them from criminal activity. James Q. Wilson and Allan Abrahamse conclude that the RIS offenders do not act rationally, as deterrence theory requires.[10]

Now let us turn our attention to some policies designed to deter crime and see what we can learn about deterrence theory in practice.

THE DEATH PENALTY

The death penalty is a good subject for examining deterrence theory for two reasons. First, many people believe that capital punishment deters crime; second, considerable research has been done on the subject.

Sorting Out the Issues

We can debate the merits of the death penalty in terms of three separate issues.[11] First is the moral question of whether it is a just form of punishment. Some people firmly believe it is a morally justifiable form of punishment for murder, whereas others believe it is morally wrong. This debate involves basic conceptions of morality and justice and is not subject to empirical proof one way or the other.

The question of whether the death penalty is constitutional is the second issue. Constitutional challenges began in the 1960s and eventually led to the 1972 *Furman v. Georgia* decision in which the U.S. Supreme Court ruled that the death penalty had been applied in an unconstitutionally arbitrary and capricious fashion.[12] It rejected the argument that capital punishment is inherently cruel and unusual. Four years later, in *Gregg v. Georgia*, the Court upheld the constitutionality of the death penalty where there were guidelines to control its application.[13]

The third issue is whether the death penalty deters crime. That is the focus of our discussion here. The moral and constitutional questions are extremely important and covered in many other books, but they are not the focus of our discussion here.

Executions and Crime: Sellin's Studies

Some of the first attempts to study the deterrent effect of capital punishment were relatively simple comparative and longitudinal studies. The noted criminologist Thorsten Sellin compared neighboring states, two with and one without the death penalty. As Table 6.1 indicates, Ohio and Indiana, two death penalty states, did not have lower crime rates than Michigan, which does not have the death penalty. Murder rates in all three states changed in roughly the same direction, decreasing from the 1930s to the early 1960s and then rising sharply. This suggests that broad social factors common to all states, rather than executions, were the primary causal factors in homicide rates.[14]

Sellin also examined individual states over time. Kansas, which had earlier abolished the death penalty, restored it in 1935. Its homicide trends were nearly identical to those in Missouri and Colorado, which had kept the death penalty throughout the period.

Sellin's research did not conclusively demonstrate the absence of a deterrent effect. His fairly simple methodology did not control for all the variables that might influence homicide rates. Now let us turn our attention to one controversial study that did attempt to.

Dr. Ehrlich's Magic Bullet

The debate over the deterrent effect of the death penalty entered a new phase in 1975 when economist Isaac Ehrlich produced a study of crime and executions between 1930 and 1969 purporting to prove that each execution deterred seven or eight murders.[15] If his analysis is correct, the death penalty has a powerful deterrent effect.

Did Ehrlich prove his case? His major contribution to death penalty research was his sophisticated formula that attempted to control for all of the variables that might have affected the murder rate. This included the probability of apprehension, the probability of conviction for murder, the probability of execution, the unemployment rate, the labor force participation of adults, the real per capita income, and the proportion of the population between the ages of fourteen and twenty-four. He explicitly embraced the rational choice theory of human behavior, explaining that "the propensity" to commit crimes "crimes is influenced by the prospective gains and losses associated with their commission."[16]

Critics, however, quickly found flaws in his analysis. His sophisticated mathematical formula, which appeared to be the strongest part of his approach, also turned out to be his greatest weakness. The formula is highly sensitive to problems with the reliability of the data. Critics focused on the 1960s, when executions stopped and violent crime increased. As we already noted, this pat-

Table 6.1 Homicide rates in death penalty states (Ohio, Indiana) and in a state without the death penalty (Michigan), 1920–1974 (homicides per 100,000 population)

Five-year periods	Michigan Rates	Ohio Rates	Ohio Number of executions	Indiana Rates	Indiana Number of executions
1920–1924	5.5	7.4	45	6.1	5
1925–1929	8.2	8.4	40	6.6	7
1930–1934	5.6	8.5	43	6.5	11
1935–1939	3.9	5.9	29	4.5	22
104--1944	3.2	4.3	15	3.0	2
1945–1949	3.5	4.8	36	3.8	5
1950–1954	3.8	3.8	20	3.7	2
1955–1959	3.0	3.4	12	3.0	0
1960–1964	3.6	3.2	7	3.2	1
1965–1969	6.6	5.1	0	4.7	0
1970–1974	11.3	7.8	0	6.4	0

SOURCES: National Office of Vital Statistics, *Vital Statistics of the United States*; William J. Bowers, *Executions in America* (Lexington, MA: Heath, 1974), Appendix A; Thorsten Sellin, *The Penalty of Death* (Beverly Hills, CA: Sage, 1980), p. 144.

tern leads many people to believe that the death penalty does deter crime. In their own analyses, Brian Forst, Peter Passell, and William Bowers and Glenn Pierce all argue that when you exclude the years from 1962 to 1969, the deterrent effect claimed by Ehrlich vanishes.[17] His formula does not explain the trends between the 1930s and the early 1960s, when executions declined while the crime rate either declined or remained stable.

We might add that the murder rate increased dramatically in the late 1980s at the same time that executions increased. The number of homicides increased from 18,980 in 1985 to 24,530 in 1993, despite an average of almost twenty executions per year in that period, with a peak of thirty-one in 1992.[18] The lesson here is that it is often easy—but inappropriate—to try to prove an argument by selecting a certain time period when the trends favor your position.

Ehrlich's critics also found serious problems with the official UCR data he used. The data on crime and arrests indicate that the certainty of apprehension declined from the 1930s through the 1960s. We have good reason to believe, however, that because of the lack of professionalism in most departments, these data seriously undercount the amount of crime. In New York City alone, for example, at least two well-documented episodes (in 1955 and 1965) occurred in which administrative changes in the police department produced huge increases in officially reported crime. In Chicago, meanwhile, reporters in 1983 caught the Chicago police unfounding a substantial number of crimes.[19] In other words, the apparent risk of apprehension was higher in the pre-1960 years because police record keeping kept the number of reported crimes artificially low. Consequently, the real risk of apprehension had not declined as much between 1930 and 1969 as Ehrlich asserted.

Research on the deterrent effect of the death penalty continues. The safest conclusion we can draw at this point is that no convincing evidence has surfaced indicating that the death penalty deters crime. This point leads us to the following proposition:

PROPOSITION 12
The death penalty does not deter crime.

DELAYS AND DETERRENCE

Death penalty advocates reply to the critics by arguing that the deterrent effect is undermined by long delays in carrying out executions. In fact, the average time between conviction and execution is over eight years. Appeals in some cases take fifteen years or more. Also, many death sentences are vacated, through appeal, executive clemency, or death by natural causes. In 1995, for example, 56 offenders were executed while nearly twice as many (105) were removed from death row by other causes.[20] Death penalty advocates argue that these factors undermine both the certainty and the swiftness of the death penalty. If we would eliminate these obstacles, the argument continues, the deterrent effect would work.

Long delays in death penalty cases are to be expected. Someone sentenced to die is going to explore every possible avenue of appeal. The process of appeal is an essential part of the criminal justice system, designed to protect against errors in the process. And mistakes do happen. Hugo Bedau and Michael Radelet identified a total of 350 miscarriages of justice in potentially capital cases since 1900. They define *miscarriage of justice* as a case in which "the defendant was erroneously convicted of a capital crime." Of the 350 cases they identified, 139 were given death sentences, and 23 were actually executed.[21]

The U.S. Supreme Court has substantially reduced the right of death row inmates to challenge their sentences in recent years. As a result, the pace of executions has increased. In 1995, fifty-six persons were executed, the largest number since 1960 when fifty-six were also executed.[22] Some advocates of the death penalty will argue that this increase is responsible for the drop in the crime rate in the mid-1990s. Yet, as we already noted, homicides increased in the late 1980s at the same time as the number of executions was increasing. In short, you cannot cite trends over a short period of time and assume that a cause-and-effect relationship exists.

Brutalization Theory?

In a different challenge to deterrence theory, Bowers and Pierce argued that capital punishment may actually encourage crime. According to their "brutalization" theory, each execution is followed by a two- to threefold increase in the number of homicides the next month. They found in three California counties a "slight but discernible" increase in the number of murders in the ten days following an execution (0.25 per execution). A greater increase (1.6 per execution) in homicides occurred in Philadelphia within two months after an execution. Bowers and Pierce contend that the effect is felt among a limited group of people who, independently, have "reached a state of 'readiness to kill,'" in the sense of having an intended victim already in mind. The legal execution conveys the message that vengeance is justified.[23]

Bowers and Pierce concede that "there is room to quarrel" with their analysis, but Brian Forst reached a similar conclusion in his own study. Examining the years 1960 through 1970, he found no evidence that executions prevented crime and some evidence that they actually "provoked" homicides.[24]

Summary

Research on the effect of the death penalty on crime is extremely mixed. Because so many different factors influence criminal behavior, it may never be possible to determine the extent of any deterrent effect. For the moment, then, we can say that the advocates of capital punishment have not persuasively established the existence of a deterrent effect. We should also recall the original ground rules for this book. We are looking for policies that might reduce robbery and burglary. The death penalty applies to neither crime, and it is not directly relevant for our purposes.

DETERRING THE DRUNK DRIVER

One of the most popular applications of deterrence theory involves drunk driving. A national crusade against drunk driving arose in the 1980s. Spurred by a wave of public outrage, virtually every state enacted new laws and policies. The most important of these were deterrence oriented: to reduce drunk driving through tougher punishment, in the form of either mandatory imprisonment or longer sentences, or both.[25]

Leading the national crusade was MADD (Mothers Against Drunk Driving), organized by Candi Lightner, whose thirteen-year-old daughter, Cari, was killed in a crash involving Clarence Busch, who had two previous drunk driving convictions and was then out on bail on a third drunk driving charge. Cari Lightner's death confirmed the belief of many people that repeat drunk drivers beat the system.

The "Killer Drunk" and Other Myths

Like so many aspects of criminal justice, the subject of drunk driving is dominated by myths that inhibit the development of sound and effective policies. It is widely believed, for example, that drunk drivers are responsible for half of all traffic fatalities. One Justice Department report repeated the widely publicized claim that drunk driving kills 50,000 people every two years—"almost as many American lives as were lost in the entire ten years of the Vietnam war."[26] This "fact" originated in a 1968 report by the Department of Transportation (DOT) and has been widely repeated ever since. Most experts in the field argue that the role of alcohol in traffic fatalities has been greatly exaggerated.

Even the DOT's current figures estimate that only 40.8 percent of all traffic fatalities in 1994 were "alcohol related," meaning that the driver tested positive for alcohol.[27] But alcohol was not necessarily the *cause* of each of those accidents. There is an important distinction between drivers who have been drinking and those whose driving is *impaired* by drinking. James B. Jacobs argues that only 30 percent of all traffic deaths are associated with drunk driving, whereas H. Laurence Ross believes that about a quarter of all fatalities involve a driver who is clearly drunk (that is, with a blood alcohol content of 0.10 percent or higher).[28]

The dominant myth about drunk driving involves the so-called "killer drunk": the person with a serious drinking problem, who has many arrests but always seems to beat the system.[29] The myth of the killer drunk has several elements. First, it places the blame on a small number of dangerous people. Second, it emphasizes the killing of innocent people. Third, it puts much of the blame on the criminal justice system for not punishing them and keeping the "killer drunks" off the road. Fourth, it makes criminal punishment the primary focus of efforts to reduce traffic fatalities.

Ross argues that each of these elements distorts the reality of alcohol-related fatalities. First, the problem is not confined to a few dangerous people. Driving after drinking is fairly common. Ross estimates that about 20 percent of all drivers, or 33 million people, drive after drinking every year. That is a lot of people. Moreover, because about 20 to 30 percent of the population do not drink at all, the percentage of drinkers who drive after drinking is higher than 20 percent. Ross's point is that drinking and driving is a predictable and understandable part of our society in which driving is nearly universal (and practically necessary in terms of work) and drinking is an acceptable social custom. In short, we cannot address the problem by assuming that only a handful of people are responsible for it.[30]

Second, innocent drivers or bystanders are not the typical victims of alcohol-related crashes. About half of all the people killed are the drunk drivers themselves, and another 20 percent are passengers in their cars. Additionally, a large percentage of pedestrians who are killed are drunk themselves.[31]

Third, the argument that the criminal justice system is "soft" on drunk drivers is the same one that arises with respect to all serious crime. We have already discussed this issue. We will take a close look at the alleged loopholes in the criminal justice system in Chapter 8. Later in this chapter, we will look specifically at the handling of drunk driving cases.

One major problem is that most of the drivers killed in alcohol-related crashes do not have a history of drunk driving. It is not possible, therefore, to spot them in advance. This is one more manifestation of the prediction problem in criminal justice. The crash that killed Cari Lightner, involving an innocent victim and a driver with a long record, is the classic "celebrated case" at the top of our Criminal Justice Wedding Cake.

Fourth, and perhaps most important in terms of developing effective responses to drinking and driving, both Ross and Jacobs argue that many different kinds of policies can contribute to reducing alcohol-related traffic fatalities. It is a mistake to focus only on the criminal justice system and think that punishment alone can solve the problem.[32]

Deterrence and Drunk Driving

Deterrence-oriented efforts to reduce drunk driving involve both short-term enforcement "crackdowns" and long-term changes in sentencing policy.[33] There are several reasons for thinking that tougher punishment is more likely to work with drunk driving than, for example, robbery or burglary. Because people who drink and drive are more representative of the general population, more of them will have a stake in society and therefore feel threatened by the stigma of arrest and the impact on their jobs and families. Reasons also abound for thinking that the probability of arrest is higher for drunk driving. It is one of the least surreptitious crimes, occurring on public streets over an extended period of time. The evidence does not necessarily support these assumptions, however.

One of the first and most famous drunk driving crackdowns involved the 1967 Road Safety Act in England. The law empowered the police to require a breath test of any driver and specified that refusal to submit to the test was punishable as an actual failure. It attempted to increase the certainty of apprehension, without changing the severity of punishment.[34]

As Figure 6.1 indicates, weekend traffic fatalities and serious injuries dropped to one-third of their previous levels after the law went into effect. Some observers claimed that this was evidence of the deterrent effect of the new law. But it is also obvious that the effect gradually wore off. Within three years fatalities had returned to their previous level. This decay appears to be a general phenomenon in enforcement crackdowns. A 1984 Justice Department evaluation of four anti–drunk driving campaigns found similar results and concluded that the deterrent effects of an enforcement effort, even when it exists, "appear to diminish over time."[35]

The British crackdown illustrates a phenomenon known as the "announcement effect." The publicity surrounding a crackdown causes people to alter their behavior: people decide not to have another drink, or they ask someone else to drive them home; a bartender refuses to serve a drink, or friends tell someone that he or she has had enough to drink. In short, people do perceive the threat of punishment and make rational decisions to alter their behavior. In some instances, these changes occur before the law actually goes into effect as people's awareness of the potential penalty rises.

The announcement effect may also change the behavior of police officers, causing them to become more active in stopping drunk drivers. A Justice

FIGURE 6.1 The effect on traffic fatalities and serious injuries of a crackdown on drunk driving, United Kingdom, 1966–1970.

SOURCES: Reprinted by permission of the publisher, from *Deterring the Drinking Driver: Legal Policy and Social Control*, by H. Laurence Ross (Lexington, MA: Lexington Books, D. C. Heath and Company). Originally appeared in Ross, 1973, *Journal of Legal Studies*, University of Chicago Press.

Department evaluation of four anti–drunk driving campaigns, for example, found that arrests went up in three of them but not in the one in which "relatively little publicity" was made about the mandatory imprisonment law.[36]

As the publicity surrounding an enforcement effort diminishes, however, the effect wears off. Drinkers are less conscious of the risks and revert to their normal behavior. Police officers return to their normal levels of enforcement activity.

The major problem in trying to deter drunk driving through an enforcement crackdown is that the risk of arrest is extremely low. In his evaluation of the British experiments, H. Laurence Ross estimates that the probability of being asked to submit to a breath test is one per million vehicle miles driven. The risk is higher for drinking drivers because their behavior attracts the attention of the police, but it is still "low by any reasonable criterion." The U.S. Department of Transportation estimates that someone would have to drive drunk between 200 and 2,000 times to be apprehended—and even then would face only a 50 percent chance of being punished.[37]

Most people, moreover, believe the risk is low. A survey of Minneapolis and St. Paul residents found that 75 percent thought their chances of being arrested if they drove drunk were "unlikely" or "very unlikely."[38] If both the actual and perceived risks are low, the deterrent effect does not work.

We can understand why the risk of arrest is so low when we look at enforcement from the perspective of the police officer. Two groups of officers are theoretically on the lookout for drunk drivers: regular patrol officers and traffic enforcement officers. Regular patrol officers, however, have many responsibilities—law enforcement, order maintenance, and service—and are primarily concerned with answering calls for service. Moreover, as we learned in the previous chapter, they are spread very thinly and are responsible for patrolling streets that are not prime "hunting grounds" for drunk drivers. Traffic units, meanwhile, comprise no more than about 10 percent of the sworn officers in a department. They also have other responsibilities, such as watching for speeders. Drunk driving is heaviest at those hours when the police are busiest with other assignments. In short, not that many police officers are concentrating exclusively on drunk driving.

In addition, certain disincentives exist for aggressive traffic enforcement. Traffic stops are unpleasant and occasionally dangerous experiences for police officers. Citizens resent them and sometimes let the officer know it. Traffic situations are the fourth most hazardous situation for police officers in terms of officers killed on duty (and these situations include accidents resulting from pursuits).[39] In the absence of any strong incentives, such as ticket quotas, most cops prefer to avoid traffic stops except in the most serious cases.

When police do make arrests, the law of diminishing returns comes into play. Processing an arrest may take up to two hours (or more depending on local procedures). Thus, each arrest removes the police officer from the street. Some gain in specific deterrence related to the person arrested may be achieved, but there is an offsetting loss in general deterrence as the police officer is no longer patrolling.

If the hunters are few, the hunted are many and well hidden among law-abiding drivers. Experts estimate that even during the peak drunk driving hours (Friday and Saturday nights), only about 3 to 4 percent of all drivers are legally drunk.[40] Perhaps another 5 percent have some detectable level of alcohol in their blood. But drivers who are legally drunk may not be impaired, and their driving may not attract the attention of the police. The drive home from a neighborhood bar may be very short, leaving a small "window of opportunity" for detection.

Drunk Drivers in Court

Another factor undermining the deterrent effect of a crackdown is the fate of drunk driving cases in court. James B. Jacobs estimates that about 90 percent of all arrested drunk drivers are convicted through guilty pleas.[41] In this respect, the prosecution of drunk driving offenses closely resembles the handling of other criminal cases. Those data, however, reflect only convictions.

The main purpose of crackdowns is to deter drunk driving by increasing the severity of punishment, usually through a mandatory jail or prison sentence.

Mandatory sentencing provisions can be evaded through dismissal, plea bargaining, or blatant disregard for the law. H. Laurence Ross and James P. Foley examined the implementation of new mandatory sentencing laws enacted in New Mexico and Indiana in the 1980s. The New Mexico law required a jail term of not less than forty-eight hours for offenders with a prior drunk driving conviction and prohibited suspended sentences. Ross and Foley found that in 238 cases the mandated sentence was imposed and served in only 106, or 45 percent of the total. In another sixty cases (25 percent) the mandatory sentences were imposed but there was no documented proof that the offenders served them. In 10 percent of the cases, the judge suspended the sentence, and in another 20 percent the offender served no jail sentence. The Indiana law mandated five days in jail, with at least forty-eight consecutive hours, or a minimum of eighty hours of community service, for offenders with a prior drunk driving conviction. Yet, 30 percent of the convicted offenders did not serve the mandated sentence. Of 753 cases, 64 percent served the forty-eight consecutive hours, and another 6 percent did the required eighty hours of community service.[42]

Ross and Foley offer several possible explanations for this evasion of mandatory sentences. In some cases, the judges may have been ignorant of the offender's prior record. (We might ask whether they chose not to find out as a deliberate strategy for evading the mandatory sentencing provision.) In others, judges may have chosen to interpret the law as covering only certain kinds of prior convictions (for example, felonies and not misdemeanors). Judges may have simply ignored the law in some cases. For some sentenced offenders, the term "forty-eight hours" may not have been interpreted literally. Correctional officials may have counted a few hours a day as representing the entire day; if the offender spent a few hours in jail spanning midnight, he might have been credited with having served both days. Similar evasions of mandatory sentencing have been found in studies of other crackdowns.

Evasion of the law by justice officials is not universal by any means. The Justice Department's evaluation of enforcement efforts in Seattle found that the incarceration rate for convicted drunk drivers went from 9 to 97 percent. In Memphis, it went from 29 to almost 100 percent.[43] A 1982 California law increased the statewide jail incarceration rate for second-time offenders from 83 percent in 1980 to 97.5 percent in 1984. In Sacramento County the percentage of first-time drunk drivers sent to jail went from 10 percent to more than 50 percent. These data make it clear that second offense drunk drivers were not getting off easy before passage of the new law. The most significant effect of the California law was on first-time offenders; the percentage going to jail increased from about 10 percent to over 50 percent.[44]

Nonetheless, as the Ross and Foley study suggests, a certain amount of evasion of mandatory sentencing persists in some jurisdictions that undermines both the certainty and severity of punishment. This compounds the low perceived and actual risk of arrest. In the end, most experts believe that enforcement crackdowns are not likely to deter drunk driving. After reviewing all the evidence, Ross concludes that "deterrence-based policies are questionable in the long run. No such policies have been scientifically demonstrated to work over time."[45] Jacobs agrees but adds that deterrence-based laws play a symbolic role in expressing society's moral condemnation of drunk driving.[46] Our conclusion can be stated as follows:

> ### PROPOSITION 13
> #### Enforcement crackdowns will not deter drunk driving.

Crackdown Costs

When a drunk driving crackdown does result in more punishment, it imposes significant costs on the criminal justice system. The most direct impact is on local jails and courts. Additional judges were needed in Seattle to handle the increase in cases. Cincinnati had to add an additional daily traffic court. In Sacramento County, California, more defendants insisted on going to trial, with the result that convictions at trial decreased. In Seattle, the county had to open a new jail facility just to handle the drunk drivers. In Memphis, some offenders had to wait six or seven months to serve their jail sentences. In two California counties, the jails became so overcrowded that courts found jail conditions unconstitutional.[47]

In short, as with other "get tough" policies, drunk driving crackdowns not only may not achieve their intended goals but may also impose unintended costs on the justice system.

ALTERNATIVE STRATEGIES FOR
DEALING WITH DRUNK DRIVERS

And Now for Some Good News

Actually, there is some substantial good news about traffic fatalities, including alcohol-related ones. Traffic fatalities have been declining steadily for decades: from 54,633 in 1970 to 41,274 in 1994, a decline of 25 percent. When we look at motor vehicle death *rates*, the long-term decline is startling. As Table 6.2 indicates, the death rate per 100,000 vehicle miles has dropped from 15.97 in 1930 to 3.50 in 1980 and 2.8 in 1990. The decline in the death rate is obscured by a steady increase in the number of cars on the road and the number of miles driven each year.[48]

The long-term decline since 1930 is substantial, and the nearly 50 percent reduction since 1980 is a particularly significant achievement. If we had cut the robbery and burglary rates in half over the past twenty years, we would be dancing in the streets—and the streets would be a lot safer for dancing, too.

Table 6.2 Motor vehicle death rates

Year	Number of deaths	Death rate per 100,000 vehicle miles
1930	32,900	15.97
1940	34,501	11.42
1950	34,763	7.59
1960	38,137	5.31
1970	54,533	4.88
1980	53,172	3.50
1990	45,800	2.18

SOURCE: National Safety Council, *Accident Facts 1992* (Washington, D.C.: National Safety Council, 1992), pp. 72–73.

How do we explain this success, especially in light of our conclusion that enforcement crackdowns do not work? The answer is that some things do work. Tougher enforcement by the criminal justice system undoubtedly contributed to this decline, but both Ross and Jacobs argue that at best it was only one factor. To deal with the problem of drinking drivers, we need to look beyond the criminal justice to other social policies.

One of the most important strategies involves safer cars. Seat belts are required on all new cars, and their use is mandatory in most states. The National Safety Council estimates that seat belts saved 18,000 lives through 1990.[49] (Air bags and antilock brakes are also widely used, but new evidence has raised questions about whether they reduce accidents and save lives. Air bags, in fact, have been responsible for the deaths of some children).

As a result of federal law, all states have raised the legal age for drinking to twenty-one. Although this measure has not necessarily curbed teenage drinking, it may have helped to reduce drunk driving by teenagers. The Department of Transportation estimates that it saved a total of 13,152 lives between 1975 and 1992.[50]

Another strategy is administrative license revocation, in which a police officer can revoke a driver's license on the spot if he or she fails a breath test. It is important to point out that this is a *civil* law rather than a criminal law approach. It rests on the theory that a driver's license is essentially a privilege that can be withdrawn without resort to the full criminal process. Ross argues that it is both swift and certain, resulting in the immediate incapacitation of the offender (in the sense that the person cannot drive legally (although obviously some people drive without a license). He cites studies indicating that this approach has been effective in reducing alcohol-related accidents and fatalities.[51]

Some of the long-term reduction in fatalities may be due to socialization. It is possible that the national anti–drunk driving crusade, with all of the attendant publicity, has had a long-term effect on attitudes and behavior. Public opinion surveys have found that the percentage of people saying they "sometimes" drive after drinking fell from 25 percent in 1983 to 16 percent in 1995. The percentage indicating that they "never" did rose correspondingly.[52] We have good reason to assume that these attitudes reflect real changes in behavior. Not only has the number of traffic fatalities fallen, but the percentage that are alcohol related fell from 57.3 in 1982 to 40.8 in 1994.[53]

In other words, some real long-term changes may have occurred in attitudes and behavior related to drinking and driving. We will also examine the issue of long-term behavioral changes when we discuss drug policy in Chapter 13. Other examples of such long-term changes are evident. Consumption of red meat has declined, and consumption of fresh fruits and vegetables has increased since 1970.[54] Smoking among adults is down substantially. These changes are a result of public concern about health. Safe-sex education programs, meanwhile, have produced a sharp decline in the incidence of new AIDS cases among gay men (but not among needle-drug users). In short, behavior does change over time, and some of those changes are the result of national-level efforts. But, as James B. Jacobs argues, there "are limits to what can be accomplished through directed social change."[55] We cannot force people to change, particularly through the criminal law. But a variety of factors induce change over the long term.

DETERRING BURGLARS AND ROBBERS

So far, we have discussed deterrence with respect to the death penalty and drunk driving. But what about burglars and robbers? Are they deterred by harsher punishments? Considerable research has been done on this question using aggregate data on crimes and punishments. Unfortunately, specifying the causality in this type of research poses many problems. Most of the social psychological literature involves research on undergraduates, or what some scholars have called "the science of sophomores."[56] What about real criminals? There has been surprisingly little research about deterrence involving actual offenders.

In an imaginative study, Scott Decker and his colleagues interviewed a group of forty-eight active residential burglars and a control group of forty nonoffenders drawn from two job training and recreation centers in the same city. Procedures were taken to ensure the anonymity of the active burglars (unlike subjects in most of the career criminal research, these individuals were not currently prison inmates). Both groups were given hypothetical situations that altered the risk of apprehension, the reward from doing the burglary, and the penalty if caught.[57]

Including the expected reward in the equation added an important element. As we already noted, deterrence theory assumes a rational choice between the relative costs *and* gains from doing crime. Virtually all of the deterrence research has focused only on the cost side: the effect of different punishments. Because the theory assumes a choice between alternatives, it is necessary to include the expected gains as well.

Decker and his colleagues found a "clear and highly significant difference" between the burglars and the control group.[58] The active burglars were much more likely to commit a crime than were members of the control group. This difference persisted despite changes in either the expected penalty or the gain. Increasing the risk of apprehension lowered the willingness to commit a burglary for both groups. But only 10 percent of the controls indicated a willingness to commit a burglary when told that the risk of apprehension was only 1 percent. Meanwhile, even with a 50 percent chance of apprehension, slightly more than half (55.2 percent) of the active burglars would still commit a burglary.

For the active burglars, an increase in the severity of the penalty had some effect on their willingness to commit a burglary, but it was surprisingly modest. When the punishment was described as two years' probation, 61.5 percent said they would commit a burglary; increasing the penalty to five years in prison only reduced it to 52.5 percent. The burglars were more influenced by changes in the relative gain from the burglary; that is, they indicated a greater willingness to commit crime when the expected gain was higher than what they had previously believed it to be.

The study provides little support for traditional deterrence theory. Decker and his colleagues concluded that neither the burglars nor the control group "were significantly affected by the severity of the threatened penalty on its own."[59] Certainty of apprehension did have some effect, but, as we learned in the previous chapter, the prospects for increasing clearance rates are not good.

The Rand Inmate Survey

The Rand Inmate Survey asked prisoners in three states (California, Michigan, Texas) to estimate the probable results of doing crime. Well over 80 percent believed they had an "even chance" of being arrested, imprisoned, or being injured or killed. Over 60 percent believed they had a "high chance" of arrest and imprisonment or that it was "certain." In short, they were extremely fatalistic about the consequences of criminal activity. Significantly, they were only half as likely to expect a high chance or certainty of enjoying the good outcomes of crime ("high living," having "expensive things," or "being own man").[60]

In their analysis of these data, James Q. Wilson and Allan Abrahamse posed the obvious question: if their estimate of bad consequences is so high and their estimate of good consequences so much lower, why do they commit crime? (Remember, these were imprisoned offenders, some of whom were classified as "high-rate" offenders). The answer is that they do not act on the basis of a rational calculation of costs and benefits. Wilson and Abrahamse, for example, found that they consistently overestimate the financial rewards of crime. They act impulsively and overestimate the immediate, short-term gains of crime and underestimate unpleasant consequences, such as imprisonment, which lies in the future.[61] They also may have felt that they have no alternatives in terms of legitimate work—in other words, that they perceived no positive rewards for a law-abiding lifestyle.

Like Decker's study of active burglars, the Rand Inmate Survey provides little support for traditional deterrence theory. Actual offenders do not appear to make their decisions about criminal activity on the basis of a rational and carefully calculated assessment of the costs and benefits.

DETERRING DOMESTIC VIOLENCE

Another area that has seen considerable research on the deterrent effect of punishment is arrest for domestic violence. Traditionally, police officers avoided arrest in domestic violence situations, especially when married couples were involved. In the 1970s, the women's movement challenged this practice, arguing that failure to arrest left the female victim vulnerable to further violence. Women's groups successfully sued the New York City and Oakland police departments on equal protection grounds and won settlements that included mandatory arrest policies. By the 1980s, a national movement was under way toward mandatory arrest or arrest-preferred policies. These have been implemented either through police department policy or state law.[62]

Most advocates of mandatory arrest for domestic violence believe that it deters future violence. The first study of this issue, the Minneapolis Domestic Violence Experiment, became one of the most publicized and influential experiments in criminal justice history. The experiment tested the effect of three different police actions: arrest, separation, and mediation. Through official police records and interviews with victims, it found lower rates of repeat violence over the following six months as a result of arrest compared with either of the other two alternatives. The experiment seemed to indicate that arrest deterred domestic violence. The authors of the experiment were careful to point out that the persons arrested were rarely prosecuted or incarcerated; the "punishment" was usually nothing more than arrest, or at most a night in jail.[63]

These findings had an enormous impact on public policy. Over the next few years most police departments adopted mandatory arrest policies. By 1988, 60 percent of all big-city police departments mandated arrest, and another 30 percent specifically encouraged it.[64]

Replications of the Minneapolis experiment in Omaha, Charlotte, Miami, and Milwaukee, however, found no consistent evidence that arrest deters future violence. Moreover, the Milwaukee experiment found that arrest had different effects on different kinds of offenders. It seemed to increase the level of repeat violence among unemployed men compared with employed. It is probably that employed men have a greater stake in social conformity and are more likely to be deterred by the sanction of arrest than are unemployed men who have less of a stake in conformity.[65]

Lawrence Sherman, principal investigator on the original Minneapolis experiment, now argues that the impact of arrest in domestic violence situations is an extremely complicated matter and that we cannot assert conclusively that arrest deters violence.

The evidence regarding the death penalty, drunk driving, burglary and robbery, and domestic violence leads us to the following general conclusion:

PROPOSITION 14
Deterrence-oriented policies that rely exclusively on the criminal justice system will not reduce crime.

CONCLUSION

The commonsense notion that people will avoid unpleasant things and that we can influence their decisions by increasing the unpleasantness does not necessarily work in the real world of criminal justice. Let us be careful about exactly what we are saying. As in so many other areas, it is not true that "nothing works." The criminal law does have some deterrent effect. Most of us, after all, do not become career criminals. The threat of punishment, however, probably plays a relatively minor role in influencing the behavior of law-abiding people. The threat works, but it just is not the major factor. In terms of controlling behavior, the broader processes of socialization are the primary factors. As Leslie Wilkins put it, there are "those of us who have never needed a deterrent."[66] When these processes have broken down, we should not expect the criminal justice system—and deterrence-oriented policies in particular—to fix the problem.

NOTES

1. The best treatment of the subject is still Franklin E. Zimring and Gordon J. Hawkins, *Deterrence: The Legal Threat in Crime Control* (Chicago: University of Chicago Press, 1973).

2. David P. Farrington and Patrick A. Langan, "Changes in Crime and Punishment in England and America in the 1980s," *Justice Quarterly* 9 (March 1992): 5–46.

3. Scott Decker, Richard Wright, and Robert Logie, "Perceptual Deterrence Among Active Residential Burglars: A Research Note," *Criminology* 31 (February 1993): 135.

4. Zimring and Hawkins, *Deterrence*, pp. 92–248.

5. Ibid., pp. 13–14.

6. Ronald L. Akers, "Rational Choice, Deterrence, and Social Learning Theory in Criminology: The Path Not Taken," *Journal of Criminal Law and Criminology* 81 (Fall 1990): 653–676.

7. See, for example, the extremely influential conservative argument in Charles Murray, *Losing Ground: American Social Policy, 1950–1980* (New York: Basic Books, 1984).

8. Dallin Oaks, "Studying the Exclusionary Rule in Search and Seizure," *University of Chicago Law Review* 37 (Summer 1970): 665–757.

9. Bureau of Justice Statistics, *Spouse Murder Defendants in Large Urban Counties* (Washington, D.C.: Government Printing Office, 1995).

10. James Q. Wilson and Allan Abrahamse, "Does Crime Pay?" *Justice Quarterly* 9 (September 1992): 359–377.

11. Raymond Paternoster, *Capital Punishment in America* (Lexington, MA: Lexington Books, 1991), Part IV, "Arguments for and Against the Death Penalty," pp. 185–270.

12. *Furman v. Georgia*, 408 U.S. 238 (1972).

13. *Gregg v. Georgia*, 428 U.S. 153 (1976).

14. Thorsten Sellin, *The Penalty of Death* (Beverly Hills, CA: Sage, 1980).

15. Isaac Ehrlich, "The Deterrent Effect of Capital Punishment: A Question of Life and Death," *American Economic Review* 65 (1975): 397–417.

16. Isaac Ehrlich, "Participation in Illegitimate Activities: A Theoretical and Empirical Investigation," *Journal of Political Economy* 81 (1973): 521.

17. Brian Forst, "Capital Punishment and Deterrence: Conflicting Evidence," *Journal of Criminal Law and Criminology* 74 (Fall 1983): 927–942; Peter Passell, "The Deterrent Effect of the Death Penalty: A Statistical Test," *Stanford Law Review* 28 (November 1975): 61–80; William J. Bowers and Glenn Pierce, "The Illusion of Deterrence in Isaac Ehrlich's Research on Capital Punishment," *Yale Law Review* 85 (1975): 187–208.

18. Bureau of Justice Statistics, *Sourcebook of Criminal Justice Statistics—1995*, pp. 324, 609.

19. Robert Hood and Richard Sparks, *Key Issues in Criminology* (New York: McGraw-Hill, 1980), pp. 40–41; Zimring and Hawkins, *Deterrence*, p. 334; Philip Wattley, "City Hit on Crime Data," *Chicago Tribune* (April 28, 1983), pp. 1–2.

20. Bureau of Justice Statistics, *Capital Punishment 1995* (Washington, D.C.: Government Printing Office, 1996), Table 11.

21. Hugo Adam Bedeau and Michael L. Radelet, "Miscarriages of Justice in Potentially Capital Cases," *Stanford Law Review* 40 (November 1987): 21–179.

22. Bureau of Justice Statistics, *Capital Punishment 1995*.

23. William J. Bowers and Glenn L. Pierce, "Deterrence or Brutalization? What Is the Effect of Executions?" *Crime and Delinquency* 26 (October 1980): 453–484.

24. Forst, "Capital Punishment and Deterrence."

25. The two best surveys of the subject are H. Laurence Ross, *Confronting Drunk Driving: Social Policy for Saving Lives* (New Haven, CT: Yale University Press, 1992), and James B. Jacobs, *Drunk Driving: An American Dilemma* (Chicago: University of Chicago Press, 1989).

26. Bureau of Justice Statistics, *Jailing Drunk Drivers: Impact on the Criminal Justice System* (Washington, D.C.: Government Printing Office, 1984).

27. Department of Transportation, *Traffic Safety Facts 1994* (Washington, D.C.: Government Printing Office, 1995), p. 32.

28. Jacobs, *Drunk Driving*, pp. 27–28; Ross, *Confronting Drunk Driving*.

29. Ross, *Confronting Drunk Driving*, pp. 21–22, 168–170.

30. Ross, *Confronting Drunk Driving*.

31. Department of Transportation, *Traffic Safety Facts 1994*, p. 32.

32. Jacobs, *Drunk Driving*; Ross, *Confronting Drunk Driving*.

33. Lawrence W. Sherman, "Police Crackdowns: Initial and Residual Deterrence," in Michael W. Tonry and Norval Morris, eds., *Crime and Justice: An Annual Review of Research*, vol. 12 (Chicago: University of Chicago Press, 1990), pp. 1–48.

34. H. Laurence Ross, *Deterring the Drinking Driver: Legal Policy and Social Control*, rev. ed. (Lexington, MA: Lexington Books, 1984), pp. 24–34.

35. Bureau of Justice Statistics, *Jailing Drunk Drivers*, p. 2.

36. Ibid.

37. Ross, *Deterring the Drinking Driver*, pp. 33, 105.

38. Donald E. Green, "Past Behavior as a Measure of Actual Future Behavior: An Unresolved Issue in Perceptual Deterrence Research," *Journal of Criminal Law and Criminology* 80(3) (1989): 781–804.

39. Federal Bureau of Investigation, *Law Enforcement Officers Killed and Assaulted, 1994* (Washington, D.C.: Government Printing Office, 1995).

40. Jacobs, *Drunk Driving*, p. 47.

41. Ibid., pp. 98–100.

42. H. Laurence Ross and James P. Foley, "Judicial Disobedience of the Mandate to Imprison Drunk Drivers," *Law and Society Review* 21(2) (1987): 315–323.

43. Bureau of Justice Statistics, *Jailing Drunk Drivers*, p. 2.

44. Rodney Kingsworth and Michael Jungsten, "Driving Under the Influence: The Impact of Legislative Reform on Court Sentencing Practices in Drunk Driving Cases," *Crime and Delinquency* 34 (January 1988): 3–28.

45. Ross, *Deterring the Drinking Driver*, p. 111.

46. Jacobs, *Drunk Driving*, p. 126.

47. Bureau of Justice Statistics, *Jailing Drunk Drivers*; Kingsworth and Jungsten, "Driving Under the Influence."

48. National Safety Council, *Accident Facts 1992* (Washington, D.C.: NSC, 1992); Bureau of the Census, *Statistical Abstract of the United States, 1995*, Table 1035, p. 639.

49. National Safety Council, *Accident Facts, 1992*, p. 57.

50. Department of Transportation, *Traffic Safety Facts 1992*, "Alcohol" (Washington, D.C.: Government Printing Office, 1993), p. 4.

51. Ross, *Confronting Drunk Driving*, pp. 63–67.

52. Bureau of Justice Statistics, *Sourcebook of Criminal Justice Statistics—1995* (Washington, D.C.: Government Printing Office, 1996), p. 302.

53. Ibid., p. 303.

54. *Statistical Abstract of the United States, 1995*, Table 225, p. 147.

55. Jacobs, *Drunk Driving*, p. 191.

56. Raymond Paternoster, "The Deterrent Effect of the Perceived Certainty and Severity of Punishment: A Review of the Evidence and Issues," *Justice Quarterly* 4 (June 1987): 173–217.

57. Decker et al., "Perceptual Deterrence," pp. 135–147.

58. Ibid., p. 139.

59. Ibid., p. 145.

60. Wilson and Abrahamse, "Does Crime Pay?" p. 373.

61. Ibid., pp. 372–373.

62. Lawrence W. Sherman, *Policing Domestic Violence: Experiments and Dilemmas* (New York: Free Press, 1992).

63. Ibid.

64. Ibid.

65. Ibid.

66. Quoted in Zimring and Hawkins, *Deterrence*, p. 97.

7

Lock 'Em Up

GETTING CRIMINALS OFF THE STREET

The main conservative crime control strategy is to get criminals off the street. This includes three "lock 'em up" proposals: preventive detention, incapacitation, and mandatory sentencing. All three are based on the assumption that the criminal justice system turns dangerous criminals loose on society where they prey on law-abiding citizens. The new "three strikes and you're out" laws are the ultimate lock 'em up policy.

All of the lock 'em up strategies seek to limit the discretion of judges.[1] The underlying assumption is that judges have too much discretion to release dangerous criminals on bail, grant them probation, or sentence them to inappropriately short prison terms. Conservatives believe that the misuse of judicial discretion is the result of two factors. First, too many judges are "bleeding hearts" who are too lenient with convicted offenders. Second, many of our policies encourage not locking people up. American law traditionally embodied the principle of a right to bail. The philosophy of rehabilitation, meanwhile, encourages alternatives to prison for convicted felons. Conservative proposals attack these laws and policies as being soft on crime.

PREVENTIVE DETENTION

Conservatives believe that people released on bail commit a large number of crimes. President Ronald Reagan's Task Force on Victims of Crime declared in 1982, "A substantial proportion of the crimes committed in this country are committed by defendants who have been released on bail or on their own recognizance."[2] Conservatives believe that preventive detention, a policy that allows denying bail to high-risk criminal defendants, can prevent these crimes.

Preventive detention raises both *constitutional* and *empirical* questions. The constitutional question is whether the Eighth Amendment to the U.S. Constitution prohibits detaining someone solely for the purpose of preventing crime. The Eighth Amendment guarantees that "[e]xcessive bail shall not be required." As with many other parts of the Bill of Rights, the exact meaning of the Eighth Amendment is ambiguous. Traditionally, it was interpreted to mean that all criminal defendants have a right to bail, with the exception of persons accused of "capital" crimes, or those crimes punishable by the death penalty. The purpose of bail in Anglo-American law was to ensure the defendant's appearance at trial. Preventive detention, then, represents a fundamental change in the purpose of bail.[3]

The Supreme Court answered the constitutional question in 1987 when it upheld the preventive detention provision of the 1984 federal Bail Reform Act. In *United States v. Salerno*, the Court ruled that there is no absolute right to bail and that preventive detention is a legitimate "regulatory" measure.[4]

The empirical question that is central to our inquiry involves the amount of crime committed by people released on bail. How much crime will we prevent by keeping certain offenders in jail?

A Short History of Bail Reform

The demand for preventive detention is a backlash against the bail reform movement of the 1960s. The civil rights movement focused public attention on the plight of the poor in the criminal justice system. The President's Crime Commission found that 52 percent of all people in jail were awaiting trial. Critics labeled America's jails the "new poorhouses." Wealthy organized crime figures easily raised large bail amounts, whereas poor people remained in jail.[5] Caleb Foote's pioneering studies of bail in Philadelphia in the 1950s found that defendants not released on bail were more likely to be convicted and imprisoned.[6] Thus, the money bail system compounds the denial of a basic constitutional right by increasing the chance of conviction and imprisonment. Unnecessary pretrial detention also raises the cost of operating the jails and often results in jail overcrowding.

Current data support Foote's earlier finding about the impact of pretrial detention. According to the National Pretrial Reporting Program (NPRP), 79 percent of those detained in 1992 were convicted, compared with only 61 percent who were released. Additionally, 70 percent of those detained were convicted of a felony, compared with only 45 percent of those released. Finally, among those convicted, 89 percent of those who had been detained were sentenced to incarceration, compared with only 59 percent of those who were released.[7]

The bail reform movement sought to correct these problems with programs to facilitate pretrial release. The most popular innovation was release on recognizance (ROR), which allows a defendant to be released without any financial considerations. Evidence of a job, family ties, or other roots in the community are used to evaluate whether the person is likely to appear for scheduled court dates. The 1966 federal Bail Reform Act directed federal courts to develop ROR procedures. Many states, meanwhile, developed their own ROR programs and/or adopted 10 percent plans that allowed defendants to post 10 percent of the formal bail amount.[8]

The bail reform movement achieved many of its goals. The percentage of people in jail who were being held for trial dropped from 52 percent in 1967 to 33 percent in 1971. In some cities, reform had a dramatic impact. The percentage of defendants held for more than twenty-four hours in Philadelphia dropped from 75 percent in 1954 to only 25 percent in 1975. Similar reductions were also found in other cities. Some evidence, however, indicates that the "get tough" policies of recent years have reversed these trends. In 1992, 50 percent of all jail inmates were defendants awaiting trial.[9]

The first bail reform movement did not achieve all of its goals, however. Because employment status is a major criterion for ROR, it discriminates against the unemployed and the marginally employed. Nearly three-quarters (72 percent) of employed defendants were released in 1990, compared with 46 percent for unemployed.[10] Bail reform also did not eliminate the practice of detaining certain defendants by simply setting high bail.

The first bail reform movement coincided with the great rise in serious crime. Between 1963 and 1973, the robbery rate tripled, while the burglary rate went up two and a half times. Conservatives argue that bail reform contributed to this by releasing many dangerous offenders.

The focus of the backlash was Washington, D.C. Because of rising crime rates, Congress passed a preventive detention law for the District of Columbia in 1970. By the 1980s, public support for preventive detention was widespread, and nearly all states had adopted it. Some states amended their state constitutions to limit the right to bail. The Michigan constitution allows preventive detention in four kinds of crimes when the judge finds a possibility of "danger" if the defendant were to be released.[11]

Let us take a look at how preventive detention works in practice.

Preventive Detention in Operation: Washington, D.C.

The 1970 District of Columbia law offered the first evidence of how preventive detention might work. The law allowed a judge to hold without bail for sixty days a defendant charged with a crime of violence or a dangerous crime. Several procedures were designed to protect defendants's rights. A formal hearing was required to determine that substantial probability of guilt existed and that no other release procedure could guarantee public safety. The defendant must have been convicted of a crime in the preceding ten years, be a narcotics addict, or currently be on pretrial release, probation, or parole. Finally, if the trial were not held within sixty days, the defendant had a right to release on bail.

Something funny happened in Washington, however: the law was hardly ever used. Judges detained very few defendants without bail. A study by Georgetown University and the Vera Institute found that in the first six months prosecutors filed detention motions against only 20 of 6,000 felony defendants (or less than one-third of 1 percent!). These motions resulted in nine formal hearings and eight actual detentions. Another two defendants were detained through judicial initiative. Thus, only ten defendants were detained in six months.[12]

This is not the end of the story, however. Five of the ten detentions were reversed on appeal or reconsideration. Another was dismissed when the grand jury refused to indict the suspect. Thus, a grand total of four people were fully detained during the entire ten-month period.

What happened? Federal prosecutors in the District of Columbia had full discretion to use or not use the law. It is easy to explain why they chose not to. In most cases they did not need to. They could detain someone simply by setting bail at a level beyond his or her financial means. Because most robbers are poor, unemployed, or marginally employed, establishing an inaccessible bail amount is not hard to do. Setting bond at a high figure is the traditional means by which the courtroom work group has covertly undermined the nominal right to bail. In effect, it says, "Sure you have a right to bail—how much *can't* you afford?" Remember from our discussion of the courtroom work group in Chapter 3, disagreement rarely erupts over bail.[13] In other words, all members of the work group are in agreement over the real impact of a high bail amount.

This practice continues today. In 1992, the median bail for all robbery defendants was $10,000. Those who succeeded in obtaining release, however, faced a median bail of only $5,000. Under a 10 percent plan they would only need to post $500. Those who did not obtain their release faced a median bail of $20,000. In short, robbery defendants can be categorized into two classes: one group gets relatively low bail, whereas the other, which the courtroom work group wants to detain, gets high bail and is not released.[14]

The 1984 Federal Bail Reform Act

The 1984 Bail Reform Act allows federal judges to detain a defendant without bail if "no condition or combination of conditions" "will reasonably assure...the safety of any other person and the community." The law has had a very different impact than the 1970 law. Federal judges are using it very extensively. The number of defendants detained by federal judges increased from 2,733 in the first six months of 1987 (before the Supreme Court upheld the law) to 4,470 in the last six months of 1988. The war on drugs accounted for much of this increase: more people were arrested for drug offenses, and prosecutors requested detention for drug defendants far more often than for other crimes. Between 70 and 75 percent of the prosecutors' requests for detention were granted.[15] The heavy use of the 1984 law, compared with the 1970 one, is an index of the "get tough" mood of the period.

Closer inspection, however, reveals that the overall detention rate did not increase greatly. The percentage of all federal defendants detained before trial only increased from 24 percent to 29 percent. The major change was a shift in the *method* of detention. Before the 1984 law, virtually all of the detained defendants remained in jail because they could not raise sufficient bail. Of the 29 percent detained after the law went into effect, 19 percent were detained under the preventive detention law, and 10 percent were detained because they could not raise bail.[16] In short, the 1984 law gave judges legal authority to do what they had previously done covertly.

The important question, from our perspective, is whether preventive detention has helped reduce crime. None of the studies of bail reform evaluates the impact on the overall crime rate. Evaluations have focused on crime by persons released on bail and have found no significant impact on pretrial crime. The percentage of released defendants who were rearrested for a felony increased from 1.2 percent in 1983 to 1.3 percent in 1985. The percentage arrested for misdemeanors went from 0.6 percent to 0.7 percent. By 1992, 1.8 were rearrested for a felony.[17] It is important to note how small a percentage of defendants were being rearrested before 1984. If anything, the percentage should have gone down, since judges were now able to detain suspected repeat offenders. These data force us to take a closer look at the whole question of crime by persons out on bail.

Crime on Bail: Myths and Reality

The failure of the Bail Reform Act to reduce pretrial crime comes as no surprise to most experts. Substantial research has found that, contrary to popular belief, the amount of crime committed by persons out on bail is relatively small. Let us take a look at success and failure of defendants on pretrial release.

A defendant released on bail can "fail" in one of two ways: either by committing a crime or by failing to appear (FTA) at a scheduled court hearing. Both types of failure are complex, and it is necessary to examine the data carefully.

Not all crimes by persons on bail are equally serious. In terms of the "cost" to society, a felony is far more serious than a misdemeanor, and a violent crime is more serious than a property crime. Arrest, meanwhile, is not the same as conviction. If you use the total number of failures—*all* arrests and *all* FTAs— the failure rate for people on bail will be relatively high. It will be much lower, however, if we only measure convictions for a violent offenses.

The National Pretrial Reporting Program (NPRP) reports that in 1992, 14 percent of all felony defendants released before trial were rearrested in the next twelve months; 10 percent were rearrested for a felony and about 3 percent for a misdemeanor (Table 7.1). Interestingly, persons originally charged with a violent crime were rearrested at a slightly lower rate (12 percent) than were persons charged with property (14 percent) or drug (16 percent) offenses. Of all those who were rearrested, 61 percent were convicted on the

Table 7.1 Felony defendants arrested while on pretrial release in the seventy-five largest counties, by selected defendant characteristics, 1992[a]

Defendant characteristics	Number of defendants	Not re-arrested	Percentage of felony defendants		
			Rearrested		
			Total	Felony	Mis-demeanor
All released defendants	30,051	86%	14	10	3
MOST SERIOUS ORIGINAL ARREST CHARGE					
Violent offenses	6,991	88	12	8	3
Property offenses	10,147	86	14	11	4
Drug offenses	10,146	84	16	13	4
Public-order offenses	2,765	91	9	7	2
SEX					
Male	24,839	85	15	11	3
Female	5,164	91	9	6	3
RACE					
Black	15,830	85	15	12	4
White	11,329	89	11	8	3
Other	365	95	5	5	0
RACE/HISPANIC ORIGIN[b]					
Non-Hispanic					
Black	11,292	85	15	11	4
White	6,313	91	9	7	3
Other	361	94	6	6	0
Hispanic, any race	5,126	84	16	12	4
NUMBER OF PRIOR CONVICTIONS					
10 or more	1,154	62	38	27	11
5 to 9	2,393	74	26	19	7
2 to 4	4,691	82	18	14	4
1	4,122	86	14	10	4
None	15,670	91	9	7	2

NOTE: See note, Table 5.63. Rearrest data were collected for one year. Rearrests occuring after the end of this one-year study period are not included in the table. Information on rearrests in jurisdictions other than the one granting the pretrial release was not always available. Rearrest data were available for 94 percent of released defendants.
[a]Detail may not add to total because of rounding.
[b]Data on race combined with Hispanic origin were available for 77 percent of defendants.

SOURCE: U.S. Department of Justice, Bureau of Justice, *Pretrial Release Defendants, 1992*, Bulletin NCJ-148818 (Washington, D.C.: U.S. Department of Justice, 1994), p. 11.

new charge, but only 45 percent were convicted of a felony. Thus, only about 6 percent of all defendants released before trial were convicted of a new felony.[18]

Although the overall reconviction rate is fairly low, it is clear that some types of defendants are rearrested and reconvicted at fairly high rates. Not surprisingly, 38 percent of those with ten or more prior convictions were rearrested, compared with only 9 percent of those with no prior convictions.

Now let us look at the failures to appear. Most FTAs are not intentional. Usually, the defendant forgets the date or is confused about the court proceedings. The really serious FTAs, which we should be concerned about, are those in which the defendant deliberately flees. In 1992, 25 percent of all felony defendants failed to appear in court. Yet about two-thirds of these were eventually returned to court. Thus, only 8 percent of all defendants released before trial were actual fugitives from justice.[19]

The Prediction Problem Revisited

The relatively low rearrest and reconviction rates bring us back to the prediction problem that we discussed in Chapter 4. The problem facing a judge is to spot in advance the defendants likely to commit a crime on bail. The point of preventive detention is to detain them and *only* them. How successful are judges likely to be in this effort?

Predicting Dangerousness: A Natural Experiment   A 1984 Supreme Court case on preventive detention for juveniles produced a natural experiment in predicting dangerousness. A New York law authorized preventive detention of juveniles who posed a "serious risk" of committing another crime if released. The law was challenged, and in 1981 a federal district court judge declared it unconstitutional and enjoined its operation. New York appealed, and in 1984 (*Schall v. Martin*) the U.S. Supreme Court ruled that preventive detention for juveniles was constitutional.[20]

The lower-court decision had a quirk, however. The district court judge only enjoined the commissioner of corrections from holding allegedly dangerous juveniles but not the judges who ordered them held. Thus, judges continued to order some juveniles detained. These kids were turned over to the commissioner of corrections, who was forced to release them. This produced a natural experiment that allows us to examine how accurate the judges were in predicting the dangerousness of a small group of juvenile defendants.[21]

Jeffrey Fagan and Martin Guggenheim identified sixty-nine juveniles who were judged "at risk," ordered detained by judges, but then released. These juveniles were compared with a control group of sixty-four who had similar backgrounds and were not ordered held. After ninety days, 40 percent of the at-risk group had been rearrested, compared with only 15.6 percent of the control group. In short, the judges were reasonably accurate in identifying juveniles who posed a higher risk than comparable offenders. This was achieved, however, at the cost of false positives: 60 percent of the at-risk group were not rearrested. Moreover, only 19 percent were rearrested for a violent crime, so the judges were even less successful in predicting violent behavior.

As Fagan and Guggenheim argue, the goal of policy reform is to improve on current practice, to make some *marginal* improvement in predictive accuracy. If you used an actuarial method for making preventive detention decisions, based on objective criteria, and applied it to all the juveniles in their study, you would detain members of the control group. Remember, they were comparable to an "at-risk" group in terms of their background characteristics (about 90 percent of both groups had some prior criminal record, for example). Yet, only 15.6 percent of the control group were arrested within ninety days (think of them as false negatives). Applying the same objective prediction formula to the control group would result in detaining the 84.4 percent of the control group who were not rearrested. This translates into five false positives for every true positive. (Recall that the Wenk prediction study we covered in Chapter 4 produced eight false positives for every true positive.)

Fagan and Guggenheim conclude that "the accuracy of prediction of dangerousness during the pretrial period remains questionable." And because of the costs and limited marginal gains likely to be achieved, "preventive detention appears to be unjustified."[22] As we will see, shortly, the Rand Corporation reached a similar conclusion regarding the prediction of high-rate criminal offenders.

The NPRP data offer another perspective on the prediction problem. As we learned in Chapter 4, Wolfgang defined career criminals as those people with five or more police contacts (but not necessarily convictions). According to the NPRP data, 26 percent of the defendants with five or more prior convictions are rearrested. But this also means that 74 percent of these supposed "career criminals" are not rearrested. The problem facing the bail-setting judge is how to identify the 26 percent who will be rearrested from among all the others with five or more prior convictions. If you detain everyone with five or more prior convictions, you get three false positives for every true positive.

Because only a small percentage of people on bail are rearrested, and because we cannot predict which ones will commit more crime, we conclude as follows:

PROPOSITION 15
Preventive detention is not a realistic strategy for reducing serious crime.

Speedy Trial: A Better Way

If we want to prevent both crime on bail and failure to appeal, speedy trial is a much better approach. The 1992 NPRP data indicate that among those who were rearrested, 8 percent were rearrested in the first week and 37 percent within a month.[23] Disposing of all cases within five to six weeks would prevent about half of the crime committed by persons out on bail (this assumes that most will be convicted and sentenced to some confinement). Speedy disposition would also reduce the FTA rate and preserve two constitutional rights: the right to bail and the right to a speedy trial. Therefore, we can draw the following conclusion:

PROPOSITION 16
Speedy trials can reduce pretrial crime while preserving constitutional rights.

Actually, we have tried this approach. Congress and many states have enacted speedy-trial laws. Yet, as Malcolm Feeley found in his research on court reform, these laws were often evaded by the courtroom work group.[24] Thus, we face another dilemma: how to achieve a desired reform in the face of resistance by the courtroom work group. One possibility might be expedited trials only for those offenders who are high risks. This would preserve their constitutional rights to both bail and a speedy trial, as well as protect the public.

INCAPACITATION

Incapacitation seeks to reduce crime by imprisoning repeat offenders. It represents the same logic underlying preventive detention: keep criminals off the street so that they cannot commit more crimes. The strategy further assumes that if we keep them in twice as long, we will prevent twice as many crimes. As a sentencing philosophy, incapacitation does not try to rehabilitate offenders; it is only intended to get them off the street.[25]

There are actually two kinds of incapacitation. *Selective* incapacitation is designed to lock up only the few "high-rate" offenders or "career criminals." Like preventive detention, it builds on Wolfgang's career criminal research, which we discussed in Chapter 4. The alternative is *gross* incapacitation, which involves locking up large numbers of people, without distinction regarding their criminal histories. The new three-strikes laws are the ultimate form of gross incapacitation.

Selective Incapacitation: The Rand Formula

Selective incapacitation was one of the hot ideas in criminal justice in the 1970s and 1980s. James Q. Wilson endorsed it in his 1975 book, *Thinking About Crime*, claiming that serious crime could be reduced by *one-third* if each person convicted of a serious crime received a mandatory three-year prison sentence. He cited an earlier study that claimed that selective incapacitation could reduce crime by 80 percent.[26]

These extravagant claims generated much excitement, and a number of criminologists attempted to develop more sophisticated selective incapacitation policies. The most notable was a 1982 study, *Selective Incapacitation*, by Peter Greenwood and his associates at the Rand Corporation.[27] We have already discussed this work in Chapter 4 on the subject of career criminals. Let us take another look at it from the perspective of sentencing policy.

Selective Incapacitation estimated that a fine-tuned sentencing policy could reduce robbery by 15 percent while also reducing prison populations by 5 percent (an *un*selective policy would have to increase the prison population by 25 percent to achieve the same reduction in crime). The reduction in the prison population (with the resulting cost savings) would be achieved because the longer prison terms for career criminals would be offset by reduced punishments for low-risk offenders (shorter prison terms or probation).[28] Like so many crime control proposals, the policy seems to offer the best of all possible worlds: more effective crime control at less cost.

As we mentioned in Chapter 4, the Rand proposal is based on the earlier Rand Inmate Survey (RIS). Interviews with 2,190 prison and jail inmates in California, Texas, and Michigan are used to develop estimates of the *average annual offending rates* for offenders.[29] These estimates are the subject of considerable controversy, and the particular rate you choose has enormous policy implications. If the average career criminal commits more than a hundred crimes a year, incapacitation will achieve significant crime reduction. But if the average is only about five a year, the payoff will be relatively small.[30] Think of it in terms of Wolfgang's birth cohort, which we studied in Chapter 4: an ideal selective incapacitation policy would successfully identify and incarcerate the 6 percent of the cohort who are the career criminals, and only that group.

Rand developed a prediction instrument by correlating inmates' background characteristics with their self-reported criminal behavior. The result is a seven-point scale of factors associated with high rates of criminal behavior (see Table 4.3, p. 68). Offenders are then classified as low risk (one point), medium risk (two to three points), and high risk (four to seven points).

Rand then correlated inmates' predicted offense category with their actual self-reported level of criminal activity (see Table 4.4, p. 68). The prediction scale was correct 51 percent of the time. The 51 percent figure is calculated by adding the predicted low rate and actual low rate (14 percent), the predicted medium risk and actual medium risk (22 percent), and predicted high risk with actual high risk (15 percent). The prediction device was grossly wrong 7 percent of the time (the 4 percent who were predicted high but actually low, and the 3 percent predicted low but actually high). In the remaining 42 percent of the cases, the prediction scale was only moderately accurate.[31]

As Fagan and Guggenheim emphasize, the important question is whether any new policy is an improvement over current practice. When the Rand experts correlated their predictions with inmates' actual sentences, they found that the judges imposed a "correct" sentence (that is, a long sentence for a predicted high-rate offender) 42 percent of the time. In short, this figure is only a marginal improvement over what judges are currently doing.[32]

Why such a small marginal improvement? The Rand system has several problems. The first is our old friend the prediction problem. As other studies have found, prior criminal records and other indicators such as drug use are relatively weak predictors of future behavior. We consistently get significant numbers of false positives and false negatives. In fact, in the face of widespread criticism, Rand took another look at its own proposal five years later and admitted that its earlier estimates were "overly optimistic." It concluded that "there are no reliable methods for either measuring or predicting future offense rates."[33]

One of the problems with selective incapacitation schemes involves the estimated annual offending rates. The overall rates are *averages* that are inflated by the extremely high rates for the very worst offenders. The Rand report observes that "most offenders reported fairly low rates of crime." The median robbery rate was only five per year, but the worst 10 percent (or the 90th percentile) averaged eighty-seven per year![34] Incapacitating a member of the 90th percentile will produce a significant crime reduction, but the payoff for locking up all the others is relatively small.

The most shocking aspect of the Rand prediction scale is the use of employment history as a criterion for sentencing. An offender acquires one point for having been unemployed for more than half of the two preceding years. It carries the same weight as a prior conviction for the same offense. Under the formula, an additional point might reclassify the offender from a low-risk to a medium-risk offender, and thus it would mean the difference between jail and prison.

When you take out any one of the seven factors in the prediction scale, the entire scheme begins to collapse. With only six factors, the success rate will fall below the 51 percent that Rand estimates. You would then be doing no better than judges currently do, using a combination of presentence investigations and pure hunch.

It is outrageous that imprisonment might be contingent on unemployment. The Rand formula takes us back two hundred years to the days of imprisonment for debt. Even if such a policy were to become practice somewhere, it would immediately be challenged in court. The fact is that unemployment *is* highly correlated with criminal activity, but that correlation is not something we should translate into crime policy. An alternative response to the problem would be not to punish people for being unemployed but to provide greater employment opportunities.

Finally, the Rand *Selective Incapacitation* proposal faces a major political obstacle. The idea of not imprisoning low-risk and medium-risk offenders is exactly what liberal reformers have been advocating for decades. The National Council on Crime and Delinquency, the Edna McConnell Clark Foundation, the Sentencing Project, the Campaign for an Effective Crime Policy, and others have long maintained that we lock up too many people and for prison terms that are unnecessarily long.[35] In 1980, as the prison binge was beginning, the American Bar Association's *Standards for Criminal Justice* stated that "in many instances prison sentences which are now authorized, and sometimes required, are significantly higher than are needed in a vast majority of cases."[36] Because of the public mood, these recommendations have been consistently rejected in favor of a policy of gross incapacitation.

If selective incapacitation seems too good to be true, that is because it is. Because of the prediction problem and the political obstacles, we have to conclude as follows:

PROPOSITION 17

Selective incapacitation is not a realistic policy for reducing serious crime.

Gross Incapacitation: Zedlewski's New Math

Selective incapacitation is a fine-tuned surgical instrument that involves making careful distinctions between criminal offenders. The political reality is that we have completely ignored this approach and adopted instead a policy of gross incapacitation: locking up a lot of people and sending them to prison for long terms. This is the reason that the prison population tripled between 1980 and 1995. Let us take a look at the impact of gross incapacitation on the crime rate.

One of the most extraordinary endorsements of incapacitation is Edwin J. Zedlewski's report, *Making Confinement Decisions*.[37] He reached the startling conclusion that imprisonment actually *saves* money. Challenging the liberal conventional wisdom about the high cost of imprisonment, he calculated that for every dollar we spend imprisoning a criminal, we save $17 in total social costs. Although Zedlewski focused on the dollar costs of crime, his formula has important implications for crime reduction.

How did Zedlewski reach such an amazing conclusion? Let us take a look at his figures. First, he estimated that crime cost American society a total of about $100 billion in 1983. This included $33.8 billion for criminal justice system expenditures, $35 billion in victim losses (medical care, lost wages, property damage, and so on), $26.1 billion for private security expenses, and so forth. The NCVS, meanwhile, estimates that 42.5 million crimes were committed in 1983. Thus, Zedlewski calculated that each felony costs society $2,300 ($100 billion ÷ $42.5 million).

Using the Rand Inmate Survey (RIS), Zedlewski then estimated that each criminal commits an average of 187 crimes a year. Locking up each offender for one year, therefore, "saves" society $430,000 ($2,300 × 187 = $430,000). After you subtract the cost of imprisonment ($25,000 per year), you get a net social "savings" of $405,000 for each offender imprisoned (or about seventeen times the $25,000 cost of incarceration).

If this seems too good to be true, it is because it is. Franklin Zimring and Gordon Hawkins demolished the key assumptions underlying Zedlewski's computations.[38] The first and most serious problem is the estimate of 187 crimes a year. They point out that Zedlewski does not mention the great disagreement among career criminal specialists over annual offending rates. Many put the figure at about eighteen crimes a year, and some use an even lower estimate. If the average is only eighteen, then locking up one criminal saves only $43,000 a year according to Zedlewski's formula.

It was professionally dishonest of Zedlewski not to mention the debate over annual offending rates and to use one of the highest possible estimates. As we mentioned in Chapter 1, faith often triumphs over fact in discussions of crime policy. Here we have a case of someone deliberately misrepresenting the facts to make point.

Zedlewski also did not take into account the problem of diminishing returns. As we lock up more people, we quickly skim off the really high-rate offenders and begin incarcerating more of the less serious offenders. Because they average far fewer crimes per year (perhaps as few as five, according to the RIS), we get progressively lower returns in crime reduction and dollar savings.

The estimate of the dollar savings is also flawed. A reduction in crime does not produce a direct reduction in criminal justice system costs. If the crime rate goes down by 25 percent, we are not going to cut police department budgets by 25 percent. Also, because 80 to 90 percent of all department budgets involve personnel costs, that would really mean laying off one-quarter of all the officers. In fact, police departments have not reduced their size as crime rates have fallen in the 1990s. Police officers do a lot more than fight crime. About 70 to 80 percent of patrol work involves order maintenance and service activities.[39] These are important tasks that people want the police to continue performing. The same is true for other criminal justice system costs. If crime drops by 25 percent, the cost of running the criminal courts will not automatically decline by the same percentage.

In this regard, it is useful to remember the so-called "peace dividend." When the Soviet Union collapsed in the early 1990s and the Cold War ended, many analysts argued that we would no longer need to spend as much on national defense. The resulting "peace dividend" could be used to reduce federal government spending. In fact, the peace dividend never materialized; defense spending continues to be high even though the old "threat," the Soviet Union, has collapsed as a military power.

In the most devastating attack on Zedlewski, Zimring and Hawkins show that his own formula leads to absurd estimates of crime reduction. We have been running a natural experiment in gross incapacitation. They point out that between 1977 and 1987 the prison population increased by 230,000. If each criminal did an average of 187 crimes a year, that should have "prevented" 43 million crimes (230,000 $\times$ 187 = 43 million). Yet, this figure is more than the number of crimes that the NCVS reported as occurring in 1987. In short, Zedlewski's formula predicts the complete elimination of all crime by 1986!

We can update Zimring and Hawkins's critique with more recent data. Between 1986 and 1995, the prison population increased by about 500,000. At an annual rate of 187 crimes per offender, we should have prevented 93.5 million crimes in 1994, or about twice as many as occurred that year according to the NCVS.[40]

Crime has not disappeared, of course. The main reason is that all criminals do not average 187 crimes a year as Zedlewski estimated. Also, he did not consider the replacement factor: as some drug dealers are arrested, others take their place. And, of course, he did not even begin to discuss the social factors that lead people to become those replacements.

Incapacitation: A Sober Estimate

Having demolished Zedlewski's fantastic estimates, Zimring and Hawkins undertook their own study of incapacitation, examining incarceration and crime trends in California. Using a variety of sophisticated models, they concluded that the incarceration of each offender in California in the 1980s prevented 3.5 crimes per year. We should note that this is one-fiftieth of the 187 figure used by Zedlewski and is even lower than the estimates of many experts on career criminals. The huge increase in the state prison population (115,000) reduced the crime rate by 15 percent.[41]

As Zimring and Hawkins pursued their analysis, however, some problems surfaced. For burglary, juvenile arrests declined significantly, but adult arrests increased. This is "exactly the opposite" of what the incapacitation model would predict, because most of those incarcerated were adults. A similar pattern appeared with larceny and rape, but not robbery. Consequently, Zimring and Hawkins conclude that it is not absolutely clear that incapacitation was "the primary cause" of the drop in crime.[42]

Zimring and Hawkins also did a cross-state comparison of changes in incarceration rates and crime rates in seventeen states during the 1980s. California stood at one extreme, with the greatest increase in imprisonment and the greatest reduction in crime. Yet, Georgia had a very high increase in imprisonment but one of the highest rises in crime. Minnesota, meanwhile, had almost no increase in incarceration and virtually no change in the crime rate. In short, Zimring and Hawkins could detect "no clear patterned relationship" between incarceration rates and crime rates.[43]

Serious crime has declined in the 1990s, but we should be skeptical of claims that incapacitation is the sole or even the primary cause. Remember, we have been on the imprisonment binge for twenty-five years. Imagine you went to a doctor, got a prescription, took the medicine (two pills a day), but did not get any better. You went back to the doctor, who increased the dosage (four pills a day). But you still did not get any better. The doctor then raised the dosage again (six a day). You repeat this process for twenty years. Finally, in about the nineteenth year you begin to get better. Was it the medicine? Probably not. You cannot claim success for a prescription (pills/prisons) that failed for nineteen years and then suddenly appeared to work in the twentieth year.

Because no clear link between incarceration and crime rates is apparent, and because gross incapacitation locks up many low-rate offenders at a great dollar cost to society, we conclude as follows:

PROPOSITION 18

Gross incapacitation is not an effective policy for reducing serious crime.

MANDATORY SENTENCING

The third lock 'em up strategy for preventing crime is mandatory sentencing. Actually, mandatory sentencing is a *means* to an end. In this case there are actually two ends. Mandatory imprisonment ia a means of achieving incapacitation or deterrence or both. Mandatory sentencing usually means two things: mandatory imprisonment for a certain crime and/or a mandatory minimum prison term.

Mandatory sentencing is an extremely popular crime policy. A Justice Department report on sentencing policies found that all fifty states had some form of mandatory sentencing by 1994. Most of these laws apply to specific offenses. Forty-one states have it for repeat offenders, thirty-one for certain drunk driving offenses, thirty-two for certain drug offenses, and forty-two for some weapons offenses.[44] Meanwhile, by 1996 about twenty-two states had adopted three-strikes laws, which represent an extreme form of mandatory sentencing.[45]

The popularity of mandatory sentencing can be explained in part by the celebrated case syndrome we discussed in Chapter 2. Public opinion is heavily influenced by a few highly publicized cases. The O. J. Simpson trial convinced many people that spouse murderers are frequently acquitted at trial. But as the BJS data on spouse murder indicate (see Chapter 2), most people who murder their spouse are convicted and imprisoned. Another good example is the Polly Klass case. Twelve-year old Polly was brutally murdered by Richard Allen Davis, who was out on parole and had been twice convicted of kidnapping. The public uproar over her case led to the California three-strikes law and similar ones in other states.

Three Case Studies

Let us review three case studies of mandatory sentencing laws in practice. The three-strikes laws are a special case, and we will look at them separately.

Case 1: "The Nation's Toughest Drug Law" Most current mandatory minimum sentencing laws are modeled after a 1973 New York law, which was immediately advertised as "the nation's toughest drug law."[46] The law contained three major provisions designed to incapacitate drug offenders and deter future drug use: mandatory and long prison terms for heroin dealers, restrictions on plea bargaining for heroin dealers, and mandatory prison terms for certain categories of repeat offenders.

The prescribed prison terms were considered awesome at the time. The law established three categories of heroin dealers. Class A-I offenders (major dealers, defined as people who either sold one ounce of heroin or possessed two ounces) would serve minimum prison terms of fifteen or twenty-five years and a maximum of life imprisonment. Class A-II (middle-level dealers, defined as those who sold one-eighth of an ounce of heroin or possessed one to two ounces) would serve prison terms of at least six to eight and one-third years and a maximum of life. Class A-III offenders (minor "street" dealers, defined as anyone who sold less than one-eighth of an ounce of heroin or possessed up to one ounce) would serve a minimum prison term of at least one to eight and one-third years and a maximum term of life. In short, anyone caught selling heroin would definitely go to prison and would face the possibility of life imprisonment.

The law attempted to prevent abuse of plea bargaining. Anyone arrested for either an A-I or A-II offense could plead guilty to an A-III charge, but people originally charged with an A-III offense could not plead to anything lower. The result was a "floor" that meant at least some prison time and a potential life term. The law also included a habitual-criminal provision, imposing mandatory prison terms on anyone with a prior felony conviction. To cope with the anticipated increase in the criminal courts' workload as a result of the law, New York added forty-nine new judges, thirty-one of them in New York City.

In practice, the law was a paper tiger. An evaluation concluded that "the threat embodied in the words of the law proved to have teeth for relatively few offenders."[47] An enormous amount of "slippage" or "leakage" occurred between arrest and conviction. Between 1972 and 1976, the percentage of drug arrests leading to indictment declined from 39 percent to 25 percent. Meanwhile, the percentage of indictments resulting in a conviction fell from 86 percent to 80 percent. Thus, the overall percentage of arrests leading to conviction fell from 33.5 percent to 20 percent.

The law was not a total failure. For those who were convicted, the rate of incarceration went up from 33 percent to 55 percent. Nonetheless, if only 55 percent were going to prison, about half the defendants were evading the supposedly "mandatory" sentencing provisions. Overall, however, little changed. The percentage of people arrested for sale or heroin who went to prison was 11 percent in 1972–1973, and it was 11 percent in 1976.

The law did produce longer prison terms. Among those sentenced to prison, the percentage receiving a sentence of three years or longer rose from 3 percent of all those convicted to 22 percent.

The slippage that occurred in the application of the New York law is consistent with the long history of mandatory sentencing laws. The process can be explained in terms of the thermodynamics of the criminal justice process, which we discussed in Chapter 3. An increase in the severity of the potential punishment creates pressure to avoid its actual application. In this case, the controls over plea bargaining did not prevent a rise in dismissals. The enormous increase in the potential prison terms, meanwhile, encouraged defense attorneys to go to trial. The percentage of defendants demanding a trial increased from 6 percent to 15 percent. Because a tried case takes fifteen times as long to process as a case that is not tried, the addition of even a few trials significantly disrupts the process. Disposition time for all drug cases doubled under the new law, despite the addition of the new judgeships (and for some unexplained reason the new courts were noticeably less efficient than previously established courts were).

Finally, and most important, the law had no significant effect on crime or drug use. Heroin use in New York City was as widespread in 1976 as it had been in 1973. Serious property crime, the kind generally associated with heroin users, increased 15 percent between 1973 and 1975, but neighboring states had similar increases. Nor did the law appear to deter convicted felons from committing additional crimes. According to the National Household Survey, drug use did begin to decline in the late 1980s, but this trend was nationwide, and we cannot say that the New York law had any special impact in that state.[48]

Adaptation. As we argued in Chapter 3, the criminal justice system adapts to major changes in the going rate. Our law of thermodynamics has been clearly at work in New York in the years since the 1973 drug laws were enacted. The state has taken one step backward, another step forward, and then another step backward again.

The "nation's toughest drug law" proved to be too much for the system. In 1976 the chief prosecutor of drug cases in New York City quietly announced that he would no longer enforce the law's prohibitions on plea bargaining. Three years later, the legislature formally eliminated these same prohibitions and permitted more flexibility in sentencing. It also allowed resentencing of some offenders given extremely long sentences under the original law.[49]

An important part of the "slippage" occurs after sentencing. As states have sent more offenders to prison and for longer terms, prison have become seriously overcrowded. All prisons were 15 percent over capacity in 1995; Virginia was 40 percent over its officially rated capacity and Ohio was 70 percent over.[50] States have responded by releasing prisoners early through a variety of schemes. Some of them are overt "emergency release" procedures. But others are covert "backdoor" schemes embedded in changes in correctional practices. Pamala Griset's study of correctional trends in New York, which we discussed in Chapter 3, illustrates the extent to which this involves both a hidden form of sentencing and a device for undermining the intent of mandatory sentencing laws.[51]

New York supplemented the 1973 drug law with two additional mandatory sentencing laws in 1978, covering juveniles and certain violent felonies. Prison overcrowding resulted, and because of the state's financial problems, the needed prison cells were not constructed. The state responded in 1987 and 1989 with laws creating three early release programs: shock incarceration, earned eligibility, and CASAT (Comprehensive Alcohol and Substance Abuse Treatment). These programs transfer enormous discretion to correctional officials over how much time offenders will actually serve.

Shock incarceration, like many boot camp programs we will examine in Chapter 11, involves early release after a short six-month program. Griset found that about 40 percent of those admitted to the program had been convicted of a second felony and that about 99 percent were immediately paroled upon completing the program. Many of these offenders were technically subject to the state's mandatory sentencing law regarding second offense felons. Yet, on the basis of decisions by correctional staff—and not sentencing judges—they were released sooner than the law "mandated."

The second program, earned eligibility, speeds up an inmate's date of first eligibility for parole. Inmates who participate in treatment, educational, and work programs obtain a certificate of earned eligibility from correctional staff that grants them a virtual presumption of parole release (82 percent of those with certificates were paroled). As Griset explains, correctional staff have full discretion over whether to grant the certificate of earned eligibility.[52] Thus, actual control over the actual amount of time served passes from the legislature and judges to correctional officials.

Similarly, under the CASAT program inmates with alcohol or drug histories may be released up to eighteen months earlier than the expiration of their minimum sentence. As with the other two programs, correctional officials have full discretion to grant admission to CASAT.

The net result of these three programs, Griset explains, is that the reality of sentencing diverges from the rhetoric. New York politicians retained mandatory minimum sentencing but quietly authorized correctional officials to let prisoners out early.[53] On the one hand, this is a cynical political maneuver: talking tough about crime while not facing up to paying the bill. At the same time, it is a classic example of how criminal justice thermodynamics often undermine the intent of "tough" sentencing laws.

Case 2: Getting Tough in Florida   Florida adopted the basic elements of the New York drug law in a series of ten different laws enacted between the mid-1970s and the late 1980s. Three covered drug crimes, two applied to habitual criminals, and three covered weapons offenses. A 1975 law mandated three years in prison for using a firearm in the commission of certain other felonies. A 1988 law made persons convicted as habitual violent felony offenders ineligible for parole for fifteen years. New drug-trafficking laws imposed mandatory minimums of three, five, ten, fifteen, and twenty-five years, depending on the offense.[54]

In some important respects, many of the Florida mandatory provisions are just the opposite of the developments in New York. Whereas New York created new hidden means of reducing sentences, some of the Florida laws were designed to eliminate good-time reductions and to ensure that prisoners served the full mandatory term.

Florida's case illustrates how incredibly complex the subject of good time is. The state maintains four different kinds of good time. *Basic* good time reduces a sentence by one-third and applies the day the offender enters prison. *Incentive* good time is awarded at a rate of twenty days a month for good behavior. An inmate can then earn *meritorious* good time of up to sixty days for outstanding deeds. Finally, to maintain legally mandated limits on the prison population, officials can award *provisional credits*. Partly as a result of the different good-time provisions, Florida inmates were serving an average of 34.1 percent of their formal sentences by 1989. Other states have their own equally complex good-time laws.[55]

A series of mandatory minimum sentencing laws in Florida sought to limit the application of good-time credits for certain offenses. Persons convicted of using a firearms in the commission of a felony could not earn any good-time credits until after the minimum three-year sentence had been served. The 1977 Habitual Felony Offender law blocked the application of some types of good time but allowed some others.

The impact of mandatory minimum sentences in Florida was complex. The number of prisoners sentenced under the mandatory minimum provisions for drug trafficking increased from 4 in 1979–1980 to 1,022 in 1989–1990; the number sentenced under the habitual felony offender law increased from 21 to 1,804 in the same period. The prison population quadrupled, from about 10,000 to more than 40,000. These data seem to indicate that the mandatory sentencing laws were being applied. In other words, it is not necessarily true that mandatory sentencing provisions are always evaded by prosecutors and judges. Whether they were being applied in every potential case is another question.

The huge increase in prison population, however, provoked a serious overcrowding problem. As a result of court orders limiting the number of inmates in particular prisons and the failure of the state to build enough new prisons, officials released thousands of inmates earlier than they otherwise would have. Provisional good time was a particular useful device, and at one point some inmates were receiving sixty days of credits for every month they served. As a result, the average percentage of sentences served fell from 52.8 percent to 34.1 percent between 1987 and 1989. Thus, many offenders who had been convicted of serious crimes (robbery, for example) but were not sentenced under a mandatory minimum law were released much earlier than they would have been. As was the case in New York, the intent of "tough" sentencing laws was undermined by creative adaptations dictated by practical necessities.

Case 3: The Federal Sentencing Guidelines   The Federal Sentencing Guidelines that went into effect in 1987 include a number of mandatory sentencing provisions, and they have contributed to the increase in the federal prison population. To achieve "truth in sentencing," the guidelines reduced the range of possible sentences and abolished discretionary parole release. The percentage of convicted federal offenders sentenced to prison increased from 51 percent in 1982 to 65 percent in 1994. Also, the average prison term increased 27 percent, from an average of forty-eight to sixty-one months.[56]

A basic question is whether prosecutors and judges are complying with the Federal Sentencing Guidelines. There is mixed evidence on this issue. A study by the Federal Judicial Center found that slightly less than half of the offenders who were eligible under a mandatory minimum provision actually received it. This is a fairly high rate of "slippage" and "leakage."[57]

Another problem is plea bargaining—specifically, charge bargaining that allows defendants to plea to a lesser offense and avoid a long mandatory minimum. Section 5K1.1 of the Federal Sentencing Guidelines allows a departure from the presumptive sentence where the defendant "has provided substantial assistance in the investigation or prosecution of another person who has committed an offense."[58] In other words, a defendant can reduce his or her potential sentence by cooperating and naming other criminals.

Ilene H. Nagle and Samuel J. Schulhofer examined plea bargaining in three federal district courts and found that departures from the guidelines occurred in between 15 and 25 percent of all cases, with the national average about 17 percent. They conclude that circumvention of the guidelines is not the norm and that it is not necessarily unfair. They did, however, find some cases in which defendants won substantial sentence reductions: in one case from 168 to 21 months; in another from 69 months to 9.[59] These reductions may be excessive compared with what most defendants receive.

The point is that through prosecutorial discretion, "mandatory" sentences are not necessarily mandatory in practice. As we will see shortly, the mandatory provisions of three-strikes laws are ignored in most states. The various adaptations, moreover, because they are often hidden, increase the arbitrariness of decisions and the possibility of discrimination.

Mandatory Sentencing and Crime

The basic question, of course, is whether mandatory sentencing effectively reduces crime. A 1982 Justice Department report concluded that "it is difficult, perhaps fundamentally impossible, to substantiate the popular claim that mandatory sentencing is an effective tool for reducing crime."[60] Fifteen years later, we have much more experience with mandatory sentencing. A 1996 report on structured sentencing in a variety of states found no correlation between incarceration rates and crime rates. Changes in the crime rate in Florida were similar to changes in other states that imprisoned far fewer people.[61] Zimring and Hawkins's multistate comparison of incapacitation, which we cited earlier, also did not find any clear correlation between incarceration rates and crime rates.[62]

After reviewing all of the evidence on mandatory sentencing, Michael Tonry, one of the leading experts on sentencing, declared, "Mandatory penalties do not work."[63] In his view, they are widely circumvented, tend to shift discretion from justices to prosecutors, and often result in punishments that are "unduly harsh." We agree. Our position is as follows:

PROPOSITION 19

Mandatory sentencing is not an effective means of reducing serious crime.

The American Bar Association also agrees. Standard 18-2.1 *for Criminal Justice* recommends, "The legislature should not s[ ] tory sentence for any sentencing category or for any particula[ ] basic assumption underlying mandatory imprisonment is that [ ] tice system is "soft" on crime. We have discussed several aspects of th[ ] ment in previous chapters. In Chapter 2 we saw that offenders with substantial prior records, who are convicted of a serious crime against a stranger, are prosecuted (usually on the top charge), convicted, and imprisoned at a very high rate. We have also found that over 90 percent of the criminals who would be classified as dangerous repeat offenders are convicted and sentenced to prison. In the next chapter we will find that plea bargaining is not the loophole that many people believe it to be.

THREE STRIKES—WE ARE ALL OUT

The most popular new idea in mandatory sentencing is "three strikes and you're out." The basic concept is a mandatory life prison sentence for anyone convicted of a third felony, although in actual practice there are many variations. The state of Washington passed the first law, the Persistent Offender Accountability Act, in November 1993. The idea really caught fire after the brutal murder of Polly Klass in California by Richard Allen Davis, a man with a long criminal record who had been paroled only three months earlier. California passed its three-strikes law in March 1994. As of 1996, at least twenty-two states and the federal system had some form of three strikes.[65]

Considerable variation among three-strikes laws. The Washington law mandates life without parole for conviction to a "most serious offense" if the person had two prior convictions to "most serious offenses." These included a wide range of felonies. The California law has separate two-strikes and three-strikes provisions. The third-strike provision mandates an indeterminate sentence of between twenty-five years to life (or triple the normal sentence, whichever is greater) for persons convicted of a violent felony if they have two prior felony convictions. The two priors do not have to be to violent crimes. The second-strike provision doubles the normal sentence. Some states passed two-strikes laws: the 1994 Georgia law mandates life without parole for a second conviction to a "serious violent felony." As is clear, the factors that trigger the law vary greatly.[66]

The three-strikes idea has been almost universally condemned by criminologists and other experts on sentencing. Franklin Zimring calls it "the voodoo economics of California crime." Jerome Skolnick says it represented the values of "the dark ages." A book labels it "Vengeance as Public Policy." Princeton's John J. DiIulio is one of the few to support it, arguing that "society has a right not only to protect itself from convicted criminals but to express its moral outrage at their acts by, among other things, keeping them behind bars."[67]

Actually, the basic principle underlying three strikes is nothing new. Most states have had some kind of habitual offender law for many decades. A famous 1926 New York law mandated life in prison for conviction to a third felony. Forty-one had some kind of habitual offender law in February 1994, before the three-strikes movement took off.[68] The major difference is that the new three-strikes laws impose much longer prison terms.

Three-strikes laws raise the same questions we have already considered in this book. The first is whether the law will in fact be implemented or whether it will be evaded by the courtroom work group. The second is, assuming it is implemented, what impact it will have on the criminal justice system. The third question is whether three-strikes laws will reduce crime.

Implementation

On the first question, a study by the Center for an Effective Crime Policy found that, with the exception of California, hardly any states were using their three-strikes laws. Wisconsin had used its law only once in the first year and a half. And the laws had not been used at all in Tennessee, New Mexico, and Colorado. Georgia had imposed five life sentences in the first fifteen months.[69]

The source for this pervasive nonuse is clear: local prosecutors simply do not file the necessary charges. In some instances, it becomes a plea-bargaining tool. Many cases can be filed either as felonies or misdemeanors (say, misdemeanor assault versus felonious assault). The law gives the prosecutor a powerful weapon to get a guilty plea to a misdemeanor. In Sacramento, California, there were charge reductions in 67 percent of all the eligible cases. Even in California, application of the law varied tremendously. Two-thirds of all cases under the law originated in Los Angeles County. Officials in San Francisco, meanwhile, have publicly stated that they will not use it in certain kinds of cases, including drug cases.[70]

Impact

In the California counties where the three-strikes law has been used, the effect has rippled through the local criminal justice system. More defendants have demanded jury trials, preferring to take their chances on acquittal at trial than plead guilty to certain third-strikes sentences. In the first year, potential second and third-strike cases in Los Angeles represented 3 percent of all cases but 24 percent of jury trials. The increase in criminal trials raised the costs of handling cases (in the state of Washington, a full jury trial costs as much as $50,000, compared with $600 for a routine plea-bargained case) and caused more delays in civil cases.[71]

The increase in the number of defendants waiting trial has produced severe jail overcrowding. As a result, other offenders sentenced to short jail terms were being released early. Offenders sentenced to one-year jail terms were being released after 71 days, compared with an average of 200 days beforehand. The law had cost Los Angeles County alone an extra $169 million in just the first two years.

The Rand Corporation estimates that if the California law were fully implemented, the state would have to spend an extra $5.5 billion a year over the next twenty-five years.[72] Most of this cost involves building new prisons (at an estimated cost of $97,000 per prisoner) and operating these prisons (at an estimated cost of $20,800 per prisoner). One important factor with three-strikes laws is that the cost of incarcerating an elderly prisoner is three times the normal cost ($60,000) because of medical care and security needs of frail inmates. The number of these inmates will increase dramatically under the life terms imposed by three-strikes laws.

The Rand report does estimate that the law would reduce serious crime by 28 percent. It quickly points out that the greatest reductions would be in assaults and burglaries, but "not the murders, rapes, and robberies that many people believe to be the law's principal targets."[73] The Rand report also asks whether the estimated crime reduction would be worth the cost. In one of its budgetary projections, which assumes no increase in taxes, the cost of corrections completely wipes out the state higher education budget—in short, a 28 percent reduction in crime but elimination of all colleges and universities. The only alternatives (aside from raising taxes) would be to drastically cut K–12 education or health and welfare services.

The Rand report on the California three-strikes law reached the same conclusion as Zimring and Hawkins's study of incapacitation. Massive imprisonment does reduce crime somewhat, but at a frightful cost. Zimring and Hawkins are careful to point out that they were not completely sure that incapacitation was responsible for the reduction in crime they found.[74] In the mid-1990s, crime has been going down in California, as it has in other states. The decline began well before the three-strikes law took effect.

Many criminologists question whether long prison terms imposed by three-strikes laws will reduce crime very much. One of the basic things we know about criminal behavior is that the peak years for criminal activity are between ages fourteen and twenty-four. The middle-aged and elderly people serving life terms would commit very few crimes, if any, if they were released. With this group there would be an enormous dollar cost with no compensating crime reduction.

Three-strikes laws are the worst example of gross incapacitation. And in a classic example of the trickle-up or hydraulic effect, they sweep up many people convicted of relatively minor offenses. The first California case, in fact, involved Jerry Williams, who stole a slice of pepperoni pizza. The first woman prosecuted under the law was arrested for a $20 cocaine purchase that occurred fourteen years after her second "strike." One of the first people sentenced to life in prison in the state of Washington had stolen $151 from a sandwich shop; his two previous strikes involved robberies totalling $460. About 85 percent of those sentenced under the law in California were convicted of a nonviolent crime. In March 1996, 192 were sentenced for marijuana possession, compared with 40 for murder and 25 for rape.

Like the Federal Sentencing Guidelines, moreover, a pattern of racial disparities has appeared in the implementation of the California three-strikes law.

African Americans were being sent to prison thirteen times as often under the law as were whites.[75]

Summary: Striking Out

Three strikes represents all the worst aspects of the "get tough" approach to crime. First, it is a classic example of overreaction to celebrated cases. Second, it represents a crude, meat-ax policy that sweeps up many nondangerous criminals. Third, these laws are not consistently implemented and thus increase the arbitrariness of the administration of justice. Fourth, they upset the normal "going rate" and impose new costs on local criminal justice systems, including more trials, delays, and greater dollar costs. Finally, no clear evidence indicates that they will reduce serious crime (and some good evidence shows that they incarcerate a lot of people who will not commit any crimes at all).

PROPOSITION 20

"Three strikes and you're out" laws are a terrible crime policy.

CONCLUSION

From a commonsense standpoint, lock 'em up strategies appear to be a simple and effective way to reduce crime. Unfortunately, it is not that simple in the real world of the criminal justice system. First, we cannot precisely identify the small group of high-rate offenders. Second, gross incapacitation policies create all sorts of problems in the justice system. Third, because of these problems, the courtroom work group often finds ways to evade extremely punitive laws. Fourth, no conclusive evidence indicates that locking up a lot of people actually produces the promised reductions in crime. Finally, even where some crime reduction does occur, it is not clear that it is worth the enormous dollar cost to society.

NOTES

1. On the general subject of discretion, see Samuel Walker, *Taming the System: The Control of Discretion in Criminal Justice, 1950–1990* (New York: Oxford University Press, 1993).

2. President's Task Force on Victims of Crime, *Final Report* (Washington, D.C.: Government Printing Office, 1982), p. 22.

3. Caleb Foote, "The Coming Constitutional Crisis in Bail," *University of Pennsylvania Law Review* 113 (May 1965): 959–999 and (June 1965): 1125–1185.

4. *United States v. Salerno*, 481 U.S. 739 (1987).

5. On the background of the bail issue, see Wayne Thomas, *Bail Reform in America* (Berkeley: University of California Press, 1976).

6. Caleb Foote, "Compelling Appearance in Court: Administration of Bail in Philadelphia," *University of Pennsylvania Law Review* 102 (1954): 1031–1079.

7. Bureau of Justice Statistics, *Pretrial Release of Felony Defendants, 1992* (Wash-

ington, D.C.: Government Printing Office, 1994).

8. Thomas, *Bail Reform in America.*

9. Ibid., p. 37; Bureau of Justice Statistics, *Pretrial Release of Felony Defendants, 1992.*

10. Bureau of Justice Statistics, *Pretrial Release of Felony Defendants, 1990* (Washington, D.C.: Government Printing Office, 1992).

11. John Goldkamp, "Danger and Detention: A Second Generation of Bail Reform," *Journal of Criminal Law and Criminology* 76 (Spring 1985): 1–74.

12. *Preventive Detention in the District of Columbia: The First Ten Months* (Washington, D.C.: Georgetown Institute of Criminal Law and Procedure, 1972); Thomas, *Bail Reform in America*, pp. 231–232.

13. Frederick Suffett, "Bail Setting: A Study of Courtroom Interaction," *Crime and Delinquency* 12 (1966): 318–331.

14. Bureau of Justice Statistics, *Pretrial Release of Felony Defendants, 1992*, Table 5.

15. General Accounting Office, *Criminal Bail: How Bail Reform Is Working Selected District Courts* (Washington, D.C.: Government Printing Office, 1987); Bureau of Justice Statistics, *Pretrial Release and Detention: The Bail Reform Act of 1984* (Washington, D.C.: Government Printing Office, 1988).

16. Thomas E. Scott, "Pretrial Detention Under the Bail Reform Act of 1984: An Empirical Analysis," *American Criminal Law Review* 27(1) (1989): 1–51; Bureau of Justice Statistics, *Sourcebook of Criminal Justice Statistics—1994* (Washington, D.C.: Government Printing Office, 1995), p. 442.

17. Bureau of Justice Statistics, *Pretrial Release and Detention*, Table 9; Bureau of Justice Statistics, *Sourcebook of Criminal Justice Statistics—1994*, p. 445.

18. Bureau of Justice Statistics, *Pretrial Release of Felony Defendants, 1992.*

19. Bureau of Justice Statistics, *Pretrial Release of Felony Defendants, 1992*, p. 11.

20. *Schall v. Martin* 467 U.S. 253 (1984).

21. Jeffrey Fagan and Martin Guggenheim, "Preventive Detention and the Judicial Prediction of Dangerousness for Juveniles: A Natural Experiment," *Journal of Criminal Law and Criminology* 86(2) (1996): 415–448.

22. Ibid., pp. 445, 448.

23. Bureau of Justice Statistics, *Pretrial Release of Felony Defendants, 1992.*

24. Malcolm Feeley, *Court Reform on Trial* (New York: Basic Books, 1983).

25. Franklin E. Zimring and Gordon Hawkins, *Incapacitation: Penal Confinement and the Restraint of Crime* (New York: Oxford University Press, 1995).

26. James Q. Wilson, *Thinking About Crime* (New York: Basic Books, 1975), pp. 200–202.

27. Peter Greenwood, *Selective Incapacitation* (Santa Monica, CA: Rand, 1982).

28. Ibid., p. xix.

29. Jan M. Chaiken and Marcia R. Chaiken, *Varieties of Criminal Behavior: Summary and Policy Implications* (Santa Monica, CA: Rand, 1982).

30. Alfred Blumstein, Jacqueline Cohen, Jeffrey Roth, and Christy Visher, eds., *Criminal Careers and "Career Criminals"* (Washington, D.C.: National Academy of Sciences, 1988).

31. Ibid., p. 59.

32. Ibid., p. 60.

33. Peter W. Greenwood and Susan Turner, *Selective Incapacitation Revisited: Why the High-Rate Offenders Are Hard to Predict* (Santa Monica, CA: Rand, 1987).

34. Greenwood, *Selective Incapacitation,* Table 4.3.

35. Edna McConnell Clark Foundation, *Overcrowded Time* (New York: Edna McConnell Clark Foundation, 1982); Don C. Gibbons, *The Limits of Punishment as Social Policy* (San Francisco: National Council on Crime and Delinquency, 1988); Marc Mauer, *Americans Behind Bars: One Year Later* (Washington, D.C.: Sentencing Project, 1992); Campaign for an Effective Crime Policy, *What Every Policymaker Should Know About Imprisonment and*

the *Crime Rate* (Washington, D.C.: Campaign for an Effective Crime Policy, 1995).

36. American Bar Association, *Standards for Criminal Justice*, "Sentencing Alternatives and Procedures," Standard 18-2.1 (Boston: Little, Brown, 1980), pp. 18–25.

37. Edwin W. Zedlewski, *Making Confinement Decisions* (Washington, D.C.: Government Printing Office, 1987).

38. Franklin E. Zimring and Gordon E. Hawkins, "The New Mathematics of Imprisonment," *Crime and Delinquency* 34 (October 1988): 425–436. See also Zimring and Hawkins, *Incapacitation*.

39. Eric J. Scott, *Calls for Service* (Washington, D.C.: Government Printing Office, 1981).

40. Bureau of Justice Statistics, *Criminal Victimization 1994* (Washington, D.C.: Government Printing Office, 1996).

41. Zimring and Hawkins, *Incapacitation*.

42. Ibid., p. 126.

43. Ibid., pp. 106–107.

44. Bureau of Justice Assistance, *National Assessment of Structured Sentencing* (Washington, D.C.: Government Printing Office, 1996), pp. 24–25.

45. Campaign for an Effective Crime Policy, *The Impact of "Three Strikes and You're Out" Laws: What Have We Learned?* (Washington, D.C.: Campaign for an Effective Crime Policy, 1996).

46. U.S. Department of Justice, *The Nation's Toughest Drug Law: Evaluating the New York Experience* (Washington, D.C.: Government Printing Office, 1978).

47. Ibid., p. 18.

48. Bureau of Justice Statistics, *Drugs, Crime, and the Justice System* (Washington, D.C.: Government Printing Office, 1992), p. 30.

49. Malcolm M. Feeley and Sam Hakim, "The Effect of 'Three Strikes and You're Out' on the Courts," in David Shichor and Dale K. Sechrest, eds., *Three Strikes and You're Out: Vengeance as Social Policy* (Thousand Oaks, CA: Sage, 1996), p. 141.

50. Bureau of Justice Statistics, *Sourcebook of Criminal Justice Statistics—1995*, p. 94.

51. Pamala Griset, "The Politics and Economics of Increased Correctional Discretion over Time Served: A New York Case Study," *Justice Quarterly* 12 (June 1995): 307–323.

52. Ibid., p. 316.

53. Ibid., p. 321.

54. William G. Bales and Linda G. Dees, "Mandatory Minimum Sentencing in Florida: Past Trends and Future Implications," *Crime and Delinquency* 38 (July 1992): 309–332.

55. Ibid.; Bureau of Justice Statistics, *National Corrections Reporting Program, 1992* (Washington, D.C.: Government Printing Office, 1994). 56. Bureau of Justice Statistics, *Sourcebook of Criminal Justice Statistics—1995* (Washington, D.C.: Government Printing Office, 1996), pp. 472–473.

57. Barbara Meierhofer, *The General Effect of Mandatory Minimum Prison Terms* (Washington, D.C.: Government Printing Office, 1992).

58. U.S. Sentencing Commission, *Federal Sentencing Guidelines Manual* (St. Paul, MN: West, 1990), p. 281.

59. Ilene H. Nagel and Stephen Schulhofer, "A Tale of Three Cities: An Empirical Study of Charging and Bargaining Practices Under the Federal Sentencing Guidelines," *Southern California Law Review* 66 (1992): 501–566.

60. Department of Justice, *Mandatory Sentencing: The Experience of Two States* (Washington, D.C: Government Printing Office, 1982).

61. Bureau of Justice Assistance, *National Assessment of Structure Sentencing*, p. 117.

62. Zimring and Hawkins, *Incapacitation*.

63. Michael Tonry, "Mandatory Penalties," in Michael Tonry, ed., *Crime and Justice: A Review of Research*, vol. 16 (Chicago: University of Chicago Press, 1992), p. 243.

64. American Bar Association, *Standards for Criminal Justice*, "Sentencing Alternatives and Procedures" (Boston: Little, Brown, 1980), pp. 18–25.

65. The best collection of material on three-strikes laws is Shichor and Sechrest, *Three Strikes and You're Out*.

66. Michael G. Turner, Jody Sundt, Brandon K. Applegate, and Francis T. Cullen, "'Three Strikes and You're Out' Legislation: A National Assessment," *Federal Probation* 59 (September 1995): 16–35.

67. Jerome H. Skolnick, "Wild Pitch," *American Prospect* 17 (Spring 1994): 31–37; Shichor and Sechrest, *Three Strikes and You're Out*; John J. DiIulio, Jr., "Instant Replay," *American Prospect* 18 (Summer 1994): 12–18.

68. Bureau of Justice Assistance, *National Assessment of Structured Sentencing*, pp. 24–25; Turner et al. "'Three Strikes and You're Out' Legislation."

69. Campaign for an Effective Crime Policy, *The Impact of "Three Strikes and You're Out" Laws*.

70. Ibid.

71. Robert C. Cushman, "Effect on a Local Criminal Justice System," in Shichor and Sechrest, *Three Strikes and You're Out*, pp. 90–113.

72. Peter Greenwood, C. Peter Rydell, Allan F. Abrahmse, Jonathan P. Caukins, James Chiesa, Karyn E. Model, and Stephen P. Klein, *Three Strikes and You're Out: Estimated Benefits and Costs of California's New Mandatory Sentencing Law* (Santa Monica, CA: Rand, 1994); this selection also appears as Chapter 3 in Shichor and Sechrest, *Three Strikes and You're Out*, pp. 53–89.

73. Greenwood et al., in Shichor and Sechrest, *Three Strikes and You're Out*, p. 70.

74. Zimring and Hawkins, *Incapacitation*.

75. Campaign for an Effective Crime Policy, *The Impact of "Three Strikes and You're Out" Laws*, p. ii.

8

Close the Loopholes

onservatives believe that many dangerous criminals "beat the system" and escape punishment: their cases are dismissed, they plead guilty to lesser offenses, or if convicted they are not sent to prison. As a result, they return to the streets and commit more crimes. A major part of the conservative crime control agenda, therefore, is to close these "loopholes" in the criminal justice system.

PROSECUTE THE CAREER CRIMINAL

To make sure that the really dangerous criminals are punished, a number of prosecutors have created special "major-offender" or "career criminal" programs. The basic idea is to focus special attention on them to make sure they are prosecuted, convicted, and incarcerated. Like some of the other programs we have examined, this idea is based on Wolfgang's career criminal research, which we examined in Chapter 4.

Getting Tough in San Diego

The San Diego Major Violator Unit targets robbery and robbery-related homicide cases in which the defendant is charged with three or more separate robbery-related offenses or has been convicted of one or more serious offenses in the preceding ten years.[1] The individual prosecutor assigned a major-violator case follows it through to completion. This provides *continuity of prose-cution,* which is designed to prevent mistakes that might result from passing a case from one prosecutor to another as it moves through the system from the initial charge to preliminary hearing and eventual disposition. It is also de-signed to help maintain close contact between the prosecutor and the victim and witnesses. (Witnesses problems is one of the main reasons that cases are dismissed.) Prosecutors are involved in the preparation of the presentence in-vestigation (PSI) report, and they submit an independent sentence recom-mendation to the judge, often asking for a stiff sentence.

Like other career criminal programs, the San Diego Major Violator Unit includes restrictions on plea bargaining.[2] Prosecutors may not "charge bar-gain" and can accept a plea only to the top felony count. This is designed to prevent the defendant from avoiding prison by pleading to a misdemeanor or a lesser felony.

Despite these special procedures, however, the San Diego Major Violator Unit had only a modest impact on the prosecution of career criminals. The reason is simple: prosecutors were already very tough on serious crime.

The Major Violator Unit won conviction in 91.5 percent of its cases. This sounds very impressive until we discover that San Diego normally convicted 89.5 percent of all career criminals. The unit did increase the percentage of convicted offenders sent to prison, from 77.1 percent to 92.5 percent. This change was less significant than it might appear, however. The percentage of convicted offenders who were incarcerated (as opposed to imprisoned) in-creased only slightly, from 95.3 percent to 100 percent. This point highlights an important but often misunderstood feature of felony sentencing.[3]

The category of "incarceration" includes both sentences to prison and "split sentences" in which the offender does some time in jail followed by re-lease on probation. Split sentences are actually fairly common. Nationally, about half of all convicted felons given "probation" actually serve some time in jail. The net result is that 70 percent of convicted felons are incarcerated (prison: 44 percent; jail: 26 percent; straight probation: 30 percent).[4]

These data on sentencing are extremely important in terms of public *per-ception* of how the system works. If you look only at the percentage of con-victed offenders sentenced to prison (44 percent), the system looks somewhat weak. But when you include everyone who is incarcerated (70 percent), it looks a lot tougher. True, going to jail is not as serious as going to prison, but it is still an unpleasant experience, and these offenders are not "beating the system."

The Major Violator Unit did, however, double the average length of in-carceration. In this respect it significantly increased the severity of punish-ment. But it is important to recall that the length of prison terms has been rising across the country (particularly for serious crimes), so some of the in-crease in San Diego probably would have occurred even without the Major Violator Unit.

The important question for us is whether the San Diego Major Violator Unit had any impact on the crime rate. The evaluation of the program did not address this question. Common sense, however, suggests that it could not have had any significant effect, because the changes in the percentage of offenders convicted and the percentage incarcerated were so small.

Other Prosecution Programs

The results in San Diego were typical of outcomes in other jurisdictions. The National Institute of Justice found a similar pattern in three other career criminal programs. In Kalamazoo, Michigan, conviction rates went from 66.6 percent to 73.4 percent; in New Orleans they rose from 81.8 percent to 88.7 percent; and they went from 73.9 percent to 76.4 percent in Columbus, Ohio. Incarceration rates rose slightly in two of the cities but actually declined in New Orleans. Sentence lengths went up in two cities but went down in Kalamazoo.[5]

A Phoenix, Arizona, repeat offender program (ROP) involves police officers in the prosecution effort, working with prosecutors as a team. Detectives "walk" warrants or information about additional charges through the courts to ensure a high bond so that the defendant is not released before trial. They also attend trials inconspicuously and provide feedback to prosecutors about the reaction of jurors. ROP detectives also personally contact probation officers and provide information for the presentence investigation report.

The results of the program were similar to those in San Diego. Over 98 percent of the ROP offenders were prosecuted, and 89.9 percent were convicted. The figures for the control group were nearly identical: 98.9 percent prosecuted and 86.4 percent convicted. The percentage incarcerated is almost the same, although a slightly higher proportion were sent to prison rather than given a split sentence.[6]

These data on the prosecution of so-called career criminals reveal an important point. Local prosecutors, without the benefit of a special program, are generally tough on major offenders—and have been getting tougher since the 1970s. They rely primarily on two important commonsense criteria: the seriousness of the offense and the defendant's prior record.[7]

Most people are surprised to find that the system is consistently tough on career criminals. This misperception can be explained in terms of our criminal justice wedding cake (Chapter 2). Public perception is heavily influenced by a few celebrated cases in the top layer: the armed robber who got probation; the rapist who plead guilty to misdemeanor assault; the O. J. Simpson trial. The typical career criminal case, however, falls into the second layer: successful prosecution, conviction, and a prison term. Additional public misunderstanding arises from aggregating second- and third-layer felonies. The relatively softer treatment of third-layer cases masks the tough response to the career criminals in the second layer.

In the end, it turns out that the alleged "loophole" of being soft on dangerous offenders does not exist. Therefore, we have to draw the following conclusion:

PROPOSITION 21

Career criminal prosecution programs do not produce either higher conviction rates or lower crime rates.

ABOLISH THE INSANITY DEFENSE

John W. Hinckley never succeeded at much in life, but he is single-handedly responsible for some significant changes in American criminal justice. His acquittal for the attempted assassination of President Ronald Reagan in 1981 sparked a national outcry over the insanity defense.[8] In the next five years, in what one study called a "rush to reform," over thirty states revised their insanity defense laws. Two states—Utah and Idaho—abolished it completely. By 1990, only eight states had not made any change in their laws.[9]

Hinckley's acquittal touched one of the raw nerves of public opinion: the sight of a guilty person "beating the rap" and "getting off" because of a "technicality." There was no question about whether John Hinckley shot and wounded the president; we all saw it on television. People were outraged over the Hinckley verdict of not guilty by reason of insanity (NGRI), which appeared to let him off. The fact is that he was institutionalized—in a hospital rather than a prison—and remains there today. Moreover, his notoriety will probably keep him there longer than if he had shot an ordinary person, pled guilty, and gone to prison.

For many people, the insanity defense is the classic "loophole." It conjures up images of criminally insane persons roaming the streets in search of more victims. Insanity defense proceedings also anger many people. The parade of psychiatrists and expert witnesses on both sides of the case creates the impression that you can always find an expert somewhere to say what you want said. Like the O. J. Simpson trial, the Hinckley case supports the impression that the wealthy can buy lawyers and experts who will win them acquittal. In one public opinion survey, 87 percent of the respondents felt that the insanity defense is a loophole; about 40 percent regard it as a "rich person's defense."[10]

The conservative response to these perceptions is to try to close the loophole. The changes inspired by the Hinckley verdict fall into six categories: (1) two states abolished the insanity defense altogether; (2) Congress and thirteen states changed the test of insanity; (3) Congress and twenty states shifted the burden of proof to the defendant (instead of the state having to prove criminal intent, the defendant has to prove mental illness); (4) eleven states created a new "guilty but mentally ill" (GBMI) verdict; (5) seven states revised their trial procedures, involving the way an insanity plea is raised; and (6) thirty-four states changed the procedures for committing a person found not guilty by reason of insanity.[11]

Sorting Out the Issues

Changing the law on the insanity defense raises four separate issues. The first concerns the extent of the use of the defense. How many criminal defendants successfully win verdicts of not guilty by reason of insanity? A second issue involves the fate of those who do win acquittal. Do they return to the streets? How soon? Do they endanger the public? The third issue is predicting dangerousness. If some offenders are dangerous, how can we identify them? How can we tell when it is safe to release them? The fourth issue is the effect of abolishing the insanity defense. What is the impact on crime and the criminal justice system?

The Reality of the Insanity Defense

Despite all the attention it receives, the insanity defense is an extremely rare event. Very few defendants even try to use it, and few of them succeed. In the most comprehensive study of the subject, Henry J. Steadman and his colleagues found that in four states (California, Georgia, Montana, New York), the insanity defense was *raised* in slightly less than 1 percent (0.90 percent) of all felony indictments. Only about 23 percent of these *succeeded* in getting an NGRI verdict. Thus, the insanity defense is successful in about two-tenths of 1 percent of all felony indictments.[12]

The American Psychiatric Association (APA) Insanity Defense Work Group concluded, "While philosophically important for the criminal law, the insanity defense is *empirically unimportant* (involving a fraction of 1 percent of all felony cases").[13] If this alleged loophole were completely closed, the effect would not be noticed. Moreover, there would be absolutely no impact on robbery and burglary cases. The few successful insanity defense cases are the classic "celebrated cases" in the top layer of the criminal justice wedding cake. They are completely unrepresentative and tell us nothing about how most serious crimes are routinely handled.

The extent of public misunderstanding about the frequency of the insanity defense is extraordinary. An Illinois poll found that people believed nearly 40 percent of all criminal defendants used the insanity defense. This misunderstanding explains the fact that nearly half of the respondents wanted the insanity defense abolished.[14]

Most successful uses of the insanity defense are the result of a plea bargain or a stipulated finding. That is, the prosecutor, defense attorney, medical experts, and judge all agree that the defendant is mentally ill. Eighty percent of the insanity defense verdicts in Oregon and all thirty of the cases in Knoxville, Tennessee, between the years 1978 and 1984 were stipulated verdicts.[15] The main point is that the prosecutor agrees with this verdict. The defendant is not "beating the system."

Another popular myth about the insanity defense is that the people who use it are violent and dangerous. Not all of the defendants committed to mental health institutions by way of an insanity verdict have committed a violent offense, however. Of the 500 men in the Bridgewater (Massachusetts) State

Hospital for the Criminally Insane, more than 100 had been charged with vagrancy.[16] These people are not dangerous sociopaths. Many are pathetic individuals who have serious mental health problems and cannot cope with their lives. Most sank through the various safety nets and ended up on skid row, where they finally were arrested.[17]

Aftermath of Acquittal

What happens to defendants who are committed to mental institutions after winning NGRI verdicts is a matter of much controversy. Liberals generally contend that they are likely to spend more time in a mental hospital than if they had been found guilty of the crime and sent to prison. Conservatives argue that they get out too soon.

Several years ago there was considerable truth to the liberal argument. Many allegedly mentally ill people were hospitalized for years, even decades without any treatment or any evidence that they were really dangerous. Supreme Court decisions and new state laws, however, have led to greater protection of the rights of the confined. One of the most important is a mental patient's right to periodic review of his or her condition to determine whether continued confinement is justified. The landmark case of *Baxstrom v. Herold* (1966) forced the release of persons held for long periods of time in the New York State Hospital for the Criminally Insane and necessitated the development of new procedures for continued confinement.[18]

Nonetheless, persons hospitalized after being found not guilty by reason of insanity still spend more time confined in hospitals than comparable offenders spend in prison after being found guilty of the crime. Henry Steadman and his associates found that in New York, 88 percent of all NGRIs were hospitalized; of the 12 percent immediately released, a disproportionate share were women. Those who were charged with murder but found not guilty by reason of insanity spent an average of 6.4 years in the hospital; those acquitted of other violent crimes were hospitalized for an average of 5.2 years; for nonviolent crimes, hospital stays averaged 2.8 years. For all the crimes except murder, these terms of confinement were longer than for offenders found guilty of similar crimes.[19]

In an earlier study, Steadman studied a group of defendants found incompetent to stand trial to see whether they "beat the rap." A defendant who is too mentally ill to comprehend the nature of a criminal trial is committed to an institution until he or she is able to understand the proceedings, at which point the criminal process resumes. Steadman found that those defendants deemed "nondangerous" spent less than two years in mental institutions, whereas the "dangerous" were confined an average of two years and two months. If they were subsequently convicted at trial, they faced the possibility of additional prison time. Do you "beat the rap" by taking the mental health route? Steadman argues not: "Mental hospitals are simply an alternative place to do time."[20] In short, the system is not turning hordes of dangerous psychotics loose on society.

Danger to the Community

How dangerous are the criminally insane? We have had some "natural experiments" on this question as a result of court decisions that forced the release of criminal defendants. A 1971 decision forced the clinical reassessment of 586 inmates of Pennsylvania's Fairview State Hospital for the Criminally Insane. More than two-thirds were eventually released. Over the next four years, 27 percent were rearrested, but only 11 percent for a violent crime. Including some others who were rehospitalized for a violent act, a total of 14.5 percent of those released proved to be dangerous.[21]

Once again we encounter the prediction problem. A decision to release or confine persons alleged to be criminally insane involves a prediction about their future behavior. Do they pose a danger to the community? The success rate in predicting the dangerousness of the criminally insane is no better than in other areas of criminal justice. Because only 14.5 percent of the Fairview inmates committed another violent act, you could argue that the experts were wrong about the other 85.5 percent. This translates into six false positives (people unnecessarily locked up) for each true positive.

The Impact of Abolition

For many people, "abolishing" the insanity defense (like "abolishing" plea bargaining or parole) is a slogan. As we have seen, changing the law on the insanity defense can be done six different ways. Each of these changes involves complex legal and practical problems.

Abolishing or modifying the insanity defense raises fundamental issues about the criminal law. Our justice system rests on the principle that the accused is innocent until proven guilty and that the prosecution must prove guilt beyond a reasonable doubt. To prove guilt, the prosecution must establish three things: the accused committed the act (*actus reus*), the accused had criminal intent (*mens rea*), and a connection exists between the two (that is, that the accused did it and intended to do it).[22]

The key issue with the insanity defense is the *mens rea* requirement. The criminal law has long recognized different degrees of intent. The law distinguishes between a planned murder (first degree) and one committed in the heat of passion (second degree). It further recognizes that some homicides occur without any criminal intent (manslaughter). Differences in the degree of intent are reflected in the severity of the punishment. First-degree murder carries the a potential death sentence in many states.

The law has historically recognized that some people lack full criminal intent because they do not understand what they are doing. One example is the five-year-old who picks up the loaded handgun and accidentally kills his brother. This child does not have criminal intent; he does not understand the nature and consequences of firing the gun. Another example is the truly deranged person who kills because she hears voices from another planet. Like the child, this person does not appreciate the criminal nature of her act.[23]

Unfortunately, not all cases are as simple as these examples. The legal system has struggled for 150 years to develop a formula for resolving questions about the accused's mental state. The principle of insanity first entered English law in 1843 with the famous *M'Naughton* case, which established the "right-wrong test": did the accused understand the difference between right and wrong? Because this test is somewhat crude, legal scholars have attempted to develop alternatives, such as the "irresistible impulse" test. Laypersons are often mystified by the arcane distinctions among those alternatives, none of which resolves the basic problem created by the intersection of medical diagnoses, with their inevitable shades of gray, and the legal system, with its requirement of an absolute verdict of guilt or innocence.[24]

Attempts to abolish the insanity defense run up against the *mens rea* requirement. Suppose a state adopted a law that said "mental condition shall not be a defense to any charge of criminal conduct." This might be interpreted as abolishing the *mens rea* requirement altogether. The prosecution would not have to prove anything about the accused's mental state, only that he or she did the crime. Among other things, it would wipe out the distinction between first-degree murder, second-degree murder, and manslaughter. It is doubtful that even the most ardent opponents of the insanity defense seriously want to take this approach. It would probably be found unconstitutional. Wisconsin (1909) and Mississippi (1928) abolished the insanity defense early in this century. In both cases, the new laws were declared unconstitutional under the due process clauses of their state constitutions.[25]

A more limited interpretation of "mental condition shall not be a defense to any charge of criminal conduct" would be that an affirmative plea of not guilty by reason of insanity could not be raised. The crucial distinction here is between affirmative and ordinary defenses. An *ordinary* defense is simply an attempt to show that the prosecution has failed to connect the accused with the crime. An *affirmative* defense is that, yes, the accused did kill the victim and intended to, but he or she does not have criminal responsibility for the act (because of self-defense, duress, insanity).

What would happen if we abolished insanity as an affirmative defense? Put yourself in the shoes of a defense attorney, and the answer is obvious. You would attack the prosecution's case head-on, on the basic *mens rea* requirement, and argue that your client lacked the necessary criminal intent. You would not win every time, of course, but you might win some of the time, with the net result that your client would be fully acquitted. The people who oppose the insanity defense would find this outcome even more outrageous than our current situation. Even if you did not win, you would force the prosecution to address your client's mental state. In short, the basic issues underlying the insanity defense would reappear in a different form. The *mens rea* requirement is a bedrock principle of our legal system; there is no getting around it.

The guilty but mentally ill (GBMI) alternative has three serious flaws. First, it strikes indirectly at the *mens rea* requirement, introducing the slippery notion that the accused had partial, but not complete, criminal intent. Second, it creates a lesser and included offense that judges and juries may choose simply as a compromise verdict. They may decide that the accused probably did something wrong and deserves some punishment, but they are unwilling to bring in a verdict of guilty on the top charge. The GBMI option would allow them to split the difference and choose the lesser verdict. Finally, the GBMI verdict does not guarantee treatment for the person who has been declared mentally ill.

Prisons, most of which are overcrowded, cannot handle their current inmates with mental problems. They are in no position to accept more inmates with even worse problems. We can imagine the sequence of events. The convicted offender is sentenced to prison, where his behavior becomes a problem. He is then transferred to the state mental hospital for treatment. After his behavior stabilizes, he is transferred back to prison, where because of the brutal conditions, his behavior again deteriorates. The cycle then repeats itself. This is not to suggest that our mental hospitals are models of effective treatment and humane custody. They are not, and much of the "treatment" is meaningless. But sending an allegedly mentally ill person to prison is an even worse solution.

The GBMI option has already proved to be a bogus reform. A 1981 Illinois law added GBMI as an additional verdict, retaining the traditional insanity defense. In Cook County (Chicago), NGRI verdicts actually increased from 34 to 103 between 1981 and 1984. At the same time, GBMI verdicts went from sixteen in 1982, the first year the option was available, to eighty-seven in 1984. This represents a "hydraulic" effect that is contrary to the law's intent. GBMI verdicts appear to have involved people who would otherwise have been found guilty, not defendants who would have been found not guilty by reason of insanity.[26]

The Illinois GBMI law also failed to provide medical treatment for GBMI defendants. An evaluation found that "not a single GBMI offender has been transferred from the Department of Corrections to the Department of Mental Health" for treatment. The law only "complicated rather than resolved [the] fundamental issues surrounding the insanity defense."[27] A study of the GBMI verdict in another state reached similar conclusions: there was no reduction in the number of insanity pleas, jurors were more likely to be confused about the legal issues, many offenders receiving a GBMI verdict were placed on probation, and offenders had no assurance that they would receive any medical treatment.[28]

The real function of the guilty but mentally ill option is symbolic, to appease public opinion. The public has little concern for the details of what actually happens to a mentally ill criminal defendant. Basically, it wants a symbolic statement of "guilty." In practice, as Richard Moran points out, the GBMI verdict has as much meaning as "guilty but brown eyes."[29]

In sum, the various proposals to abolish or modify the insanity defense fail on two counts. Not only do they fail to reduce crime, because the insanity defense is so rare, but they create new problems for the criminal justice system. We can state unequivocally:

> ### PROPOSITION 22
> **Abolishing or limiting the insanity defense will have no impact on serious crime.**

Richard Moran offers the best verdict on this issue: "The insanity defense has been misinterpreted and abused"—not by criminal defendants but "by politicians and journalists who mistakenly attack it as a major loophole in the law."[30]

ABOLISH PLEA BARGAINING

Everyone seems to dislike plea bargaining. Conservatives believe it is a major loophole through which criminals beat the system and avoid punishment. Liberals, meanwhile, believe that it is the source of grave injustices: prosecutors deliberately "overcharge"; defense attorneys make deals rather than fight for their clients; defendants are coerced into waiving their right to a trial; some defendants get much better deals than others.[31]

In many instances, the process of plea bargaining makes a mockery of justice. In court the judge goes through the charade of asking the defendant whether any promises have been made in return for the guilty plea, and the defendant answers no. But, of course, a deal has been made.[32]

For a few years in the 1970s, calls were made for abolishing plea bargaining. Public outrage reached its peak in 1973, when Vice President Spiro Agnew, in perhaps the most famous plea bargain of all time, avoided going to prison on extortion charges by pleading no contest to a lesser charge. In 1973 the National Advisory Commission on Criminal Justice Standards and Goals recommended that plea bargaining be abolished within five years.[33]

Plea bargaining, of course, continues to survive. In 1992, 92 percent of all felony cases in state courts were settled by a guilty plea.[34] When we take a closer look at plea bargaining, including some of the attempts to abolish it, we can understand why.

Alaska Bans Plea Bargaining

The most ambitious attempt to abolish plea bargaining occurred in Alaska, when Attorney General Avrum Gross abolished plea bargaining in the entire state.[35] On July 3, 1975, he issued a memorandum that read, in part, as follows:

> I wish to have the following policy implemented with respect to all adult criminal offenses in which charges have been filed on or after August 15, 1975:
>
> (1) District Attorneys and Assistant District Attorneys will refrain from engaging in plea negotiations with defendants designed to arrive at an agreement for entry of a plea of guilty in return for a particular sentence. . . . (4) . . . While there continues to be nothing wrong with

reducing a charge, reductions should not occur simply to obtain a plea of guilty. (5) Like any general rule, there are going to be some exceptions to this policy [which must be approved by the attorney general's office].

The new policy attacked plea bargaining in three ways: abolishing "sentence bargaining" (paragraph 1), abolishing "charge bargaining" (paragraph 4), and establishing procedures for supervising plea negotiations.

Gross's action was possible in part because of the structure of Alaska's criminal justice system. Local prosecutors are appointed by and work under the supervision of the state attorney general. In other states, local prosecutors are elected and enjoy almost complete political and administrative independence.

What happened when Alaska banned plea bargaining? Contrary to popular expectations, the criminal courts did not collapse. The traditional defense of plea bargaining is that it is necessary to handle the heavy load of cases and that the courts would grind to a halt if it were abolished. The Alaska courts, however, continued to function pretty much as they had before with little change in the rate of guilty pleas. Trials increased, from 6.7 to 9.6 percent of all cases. True, this is about a 50 percent increase, but the total remains less than 10 percent of all cases.[36]

Other dire predictions also did not come true in Alaska. Many experts argue that discretion cannot be eliminated and that attempts to abolish it only serve to move it to other parts of the justice system. Restricting a prosecutor's discretion to accept guilty pleas, according to this argument, will shift discretion "upstream" to police officers or "downstream" to judges.[37] Specifically, some experts believe that banning plea bargaining will give judges more discretion and lead to more sentence bargaining.

No radical shift in discretion occurred as a result of the ban in Alaska. One way to measure this effect is to examine the pattern of rejections and dismissals of cases. Some experts believe if a prosecutor cannot settle cases by accepting pleas to lesser offenses, more cases will be dismissed altogether. The rate of dismissals in Alaska, however, remained consistently high—about 52 percent before and after the ban. Dismissals in drug possession and morals cases increased, but this seemed to be a function of the low priority prosecutors gave these cases rather than anything related to the ban on plea bargaining.[38]

One surprising result of the ban was that cases were processed faster than before. This was contrary to the expectation that there would be more delay because of more trials and a greater backlog of cases. In Anchorage, the mean disposition time for felony cases dropped from 192.1 months to 89.5 months. Case processing time also dropped in Fairbanks and Juneau. This unexpected effect has an obvious explanation. Restrictions on plea bargaining eliminate certain alternatives. With less to negotiate, the prosecutor and defense attorney reach agreements more quickly.[39]

The ban on plea bargaining had no apparent impact on cases involving defendants charged with serious crimes or those with substantial criminal records. An evaluation concluded that "the conviction and sentencing of persons charged with serious crimes of violence such as murder, rape, robbery, and felonious assault appeared completely unaffected by the change in policy."[40] Dangerous offenders had not been beating the system beforehand through plea bargaining (any more than they had in San Diego), and the ban did not make the system either weaker or tougher than before.

The ban did have an unexpected effect on the disposition of less serious cases, producing more severe sentences. A similar effect has been found in other reforms, called the "trickle-up" or "hydraulic" effect. Our wedding cake model helps explain this process. Policies directed toward second-layer cases actually have their greatest impact on third-layer cases. Under normal circumstances, third-layer cases—low-level assaults or burglaries where little of value is stolen—are often settled with pleas to even lesser offenses and sentences of probation. A get-tough policy, such as a ban on plea bargaining however, closes off this avenue of mitigation and produces both convictions on more serious charges and harsher sentences than would normally be the case. This process is characterized as a hydraulic effect because it lifts third-layer cases into the second layer. The problem, of course, is that these third-layer cases were not the original target of the policy change.

From the standpoint of our inquiry, the important question is whether the Alaska ban on plea bargaining affected the crime rate. The evaluation did not examine this issue. Nonetheless, the mere fact that the ban had no real effect on the disposition of cases involving serious crimes suggests that it probably had no impact on the crime rate.

Other Experiments

Other attempts to ban plea bargaining have focused on specific crimes. When Michigan enacted a law mandating prison terms for people convicted of gun-related crimes ("one with a gun gets you two"), the Wayne County (Detroit) prosecutor supplemented it with a ban on plea bargaining. They would no longer drop gun-related charges in return for a guilty plea. This seemed to be an important step, because many people believe that weapons charges are frequently dropped in return for a plea to a nongun charge (for example, from armed robbery to simple robbery) as a way of avoiding a prison sentence. Some people believe this is how "mandatory" sentencing laws are evaded.[41]

An evaluation of the Michigan law found no significant change in the minimum sentences for homicide and armed robbery cases. The going rate for armed robbery was about six years in prison both beforehand and afterward. In other words, Wayne County prosecutors had not been lenient in plea bargaining with defendants charged with robbery beforehand. Once again, there was no "loophole" to be closed.

The Michigan policy had a trickle-up or hydraulic effect, however. Persons charged with aggravated assault began to receive higher minimum sentences. Prosecutors had previously treated aggravated assaults as third-layer cases, accepting pleas to lesser charges. The new law closed off this avenue and (as in Alaska) produced convictions on higher charges and longer sentences.

The 1973 New York drug law, which we examined in the previous chapter, also restricted plea bargaining. Persons charged with a Class A-I drug felony (a mandatory penalty of fifteen or twenty-five years to life imprisonment) could not plead to a lesser felony. Persons charged with a lesser drug-related felony could not plead to a misdemeanor. As we learned, the law did not reduce drug use or violent crime.[42]

Meanwhile, in Hampton County, Iowa, a local prosecutor was elected on a platform promising "no deals with dope pushers." His policy did move discretion further back in the system. In 1972, before it went into effect, 107 of 109 drug sale cases were settled through guilty pleas; 88 involved pleas to a reduced charge (see Table 8.1). By 1974, a year after the policy went into effect, all of the guilty pleas were to the original charge. But there were only forty-one drug sale cases (thirty-seven settled with a plea; four by trial), a drop of more than 60 percent. Only part of this decline can be attributed to outright dismissals (the dismissal rate increased slightly, from 31 percent to 35 percent). More significant was the decline in cases filed in the first place— from 157 in 1972 to 63 in 1974. "Getting tough" in this instance produced adaptations by the courtroom work group that resulted in fewer prosecutions and convictions.[43]

In Search of Plea Bargains

Plea bargaining has proven to be a phantom loophole. Despite the criticisms, it is not a device by which large numbers of serious offenders are beating the system. Attempts to abolish it either have no effect whatsoever or produce changes that are contrary to the intended result.

Table 8.1 Prosecution of drug cases, Hampton County, Iowa

	1972	1974
Total drug cases filed	157	63
Dismissed	48	22
Percentage dismissed	30.5	34.9
Prosecuted	109	41
Guilty pleas	107	37
To lesser charges	88	0
Trials	2	4

SOURCE: Adapted from Thomas W. Church, "Plea Bargains, Concessions, and the Courts: Analysis of a Quasi-Experiment," *Law and Society Review* 10 (Spring 1976): 377–401.

Our discussion of the criminal justice wedding cake (Chapter 2) and the role of the courtroom work group (Chapter 3) helps explain why plea bargaining survives. As Malcolm Feeley suggests, we should think of the criminal courts as supermarkets, handling a high volume of business with fixed prices.[44] Once the work group reaches a consensus about the proper "going rate" for different kinds of cases, not much actual bargaining is necessary.

Virtually all of the studies of plea bargaining have found a high degree of regularity and predictability in the disposition of cases. One of the most systematic studies concluded that you would predict the outcome if you knew the seriousness of the top charge and the defendant's prior record. Charges were not changed in 60 percent of the guilty plea cases; there was some reduction in 26.7 percent but some enhancement of the charges in 13.3 percent. The system was both predictable and relatively tough.[45]

In short, plea bargaining is not a loophole that lets lots of offenders beat the system. Therefore, we can safely make the following conclusion:

PROPOSITION 23

Abolishing plea bargaining will not reduce serious crime.

RESTRICT APPEALS

Conservatives believe that postconviction appeals undermine the criminal justice system in several ways. First, some offenders win and thereby escape punishment altogether. Second, appeals delay final resolution of a case and undermine the deterrent effect of the law. Deterrence theorists argue that punishment needs to be swift and certain. Third, appeals transform the criminal process into a "sporting contest," a game rather than a search for truth. Liberals, on the other hand, see the absence of finality as a virtue. Protection of individual rights requires recognition of the possibility of error in the criminal justice process.[46]

Years ago, Judge Macklin Fleming argued that our obsession with post-conviction appeals represented a quixotic search for "perfect justice." He listed twenty-six possible challenges available in California on search-and-seizure grounds alone, including moving for dismissal of all charges at the preliminary examination; appealing a denial of that motion to the state supreme court; moving to have the case transferred to federal court on grounds that federal civil rights had been violated; objecting to admission of the evidence at trial; if convicted, appealing for postconviction relief in the state supreme court; and if that fails, appealing the conviction in federal court.

Nor is this all. Fleming points out that "in almost every one of the foregoing steps the losing defendant can petition for a rehearing or reconsideration by the particular court that ruled against him."[47] Thus, innumerable potential challenges to a criminal charge can be made just on Fourth Amendment search-and-seizure issues. If these fail, many postconviction appeals are possible, for example, on grounds of inadequate assistance of counsel in violation of the Sixth Amendment. For the imaginative and determined offender, the possibilities are seemingly endless.[48] As we shall see, however, the key word here is *seemingly*.

Limiting Appeals

Conservatives believe that postconviction appeals are another loophole that undermines the criminal justice system. The 1981 Attorney General's Task Force on Violent Crime recommended a three-year statute of limitations on habeas corpus petitions and a prohibition on federal courts' holding evidentiary hearings "on facts which were fully expounded and found in the state court proceeding."[49]

Habeas corpus is one of the cornerstones of Anglo-American law. The British Parliament formalized it with the Habeas Corpus Act of 1679, and Americans wrote it into the U.S. Constitution. Article III, Section 9, of the Constitution reads, "The privilege of the writ of habeas corpus shall not be suspended, unless when in case of rebellion or invasion the public safety may require it." The writ of habeas corpus is a device to challenge the detention of a person taken into custody. A person under arrest or in prison may demand an evidentiary hearing before a judge to examine the legality of the detention. The writ of habeas corpus is purely procedural: it guarantees only a right to a hearing and says nothing about the substance of the issues in the case.

The Supreme Court greatly expanded the ability of an offender convicted in a state court to obtain a rehearing in federal court in the 1963 decision *Fay v. Noia*. One of the underlying issues here is the role of the Supreme Court in a federal system. Conservatives have long argued that the Court, particularly under Chief Justice Earl Warren, intruded into matters that should be left to the states and to legislatures. Liberals, on the other hand, saw the Court as the principal guardian of individual rights.

Appeals in Practice

In actual practice, appeals play a very minor role in the administration of criminal justice. A national study of 10,000 habeas corpus petitions filed in federal district courts by offenders challenging their convictions found that only 1 percent succeeded. Federal judges dismissed 63 percent (usually for failing to exhaust state remedies) and ruled against the offender on the merits of the case in 35 percent. The typical habeas corpus petition was filed by someone convicted of a violent offense (23 percent had been convicted of murder) and sentenced to a long prison term. The most frequent claim raised was ineffective assistance of counsel.[50]

How many convicted offenders "abuse" the right to appeal? The study found a rate of fourteen habeas corpus petitions for every 1,000 prisoners—or only 1.4 percent of all imprisoned offenders. This confirms what we have already learned: that most convictions are obtained through plea bargains in which the facts of the case are not seriously contested. The study also found that the impact of habeas corpus petitions on the work load of the courts has been greatly exaggerated. These appeals represented only 4 percent of the civil case filings in U.S. District Courts.

In short, Macklin Fleming's nightmare vision of convicted offenders endlessly filing appeals on all of the theoretically possible issues is pure fantasy. Appeal of a felony convictions through habeas corpus petitions is very much like the insanity defense: a procedure that is rarely used and even more rarely successful. There are two exceptions to this rule. People on death row do exhaust every possible appeal, and many appeals drag on for as long as fifteen years, or even longer. A second exception involves the so-called "writ writers," prisoners who file innumerable appeals in federal court challenging their conviction or prison conditions. Both of these exceptions, however, are examples of celebrated cases; they do not represent the general flow of business in the criminal justice system.

Our concern here, of course, is with crime control. The available facts about the use of appeals do not support the conservative argument that multiple appeals contribute to crime. Conservatives argue that appeals delay "finality" and thereby undermine the deterrent effect of the criminal process. Several things are wrong with this argument. First, appeals are filed in so few cases that they cannot have any broad impact on criminal justice. Second, as we have also learned, many factors affect the deterrent effect (low probability of arrest, a relatively high probability of the charges being rejected or dismissed, whether the threat of punishment even works for certain categories of offenders, and so forth). Appeals are at best a very minor factor.

Like the insanity defense, postconviction appeals are mainly a *symbolic* issue. On occasion a convicted offender is released through a successful appeal. But these are the few celebrated cases that do not represent the general pattern in the criminal justice system. Therefore, our proposition is this:

PROPOSITION 24
Limiting habeas corpus appeals of criminal convictions will have no effect on serious crime.

CONCLUSION

We will not reduce serious crime by trying to close alleged loopholes in the criminal justice system. The reason for this is simple: those loopholes do not exist. The idea that thousands of criminals beat the system through the insanity defense, or plea bargaining, or some other loophole is a perception based in a very small number of unrepresentative celebrated cases. The justice system is actually fairly harsh in dealing with those serious offenders who are arrested.

NOTES

1. U.S. Department of Justice, *An Exemplary Project: Major Violator Unit—San Diego, California* (Washington, D.C.: Government Printing Office, 1980).

2. Some examples are described in William F. McDonald, *Plea Bargaining: Critical Issues and Current Practices* (Washington, D.C.: Government Printing Office, 1985).

3. Ibid.

4. Bureau of Justice Statistics, *Felony Sentences in State Courts, 1992* (Washington, D.C.: Government Printing Office, 1995), Table 2.

5. Eleanor Chelimsky and Judith S. Dahmann, *National Evaluation of the Career Criminal Program: Final Report* (McLean, VA: MITRE, 1979).

6. Allan F. Abrahamse, Patricia A. Ebener, Peter W. Greenwood, Nora Fitzgerald, and Thomas E. Kosin, "An Experimental Evaluation of the Phoenix Repeat Offender Program," *Justice Quarterly* 8 (June 1991): 141–168.

7. Michael R. Gottfredson and Don M. Gottfredson, *Decision Making in Criminal Justice: Toward the Rational Exercise of Discretion*, 2d ed. (New York: Plenum, 1988).

8. Jack Hinckley, *Breaking Points* (Grand Rapids, MI: Chosen Books, 1985).

9. Henry J. Steadman, Margaret A. McGreevy, Joseph P. Morrisey, Lisa A. Callahan, Pamela Clark Robbins, and Carmen Cirincione, *Before and After Hinckley: Evaluating Insanity Defense Reform* (New York: Guilford, 1993), pp. 1–3; Table 3-1, p. 37.

10. Reported in Rita J. Simon and David E. Aaronson, *The Insanity Defense: A Critical Assessment of Law and Policy in the Post-Hinckley Era* (New York: Praeger, 1988), p. 166.

11. Ibid., Table 3.2, p. 40.

12. Ibid., pp. 27–28.

13. American Psychiatric Association, *American Journal of Psychiatry* 140 (1983): 681–688.

14. Valerie Hans, "An Analysis of Public Attitudes Toward the Insanity Defense," *Criminology* 24 (May 1986): 393–414.

15. Richard Moran, "The Insanity Defense: Five Years After Hinckley," in Robert J. Kelly and Donal E. J. MacNamara," eds., *Perspectives on Deviance: Dominance, Degradation, and Denigration* (Cincinnati: Anderson, 1991), p. 79.

16. *Newsweek* (May 24, 1982).

17. For a good study of this subject, see Egon Bittner, "Police on Skid Row: A

Study in Peacekeeping," *American Sociological Review* 32 (October 1967): 694–715.

18. *Baxstrom v. Herold*, 383 U.S. 107 (1966).

19. Steadman et al., *Before and After Hinckley*, pp. 58–61 (California), 97–99 (New York).

20. Henry J. Steadman, *Beating a Rap? Defendants Found Incompetent to Stand Trial* (Chicago: University of Chicago Press, 1979), p. 104.

21. Terence P. Thornberry and Joseph E. Jacoby, *The Criminally Insane: A Community Follow-up of Mentally Ill Offenders* (Chicago: University of Chicago Press, 1979). For another study with similar results, see Henry J. Steadman and James J. Cacozza, *Careers of the Criminally Insane* (Lexington, MA: Lexington Books, 1974).

22. Norval Morris, *Madness and the Criminal Law* (Chicago: University of Chicago Press, 1982).

23. Ibid.

24. Ibid.

25. Grant H. Morris, *The Insanity Defense: A Blueprint for Legislative Change* (Lexington, MA: Lexington Books, 1974).

26. John Klofus and Ralph Weisheit, "Guilty but Mentally Ill: Reform of the Insanity Defense in Illinois," *Justice Quarterly* 4 (March 1987): 39–50.

27. Ibid.

28. Kurt M. Bumby, "Reviewing the Guilty but Mentally Ill Alternative: A Case of the Blind 'Pleading' the Blind," *Journal of Psychiatry and the Law* 21(2) (1993): 191–220.

29. Moran, "The Insanity Defense," p. 81.

30. Ibid., pp. 77–78.

31. The most critical view of plea bargaining is Abraham Blumberg, *Criminal Justice: Issues and Ironies*, 2d ed. (New York: New Viewpoints, 1979). The best recent study is McDonald, *Plea Bargaining*.

32. On the "cop-out" ceremony, see Jonathan D. Casper, *American Criminal Justice: The Defendant's Perspective* (Englewood Cliffs, NJ: Prentice Hall, 1972), pp. 81–86.

33. National Advisory Commission on Criminal Justice Standards and Goals, *Courts* (Washington, D.C.: Government Printing Office, 1973), p. 46.

34. Bureau of Justice Statistics, *Felony Sentences in State Courts, 1992* (Washington, D.C.: Government Printing Office, 1995), pp. 9–10.

35. Michael L. Rubinstein, Stevens H. Clarke, and Teresa J. White, *Alaska Bans Plea Bargaining* (Washington, D.C.: Government Printing Office, 1980).

36. Ibid.

37. Norval Morris and Gordon Hawkins, *Letter to the President on Crime Control* (Chicago: University of Chicago Press, 1977), p. 61.

38. Rubinstein et al., *Alaska Bans Plea Bargaining*.

39. This point is argued in Samuel Walker, *Taming the System: The Control of Discretion in Criminal Justice, 1950–1990* (New York: Oxford University Press, 1993), pp. 95–96.

40. Rubinstein et al., *Alaska Bans Plea Bargaining*, p. viii.

41. Colin Loftin and David McDowall, "One with a Gun Gets You Two: Mandatory Sentences and Firearms Violence in Detroit," *Annals of the American Academy of Political and Social Science* 455 (May 1981): 150–167.

42. U.S. Department of Justice, *The Nation's Toughest Drug Law: Evaluating the New York Experience* (Washington, D.C.: Government Printing Office, 1978).

43. Thomas W. Church, "Plea Bargains, Concessions, and the Courts: Analysis of a Quasi-Experiment," *Law and Society Review* 10 (Spring 1976): 377–401.

44. Malcolm W. Feeley, "Perspectives on Plea Bargaining," *Law and Society Review* 13 (Winter 1979): 199.

45. Peter F. Nardulli, James Eisenstein, and Roy B. Flemming, *The Tenor of Justice: Criminal Courts and the Guilty Plea Process* (Urbana: University of Illinois, 1988).

46. Herbert Packer, "Two Models of the Criminal Process," in Packer, *The Limits of the Criminal Sanction* (Stanford, CA: Stanford University Press, 1968), pp. 149–173.

47. Macklin Fleming, *The Price of Perfect Justice* (New York: Basic Books, 1974).

48. Ibid.

49. Department of Justice, *Attorney General's Task Force on Violent Crime* (Washington, D.C.: Government Printing Office, 1981), p. 58.

50. Bureau of Justice Statistics, *Federal Habeas Corpus Review: Challenging State Court Criminal Convictions* (Washington, D.C.: Government Printing Office, 1995). See also Victor E. Flango, *Habeas Corpus in State and Federal Courts* (Williamsburg, VA: National Center for State Courts, 1994).

PART III

The Middle Ground:
Guns and Victims

On one thing, conservatives and liberals agree: guns are a major part of the crime problem. They disagree, however, over the exact nature of the problem and the solution to it. Liberals focus on guns and want to limit their availability. Conservatives focus on criminals who use guns and want to get tough with them. The policies each side recommends reflect their fundamentally different assumptions about crime and criminals. There is also a certain amount of agreement with respect to crime victims. Both sides support certain programs designed to assist victims. In this section we will examine policies directed toward the victims of crime, guns, and gun-related violence.

Protect the Victims

VICTIMS OF CRIME

In early 1997, at the start of his second term as president, Bill Clinton proposed a constitutional amendment to protect the rights of crime victims. The amendment would guarantee a victim the right to court-ordered financial restitution from offenders; to a speedy trial; to express objection to an offender's release on bail, plea bargain agreement, or sentence; to attend trials and parole hearings; and to be notified about all court proceedings.[1]

The proposal for a victims' rights amendment represents the culmination of a twenty-year movement on behalf of crime victims. The movement emerged in the 1970s and reached its peak in the 1980s. President Ronald Reagan declared a national Crime Victims' Week, the first ever, in 1981. A year later his President's Task Force on Victims of Crime offered sixty-eight policy recommendations designed to help victims.[2] The 1992 Attorney General's Report on Violent Crime made six recommendations related to crime victims.[3] They are listed in Figure 9.1.

The fact that President Clinton endorsed a victims' rights amendment is significant. Victims' rights has been primarily a conservative crime policy issue. Emilio Viano, one of the leading experts in the field, points out that national concern about crime victims is largely due to "the prevalence of conservative ideology in the 1980s."[4] Clinton's position is another indication of the extent to which, on this issue as on others, liberals have now adopted much of the traditional conservative crime policy agenda.

VI. Respecting the victim in the criminal justice process

19. Provide for hearing and considering the victims' perspective at sentencing and at any early release proceedings.

20. Provide victim–witness coordinators.

21. Provide for victim restitution and for adequate compensation and assistance for victims and witnesses.

22. Adopt evidentiary rules to protect victim-witnesses from courtroom intimidation and harassment.

23. Permit victims to require HIV testing before trial of persons charged with sex offenses.

24. Notify the victim of the status of criminal justice proceedings and of the release status of the offender.

FIGURE 9.1 Recommendations related to crime victims.

SOURCE: U.S. Department of Justice, *Combating Violent Crime* (Washington, D.C.: Government Printing Office, 1992), p. xii.

The Victims' Rights Movement

The crime victim was long the "forgotten person" in American criminal justice. Under current Anglo-American law, the crime victim has no formal role in the criminal process. The prosecutor represents the public interest, including that of the victim. This is why, in some states, cases are formally titled "The People versus . . . ." As an ACLU handbook on *The Rights of Crime Victims* explains, "The victim is not a formal party to a criminal proceeding."[5]

It was not always this way. Until the mid–nineteenth century, crime victims represented themselves, bringing their own cases before magistrates and judges. The office of the modern prosecutor gradually emerged in the nineteenth century, assuming the role of representing the public in general and crime victims in particular.[6]

Having a professional public official handle criminal cases serves two important purposes. First, it establishes the idea that a crime is an offense against society as a whole and not just an individual. Second, it removes the element of vengeance from the handling of a case. A public official is more likely to be free of anger and personal animosity toward the offender. The desire to keep emotionalism out of the criminal process explains why in two cases the U.S. Supreme Court has ruled that victim impact statements at sentencing in death penalty cases are unconstitutional.[7]

Another reason that crime victims have had no formal role in the criminal process is that Anglo-American law places a high priority on protecting individual rights against possible violations by the state. For this reason, the Bill of

Rights includes specific protections for criminal suspects and defendants: due process of law, the right to an attorney, protection against self-incrimination, and so on.

By the 1970s, however, a new victims' rights movement emerged, arguing that the victim was neglected by the criminal justice system. The movement found fault with all parts of the system: police and prosecutors did not inform victims about the progress of cases; victims had no say in plea bargain agreements, sentencing, or parole decisions. A survey conducted as the movement was just beginning found that in Alameda County, California (Oakland), only about 12 percent of victims had ever been notified that an arrest had been made in their case. Also, 45 percent of those who appeared in court had not been informed of the nature of their appearance, and about 42 percent were never notified of the outcome of the case.[8] In 1982, the chair of the President's Task Force on Victims of Crime declared, "The neglect of crime victims is a national disgrace."[9]

Although conservatives have dominated the victims' rights movement, groups representing other political persuasions have also been active. Feminists demanded new laws and policies to protect the victims of domestic violence and rape. Mothers Against Drunk Driving (MADD) organized an anti–drunk driving crusade primarily to protect the victims of drunk driving (see Chapter 6). The wave of "three strikes and you're out" laws was spurred by public outrage over victims such as Polly Klass, who was murdered by a recent parolee (see Chapter 7). Even the ACLU, which vigorously opposes many victims' rights proposals as unconstitutional, published a handbook on *The Rights of Crime Victims* in 1985.[10] The United Nations, meanwhile, adopted a Declaration of Basic Principles of Justice for Victims of Crime and Abuse of Power in 1985.

The Costs of Crime

The victims' rights movement has spurred interest in estimating the total cost of crime. A 1996 Justice Department report reached an estimate of $450 billion a year (based on 1987–1900 National Crime Victim Survey [NCVS] data).[11] The study took a comprehensive view of the costs of crime and included property loss, medical care, mental health care, loss of productivity at work, and the costs of police, fire, and victim assistance services. Most controversially, it included an estimate of the intangible "quality of life" costs. This category comprised 75 percent ($345 billion) of the total costs.

New Laws and Programs

The victims' rights movement has been enormously successful in achieving its legislative goals. State and local governments have passed over 5,000 laws designed to benefit victims.[12]

Typical of many new state laws is the 1986 North Carolina Fair Treatment for Victims and Witnesses Act. The law guarantees a victim's right to information about emergency medical assistance, protection from harm, and financial compensation; a secure area in the courthouse; the right to make a victim impact statement at sentencing; information about the final disposition of the case; and notification about the offender's release or escape.[13]

Congress has passed a series of federal laws, including the 1970 Crime Insurance Act, the 1982 Victim Witness Protection Act, the 1984 Victims of Crime Act, the 1984 Justice Assistance Act, the 1990 Victims' Rights and Restitution Act, and the 1994 Violent Crime Control Act, which authorizes funds for battered women's shelters and other services for female victims.

Critics of the Movement

The victims' rights movement has many critics. Civil libertarians in particular have criticized proposals to limit individual rights in the name of helping crime victims. The most sweeping criticism has been made by Robert Elias. In a series of books, he has argued that victims have been manipulated to serve a conservative political agenda, that most of the new victims' rights laws and policies have not provided much in the way of tangible help, and that many serious forms of victimization (workplace injuries, environmental pollution, unsafe products, false advertising, among others) have been ignored despite their enormous toll in terms of human suffering and dollar cost. As Elias sees it, the victims' rights movement has been largely an exercise in "symbolic politics" that leaves crime victims "victims still."[14]

SORTING OUT THE ISSUES

The victims' rights movement does not have a single agenda. A variety of groups has recommended many different proposals. To make sense of all these proposals, it is useful to divide them into three general categories.

Victims' services. One set of proposals involves services for crime victims. The most important are include financial compensation and counseling. Women's groups have led the fight for rape and domestic violence hot lines, counseling programs, and shelters.

Victims' voice laws. A second set of proposals include laws to enhance the role of victims in the criminal justice system, in particular to allow them to make a statement about bail setting or plea bargain agreements, or at sentencing or parole hearings.

"Get tough on crime." A third set of proposals are "get tough on crime" ideas similar to ones we have considered in other chapters. These include proposals to deny bail to dangerous offenders, close loopholes in the criminal justice system, and give longer prison sentences. They usually do not mention crime victims directly. The underlying assumption is that by getting criminals off the streets, there will be fewer crimes and crime victims.

The six recommendations of the Attorney General's Task Force on Violent Crime listed in Figure 9.1 include three in the area of victims' services, one related to victims' voices, and two designed to get tough on crime.

Criteria for Evaluation

What criteria should we use to evaluate the various crime victims' laws and policies?[15] Three different criteria are appropriate.

Crime reduction. It is important to remember the purpose of this book: to search for sensible policies that are likely to reduce crime. Some of the proposals we will examine may be sound, humane ideas that will genuinely help victims deal with their suffering. They should be supported for that reason. But the relevant question for us is whether they will reduce crime.

Implementation. A second criterion is whether a law or policy is in fact being implemented or is likely to be implemented. As we have learned, the courtroom work group has tremendous power to block or frustrate new policies if it upsets the established going rate. If a victims' rights law is not implemented, it will not have any impact on crime.

Impact on the criminal justice system. Some laws and policies designed to help crime victims may have undesirable effects on the criminal justice system. Many, for example, call for radical changes in constitutional law. Even if they might reduce crime or help victims, the cost to the justice system may be too great. Remember, our goal in this book is to find policies that are effective, practical, and sound.

VICTIM ASSISTANCE PROGRAMS

Perhaps the most popular victims' rights idea has been victim-witness assistance programs. By the late 1980s an estimated 4,000 such programs existed around the country. The 1984 Victims of Crime Act provides about $50 million a year for local programs; by 1987, 1,364 programs were receiving federal funds. By 1993, nearly half of all city police departments (46 percent) and sheriffs' departments (49 percent) had a special unit for victim assistance.[16]

Table 9.1 presents the range of services required by law in 2,282 prosecutors' offices in 1994. Note that the survey only asked prosecutors what services they were required to provide. It is not clear that all of these services are in fact provided. The survey found, for example, that some information, although required, was provided only upon the request of a victim.[17]

Victim-witness programs vary widely. Many provide emergency services in the form of shelter, security repair, financial assistance, and on-the-scene comfort. One national survey found that most provide follow-up counseling. Nearly all have some form of advocacy and support services, such as intervening with the victim's employer or landlord. Many help with insurance claims or efforts to obtain restitution. Nearly all provide court-related services concerned with being a witness for the prosecution, such as orienting victims or witnesses to court procedures, notifying them of court dates, giving transportation to court, escorting them at the court, and providing child care.

How well do these programs work? A survey of sixty-two victim service programs in North Carolina found that the state's 1986 Fair Treatment for Victims and Witnesses Act was meeting the needs of victims "only minimally."[18] Almost all of the programs were providing referral to social, restitution, and compensation services; notification about court cases; and allowances for victim impact statements. Nonetheless, 59 percent of crime victims surveyed in the state expressed dissatisfaction with the criminal justice system. Particularly significant was the fact that about one-third were not even aware of their right to make a victim impact statement. This suggests that a major provision of the law was not being fully implemented. An evaluation concluded that the programs primarily provided *witness* assistance rather than crime *victim* assistance.

What about the impact of victim-witness services on crime? Because most victim assistance programs operate after the crime has occurred, we have little reason to assume that they will reduce crime. We should not ignore one possible exception to this rule. Shelters for the victims of domestic violence may in fact protect women from immediate violence. This aspect of shelters has not been evaluated, however.

Even if they prove effective, shelters have no relationship to the crimes of robbery and burglary, which are the focus of this book. This leads us to the following proposition:

Table 9.1 Victim services that jurisdictions require prosecutors' offices to provide, 1994

Type of service	Percentage of offices			
		Full-time office (population served)		
	All offices	500,000 or more	Less than 500,000	Part-time office
NOTIFICATION/ALERT				
Notify victim	82	87	85	73
Notify witness	55	67	59	42
ORIENTATION/EDUCATION				
Victim restitution assistance	60	62	62	55
Victim compensation procedures	58	73	65	41
Victim impact statement assistance	55	78	60	40
Orientation to court procedures	41	57	48	24
Public education	15	20	17	9
ESCORT				
Escort victim	23	39	28	9
Escort witness	17	31	19	9
COUNSELING/ASSISTANCE				
Property return	38	46	39	35
Referral	32	46	37	18
Personal advocacy	17	26	22	5
Counseling	10	21	12	5
Crisis intervention	10	19	14	0
Number of offices	2,282	119	1,480	683

NOTE: Zero indicates no cases in the sample. Survey question: Does your jurisdiction require your office to provide any of the following services to victims?

SOURCE: Bureau of Justice Statistics, *Prosecutors in State Courts, 1994* (Washington, D.C.: Government Printing Office, 1996), p. 9.

PROPOSITION 25

With the possible exception of domestic violence shelters, social service programs for crime victims will not reduce serious crime.

Police-Victim Recontact

A variation on the theme of victim services is to provide more contact between the police and crime victims. The President's Task Force on Victims of Crime recommended that police departments establish procedures for informing victims of violent crime about the status of the investigation of crimes.[19] Known as victim recontact programs, they are designed to overcome the problem of victims feeling alienated from the system because they never hear from the police.

Victim recontact is a sound and humane idea that is probably long overdue. There is absolutely no reason that the police should not keep victims informed and many reasons that they should. Mainly it would help build positive police-community relations. By 1993, about half of all city police departments and county sheriffs departments had some kind of victim assistance program.[20] Meanwhile, almost all state prosecutors (93 percent) reported in 1990 that they inform victims of the outcome of cases. This compares with only 35 percent in 1974.[21]

Victim recontact may not deliver what its advocates expect, however. In one component of the Houston "fear reduction" experiment, police officers contacted crime victims to express sympathy and ask whether they needed any further assistance or information. An evaluation found that the program achieved none of its goals. Victims who were contacted did not express any less fear of crime or greater confidence in the police, compared with victims who were not contacted. Victims with poor English skills were actually more fearful than those who were not recontacted. They did not understand why the police were contacting them and became more fearful as a result.[22]

The Houston data suggest that perhaps victims' rights advocates have misinterpreted the victims' alienation from the criminal justice system. Many people may prefer just to be left alone. We should remember that according to NCVS, victims do not report 61 percent of all crimes. Many regard the crime as a private matter or say that it just was not important enough. In other words, even though something bad has happened to them, these people do not want any involvement with the criminal justice system.[23]

Most important, as far as we are concerned, victim recontact is not going to reduce crime. This leads us to another proposition:

PROPOSITION 26
Victim recontact programs will not reduce crime.

Victim Compensation

The most popular victims' rights program involves financial compensation. California passed the first crime victims' compensation law in 1965. By the 1980s, forty-four states and the District of Columbia had similar laws. The 1984 Victims of Crime Act provides federal financial support for state and local programs.

Victim compensation can be seen as a government-supported insurance program, providing funds to help people recover from their losses. (The 1970 Crime Insurance Act was passed to provide insurance for businesses and individuals in high-crime areas who could not get coverage through private insurance companies.)[24] These losses include medical bills, lost wages, and other expenses. The Justice Department estimates that medical costs of crime are $18 billion a year.[25] State programs typically provide between $10,000 and $25,000, although at least two have no upper limit. Many programs limit compensation to victims of particular crimes, and virtually all have time limits on when people must file claims, as well as procedures for documenting actual losses.

Evaluations of victim compensation programs have not been overly favorable. Many requests are denied. The New York State Crime Victims Board denied as many as 60 percent of all requests in the late 1980s. The most common reason for denying claims is the failure to provide sufficient documentation.[26]

Even more disturbing, according to William Doerner's study of Florida crime victims, those who did receive compensation did not have more favorable attitudes toward the criminal justice system than did victims whose claims were denied.[27] This failure to affect the attitudes of crime victims is one of the reasons that Robert Elias feels that the victims' rights movement is largely an exercise in symbolic politics.[28]

Despite these problems, victim compensation is a worthy idea that is long overdue. The heavy toll that crime takes on people gives the government good reason to maintain some kind of insurance or compensation program. Yet, we have no reason to believe that compensation will reduce crime in any way.

PROPOSITION 27

Victim compensation programs may help crime victims but will not reduce serious crime.

EXPANDING THE VICTIM'S VOICE

One of the major goals of the victims' rights movement has been to expand the role of the victim in the criminal process, giving him or her a greater voice in bail decisions, plea bargains, sentencing, and parole release decisions. The President's Task Force of Victims of Crime recommended amending the Sixth Amendment to read, "Likewise, the victim in every criminal prosecution shall have the right to be present and to be heard at all critical stages of judicial proceedings."[29] President Clinton's proposed constitutional amendment in 1997 embodied the same idea.

The idea of expanding victims' voices has two goals. One is to give crime victims a feeling of participating in the justice system and to end their feelings of isolation and alienation. We should see this as a victim service program. The other goal is ensure that offenders are properly punished and not allowed to get off too easily. The assumption is that the victim will object to a too lenient plea bargain or sentence. We should see this as a "get tough on crime" program.

Several states have enacted victims' voice laws. Proposition 8, adopted by California voters in 1982, provided that "the victim of any crime, or the next of kin of the victim . . . has the right to attend all sentencing proceedings . . . [and] to reasonably express his or her views concerning the crime, the person responsible, and the need for restitution."[30] The judge is required to take the victim's views into account in imposing sentence.

Opponents of victims' voice laws fear that it brings vengeance (as opposed to justice) into the criminal process. One of the functions of a professional criminal-justice bureaucracy is to ensure fair and impartial treatment of all accused persons. A professional is someone who is not emotionally involved in a case and acts impersonally on the basis of the facts and circumstances. A lawyer, for example, has a professional obligation to prosecute or defend a criminal defendant regardless of his or her personal feelings about the person or what he is accused of doing.

The Supreme Court has shared some of these fears about the danger of vengeance and emotionalism distorting the criminal process. In *Booth v. Maryland* (1987) and *South Carolina v. Gathers* (1989), the Court reversed death sentences because of statements read to the jury about the victim. In *Gathers*, for example, the prosecutor read from religious material that had been in the possession of a murder victim and also mentioned that he was a registered voter.[31] The Court ruled that this information was not related to the circumstances of the crime. Two years later, however, in *Payne v. Tennessee* (1991), the Court ruled that victim impact statements were not unconstitutional.[32]

The Impact of Victims' Voice Laws

There is very mixed evidence about the impact of victims' voice laws. On the one hand, many victims do not take advantage of the opportunities to participate in the process. Also, those who do are not always seeking severe punishment. Nonetheless, some evidence exists of harsher punishment for offenders in cases in which victims do in fact participate.

Judge Lois Forer of Philadelphia routinely invited victims to participate, but few bothered to appear. In Connecticut, only 3 percent of victims took advantage of their legal right to participate in sentencing proceedings. Exactly the same percentage of victims appeared in California under the new law. A National Institute of Justice study concluded that, overall, the victims' voice provision of Proposition 8 had "little effect."[33]

A study of 500 Ohio felony cases between June 1985 and January 1989 found several notable effects. First, victim impact statements (VISs) were submitted in about half (55 percent) of all cases. Under the program, VIS staff solicited information from victims at the time of grand jury hearings. Only 18 percent of victims appeared at trial or sentencing, and only 6 percent exercised their right to speak. Victim participation was heavily influenced by the seriousness of the crime. VISs were filed in 73 percent of "aggravated or special felony" cases, including 81 percent of sexual offenses, but only 49 percent of property crime cases, and only 13 percent of those that were handled as misdemeanors. Somewhat surprisingly, 61 percent of male victims filed a VIS, compared with only 28 percent of females.[34]

Of those who did submit a VIS, 60 percent requested that the offender be incarcerated. Convicted offenders were somewhat more likely to be incarcerated if a VIS was filed or if the victim appeared in court or requested incarceration (but, surprisingly, not if the victim only spoke in court). Also, filing a VIS statement, appearing in court, and requesting incarceration were associated with longer prison terms. The overall impact of the VIS law was somewhat limited, however. Case outcomes were primarily affected by offense severity and offenders' prior record.[35]

An earlier study of sexual assault cases in Ohio found that 60 percent of the victims made statements at sentencing. This study concluded that the statements had little effect on sentencing. A high level of agreement was noted between the sentence the victim recommended and the sentence the judge considered appropriate.[36]

A study of parole hearings in Pennsylvania, however, found that victim impact statements had a very significant effect on the chances of an offender being paroled. The Pennsylvania Board of Probation and Parole denied parole in 43 percent of 100 cases in which there was some victim input, but in only 7 percent of a comparable set of 100 cases in which there was no input.[37]

The findings on parole hearings in Pennsylvania lend support to concerns about the possible undesirable effects of victim impact statements. Whether a victim makes a statement may be a matter of chance, and it means that one offender will serve longer than another who committed the same crime because of an arbitrary factor unrelated to the crimes they committed.

In any event, apart from the satisfaction VISs may give to the victims themselves, no evidence indicates that they have any effect on serious crime. Some offenders may serve longer prison terms, but, as we have already seen, there is no evidence that they are any less likely to eventually recidivate.

PROPOSITION 28
Victim impact statements will not reduce serious crime.

Speedy Trial

Holding speedy trials is another popular victims' rights proposal. The underlying assumption appears to be that justice delayed is justice denied for the victim as well as the defendant. The irony is that the speedy trial has traditionally been seen as a defendants' rights issue. The Sixth Amendment guarantees a speedy trial for the accused.

Congress passed a federal speedy trial law in 1974 and eighteen states have followed suit. As we have already learned, however (Chapter 7), these laws have not worked as intended. Courtroom work groups frequently subvert the laws, often because attorneys on both sides often have reasons for wanting to delay the case.[38] In short, it is not true that everyone wants a speedy trial or that holding a speedy trial is in the best interest of crime victims.

As we pointed out in Chapter 7, however, speedier trials might help reduce crime. Most of the crimes committed by persons out on bail occur after the sixtieth day of release.[39] Speedy trials, particularly for robbers, might reduce the number of these crimes. We should not expect too much crime reduction here, however. As we also learned, crimes committed by persons out on bail are a small proportion of the total.

GETTING TOUGH ON CRIME

Many victims' rights proposals are essentially designed to "get tough on crime." The President's Task Force on Victims of Crime, for example, recommended legislation "to abolish the exclusionary rule," "to abolish parole," to permit hearsay evidence at preliminary hearings, and to authorize preventive detention.[40] Few of these proposals address crime victims directly. The underlying assumption is that locking up more offenders will reduce crime and, therefore, result in fewer crime victims.

We have considered many of them in other chapters. Our conclusion has been that these proposals will not reduce serious crime. In Chapter 5 we found that repealing the exclusionary rule or the *Miranda* warning will not reduce crime. In Chapter 7 we found that limiting the right to bail through preventive detention is not likely to reduce violent crime. In Chapter 11 we will examine whether abolishing parole would have any effect on crime.

Modifying the exclusionary rule may in fact backfire on victims. California's Proposition 8 attacked the exclusionary rule with a "truth in evidence" section permitting introduction of "all relevant evidence." This provision was designed to close an alleged loophole and tip the balance in favor of the prosecution. Within weeks of the proposition's enactment, it was clear that the truth in evidence clause might benefit suspects more than victims. The term "all relevant evidence" covers a lot of territory. It could include questions about a rape victim's background and character, allowing the defense to raise doubts about the victim's innocence. Although Proposition 8 specifically excludes the admission of evidence concerning a rape victim's past sexual activity, other evidence about her lifestyle is admissible. One defense attorney obtained an acquittal by introducing evidence concerning the victim's "colorful" background. The result has undermined years of progress toward the elimination of questioning about the past sexual conduct of rape victims.[41]

Equally dangerous is the President's Task Force recommendation that hearsay evidence should be admissible at preliminary hearings. The idea is that this will protect the victim from the trauma of testifying in person. Relaxing the established rules of evidence to permit hearsay testimony at any stage in the criminal process sets a dangerous precedent. Allowing it only at preliminary hearings, moreover, is silly and misleading. It will be little help in convicting the offender it is inadmissible at trial.

This leads us to the following conclusion:

> ## PROPOSITION 29
> **Laws intended to get tough on crime will not help crime victims and may instead damage the justice system.**

Mandatory Arrest for Domestic Violence

Mandatory arrest for domestic violence is designed to protect female victims of crime. Feminists argued that police failure to arrest men for domestic assault leaves women at risk of being attacked again. Women's groups successfully sued police departments over their failure to arrest, charging denial of equal protection of the law. One of the major results of this movement has been the development of mandatory arrest policies. According to the 1993 Law Enforcement Management and Administrative Statistics survey, 95 percent of all city police departments have a written policy on domestic disturbances.[42] Some of these policies are "mandatory arrest," whereas others are "arrest preferred."

The first study of the impact of arrest on domestic violence, the Minneapolis Domestic Violence Experiment, concluded that arrest deterred violence over the next six months more effectively than either mediation and separation. These findings encouraged the rapid spread of mandatory arrest policies.[43] Unfortunately, subsequent studies in Charlotte, Milwaukee, Omaha, and other cities found that arrest is not any more effective in deterring violence. The Milwaukee study, in fact, found that for certain groups of offenders, arrest actually led to higher levels of repeat violence than the other alternatives.[44]

CONCLUSION

The victims' rights movement is one of the more significant developments in recent criminal justice history. Twenty years ago there was little concern about crime victims and few programs to assist them. Today, new crime victim laws and programs are found in every jurisdiction.

Some of these laws and programs are good ideas, providing valuable assistance to people who have been harmed by crime. Some have not been fully implemented, however. Some of the others are positively dangerous, undermining important constitutional principles and likely to damage the justice system. Most important for our purposes, none of the programs we have discussed is likely to have any impact on serious crime.

NOTES

1. A critique of the proposal is in Bruce Shapiro, "Victims and Vengeance: Why the Victims' Rights Amendment Is a Bad Idea," *The Nation* (February 10, 1997): 11–19.

2. President's Task Force on Victims of Crime, *Final Report* (Washington, D.C.: Government Printing Office, 1982).

3. Office of the Attorney General, *Combatting Violent Crime: 24 Recommendations to Strengthen Criminal Justice* (Washington, D.C.: Government Printing Office, 1992).

4. Emilio Viano, "Victim's Rights and the Constitution: Reflections on a Bicentennial," *Crime and Delinquency* 33 (1987): 443.

5. James H. Stark and Howard Goldstein, *The Rights of Crime Victims* (New York: Bantam, 1985), p. 19.

6. Allen Steinberg, *The Transformation of Criminal Justice: Philadelphia, 1800–1880* (Chapel Hill: University of North Carolina Press, 1989).

7. See notes 31 and 32.

8. R. Lynch, "Improving Treatment of Victims: Some Guides for Action," in William McDonald, ed., *Criminal Justice and the Victim* (Beverly Hills, CA: Sage, 1976), pp. 165–176.

9. President's Task Force on Victims of Crime, *Final Report*, p. vii.

10. Stark and Goldstein, *The Rights of Crime Victims*.

11. Ted R. Miller, Mark A. Cohen, and Brian Wiersma, *Victim Costs and Consequences: A New Look* (Washington, D.C.: Government Printing Office, 1996), p. 17.

12. Emilio C. Viano, "The Recognition and Implementation of Victims' Rights in the United States: Developments and Achievements," in E. C. Viano, ed., *The Victimology Handbook: Research Findings, Treatment, and Public Policy* (New York: Garland, 1990).

13. Robert A. Jerin, Laura J. Moriarty, and Melissa A. Gibson, "Victim Service or Self Service: An Analysis of Prosecution Based Victim-Witness Assistance Programs and Providers," *Criminal Justice Policy Review* 7(2) (1995): 142–154.

14. Robert Elias, *Victims Still: The Political Manipulation of Crime Victims* (Newbury Park, CA: Sage, 1993), *The Politics of Victimization: Victims, Victimology and Human Rights* (New York: Oxford University Press, 1990), and *Victims of the System* (New Brunswick, NJ: Transaction, 1984).

15. Elias, *Victims Still*, p. 39.

16. Bureau of Justice Statistics, *Law Enforcement Management and Administrative Statistics, 1993* (Washington, D.C.: Government Printing Office, 1995), p. xiv.

17. Bureau of Justice Statistics, *Prosecutors in State Courts, 1994* (Washington, D.C.: Government Printing Office, 1996), p. 9.

18. Jerin et al., "Victim Service or Self Service," p. 152.

19. President's Task Force on Victims of Crime, *Final Report*.

20. Bureau of Justice Statistics, *Law Enforcement Management and Administrative Statistics, 1993*.

21. Bureau of Justice Statistics, *Prosecutors in State Courts, 1990* (Washington, D.C.: Government Printing Office, 1992).

22. Lee P. Brown and Mary Ann Wycoff, "Policing Houston: Reducing Fear and Improving Service," *Crime and Delinquency* 33 (January 1986): 71–89.

23. Bureau of Justice Statistics, *Criminal Victimization in the United States, 1993* (Washington, D.C.: Government Printing Office, 1996), pp. 104–105.

24. Data on claims are in Bureau of Justice Statistics, *Sourcebook of Criminal Justice Statistics—1995* (Washington, D.C.: Government Printing Office, 1996), pp. 390–391.

25. Miller et al., *Victim Costs and Consequences*, p. 17.

26. Andrew Karmen, *Crime Victims: An Introduction to Victimology*, 2d ed. (Pacific Grove, CA: Brooks/Cole, 1990), p. 321.

27. William Doerner, "The Impact of Crime Compensation on Victim Attitudes Toward the Criminal Justice System," *Victimology* 5(2) (1980): 61–77.

28. Elias, *Victims Still*, p. 42.

29. President's Task Force on Victims of Crime, *Final Report*, p. 114.

30. Edwin Villmoare and Virginia V. Neto, *Victim Appearances of Sentencing Under California's Victims' Bill of Rights* (Washington, D.C.: Government Printing Office, 1987).

31. *South Carolina v. Gathers*, 490 U.S. 805 (1989); *Booth v. Maryland*, 482 U.S. 496 (1987).

32. *Payne v. Tennessee*, 501 U.S. 808 (1991).

33. Villmoare and Neto, *Victim Appearances at Sentencing*.

34. Edna Erez and Pamela Tontodonato, "The Effect of Victim Participation in Sentencing on Sentence Outcome," *Criminology* 28(3) (1990): 451–474.

35. Ibid.

36. Anthony Walsh, "Placebo Justice: Victim Recommendations and Offender Sentences in Sexual Assault Cases," *Journal of Criminal Law and Criminology* 77 (Winter 1986): 1126–1141.

37. William H. Parsonage, Frances Bernat, and Jacquelin Helfgott, "Victim Impact Testimony and Pennsylvania's Parole Decision Making Process: A Pilot Study,"

Criminal Justice Policy Review 6(3) (1994): 187–206.

38. Malcolm Feeley, *Court Reform on Trial* (New York: Basic Books, 1982).

39. Bureau of Justice Statistics, *Pretrial Release of Felony Defendants, 1992* (Washington, D.C.: Government Printing Office, 1994).

40. President's Task Force on Victims of Crime, *Final Report*, pp. 17–18.

41. Cassia Spohn and Julie Horney, *Rape Law Reform* (New York: Plenum, 1992).

42. Bureau of Justice Statistics, *Law Enforcement Management and Administrative Statistics, 1993*.

43. Lawrence W. Sherman and Richard A. Berk, *The Minneapolis Domestic Violence Experiment* (Washington, D.C.: Police Foundation, 1984).

44. Lawrence W. Sherman, *Policing Domestic Violence* (New York: Free Press, 1992).

1 0

Control Gun Crimes

THE PROBLEM WITH GUNS—
AND GUN POLICY

G uns, especially handguns, are a serious problem in the United States. Over 30,000 people die every year as a result of handguns: 13,000 are murdered, and another 18,000 commit suicide. Additionally, handguns are used in over 40 percent of all robberies.[1]

Everyone agrees that we need to do something about gun-related violence, but they disagree sharply over exactly what to do. Liberals generally believe that the problem is guns, supporting a number of policies designed to reduce their availability. As they put it, "guns kill people." Conservatives, on the other hand, believe that criminals are the problem, supporting policies designed to either deter or incapacitate them. As they put it, "guns don't kill people—people kill people."[2]

Public opinion polls reveal how deeply divided the public is over what to do about gun-related violence. In one poll, about 60 percent agreed that laws governing the sale of firearms should be "more strict," whereas only about 10 percent said they should be less strict. Yet, in another poll a third of the respondents agreed with the statement that "armed citizens are the best defense against criminals" and felt that it should be easier for law-abiding people to carry concealed weapons.[3]

A series of recently enacted laws also reveals how divided the country is over guns. Federal, state, and local laws have moved in completely opposite directions. The 1993 Brady Bill attempts to limit access to handguns by mandating a five-day waiting period for the purchase of a handgun; the 1994 Violent Crime Control Act bans nineteen types of assault weapons. Several states, however, have passed "shall issue" laws requiring (as opposed to permitting) local law enforcement officials to issue permits to carry concealed weapons unless the applicant is legally disqualified (for example, if he or she has a criminal record). These laws make guns more available to the public.[4]

Gun control incites passionate opposition for several obvious reasons. With the possible exception of drinking and driving, no other issue discussed in this book directly affects so many people as the idea that we should limit ownership of guns. About 40 percent of all homes have some kind of firearm, and about 25 percent have a handgun.[5] And although no one argues that drunk driving is acceptable, many people believe they have a right to own a gun. Gun owners argue that the Second Amendment establishes a constitutional right to own a gun, although the Supreme Court has never accepted that interpretation.

GUN OWNERSHIP AND GUN-RELATED VIOLENCE

A lot of misunderstanding persists about the exact nature of the problem related to guns, gun ownership, and gun-related violence. The leaders of both sides of the issue have often distorted the evidence to support their respective positions. Let us try to clear the air by establishing a few basic facts.

Types of Guns

The first problem is that there is a lot of confusion about exactly which weapons we are talking about. A basic distinction is between rifles, shotguns, and handguns.[6] Virtually everyone agrees that handguns are the real problem with respect to crime. Ninety-six percent of the firearms used in robberies are handguns. The so-called "Saturday night special" is one particular kind of handgun, small, easily concealable, and cheap. Assault weapons, meanwhile, are rifles or pistols that are capable of rapid-fire action. We will look at specific policy proposals directed at both the Specials and assault weapons.

Gun Ownership

The Bureau of Alcohol, Tobacco, and Firearms (BATF) estimates that over 200 million firearms are in circulation in the United States. This includes about 70 million handguns. The production of new handguns adds about 1.5 to 2 million new ones each year. It is important to keep these 70 million handguns in mind throughout this chapter. They form an important part of the context for various gun control policies.

Despite the tremendous increase in the total number of firearms, the percentage of households with some kind of firearm has dropped slightly, from 47 percent in 1973 to 41 percent in 1994. Twenty-four percent had a handgun in 1994.[7] In short, the prevalence of gun ownership has not increased, but those people who already had a firearm have been buying additional weapons. Those households with a firearm have an average of about 4.5 individual weapons.[8]

Handgun ownership is higher among men (32 percent versus 19 percent for women), whites (26 percent versus 16 percent for racial and ethnic minorities), higher-income people, Protestants, and southerners. People in the Southeast are the most likely to own a handgun (32 percent), in large part because the region is very rural and there is a strong tradition of hunting. Handgun ownership is lowest in the urbanized northeast (13 percent).[9]

Handgun-Related Violence

The facts about handgun violence in the United States are grisly. In 1992, 930,700 handgun crimes were committed, which represented a significant increase over the average of 667,000 in the previous five years. This included 13,200 murders in 1992, or almost 60 percent of all murders; 11,800 rapes; 339,000 robberies; and 566,800 assaults.[10] They are also involved in about 60 percent of all suicides (or a total of about 18,000 in 1992). Another 1,409 people were killed in firearms accidents (including other kinds of firearms) in 1992.[11] Finally, two-thirds of all police officers feloniously killed in the line of duty are slain by handguns.[12]

We should add a comment about our terminology here. Note that we use the term *gun-related fatalities*. To say that guns "are responsible for" or "caused" deaths is to accept the liberal gun control position on this issue. *Gun-related* is policy-neutral.

As we mentioned in Chapter 1, the most alarming development in recent years has been the sharp increase in gun-related homicide among juveniles.[13] The murder rate among people aged twenty-four and older has remained stable, whereas the rate among people ages under the age of 18 more than doubled between 1985 and 1995 (see Figure 1.1, p. 4). Virtually all of the increase involves gun-related murders. The rate of nongun murders among ten- to seventeen-year-olds has remained stable.[14]

The profile of handgun crime victims closely resembles the profile of gun crime users. Both groups are disproportionately young, African American males. Juveniles are currently more likely to carry a gun than are adults. Analyzing data from the Drug Use Forecasting (DUF) survey, Scott Decker and his colleagues found that whereas 14 percent of all arrestees carried a gun all or most of the time, 20 percent of the juvenile males and 31 percent of gang members did.[15]

Handguns as Self-Protection

Two-thirds of all arrestees say they carry a weapon for protection or self-defense. The result is a self-perpetuating gun culture. As more juveniles carry guns, their peers feel the need to carry one also for self-protection. As James D. Wright explains, these men "live in a very hostile and violent environment, and many of them have come to believe, no doubt correctly, that their ability to survive in that environment depends critically on being adequately armed."[16] They are "highly motivated gun owners who are not easily persuaded that they should not have one."

Although many people say that they have a gun for self-protection, crime victims rarely use a weapon. In fact, handguns are fired in only 13 percent of all the robberies in which they are used, and the victim is actually struck by a bullet in only about 15 percent of these incidents (or 2 percent of all robberies). Handguns are primarily used to intimidate victims, and in this regard they are extremely efficient.[17] They are used in 78.8 percent of all the *completed* robberies and 48.7 percent of the *completed* rapes.

Analyzing NCVS data from 1979 to 1985, Gary Kleck and Miriam DeLone found that robbery victims used a gun to resist the offender in only 1.2 percent of all robberies (this figure included both completed and attempted robberies). Very few of these incidents involved a shoot-out between victim and offender. In 70 percent of the cases when the victim was armed, the robber was not. Nonetheless, Kleck and DeLone argue that when victims do use guns, they are frequently successful in preventing a completed robbery. In short, victims use them in the same way armed criminals do: to intimidate the other person.[18]

GUN-RELATED LAWS

It is a myth that the United States has no gun-related laws. In fact, we have innumerable federal, state, and local laws regulating ownership and use of guns.[19] The real question is whether these laws are effective in accomplishing their stated purposes. (We should note here that we are using the term *gun-related laws*, because many laws are directed at gun use by criminals and not gun ownership.)

The main reason that we have so many laws is the federal structure of the American political system, which divides responsibility among federal, state, and local governments. Other countries have a single, national law related to gun ownership. Historically, federal gun laws have been very weak. The 1934 and 1938 firearms acts involved some limited controls over the interstate sale of weapons. The 1968 Gun Control Act tightened the licensing of gun dealers. Some of these earlier restrictions, however, were weakened by the 1986 Firearms Owners Protection Act.

State and local laws vary considerably. The most important features include restrictions on who can purchase and own them, and background checks and waiting periods for purchasers. Some cities have banned the ownership of handguns, and at least fourteen have outlawed the sale of Saturday night specials. The end result is that some states and cities have far more restrictive laws than others. Thus, someone can easily buy a handgun in a state with weak regulations and carry it to a state or city with very restrictive laws. A Congressional report issued in 1997 found that many guns sold in Virginia, Florida, South Carolina, Georgia, and Texas—states with some of the weakest laws—ended up being seized in other states. In one report, the BATF identified 1,234 guns sold in Florida that were later used by criminals in other states, including 181 in New York.[20]

The Policy Alternatives

The question is, What should we do to reduce gun-related violence? Generally, liberals want to reduce the availability of firearms, especially handguns. They cite the fact that compared with other countries, the United States has both the most permissive gun ownership laws and the highest rates of gun-related violence. These facts lead them to the conclusion that reducing gun availability would reduce violent crime. Mark Moore characterizes this as a "supply reduction" strategy.[21]

Conservatives argue that criminals, not guns, are the problem and that we have high rates of violent crime because we fail to punish offenders who use firearms. They want tougher penalties as a way of both deterring crimes and incapacitating criminals. The most popular approach involves mandatory prison terms for criminals who use guns. Moore calls this a "demand reduction" strategy.

We will encounter the same distinction between supply reduction and demand reduction when we discuss drug policy in Chapter 13. As Moore suggests, it is helpful to think comparatively about strategies for controlling guns, drugs, and alcohol.

Pro-gun advocates have introduced a new issue in the gun policy debates, supporting laws that permit the carrying of concealed weapons. They believe that the greater availability of guns will prevent crime.

Public Attitudes Toward Gun Control

It is often reported that a majority of Americans favor gun control. This is only partly true. It depends on exactly which gun control policy you are referring to.

The percentage of Americans favoring a ban on the possession of handguns has remained steady at about 40 percent since the early 1980s.[22] A large majority of the public supports regulation of gun ownership. In 1994, for example, 78 percent supported requiring a police permit to buy a gun (up from 70 percent in 1972).[23] Meanwhile, 90 percent favor a waiting period of seven to twenty-one days for a purchase. At the same time, many people endorse tough penalties for criminals who use guns: 83 percent support mandatory prison sentences for gun crimes.[24]

We have to be very careful in interpreting public opinion poll data. When some people say they favor "gun control," they may mean only restrictions on the purchase of guns rather than a ban on ownership, or they may actually mean tough penalties for criminals who use guns.

Now let us review the various policy alternatives and see whether any evidence indicates that they work or might work.

BAN HANDGUNS

The most extreme gun control proposal is to ban handguns. The idea of "banning" handguns actually consists of several different policies: outlawing possession, outlawing bullets, prohibiting the manufacture and sale of handguns, and banning only Saturday night specials or assault weapons. Let us take a look at each of these approaches.

Ban Possession

A few cities have actually banned the possession of handguns. Their experience gives us some idea of what this approach can and cannot accomplish.

The District of Columbia banned the purchase, sale, transfer, and possession of all handguns in 1975. It exempted handguns and long guns previously registered under a 1968 gun registration law. The nation's capital represents a tough test of banning handguns because it is a major city with a lot of violent crime.

What happened as a result of the law? The U.S. Conference of Mayors, a leading gun control advocate, claimed that the law was responsible for a "significant reduction in both firearm and handgun crime." Other analysts, however, believe that the mayors' report was flawed and inconclusive. Edward Jones found that comparable cities experienced even greater reductions in gun-related crime during the same period, without the benefit of gun control. Jones conceded that the law may have made some contribution to reducing handgun crime, but it was impossible to argue that it was the only or even the most important cause.[25]

Murder trends in Washington over the last twenty years clearly suggest that the 1975 law was not effective. Murders declined significantly in the late 1970s and early 1980s, reaching a low of 147 in 1985. They skyrocketed to 482 by 1991, mainly as a result of the arrival of crack. Clearly, young men in Washington who wanted to obtain a handgun had little trouble getting one.

Evanston, Illinois, enacted what Gary Kleck calls "the toughest gun law in America" in 1982.[26] It banned the possession of handguns within the city limits (except for possession by police, private security guards, licensed gun dealers, and a few gun collectors). The impact of the law on crime was insignificant. Between 1981 and 1984, trivial increases in murder and assault occurred, and armed robbery decreased slightly.

The Limits of "Banning" Handguns

The Washington, D.C., and Evanston experiences illustrate the limits of attempting to outlaw possession of handguns. The main problem is the 70 million handguns that already exist. No one has offered a realistic plan for how they might be removed from circulation. As law professor John Kaplan once pointed out, crusaders who seek to outlaw a product (alcohol, drugs, guns) always focus on the alleged dangers of the item and spend "little time and energy" estimating the costs of enforcement and the likelihood of effectiveness.[27]

A sizable black market in handguns and other weapons already exists. A majority of the arrestees in the DUF survey indicated that they obtained their guns through the illegal firearms market. Over half (55 percent) said that guns are easy to obtain: more than a third (37 percent) said they could obtain one in less than a week, and 20 percent said they could get one in a day or less. Thirteen percent said that they had stolen a gun at some point in their life.[28] A federal ban on handgun possession would only foster the growth of the black market, just as the prohibition of alcohol (1920–1933) stimulated the growth of organized crime.

A truly effective ban on ownership would require a federal law. However, no strong support for such a law exists at present. Second, it is safe to predict that millions of gun owners would refuse to turn in their weapons. In Evanston, Illinois, only 116 handguns were voluntarily turned in after the 1982 ban went into effect, despite the fact that there were over 5,000 admitted handgun owners.[29] Not only do 25 percent of all American households currently have handguns, but many of those people fiercely believe that they have a constitutional right to own those weapons. A federal law would create a situation resembling Prohibition in the 1920s when tens of millions of people drank alcoholic beverages despite a constitutional amendment. Any attempt to enforce such a ban would require highly intrusive measures by the police. Many right-wing groups already express intense hostility toward the BATF, and a federal ban would only inflame the situation further.

Ban Bullets

Some groups, including the U.S. Conference of Mayors and the Consumer Product Safety Commission, have recommended banning the manufacture and sale of bullets on the grounds that they are a health hazard. This is a politically motivated strategy designed to sidestep the strong public opposition to outlawing guns themselves. The obvious problem with this approach is that bullets are easily made at home. Many hunters already pack their own. Outlawing bullets would only stimulate a large cottage industry in homemade bullets and a black market.

A variation of the bullet ban is a 1986 federal law prohibiting the manufacture, importation, and sale of so-called "cop-killer" bullets. These bullets are made of hard metals capable of piercing the bulletproof vests worn by police officers. Law enforcement organizations actively supported the law. When pressed, however, advocates of the law could not cite any cases of a police officer actually being killed by one of these bullets. Meanwhile, only eighteen cases were reported of criminals caught in possession of such bullets over an eighteen-year period![30]

The cop-killer bullet issue is a classic example of a general phenomenon in crime control policy debates: the habit of some activists and politicians to seize on a small but seemingly important part of the problem. It is usually a cop-out: a way of appearing to have a solution to the problem while actually ignoring the hard questions related to the larger problem.

Ban the Manufacture and Importation of Handguns

Another way to reduce the availability of handguns in the United States is to outlaw their manufacture and importation. This approach is designed to dry up the supply of handguns over the long run. In practice, however, it would only stimulate an international black market like the one that already dominates the drug trade. Also, it has been estimated that the current supply of handguns is enough to last for the next hundred years.[31]

Buy Back Handguns

Another strategy for drying up the supply is for law enforcement officials to buy back handguns. A number of cities have tried buy-back programs. With the aid of federal funds, Baltimore offered to buy back handguns at $50 apiece in 1974. The city eventually bought 8,400 guns, or about one-fourth of the estimated number in the city.[32]

The buy-back approach has serious drawbacks. The available supply is so huge, that it could never remove all of the guns. It may also absorb guns from other jurisdictions. Some critics suggested that the $50 offered by Baltimore was too high for many small guns and may only have allowed some people to trade up to a more expensive and more deadly weapon. Finally, and most important, anyone currently engaged in crime, or who has plans to commit a crime, is not going to sell his or her gun.

Ban Saturday Night Specials

A compromise strategy for banning handguns advocated by some liberals is to outlaw only the so-called Saturday night specials.[33] The BATF defines the special as a gun of 0.32 caliber or less, with a barrel less than three inches in length, and priced at $50 or less. In 1996 Los Angeles became the fourteenth city in the United States (along with the state of Maryland) to outlaw the sale of specials, specifically prohibiting twenty-three different weapons.[34] Advocates of outlawing the specials believe these weapons are favored by criminals because of their price and concealability.

Outlawing only Saturday night specials probably will not accomplish what many people think it would. The role of the specials in crime has been greatly exaggerated. Gary Kleck found that, far from being the "preferred" weapon of criminals, they represent only between 10 and 27 percent of all handguns used in crimes (and only 13 percent of all the weapons confiscated in Los Angles in 1995).[35] Banning only the specials might produce a "substitution effect," in which criminals simply move up to a larger weapon.

Kleck further argues that specials are the primary self-defense weapon for low-income people. Banning them would deprive poor people, who are victimized by violent crimes more than middle-class people, of one of their principal means of self-protection.[36]

The proposal to ban only the Saturday night specials is essentially a political cop-out. It allows people to appear to be doing something about the gun problem without directly threatening most gun owners. The same can be said about banning cop-killer bullets: it focuses on a small part of the problem, one that has high symbolic power, while avoiding the hard questions associated with the real problem.

Ban Assault Rifles

The rise of gang-related violence in the 1980s aroused public concern about so-called assault weapons. Much publicity was generated about gangs being heavily armed with Uzis, AK-47s, and similar weapons. The term *assault weapon* generally refers to "semiautomatic firearms with a large magazine of ammunition that [are] designed and configured for rapid fire and combat use."[37] They can be pistols, rifles, or shotguns. The BATF estimated in 1993 that about 1 percent of the 200 million guns in private hands were assault weapons. Many people want to ban them because they are not legitimate hunting weapons and have no purpose other than killing people. The 1994 Violent Crime Control Act outlawed the manufacture and sale of nineteen specific types of assault weapons.

As with Saturday night specials, the importance of assault weapons has been greatly exaggerated. Kleck points out that the ordinary handgun remains the gun of choice among robbers. Virtually all of the police officers feloniously killed are killed with handguns. In short, although extremely deadly, assault weapons are not the real problem in gun-related crimes.[38]

Summary

All of the policies designed to eliminate the possession of handguns or certain types of guns run up against the same basic problems: millions of these weapons already are in circulation, there is no practical plan for eliminating them, a black market already exists, and any kind of ban would only foster the growth of the black market. This leads us to the following conclusion:

> **PROPOSITION 30**
>
> **Attempts to ban all handguns, or certain kinds of guns, or bullets will not reduce serious crime.**

REGULATE THE SALE AND POSSESSION OF HANDGUNS

The basic American strategy for controlling handguns is to regulate their sale, purchase, and ownership. Innumerable federal, state, and local laws are designed to keep handguns out of the hands of convicted offenders, people with a history of mental illness, and juveniles. The 1993 Brady Law requires a five-day waiting period, which is designed to give local officials sufficient time to conduct a records check on the applicant. The Youth Handgun Safety Act of 1994 outlaws possession of handguns by juveniles and the private sale or transfer of a handgun to a juvenile.[39] A 1996 law, meanwhile, outlaws gun ownership by anyone with a domestic violence conviction. (This law creates enormous problems for police officers and members of the military who have such convictions but who must use weapons as part of their jobs.)

Prohibiting certain people from owning guns is essentially a "bad-person" strategy. It is similar to the long-standing policy on driving, in which the registration of vehicles and the licensing of drivers are required as ways of keeping unfit drivers off the road.

The bad-person strategy can only be described as a monumental failure. All of the evidence indicates that active criminals either have weapons or can readily obtain them if they want to. To be sure, it probably works in a certain number of cases, in which a person applies for a gun permit and is turned down because of a criminal record or some other problem. In the first year following passage of the Brady Bill, about 3 percent of all applications for gun purchases were denied—an average of about 7,000 people every month.[40] Some of these people will undoubtedly stop at that point, but many others will simply turn to the black market and obtain a gun.

We have already discussed the problem of the black market in guns. Mark H. Moore estimates that between 500,000 and 750,000 gun transactions take place between private individuals every year.[41] Many of these do not involve active or potential criminals: they are sales or gifts between friends, family members, gun collectors, and hunters. But many do involve illegal sales among active criminals. James D. Wright found that only one-sixth of all gun-using felons acquired their guns through legal, retail transactions. Half had stolen a gun at one time or another.[42] An estimated 341,000 firearms are stolen every year, 180,000 of which are handguns. By definition, these guns go directly into the hands of people (thieves) who are barred from owning them.[43]

We have also noted already how murders rose spectacularly in Washington, D.C., ten years after the 1975 gun possession ban. The case of New York City offers additional evidence of the failure of gun permit laws. The 1911 Sullivan Law requiring a gun permit was for many decades the strictest law in the country. Yet, law enforcement officials have estimated that the city has at least 2 million illegal handguns. The BATF's Project Identification found that 57 percent of the illegal guns seized in New York City were purchased in just four states: Florida, Georgia, South Carolina, and Virginia.[44]

Attempts to prevent certain kinds of people from owning guns run up against some basic information problems. Criminal history data are far from complete or fully accurate. Thorough background checks assume the ability to check an applicant's possible criminal record not only in the state of purchase but in other states as well. In late 1996 it was estimated that no state had computerized all of its criminal records, and two states had computerized none of them. A Maine official admitted that administrators were still compiling records by hand, "the same way we did it in the 1930s."[45] The most serious problem is with offenders whose records do not show up in the files (think of these as false negatives). There are also false positives: people inaccurately listed as having a criminal record (a mistaken identity, data that were entered inaccurately, mistakes that were not expunged, and so forth).

The mentally disturbed gun buyer represents an even more serious problem. There is no national data file of people with mental health problems—and some serious civil liberties questions exist about whether we would want such a file. What is meant by having a history of mental illness? Being hospitalized? That only covers a small number of people with problems. What about people who were treated by a private physician or counselor? Requiring these professionals to report all of their clients would be a serious invasion of privacy. And what level of seriousness would trigger the ban on gun ownership? Mild depression? That covers a lot of the public. And of course millions of people with serious mental health problems never see a doctor or counselor.

Waiting Periods: The Brady Bill

To facilitate background checks, many states and cities have required waiting periods between applying for and granting a permit to purchase a gun. Gun control advocates won a major victory with passage of the federal Brady Bill in 1993, which requires a five-day waiting period in those jurisdictions that do not already have any waiting period. (In 1998 the waiting period will be replaced by an instant records check.) The law is named after James Brady, the press secretary who was seriously injured in the 1991 assassination attempt against President Ronald Reagan. (The constitutionality of the law has been challenged by some local law enforcement officials, and its fate is not clear as this book is being written.)

Supporters of the Brady Bill believe it has been a tremendous success. About 3 percent of all applications were denied.[46] But as we have already mentioned, we cannot know how many of these people simply turned to the black market. James D. Wright concludes quite appropriately that "the national five-day waiting period will have no effect on the acquisition of guns by criminals because that is not how the bad guys get their guns in the first place."[47]

Summary

For all of the same reasons that banning ownership of handguns seems futile, regulations designed to deny ownership to certain categories of "bad" people are not likely to succeed. Seventy million handguns are in existence, an active black market thrives in guns, and criminals themselves say that they have or would have no trouble quickly obtaining a weapon. People intent on committing a crime are particularly motivated to obtain a gun. James D. Wright sums it up very well when he argues that it is not very efficient or sensible to try to control ownership of guns by the public at large when the real problem is the behavior of a very small part of the population—violent criminals.[48]

PROPOSITION 31

Attempts to deny ownership of handguns to certain "bad" people are not likely to either limit ownership or reduce serious crime.

RESTRICT THE USE OF HANDGUNS

Instead of attempting to deny ownership of handguns, another serious group of policies are aimed at limiting how people *use* handguns. Let us take a look at this approach.

Restrict the Carrying of Handguns

Most states have traditionally had laws regulating the carrying of handguns outside the home, usually by prohibiting the carrying of concealed weapons or by requiring some kind of permit. The most famous variation of this approach was the 1975 Massachusetts Bartley-Fox law, which mandates a one-year prison term for people who are caught carrying a handgun outside their homes without a permit. The law prohibits plea bargaining to a lesser offense and denies the possibility of either probation or parole. The intent was simple: "If you are caught with a gun, you will go to prison for a year and nobody can get you out."[49]

The Bartley-Fox law is closely related to other crime control policies we discuss in this book. On the one hand, it is an exercise in mandatory sentencing (Chapter 7). It is also a strategy of deterrence, seeking to prevent crime through the threat of certain punishment (Chapter 6). Finally, it is an attempt to close the alleged loophole of plea bargaining (Chapter 8). Here we are primarily interested in its impact on crime and on gun-related crime in particular.

As a gun control measure, Bartley-Fox is a strategic compromise. It does not challenge people's right to own guns and keep them at home. Thus, it sidesteps much of opposition from gun owners. It attempts to reduce gun-related crime by keeping the guns at home. This strategy has strong empirical support. Many violent crimes are unplanned, spontaneous events: the person left home with no intention of committing a crime. As interviews with criminals have found, most carry a gun for self-defense. Nonetheless, some of these people end up committing a gun crime. Having the gun may have emboldened them to commit a crime once a situation arose. As we have already argued, guns are terribly efficient as threats. Without the gun a robber may not have attempted or completed the crime. Thus, a strategy to deter people from carrying a gun in the first place might reduce crime.

Bartley-Fox has been intensively evaluated. The data on crime trends indicated that in Boston assaults with a gun declined by 13.5 percent between 1974 and 1975 and by 11.7 percent between 1974 and 1976. Four other cities, however, experienced even greater reductions in gun assaults without the benefit of a similar law. They went down 21.3 percent in Philadelphia and 26 percent in Chicago. Meanwhile, in Boston assaults with other kinds of weapons went up by 40.4 percent between 1974 and 1976. Thus, there may have been a "substitution effect," as people kept their guns at home and shifted to other weapons.[50]

Gun robberies in Boston went down a substantial 35.5 percent in the 1974–1976 period, whereas robberies committed without guns increased slightly. Again, however, other cities that did not have a similar law experienced even greater reductions. Armed robberies went down 43.5 percent in Chicago and 36.7 percent in Philadelphia. Meanwhile, gun murders declined by 55.7 percent in Boston. This decrease was part of a national decline in murders; the comparison cities had reductions of between 30 and 45 percent. An "announcement effect" (see Chapter 6) may have been at work. Gun-related crimes began to decline in the months just before the law went into effect, perhaps as a result of all the publicity (as has been the case in some drunk driving crackdowns), but this point is not entirely clear.

Some evidence indicates that officials undermined the "mandatory" provisions of Bartley-Fox. Police officers reportedly became a little more cautious about frisking people for weapons. Police reports on gun incidents declined by 25 percent in Boston between 1974 and 1976. Seventy of seventy-nine officers interviewed admitted to being more selective because they did not want to catch "otherwise innocent" people violating the law. This is a classic example of how police officers' discretion reflects their judgment about the moral character of possible suspects. Meanwhile, the percentage of cases dismissed went from 18 percent to 38 percent. Despite its attempt to close plea-bargaining loopholes, the law did not restrict outright dismissal. Acquittals in the remaining cases increased from 16 percent in 1974 to 40 percent in 1975 and then declined to 33 percent in 1976. Finally, the number of appeals of convictions went from 21 percent to 96 percent.[51]

The net effect was that fewer people were sentenced for carrying a gun. The percentage of defendants actually sentenced dropped from 41 percent in 1974 to only 17 percent in 1976. This appears to be a classic illustration of criminal justice thermodynamics at work: as the nominal punishment went up, actual punishment went down. A follow-up study of the law in six Massachusetts counties found that it was still being implemented, with no evidence of systematic lowering or dropping of charges.[52]

PROPOSITION 32

Bartley-Fox laws restricting the unauthorized carrying of handguns, if vigorously implemented, may help reduce gun violence.

Airplanes and Schools

Another set of laws attempts to keep people from carrying guns in certain places such as airplanes and schools. A federal law prohibits the carrying of a weapon on an airplane, and all passengers are electronically screened at the gate. The electronic screening at airports makes enforcement fairly effective. Every year about 2,500 firearms are confiscated.[53] Many of the people carrying them apparently forgot that they had a gun with them. This point is a testimony to the prevalence of guns in American society, the casualness with which they are carried around, and the limited deterrent effect of a well-known law. Nonetheless, the law has been effective in curbing airplane hijacking. The number of hijackings decreased from forty in 1969 to only one attempted hijacking each in both 1990 and 1991, and none in either of the next two years.[54]

It is important to remember, however, that airports are special locations and airplane hijackings are a special kind of crime. The prevention of hijacking has almost no relevance to the main purpose of this book: the reduction of ordinary robbery and burglary.

Another problem involves guns in school. This is part of the problem of escalating gun violence among teenagers. A national survey of students in 1994–95 found that 93.9 percent had never taken a gun to school. Nonetheless, the fact that about 6 percent had at some point (1.9 percent said they took a gun to school "a lot") translates into a large number of students.[55] Six percent of the 14 million high school students in 1993 would be 840,000. About 200,000 students carry a gun to school "a lot."[56]

The 1994 Gun Free Schools Act requires schools receiving federal education funds to have a policy mandating the expulsion of students who bring firearms to school. We do not know to what extent this law effectively deters students from bringing guns to school. With respect to the purpose of this book, we also do not know to what extent the law indirectly prevents robberies and burglaries.

Get Guns Off the Street: The Kansas City Experiment

The most innovative recent approach to reducing gun crimes is the Kansas City Gun Experiment.[57] The experiment involved intensive enforcement of existing laws on the illegal carrying of handguns. Funded by the federal Weed and Seed program, it represents a combination of two important innovations in policing: "problem-oriented policing," in which the police focus on a specific problem, and "hot spots," in which patrols focus on a particular area (see Chapter 5).[58]

The experiment was conducted in a particularly high-crime-rate precinct in Kansas City, where the 1991 murder rate was 177 per 100,000, or about twenty times higher than the national average. Two two-officer patrol cars, working overtime, patrolled for six hours every night, concentrating exclusively on detecting and seizing illegally possessed guns. The officers would stop cars on legitimate legal grounds (for example, a traffic violation) but focus on weapons seizures. Almost half (45 percent) of all the guns eventually seized were found through a search incident to arrest, another 21 percent were found in plain view, and 34 percent were found in frisks as authorized by the Supreme Court in the 1968 *Terry* decision.

Over the course of twenty-nine weeks, the gun unit officers seized a total of twenty-nine guns. Meanwhile, regular patrol officers in the target beat seized another forty-seven guns, for a combined total of seventy-six. The number of gun crimes in the target beat declined by 49 percent, but only by 4 percent in a control beat. The experiment controlled for a possible displacement effect and found that gun crimes went up in some of the neighboring beats and down in others. The reduction in gun crimes could have occurred as a direct result of removing guns from the area, or through deterrence, or through the incapacitation of potential offenders who were arrested and imprisoned.

The Kansas City Gun Experiment seems to suggest that a clearly focused program to remove guns from the streets can reduce gun-related crime. A number of questions about the program remain, however. It is extremely expensive when measured in terms of the cost per gun seized or crime prevented. It is not clear that a police department could afford to run such a program as a part of normal operations. Also, when Sherman replicated the program in Indianapolis, some serious questions were raised about the data and some of the claims made for its success.[59]

The safest conclusion at this point is that the gun seizure approach may prove to be an effective strategy for reducing gun-related violence, but more research is needed.

PROPOSITION 33

Focused, proactive police programs to remove illegal guns from the streets may prove to be an effective way to reduce serious crime.

More Guns?

Some gun owners believe that the best way to reduce crime and protect law-abiding citizens is to have more guns on the street. The debate over guns and crime took a new direction in 1996 with a paper by University of Chicago professors John R. Lott and David B. Mustard arguing that "allowing citizens to carry concealed weapons deters violent crimes and it appears to produce no increase in accidental deaths."[60]

The idea that more guns should be on the street (at least in the hands of law-abiding people) flies directly in the face of policies such as the Bartley-Fox Law and the Kansas City Gun Experiment. A fair amount of support is expressed for it. Between 1977 and 1992, ten states enacted "shall issue" laws related to carrying weapons. These laws create a presumptive right to a permit to carry a weapon, as opposed to the traditional approach in which law enforcement officials had broad discretion to grant or deny permits.

Using county-level data on crime, Lott and Mustard estimate that if states without "shall issue" laws adopted them, it would prevent about 1,570 murders, 4,177 rapes, and over 60,000 aggravated assaults every year. In an early critique, Frank Zimring and Gordon Hawkins raise serious questions about the crime reduction claims made for the "shall issue" laws. As was the case with Isaac Erhlich's study of the death penalty (see Chapter 6), the data have a few serious problems. Zimring and Hawkins argue that, at best, "shall issue" laws are likely to produce "modest benefits" because so few people will actually exercise their right to take out gun permits (they estimate "fewer than 2 percent" of the population doing so). "Large reductions in violence are quite unlikely," however."[61]

Lott and Mustard have, if nothing else, altered the debate over guns and crime. Their work will undoubtedly spark further research. For the moment, their claims, like those of so many other policy advocates we consider in this book, seem extravagant and unwarranted.

GET TOUGH ON WEAPONS OFFENSES

The primary conservative policy on gun-related crimes is to get tough on offenders convicted of using guns. This approach reflects two basic conservative views: first, that criminals and not guns commit crimes; and, second, that the criminal justice system is soft on crime and criminals. The basic policy recommendation calls for mandatory prison terms for gun-related crimes and longer prison terms. Such laws are extremely popular. In 1994 forty-one states had mandatory minimum sentencing laws for illegal weapons possession.[62] A 1975 Florida law is typical of those in other states. It imposed a mandatory minimum sentence of three years in prison for use of a weapon in the commission of certain crimes and prohibited the granting of certain types of good-time credit during the mandatory minimum period.[63]

National data indicate that, contrary to widespread belief, the criminal justice system is not soft on gun-related crimes. In 1994, 69 percent of all persons convicted of a weapons offense in state courts were incarcerated—the same figure as for drug offenses. The average prison sentence was four years, and the average jail term was six months.[64] Federal courts were considerably tougher, sentencing 77 percent to prison, for average terms of just over six years.[65] (State court sentences have been getting shorter, down from an average of fifty-six months since 1985, whereas federal prison sentences have been getting longer, up from forty-two months in 1985.) But both state and federal prisoners serve about the same amount of time: twenty-two months for state prisoners and twenty-three months for federal prisoners.[66]

Getting Tough in Detroit

In 1977, Michigan passed a law mandating two years in prison for any gun-related crime. The law precluded either probation or parole and was advertised as "one with a gun gets you two." At the same time, the Wayne County (Detroit) prosecutor announced a new policy prohibiting plea bargaining of gun charges under the new law.

An evaluation by Colin Loftin and David McDowall focused on two questions: Did the law increase the certainty and severity of punishment, and did it lower the crime rate? The key issue in regard to the severity of sentences concerned the effective minimum prison terms; that is, how much time could a convicted offender reasonably expect to do before becoming eligible for release, when reductions for both good time and parole were taken into account? They found "no statistically significant change in the expected minimum sentence" for gun-related murders and armed robberies, but a significant increase in the expected minimum sentences for gun-related assaults.[67]

Two factors—the going rate and the trickle-up phenomenon—explain what happened in Detroit. The expected minimum sentences for murder and robbery did not increase because the going rate for these crimes was already high. Armed robbers in Detroit had been serving prison terms averaging six years before the new law, and few convicted robbers ever got probation. The system was not soft on crime beforehand, and the supposed get-tough law did not change things.

Sentences for assaults increased because the going rate for those offenses had been rather low. Probation and suspended sentences were common, and incarcerated offenders got an average of six months. Much of this seeming leniency stems from the ambiguity of the crime of assault. The nature of the act is often difficult to specify with precision; it may also be difficult to determine who initiated the altercation. Moreover, as we argued in Chapter 3, criminal justice officials routinely treat assaults between people who know each other as essentially private disputes and frequently dismiss the charges or settle the case with a plea to a lesser offense. The new law raised the severity of sentences by eliminating this opportunity for mitigating punishment.

Loftin and McDowall also found that "the gun law did not significantly alter the number or type of violent offenses committed in Detroit." Murder, robbery, and assault did decline, but the decrease in the rate began five months before the law went into effect—long enough in advance to rule out the possibility of the announcement effect that has appeared with other laws toughening criminal penalties.[68]

The impact of mandatory sentences for gun crimes is extremely complex. When McDowall and Loftin (in collaboration with Brian Wiersma) pooled the results from six different studies, they reached somewhat different conclusions.[69] Mandatory sentencing appeared to reduce homicides in all six cities. In Detroit there was a 14 percent reduction, with an average of 5.5 lives saved each month. On the other hand, there were no significant reductions in gun assaults or robberies in any of the sites. The authors characterized the results as a "logical puzzle," conceding that they did not know which features of the sentencing policy were "responsible for the preventive effects." More research is clearly needed, and we should be cautious about simplistic assertions on either side of the debate: that mandatory sentencing deters crime or that it does not work at all.

Evidence from California also suggests that the system is not overly soft on gun-related crimes. Gun-related crimes were 34 percent more likely to be accepted for prosecution at the initial screening than were nongun crimes, and 24 percent more likely to be accepted at the preliminary hearing stage. Gun users were less likely to plead guilty, and 67 percent of the gun wielders who were convicted at trial went to prison, compared with only 33 percent of other offenders. Moreover, the use of a gun added nearly two years (600 days) to the average sentence. Pleading guilty did not help defendants accused of gun crimes. Seventy-four percent of those who pleaded guilty went to prison, compared with 45 percent of all others who copped a plea. And for their plea they got 400 additional days of prison time. These figures hardly paint a picture of a system soft on gun crimes.[70]

In short, the system is and always has been tough on gun-related crimes. "Getting tough," especially through mandatory sentences, will not reduce crime.

PROPOSITION 34
Trying to get tough on gun crimes, especially through mandatory sentences, will not reduce gun-related violence.

CONCLUSION

Gun-related violence is a serious problem in American society. There is no obvious solution, however. Banning guns is an empty gesture, given the number of handguns already in circulation. Trying to keep guns out of the hands of "bad" people also appears to be futile. Nor does it appear that threats of severe punishment will deter or incapacitate offenders in a way that will significantly reduce crime. Policies directed at how people use guns, such as the Bartley-Fox Law or the approach taken in the Kansas City Gun Experiment, might have some positive impact on reducing the number of guns on the street and, as a consequence, gun-related crimes.

NOTES

1. Bureau of Justice Statistics, *Sourcebook of Criminal Justice Statistics—1995* (Washington, D.C.: Government Printing Office, 1996), pp. 337–338.

2. Philip J. Cook and Mark H. Moore, "Gun Control," in James Q. Wilson and Joan Petersilia, eds., *Crime* (San Francisco: ICS Press, 1995), p. 271. The most comprehensive treatment of gun violence and gun control policies is Gary Kleck, *Point Blank: Guns and Violence in America* (New York: Aldine de Gruyter, 1991).

3. Bureau of Justice Statistics, *Sourcebook of Criminal Justice Statistics—1995*, pp. 190, 191.

4. John R. Lott, Jr., Jean Ludwig, and Michael Block, "Concealed-Carry Gun Laws and the Crime Rate," *Journal of Law and Economics* (January 1997).

5. Bureau of Justice Statistics, *Sourcebook of Criminal Justice Statistics—1995*, pp. 188–189.

6. A basic classification scheme is in Bureau of Justice Statistics, *Guns Used in Crime* (Washington, D.C.: Government Printing Office, 1995).

7. Bureau of Justice Statistics, *Sourcebook of Criminal Justice Statistics—1995*, p. 189.

8. Ibid., p. 188.

9. Ibid., p. 189.

10. Bureau of Justice Statistics, *Guns and Crime* (Washington, D.C.: Government Printing Office, 1994).

11. Bureau of the Census, *Statistical Abstract of the United States, 1995* (Washington, D.C.: Government Printing Office, 1996), pp. 99–100.

12. Federal Bureau of Investigation, *Law Enforcement Officers Killed and Assaulted* (Washington, D.C.: Government Printing Office, annual).

13. Joseph F. Sheley and James D. Wright, *In the Line of Fire: Youth, Guns, and Violence in Urban America* (New York: Aldine de Gruyter, 1995).

14. Alfred Blumstein, "Violence by Young People: Why the Deadly Nexus?" *NIJ Journal* (August 1995): 2–9; James Alan Fox, *Trends in Juvenile Violence* (Washington, D.C.: Government Printing Office, 1996).

15. Scott H. Decker, Susan Pennell, and Ami Caldwell, *Illegal Firearms: Access and Use by Arrestees* (Washington, D.C.: Government Printing Office, 1997).

16. James D. Wright, "Ten Essential Observations on Guns in America," *Society* (March/April 1995): 66.

17. Bureau of Justice Statistics, *Handgun Crime Victims* (Washington, D.C.: Government Printing Office, 1990).

18. Gary Kleck and Miriam A. DeLone, "Victim Resistance and Offender Weapon Effects in Robbery," *Journal of Quantitative Criminology* 9(1) (1993): 55–81.

19. A chart indicating the major state laws is found in Bureau of Justice Statistics,

Sourcebook of Criminal Justice Statistics—
1995, p. 120. The best discussion of gun
control laws appears in Kleck, Point Blank.

20. "Report Links Crimes to States with
Weak Gun Controls," New York Times
(April 9, 1997).

21. Mark H. Moore, "Controlling Criminogenic Commodities: Drugs, Guns, and
Alcohol," in James Q. Wilson, ed., Crime
and Public Policy (San Francisco: ICS Press,
1983).

22. Bureau of Justice Statistics, Sourcebook
of Criminal Justice Statistics—1995, p. 193.

23. Ibid., pp. 194–195.

24. James D. Wright, Peter H. Rossi, and
Kathleen Daly, Under the Gun: Weapons,
Crime, and Violence in America (New York:
Aldine de Gruyter, 1983), p. 223.

25. Edward D. Jones, "The District of
Columbia's 'Firearms Control Regulations
Act of 1975': The Toughest Handgun
Control Law in the United States—Or Is
It?" Annals 455 (May 1981): 138–149.

26. Kleck, Point Blank, pp. 408–411.

27. John Kaplan, "The Wisdom of Gun
Prohibition," Annals 455 (May 1981):
11–23.

28. Decker et al., Illegal Firearms.

29. Kleck, Point Blank, pp. 409–410.

30. Ibid., pp. 82–83.

31. Wright et al., Under the Gun, p. 320.

32. Kaplan, "The Wisdom of Gun Prohibition."

33. Robert Sherrill, The Saturday Night
Special (New York: Charterhouse, 1973).

34. "Los Angeles Bans the Sale of Inex-
pensive, Small Guns," New York Times
(September 8, 1996).

35. Kleck, Point Blank, p. 85; see also "Los
Angeles Bans the Sale of Small, Inexpen-
sive Guns."

36. Kleck, Point Blank, pp. 85–86.

37. Bureau of Justice Statistics, Guns Used
in Crime, p. 6.

38. Gary Kleck, "Assault Weapons Aren't
the Problem," New York Times (September
1, 1992); Kleck, Point Blank, pp. 70–82.

39. Office of Juvenile Justice and Delinquency Prevention, Reducing Youth Gun

Violence (Washington, D.C.: Government
Printing Office, 1996), p. 1.

40. "BJS Says Brady Law Thwarts Thousands of Gun Purchases," Law Enforcement
News (March 15, 1997).

41. Mark H. Moore, "Keeping Handguns
from Criminal Offenders," Annals 455
(May 1981): 92–109.

42. James D. Wright, The Armed Criminal
in America (Washington, D.C.: Government Printing Office, 1986); James D.
Wright and Peter H. Rossi, Armed and
Considered Dangerous: A Survey of Felons
and Their Firearms (New York: Aldine
de Gruyter, 1986).

43. Bureau of Justice Statistics, Guns Used
in Crime, p. 4.

44. Wright et al., Under the Gun,
pp. 177–181.

45. "Maine Case Shows Both Sides of '94
Gun Law," New York Times (December
14, 1996).

46. Bureau of Alcohol, Tobacco, and
Firearms, One-Year Progress Report: Brady
Handgun Violence Prevention Act (Washington, D.C.: Government Printing Office,
1996).

47. James D. Wright, "Ten Essential
Observations on Guns in America," Society (March/April 1995): 66. Wright's
article is perhaps the best short summary
of what we know about guns, gun violence, and the likely effectiveness of gun
policies.

48. Ibid.

49. Glenn L. Pierce and William J. Bow-
ers, "The Bartley-Fox Gun Law's Short-
Term Impact on Crime," Annals 455
(May 1981): 120–137.

50. Ibid.

51. Ibid.

52. Committee on Criminal Justice, The
Bartley-Fox Gun Sentencing Study: Final
Report (Boston: Committee on Criminal
Justice, 1991).

53. Bureau of the Census, Statistical Abstract of the United States, 1995, p. 657.

54. Ibid.

55. Bureau of Justice Statistics, Sourcebook
of Criminal Justice Statistics—1995, p. 280;

Bureau of the Census, *Statistical Abstract of the United States, 1995*, p. 151.

56. Bureau of the Census, *Statistical Abstract of the United States, 1995*, p. 156.

57. Lawrence W. Sherman, James W. Shaw, and Dennis P. Rogan, *The Kansas City Gun Experiment* (Washington, D.C.: Government Printing Office, 1995).

58. Herman Goldstein, *Problem-Oriented Policing* (New York: McGraw-Hill, 1990).

59. "Indy Gun-Interdiction Drive Proves an Inviting Target," *Law Enforcement News* (July 20, 1995).

60. John R. Lott, Jr., and David B. Mustard, "Crime, Deterrence, and Right-to-Carry Concealed Handguns," *Journal of Legal Studies* 26 (January 1997): 1–69.

61. Franklin Zimring and Gordon Hawkins, "Concealed Handguns: The Counterfeit Deterrent," *The Responsive Community* 7 (Spring 1997): 58–59.

62. Bureau of Justice Statistics, *National Assessment of Structured Sentencing* (Washington, D.C.: Government Printing Office, 1996), pp. 24–25.

63. William D. Bales and Linda G. Dees, "Mandatory Minimum Sentencing in Florida: Past Trends and Future Implications," *Crime and Delinquency* 38 (July 1992): 309–329.

64. Bureau of Justice Statistics, *Felony Sentences in State Courts, 1994* (Washington, D.C.: Government Printing Office, 1997).

65. Bureau of Justice Statistics, *Sourcebook of Criminal Justice Statistics—1995*, p. 470.

66. Bureau of Justice Statistics, *Weapons Offenses and Offenders*, pp. 5–6.

67. Colin Loftin and David McDowall, "'One with a Gun Gets You Two': Mandatory Sentencing and Firearms Violence in Detroit," *Annals* 455 (May 1981): 150–167.

68. Ibid.

69. David McDowall, Colin Loftin, and Brian Wiersma, "A Comparative Study of the Preventive Effects of Mandatory Sentencing Laws for Gun Crimes," *Journal of Criminal Law and Criminology* 83(2) (1992): 378–394.

70. Alan Lizotte and Marjorie S. Zatz, "The Use and Abuse of Sentence Enhancement for Firearms Offenses in California," *Law and Contemporary Problems* 49 (1986): 199–221.

PART IV

Reform:
The Liberal Prescription

Liberals take a very different approach to crime policy than do conservatives. As we indicated in Chapter 1, liberals are much more optimistic about the capacity to change both people and society in ways that would reduce crime. In the two chapters that follow, we will take a close look at the two most important components of liberal crime policy. Chapter 11 examines both the concept of rehabilitation and specific programs designed to change criminal offenders into law-abiding citizens. Chapter 12 looks at potential reforms in the criminal law and the criminal justice system that might reduce the incidence of criminality.

1 1

Treat 'Em!

REHABILITATING CRIMINALS

The Philosophy of Rehabilitation

The concept of rehabilitation is the cornerstone of traditional liberal crime control policy. Although the rhetoric has changed over the years, the basic idea remains the same: reduce crime by treating criminals and "correcting" their behavior. The terminology used by state agencies reflects the continued commitment to rehabilitation. We have departments of "corrections" but no departments of "punishment." Why do we use this terminology? Charles Logan and Gerald Gaes explain that the term *corrections* embraces "the language of medicine, psychology, and education" and that this reflects an effort to acquire "some of the perceived legitimacy and prestige of those other professions."[1]

What exactly is rehabilitation? The National Academy of Sciences defines it as "any planned intervention that reduces an offender's further criminal activity."[2] The key words here are *planned* and *intervention*. As Wolfgang's career criminal research indicates (see Chapter 4), most lawbreakers stop sooner or later. It is well established that criminal activity peaks between the ages of fourteen and twenty-four and then declines sharply. Aging is the best crime reduction policy we know about.[3] The goal of rehabilitation is to make offenders stop sooner rather than later through a program of planned intervention.

The principal strategy for rehabilitating offenders is to reintegrate them into the community. Prisons offer programs designed to facilitate this process:

academic and vocational education program, drug and alcohol counseling, and so on. Advocates of rehabilitation have traditionally preferred community-based correctional programs, primarily probation and parole, on the grounds that they are more likely to reintegrate offenders into law-abiding lives than is institutional confinement.

Our goal in this chapter is to try to identify correctional treatment programs that are relatively more effective than others and that if adopted would help reduce crime.

Political Controversy: The Willie Horton Furlough

The 1988 presidential election campaign dramatized the political controversy over rehabilitation. Republican candidate George Bush ran a television ad about a convicted murderer, Willie Horton, who had been released from prison into the community on a weekend furlough during which he raped a woman. Bush used the incident to attack his opponent, Michael Dukakis, as a liberal Democrat who was soft on crime. The fact that Horton was black and the rape victim a white woman injected a divisive racial element into the election campaign.[4]

Furloughs are a classic type of rehabilitation program, designed to reintegrate a prisoner into the community through gradual release. They have been used for many years and are very common. A 1990 survey found them operating in forty-four states, the federal system, and the District of Columbia. Florida alone granted furloughs to 96,745 inmates. Oklahoma had the second largest program, with 23,031 participants. Furlough programs appear to be quite successful. Only 31 of the 96,745 Florida offenders "failed." In Illinois all of the 13,785 participants successfully completed the program. Connecticut had the highest failure rate, but even there only 29 of 3,398 inmates furloughed were arrested for a new crime. In Massachusetts, scene of the Willie Horton incident, none of the 438 furloughed inmates was rearrested while on release.[5]

The Willie Horton story is a classic example of the celebrated case in the top layer of our criminal justice wedding cake. As David C. Anderson observes in his thoughtful review of the case, exaggerating its significance and treating it as typical of general patterns is a "gross insult to truth."[6]

The case does dramatize the political controversy over rehabilitation. Liberals believe that furloughs are an effective program for reintegrating offenders into the community and reducing crime. Conservatives believe that they are a soft-hearted and misguided method of turning dangerous people loose on the community.

THE "NOTHING WORKS" CONTROVERSY

For almost twenty-five years, discussions of rehabilitation have been dominated by the Martinson report. Criminologist Robert Martinson published an article in 1974 concluding that "with few and isolated exceptions, the rehabilitative efforts that have been reported so far have had no appreciable effect on rehabilitation."[7] His original article was titled "What Works?" but many people interpreted it to mean "nothing works." Martinson did not actually say nothing works; in fact, he found positive outcomes in 48 percent of the programs he cited. A few years later he unequivocally stated that "some treatment programs do have an appreciable effect on recidivism," adding, "The critical fact seems to be the conditions under which the program is delivered."[8]

The Martinson report is a classic example of how social science research is often misinterpreted in the political arena. Many people wanted to believe that "nothing works" because they were disillusioned with rehabilitation. They were angry over (by then) ten years of soaring crime rates. Conservatives blamed rehabilitation programs for being soft on crime, whereas liberals attacked the same programs for violating standards of due process. The disillusionment with rehabilitation was part of a more general conservative mood in the mid-1970s.[9]

The story of Martinson's report is fascinating in itself. His team reviewed all evaluations of correctional programs published in English between 1945 and 1967. They were able to find only 231 that were acceptable by rigorous scientific standards. They rejected most evaluations because they used unreliable measures, failed to specify the "treatment," did not use proper control groups, or drew questionable conclusions from the data.[10] Martinson exposed the correctional community's failure to develop a systematic process of evaluation. Programs routinely claimed "success" without any legitimate basis for doing so. The academic community shared much of the responsibility, as formal evaluations were done either by researchers under contract or by in-house professionals with academic training. Martinson disclosed a scandalous case of professional irresponsibility. Because his findings were so threatening, the state of New York did not release the report and even denied Martinson permission to publish it. He sued and eventually forced the report's release.

Was Martinson Right?

Was Martinson's assessment of correctional programs accurate? The National Academy of Sciences' Panel on Research on Rehabilitative Techniques reexamined his work and concluded that he was "essentially correct."[11] It supported his view that there was little evidence "to allay the current pessimism about the effectiveness of institutional rehabilitation programs as they now exist."

The debate sparked by Martinson continues to rage. Some, including Logan and Gaes, agree with Martinson that no convincing evidence exists regarding the effectiveness of correctional treatment.[12] Others, such as Daniel Glaser, believe that there is enough evidence of success to justify continued support for rehabilitation-oriented programs.[13]

How can we sort our way through this debate? As a first step, it is important to recognize, as Logan and Gaes point out, that the debate is as much ideological as it is empirical. Some advocates of rehabilitation regard it as a morally superior social policy regardless of the evidence about its success. Logan and Gaes, on the other hand, regard punishment as a morally legitimate social policy. "Legal punishment," they argue, is a legitimate and . . . even a noble aspect of our culture."[14] No empirical evidence is going to resolve this aspect of the debate. It is a question of what values should underlie social policies.

Criminologists, meanwhile, continue to argue over the empirical evidence on the effectiveness of correctional treatment. In defense of rehabilitation, Glaser states that "certain sentencing and correctional policies, which differ according to the criminalization of the offender, are more likely than their alternatives to reduce recidivism rates."[15] That is essentially what Martinson concluded over twenty years ago, but it glosses over some basic problems.

The Prediction Problem Revisited

Glaser's defense of rehabilitation assumes a good match between offender and treatment program. Some programs are effective for some offenders. Achieving this match, however, is more easily said than done, and the heart of the problem is our old friend the prediction problem. Sentencing a convicted offender to a community-based drug treatment program, for example, represents a prediction that he or she (1) is not a serious danger to the community (and therefore does not need to go to prison) and (2) will respond positively to the drug treatment. Drawing on the work of John Hagan, Glaser argues that some individuals are more deeply "embedded in crime" than others.[16] Those who are less deeply embedded are more "amenable" to community-based treatment.

So far, so good. The crucial question is whether judges and correctional officials can correctly identify the more "amenable" offenders and sentence them to the right treatment program. This task runs headlong into the prediction problem. We have already criticized conservative programs because of their failure to accurately predict which offenders are the really high-risk ones. As we examine probation, boot camps, and other rehabilitation-oriented programs in this chapter, the important question is whether they are any more successful in predicting behavior.

THE REVIVAL OF
CORRECTIONAL INTERVENTION?

Ted Palmer, a vigorous advocate of rehabilitation, argues that reports of its death are exaggerated and that correctional intervention revived in the 1980s. Palmer is a voice to be reckoned with. A senior researcher with the California Youth Authority, he has had considerable experience with evaluation research and has been Martinson's most effective critic. His argument deserves careful scrutiny for what it says about recent trends.[17]

Palmer primarily refers to the so-called "new intermediate punishments," including intensive probation supervision (IPS), home confinement (HC), electronic monitoring (EM), boot camps (BC), and shock incarceration (SI). These are designed to provide sentences that Norval Morris and Michael Tonry describe as being between prison and conventional probation.[18]

Do the new intermediate punishments represent a revival of rehabilitation? Palmer's own choice of words raises some doubts. He uses the term *correctional intervention* instead of *rehabilitation*. The difference is more than a matter of semantics. As we shall see later in this chapter, the new intermediate punishments emphasize surveillance and control of offenders, often with little emphasis on traditional treatment components. In short, they are more punishment than rehabilitation oriented. This reflects the extent to which recent developments in corrections have been completely dominated by the conservative crime control agenda.

Now let us examine some of the major rehabilitation programs. Probation and parole are very old and established programs; they have been joined by such new programs as electronic monitoring and boot camps. The important point is to keep our eyes fixed on the bottom-line question: Is a particular program effective in reducing serious crime?

DIVERSION

Diversion was one of the great reforms of the 1960s. The President's Crime Commission endorsed it in 1967, and an estimated 1,200 separate diversion programs were established during the 1970s.[19] Although diversion programs take many forms, they have a common goal of getting the individual out of the criminal justice system as early as possible.

Diversion was not new in the 1960s. Historically, a great many offenders have been diverted from the criminal justice system at an early stage. Police officers routinely exercise their discretion not to arrest, even when they have probable cause. Prosecutors dismiss cases when prosecution would not serve the "interests of justice." We can call these traditional practices the "old" diversion. The "new" diversion programs that appeared in the 1960s are characterized by officially stated goals, a professional staff, and treatment services.[20]

Diversion programs are designed to rehabilitate offenders (and thereby reduce crime) in two ways. First, they keep people accused of relatively minor offenses out of jails and prisons. This reflects the labeling perspective in criminological theory that holds that processing by the criminal justice system (and imprisonment in particular) accentuates the tendency toward criminal behavior. The President's Crime Commission summed up the rehabilitative goals of all community-based corrections, including diversion: "Institutions tend to isolate offenders from society, both physically and psychologically, cutting them off from schools, jobs, families, and other supportive influences and increasing the probability that the label criminal will be indelibly impressed upon them."[21] As the Wolfgang cohort data suggest, most juveniles "mature out of" criminal behavior. Diversion argues that the best approach is to intervene as little as possible.

Second, diversion programs are designed to provide social services that address the offender's real problems: drug or alcohol treatment, employment counseling, and so forth. Arrest may only aggravate those problems and overburden criminal justice agencies.

Finally, diversion programs are intended to reduce the costs of the criminal justice system. Probation is far less expensive than imprisonment.

In short, diversion promised the best of all possible worlds—more effective, more humane, and cheaper. An old adage says that if something seems too good to be true, it probably is. Let us take a look at diversion in practice.

The Manhattan Court Employment Project

The earliest and most influential diversion program was the Manhattan Court Employment Project. Sponsored by the Vera Institute, the project provided employment services to arrested persons. The basic assumption was that because unemployment is a major cause of crime, facilitating employment will reduce subsequent criminal activity.

Each day staff members of the Court Employment Project reviewed the arrest docket and identified defendants who met the program's criteria: a resident of New York City, between the ages of sixteen and forty-five, unemployed or earning less than $125 a week, and charged with a felony other than homicide, rape, kidnapping, or arson. In addition, the defendant must have not had prior jail or prison experience of one year or longer. With the prosecutor's consent, the case was suspended for ninety days, while the defendant received counseling, assistance in obtaining any short-term public assistance for which he or she might have been eligible, and referral to a job opening with one of the 400 cooperating employers. Charges were dropped completely if the defendant "succeeded" by keeping a job. If the person "failed" to secure employment, the case was prosecuted.

An early evaluation declared the Manhattan Court Employment Project a huge success. In its first three years the project accepted 1,300 clients, about half of whom (48.2 percent) succeeded. About 70 percent of these 626 people had been unemployed at the time of arrest. Fourteen months later, about 80 percent of those who could be located were still employed. Only 15.8 percent of these successful clients committed another crime in the twelve months following their release from the program. This recidivism rate was half of that for both offenders who failed in the program and a control group. The program cost only $731 per client, or $1,518 per success.[22]

A subsequent evaluation, however, reached very different conclusions. According to this report, the project did not reduce recidivism and had no discernible effect on the employment record or the behavior of its clients. Moreover, it did not reduce pretrial detention time or lower the number of convictions. A major problem was that about half of the clients served by the program would not have been prosecuted at all if there had been no court employment project.[23] This is a classic example of "net widening." Because this phenomenon affects so many well-intentioned reforms, we need to discuss it in detail.

The Net-Widening Problem

Net widening is the process by which more people are brought under some form of social control. The unwritten law of net widening is that less punitive alternatives tend to be applied to people who would otherwise not be under any social control at all: that is, they would not be arrested, prosecuted, or incarcerated.

Evaluations of early diversion programs found substantial net widening. More than half of the juveniles referred to fifteen diversion projects in California would not have entered any kind of program under traditional practice. Thomas G. Blomberg found in his review of juvenile diversion programs that they produced a 32 percent increase in the total number of juveniles under some form of control. Other evaluations have found varying degrees of expansion but an expanding net nonetheless.[24]

The dynamics of net widening are easy to understand. Officials continue to use the severe sanctions (for example, prison) for offenders they regard as really dangerous and the new less punitive program for less serious offenders. Thus, instead of offenders being diverted out of the system, new additional people are diverted in. A prosecutor, for example, worries about the public reaction if someone placed in a pretrial diversion program commits a serious crime. Additionally, if you place only the low-risk offenders in the program, the chance of a high "success" rate increases. The problem, of course, is that most of those low-risk offenders would have succeeded without the benefit of the program. In this regard, it is important to remember the purpose of our inquiry here: can we find a program that is relatively more effective in reducing crime than what we normally do?

The net-widening phenomenon suggests that the old diversion did a better job of achieving the basic goal of keeping people out of the system. When a police officer does not make an arrest, that person is truly diverted; when a prosecutor dismisses all charges, that defendant is genuinely diverted. Because many innovative programs bring more people under some form of control, some experts argue that reform always backfires.[25]

Does Diversion Rehabilitate?

The most important question for us is whether diversion effectively rehabilitates. Does it in fact "treat" the offender in a way that reduces future criminal activity? A number of evaluations have found that they do not. The Law Enforcement Assistance Administration (LEAA) touted the Des Moines (Iowa) Adult Diversion Project as an "exemplary project" that other communities should adopt. An evaluation, however, found that it had "little impact in reducing recidivism among diverted, compared to non-diverted offenders." In another program, diverted offenders had lower recidivism rates than did juveniles sent to juvenile court but, alas, had higher recidivism rates than did kids released outright without the benefit of any "treatment."[26] More recent reviews have found similarly disappointing results.

Diversion programs suffer from a number of recurring problems. The nature of the "treatment" can be vague and unspecific. Many do not actually deliver the services they claim to deliver. The early intensive probation supervision programs, for example, did not achieve a high rate of contacts between probationers and probation officers.[27] Questions also arise about the content and the impact of treatment services. Are the drug and alcohol treatment components of diversion programs effective in reducing substance abuse? How many of the offenders who succeed would have done so on their own, without the benefit of the treatment?

Additionally, if a diversion program expands the net, the promised cost savings will not result. Finally, diversion programs introduce serious due process considerations. A person who agrees to enter a treatment program in the expectation of having criminal charges dropped is, in effect, admitting guilt. Rather than contest the charge, the person is saying, "Yes, I have done something wrong, and you have a right to force me to undergo treatment." By offering a seemingly more attractive alternative to prosecution and possible incarceration, the program coerces this tacit admission of guilt in a subtle but powerful way. In addition, the selection of the program's clients may be unfair.[28]

In the end, diversion offers a false promise. It fails to achieve its own goals, may well contradict them, and does not offer a realistic solution to the problem of serious crime. For the most part, diversion is not used for persons charged with robbery or burglary. Nor is there persuasive evidence that it rehabilitates lesser offenders in a way that keeps them from becoming serious offenders.

PROPOSITION 35

Diversion programs do not reduce serious crime.

PROBATION

Probation is the most widely used rehabilitation program in the entire criminal justice system. By the end of 1994, 2.9 million adults were on probation in the United States, more than twice as many as in 1982.[29] About 25 percent of all convicted felons are sentenced to "straight probation," and another 27 percent receive split sentences, with a jail term followed by probation. Thus, over half of all convicted felons serve some time on probation.[30]

Probation embodies the philosophy of rehabilitation because it keeps convicted offenders in the community rather than sending them to prison. The "treatment" generally consists of some form of supervision and restrictions on behavior: reporting to a probation officer, drug or alcohol counseling, employment or evidence of seeking a job, and limitations on travel.

Probation serves a number of different purposes. From the perspective of making the punishment fit the crime, it is an appropriate sentence for someone who has committed a relatively less serious offense. It is also far cheaper than imprisonment—about $600 a year, compared with $17,000 to $20,000. Finally, we use probation as a matter of necessity. We simply could not afford to imprison all convicted felons even if we wanted to.

The Effectiveness of Probation

Does probation work? Is it effective in rehabilitating offenders and reducing crime? This question prompts much dispute. The Rand study of felons on probation in California found a failure rate of 65 percent; studies of other programs, however, have found failure rates as low as 12 percent (which is to say, an 88 percent success rate).[31] Where does the truth lie?

A Justice Department study of felons on probation during the 1980s found that after three years, almost half (46 percent) of all convicted felons on probation are either sent to prison or jail or have absconded (Figure 11.1). Only 38 percent completely "succeed," with neither a felony arrest nor a disciplinary hearing.[32] On the positive side, about half of the probationers succeeded, in the sense of not being sent to prison or jail or absconding; 38 percent were complete successes in that they had neither a felony arrest nor a probation disciplinary hearing after three years.

The Rand study of felons on probation in California found worse results. After forty months, 65 percent of the California probationers had been rearrested, and 51 percent were reconvicted. Moreover, one-third of those reconvicted (18 percent of the original sample) were reconvicted of a serious violent crime. Nor do they wait very long to fail. Those reconvicted of a violent crime take an average of only eight months to recidivate. Those reconvicted of property offenses take an average of only five months.[33]

The different failure rates are due in part to variations across jurisdictions. Using the same methodology as that in the California study, Gennaro Vito found a failure rate of only 22 percent among Kentucky probationers.[34] Much depends on the kind of offenders sentenced to probation, whether they are high or low risk, and the nature of the probation program. This highlights the problem of matching offenders and programs.

It is important to place probation failure rates in perspective, however. Although the failure rates for particular cohorts are high, people on probation (or parole) account for only a small proportion of all serious crime. Using data from New Orleans, Michael R. Geerken and Hennessey D. Hayes estimate that people on probation account for only 8 percent of all arrests for burglary or armed robbery; persons on parole account for only 1 to 2 percent of adult arrests for these crimes. Eliminating probation and parole, they conclude, would have only a minimal effect on the overall crime rate.[35]

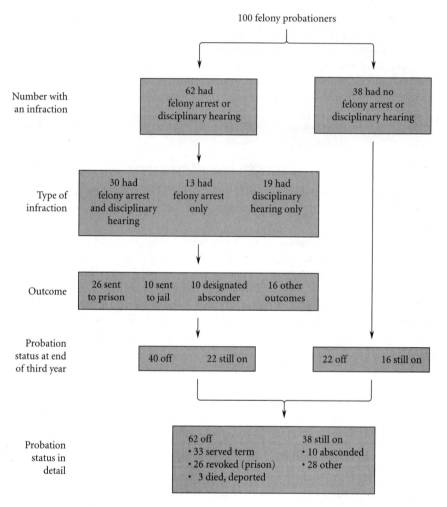

FIGURE 11.1 A hundred felons tracked
through their first three years of probation.

SOURCE: Bureau of Justice Statistics, *Recidivism of Felons on Probation, 1986–1989*
(Washington, D.C.: Government Printing Office, 1992).

The Geerken and Hayes argument, however, is not the whole story with respect to the effectiveness of community-based treatment programs. These researchers studied arrests for people on probation or parole at the time of their arrest, not taking into account those individuals who completed probation, for example, and were subsequently arrested for another crime. Probation failed in the sense that these people resumed criminal activity.

The relevant question with respect to probation is, What accounts for the success of those people who do not recidivate? Our goal is to identify the ingredients of success so that we can replicate them with larger groups of offenders. Is it the "treatment," or would successful probationers have ended their lawbreaking on their own? Are there ways to make probation more effective? We do not have good evidence to address these questions. As Todd Clear and Anthony Braga point out, evaluation research has tended to focus on special forms such as intensive probation and house arrest, and as a result we do not know much about the effectiveness of conventional probation.[36]

Many experts have serious doubts about the content of the treatment provided by traditional probation. The level of supervision has always been very minimal, involving a meeting with a probation officer (PO) once a month. The PO fills out the required reports, and that is that. Joan Petersilia found that offenders on regular probation in Los Angeles County met with their POs only once a month. Another report indicated that because of caseloads that exceeded a thousand probationers, POs in Los Angeles spent an average of one hour and forty-seven minutes *per year* with each offender.[37]

Many experts believe that probation treatment has minimal impact on offenders. Most would probably rehabilitate themselves through the process of maturing, finding a job, getting married, and so on. John Hagan, drawing on the work of Mark Granovetter and others, argues that whether a person becomes law-abiding or continues in a life of criminal activity depends on the extent to which he or she is "socially embedded" in legitimate or criminal opportunities. Some individuals have more contacts—for example, with family or people in the neighborhoods—that lead to jobs. These contacts, moreover, tend to multiply: a job results in additional contacts that lead to other and often better job opportunities. Such individuals are socially embedded in networks that lead to law-abiding lives, even when they had engaged in some initial criminal activity. This is particularly true of many white youths from blue-collar backgrounds. Other people, by contrast, have few of these positive networks. They are embedded in social circumstances that includes few contacts with people can refer them to jobs and more contacts with people are engaged in criminal activity. This is particularly true of many racial and ethnic minority youths who live in economically devastated areas where there are few jobs and relatively few people with contacts that lead to jobs.[38]

In either case, whether a person placed on probation desists or continues in criminal activity has less to do with the treatment than the social circumstances in which he or she is "embedded."

The level of probation supervision has gotten even worse because of the increase in caseloads in recent years. The total number of people on probation tripled between 1979 and 1992, from 1 to 2.9 million. The average monthly caseloads for each PO in 1994 were as high as 294 in Rhode Island, 211 in Georgia, and 135 in Illinois. California reported an astounding average of 400 per probation officer (and perhaps as high as 1,000 in Los Angeles). Among the lowest were sixty-eight in Tennessee and sixty in Arizona.[39]

PROPOSITION 36

Probation is an appropriate sentence for many offenders. Increased use of probation, however, is not likely to reduce serious crime.

Can the effectiveness of probation be improved? The traditional means of improving probation has been through intensive supervision. It is one of several so-called "new intermediate punishments," and it is often linked with other programs such as house arrest. Let us take a look at these new programs.

THE NEW INTERMEDIATE PUNISHMENTS

Intensive probation supervision is only one of several new programs referred to as the new intermediate punishments.[40] The four major programs are intensive probation supervision (IPS), home confinement (HC) or house arrest, electronic monitoring (EM), and boot camps (BC) or shock incarceration (SI).

These programs often overlap. Home confinement may also involve IPS.[41] In addition, the curfew may be enforced through electronic monitoring (EM). Thus, one offender may be on an IPS program without a curfew, while another is on IPS, with home arrest, and under electronic monitoring. Shock incarceration is really a split sentence in which the judge sentences the offender to a short term in prison or jail followed by a period of supervised probation. The short jail or prison term may involve a boot camp with military-style drill and intense physical exercise. The follow-up probation (or aftercare) may involve IPS, HC, and/or EM.

Intensive Probation Supervision

In 1992, there were 52,569 probationers under IPS, with 9,353 under electronic monitoring (these figures do not include California, however, and the actual total is undoubtedly far higher).[43]

Although often presented as a great innovation, IPS is not really new. A number of IPS (and intensive parole supervision) programs were developed in the 1960s. One of the most important was the San Francisco Project, conducted by the federal probation system. Probationers were randomly assigned to probation officers with caseloads of various sizes. Two IPS groups involved caseloads of only twenty probationers; two other groups had caseloads of forty, and another group had caseloads of several hundred clients. All other offenders were assigned to groups with normal levels of supervision, meaning that probation officers had between 70 and 130 clients.[44]

An evaluation of the program found no significant difference in the recidivism rates of offenders in the various groups. Intensive supervision did not consistently reduce the failure rate. One significant *programmatic* effect did occur, however. In the IPS groups, probation officers were more likely to cite probationers for technical violations of the conditions of probation (travel restrictions, use of alcohol, and so forth). In other words, the IPS program induced changes in the behavior of probation officers rather than of the clients.

Several problems affected the early IPS programs. Many failed to achieve the intended high rate of contacts between POs and offenders. Even more serious, the basic assumption underlying intensive supervision were flawed. The basic assumption of these early IPS programs was that the "intensity" of supervision is determined entirely by caseload size and the frequency of contact.[45] It is possible, however, that mere contact has little impact on a probationer's behavior and that increasing the number of contacts makes no difference. (In many respects, this is similar to the flawed assumptions underlying police patrol that we examined in Chapter 5: that routine patrol deters crime and, therefore, that more patrol will deter crime more effectively.)

The new IPS programs attempt to overcome some of the problems associated with the early programs. They have smaller caseloads (between nineteen and forty in three California programs) and include a much wider range of restrictions on offenders' behavior. Contacts are very frequent. One survey found that 32 percent of all IPS programs involve five to fourteen contacts per month, whereas another 38 percent involve fifteen to twenty-four contacts. Twenty-four contacts per month is almost one every day. In an experimental Los Angeles IPS program, the highest-risk clients received three to five face-to-face contacts and two telephone checks *per week*. IPS probationers are often subject to home confinement (82 percent of all programs), mandatory drug tests (76 percent), alcohol tests (74 percent), and electronic monitoring (56 percent).[46]

Are the new IPS programs effective? That is, are they more effective than traditional probation? Joan Petersilia found the results in three California programs "particularly discouraging." After one year, about 35 percent of the IPS probationers had been rearrested, another 40 percent committed technical violations of probation conditions, and only 25 percent had no violations of any sort. Admittedly, the offenders assigned to these IPS programs were "high risk," but a 75 percent failure rate after only one year is a very poor showing. Perhaps even more significant, their rearrest rates were no different from those of other probationers. This outcome suggests that the intense supervision did not stop them from committing crime. The IPS probationers did have much higher rates of technical violations. This result is hardly surprising, because that is what frequent contacts and drugs tests are designed to detect.[47]

Why do IPS programs appear to be no more successful than regular probation in reducing recidivism? The answer may be that no form of probation supervision—intensive or minimal—has any real impact on offenders' behavior. The "treatment" may not address the real problems that offenders have. Our position is as follows:

PROPOSITION 37
Intensive probation supervision is not likely to reduce serious crime.

IPS suffers from both confused goals and exaggerated promises. Its advocates claim it will rehabilitate offenders and keep them under control and reduce prison overcrowding and save money—all at the same time. As some critics point out, if all this were true, IPS would be "the wonderchild of the criminal justice system."[48] Yet, as many observers have pointed out, current

IPS programs emphasize surveillance and control rather than rehabilitation. A Justice Department report on *Performance Measures for the Criminal Justice System* argues that if the goal is surveillance and control, then a high failure rate is a positive indicator of the program's performance: offenders who violate the terms of probation or commit another crime are taken off the streets and sent to prison.[49]

Many IPS programs do not necessarily serve the clients for whom they were designed. Although generally intended for "high-risk" offenders, only 20 percent of the clients in the Georgia and New Jersey programs fit that definition. Georgia officials privately conceded that 25 percent of the IPS clients were not "true" diversions from prison. There were also rumors that New Jersey judges sentenced some offenders to prison only to make them eligible for "diversion" through IPS.[50]

The very intensity of the supervision in IPS programs has introduced an entirely new problem. Joan Petersilia reports that one-third of those offenders eligible for intensive probation in Marion County, Oregon, chose to go to prison. In New Jersey, 15 percent of those who applied for IPS withdrew their applications when they found out what IPS would be like.[51]

It is easy to see why offenders choose prison. The Oregon IPS program included home visits two or three times a week, with telephone checks on other days, unannounced searches for drugs, and periodic urine tests for drug use. Offenders were required to perform community service work and were forbidden to associate with certain people. This would last for two *years*. The alternative was a two- to four-year prison sentence that usually resulted in three to six *months* of actual time served, followed by two years of routine parole supervision, which meant only one visit per month and none of the other IPS requirements. The IPS program was far more intrusive and punitive than prison and parole.[52]

Home Confinement and Electronic Monitoring

Home confinement (HC) and electronic monitoring (EM) are designed to keep the offender in the community but under a fairly strict form of surveillance and control. HC is essentially a curfew. In some cases, the curfew is enforced through EM; in others, it is not. Critics have pointed out that both HC and EM have the same mixture of goals as does IPS. They are designed to simultaneously reduce prison overcrowding, and both control and rehabilitate the offender.

The current interest in electronic monitoring began in 1983 when Judge Jack Love of Albuquerque adopted the Gosslink system for a convicted offender. The idea quickly caught on. By 1992, there were 9,353 probationers and 2,764 parolees in EM programs.[53] An early report by the Rand Corporation gave electronic monitoring a cautiously favorable assessment. It was far cheaper than imprisonment: as low as $1,350 per year, versus $20,000 for prison. Basically two different EM technologies are available. Passive monitoring radio frequency (RF) systems place a transmitter on the offender (a tamperproof bracelet or anklet) and a dialer on the telephone. If the probationer leaves the premises, the signal is interrupted, and the dialer automatically calls the probation office. Active monitoring programmed contact (PC) systems involve periodic, usually random telephone calls to the probationer's home. The calling may be done automatically by machine or by the PO's personal phone call.

Initially, the largest group of offenders in EM programs were those convicted of major traffic offenses. By 1989, property offenders and drug offenders had become the two largest categories. This suggests that, as the program has grown, judges have felt more confident about committing different kinds of offenders to it. Sentences generally ran from 60 to 120 days. A Justice Department survey found that most failures occurred within the first two months. About 4 percent of the total sample committed a new offense, and half of those occurred in the first sixty days. About 22 percent of the sample committed a technical violation of the terms of their confinement.[54]

Many people initially opposed EM because it conjured up images of the famous novel *1984*, with Big Brother continuously monitoring everyone's private behavior. In actual practice, EM may not deliver on its promises. Gary Marx argues persuasively that it is advertised as another technological fix for the crime problem. It is the proverbial free lunch or "painless dentistry." EM systems have run into serious technical problems. Certain kinds of housing construction, for example, can disrupt the signal. Random calls in the middle of the night not only disrupt the probationer's sleep (not such a good idea if we want that person to hold a steady job) but also require that a staff person be on duty to respond to a violation.

Additionally, EM programs produce relatively small cost savings for the criminal justice system. The 12,000 offenders in EM programs in 1992 (probation and parole combined) represented a minuscule fraction of the 4.8 million under correctional supervision that year.[55]

The intensive surveillance that EM (and IPS) provides create additional problems. It is designed to detect failures, and it succeeds in doing so. More offenders are cited for technical violations than for new criminal acts, and many of them are sent to prison. As the report *Performance Measures for the Criminal Justice System* points out, disagreement persists over whether a high rate of technical violations is an indicator of success or failure. If the purpose of EM is to control offenders and detect misbehavior, then it is an indicator of success. If the purpose is to reintegrate the offender into the community, then it suggests failure.[56]

Most important for our purposes, evaluations indicate that offenders under IPS, HA, and EM have the same rearrest rate as those on regular probation. In short, they are no more effective in reducing crime than conventional prison or probation programs.

The question of effectiveness is complicated by the issue of the high rate of technical violations, however. If we assume that a technical violation of probation (for example, violation of curfew) is a predictor of more serious failures, such as committing another crime, then sending the offender back to prison for that technical violation does reduce crime. If the intermediate punishments succeed in this respect, however, it is important to see them as incapacitation rather than rehabilitation programs. In other words, we should discuss them in Chapter 7 rather than in this chapter. This still leaves us searching for an effective rehabilitation program.

Boot Camps

Boot camps are another popular innovation. By 1995, seventy-five boot camps were running in thirty-five states. The previous year they worked with a total of 11,691 offenders who served an average of 4.5 months.[57]

What exactly is a boot camp? Boot camps generally involve a short period of incarceration for first-time offenders, with program of rigorous physical, educational, and substance abuse programs, followed by intensive supervision. According to Doris MacKenzie and her colleagues, the "core components" of boot camps are "military drill and ceremony, hard labor, physical training, and strict rules and discipline."[58] Because of the short incarceration periods, boot camps are often described as shock incarceration (SI). Like the other intermediate punishments, boot camps have multiple and often conflicting goals. They are simultaneously intended to rehabilitate, punish, control, and reduce prison overcrowding.

The basic idea underlying boot camps is not entirely new. Judges have routinely given split sentences, with short periods of incarceration followed by probation. The new boot camps are distinguished from previous practices by virtue of the military rhetoric and imagery and the intensive probation supervision that usually follows release.

Boot camp programs vary considerably in terms of how participants are selected, the content of the boot camp program, and the nature of the post-release supervision. In some states, judges sentence offenders directly to boot camp; in others, correctional officials select participants. In some states, boot camp participation is voluntary; in others, it is mandatory for those sentenced to them. Offenders in some states can voluntarily drop out of the boot camp and return to prison.[59]

With respect to the content of the boot camp programs, Doris Mackenzie and her colleagues found that one of the greatest differences between the boot camps in eight states was "the amount of time in the daily schedule that is devoted to work, drill, and physical training versus such treatment-type activities as counseling, drug treatment, or academic education."[60] Some boot camps are almost entirely military-style programs, whereas others put much more emphasis on traditional rehabilitative programs.

Do boot camps work? Do their graduates commit fewer crimes than comparable offenders who are sentenced to regular probation or prison? MacKenzie and her colleagues found no consistent patterns regarding the behavior of boot camp graduates and comparable offenders in the eight states they studied. In four states, offenders who completed boot camp had lower arrest rates; in three, no differences were noted in arrest rates; and in one state, boot camp graduates tended to have higher arrest rates.[61] No consistent pattern was also apparent for revocation for program violations across the eight states.

Some important differences in the outcomes in four of the states were discerned, however. Georgia boot camp graduates had worse recidivism rates than did offenders in other states. Significantly, the Georgia program had "little treatment in the daily schedule of activities," put most of the emphasis on military drill, and released most to traditional probation. The programs in Illinois, Louisiana, and New York, on the other hand, devoted a relatively large amount of time each day (three hours or more) to treatment-oriented activities.[62]

Boot camps pose a number of problems. Some critics argue that the emphasis on military drill may be fundamentally misguided. Yelling at inmates, treating them with disrespect, and forcing them to undergo painful physical exercises may be counterproductive, teaching inmates that disrespect and verbal abuse are the keys to success in life. Such programs also value the most aggressive definition of masculinity. Finally, the legendary rigors of Marine boot camp at least offers a reward at the end: entry into the proud fellowship of the Corps. If prison boot camps offer nothing of comparable positive value at the end but only a return to the same neighborhood with the same bleak prospects (what Hagan refers to as a life socially embedded in crime), they are not likely to have a long-term positive impact on the people who pass through them.[63]

The nature of boot camps appears to be changing, however. In some states the purely militaristic aspects have been deemphasized, and more time and program effort given to traditional rehabilitation–oriented components such as substance abuse treatment. In short, a "second generation" of boot camps may be developing.[64]

Also, because they serve such a small number of offenders, boot camps are not likely to have much of an impact on prison overcrowding or prison costs. Moreover, if they result in net widening, with offenders being sentenced to expensive boot camps rather than the less expensive traditional probation, no cost savings will be achieved.

In the end, what can we say about the new intermediate punishments? First, they do not appear to be terribly effective. Second, they are not completely new but often old ideas in new dress. And third, they contain little in the way of substantive rehabilitation programs. This leads us to the following proposition:

PROPOSITION 38
Intensive probation, electronic monitoring, boot camps, and other recent innovations will not reduce crime.

PAROLE

Parole is the second most prevalent rehabilitation program. Most offenders sent to prison are released early under some form of supervision. Parole is seen as a rehabilitation program because, like probation, it seeks to reintegrate the offender into the community.

In 1992, there were 658,601 adults on parole, three times as many as in 1980. The use of parole has been declining. The percentage of all prisoners released through discretionary parole fell from 71.9 percent in 1977 to only 47.5 percent in 1992.[65] This is mainly a result of the abolition of discretionary parole release in eleven states and the federal system.[66]

Parole has historically been the unloved child of the criminal justice system. Everyone seems to criticize it. Conservatives argue that it turns dangerous offenders loose on society. Liberals, meanwhile, argue that parole release decisions are made without any scientific foundation, and the result is arbitrary and often discriminatory patterns in release.[67]

Despite these criticisms, however, parole has demonstrated a remarkable capacity to survive. It serves a number of purposes unrelated to rehabilitation: it offers prisoners an incentive to behave in prison, gives prison officials some power to control them, and serves as a safety valve for prison overcrowding.

Does Parole Work?

Do prisoners who are released on parole have lower recidivism rates than those who serve longer prison terms? Does the prospect of earning early release encourage offenders to rehabilitate themselves? Does parole supervision facilitate rehabilitation? Do some forms of parole supervision work more effectively than others?

The effectiveness of parole has traditionally been measured in terms of the recidivism rate.[68] As with probation, an offender can fail either by committing a new crime or through a technical violation of parole conditions. In terms of a new crime, it depends on whether we measure failure in terms of being re-arrested, reconvicted, or reincarcerated.

The data on parole outcomes, like those for probation, are not encourag-ing. Half (50.9 percent) of all offenders discharged from parole in 1992 suc-cessfully completed their terms. In short, half failed. These failures were divided among new prison sentences (12.7 percent), parole revocation (18.8 percent), and a pending revocation (14.7 percent).[69] These data repre-sent all the offenders leaving parole that year. Longitudinal studies of parole cohorts are even more discouraging. A study of 3,999 young parolees (aged seventeen through twenty-two) who were released in 1978 found that after six years, 69 percent were rearrested, 53 percent were reconvicted, and 49 percent were reincarcerated.[70]

These figures lend a great deal of support to the widespread belief that prison and parole are not successful in either deterring crime or rehabilitating offenders. The policy question is whether parole can be made to work more effectively.

Intensive Parole Supervision

One of the most popular strategies for improving parole success rates involves intensive parole supervision. In 1992, about 9 percent of all parolees (58,069 of 634,255) were in an intensive supervision program (this was up from 3 per-cent in 1990).[71]

As is the case with probation, intensive parole supervision is nothing new. California developed a pioneering Special Intensive Parole Unit (SIPU) pro-gram in the mid-1950s and maintained it for ten years.[72] Martinson reviewed the SIPU evaluations, however, and found that three of the four phases pro-duced no meaningful improvement in parolees' behavior. The phase involving smaller caseloads did appear to yield some positive results. Parolees in this phase appeared to be more successful because they were returned to prison more often for technical violations. Martinson concluded that this was a de-terrent rather than a rehabilitative effect. Parolees behaved themselves a little better when they knew that they faced a real prospect of being sent back to prison.[73]

Parole supervision, whether regular or intensive, suffers from the same basic problem as probation: the superficiality of the "treatment," often involv-ing routine monthly meetings with parole officers and little in the way of meaningful services.

In defense of parole, Martinson argues that parolees do no worse than the offenders who stay in prison, and therefore it makes sense to release them rel-atively early rather than imprison them for long periods.[74] More recent data

Table 11.1 Percentage of young adults in 1978 who were rearrested, by time served in prison, the number of arrests prior to parole, age when paroled, and age at first adult arrest.

	Percentage of parolees rearrested within six years of release by time served in prison[a]				
	1–6 months	7–12 months	13–18 months	19–24 months	25 months or longer
All first releases	64	66	73	67	69
NUMBER OF ARRESTS PRIOR TO PAROLE					
1	56	60	61	57	62
2–3	60	62	72	66	71
4–5	76	84	80	74	70
6 or more	99	81	99	96	95
AGE WHEN PAROLED					
17–18	60	79	72	89	87
19	76	70	85	91	65
20	69	63	70	61	64
21	55	59	68	61	70
22	56	71	82	68	73
AGE AT FIRST ADULT ARREST					
16 or younger	74	81	87	76	72
17	75	65	79	71	74
18	68	71	70	66	66
19	64	61	68	69	64
20 or older	37	58	62	42	————
Number of first releases	1,404	2,841	2,258	1,639	2,039

[a]All data refer only to "first releases," that is, new court commitments paroled for the first time on their current offense. Approximately 90 percent of the parolees in this study were first releases.
———Fewer than 20 cases.

SOURCE: Bureau of Justice Statistics, *Recidivism of Young Parolees* (Washington, D.C.: Government Printing Office, 1987).

confirm this. Failure rates in the 1978 parole cohort varied only slightly according to the amount of time they had served. As Table 11.1 indicates, the rearrest rate was 64 percent for those who served six months or less, 66 percent for those who served between six months and a year, and 73 percent for those who served between a year and a year and a half.[75]

The Prediction Problem Again

The parole reform strategy with the longest history is the attempt to improve parole release decision making. The decision to release to the community is basically a prediction that the offender will not recidivate. Criminologists have been searching for parole release formulas since the 1920s, but with little success.[76]

Parole decision making has been attacked by both liberals and conservatives. Liberals, especially civil libertarians, have criticized it as scientifically unsound and therefore inevitably arbitrary. Even though California developed a large correctional research unit in the 1950s, Martinson and others have found no evidence that California parole decision makers were more accurate in predicting offenders' behavior than were their counterparts in other states.[77] Conservatives, on the other hand, have criticized parole authorities for turning danger offenders loose on the community.

Parole release decisions represent another version of the prediction problem. The task is to identify those prisoners who represent a low risk so they can be released early and those who represent a high risk so they can be held in prison longer. Rather than reviewing the prediction problem in detail at this point, we will say that criminologists and parole authorities have available to them the same basic set of data about offenders: the offenses for which they were convicted, their prior records, evidence of violent behavior, and relevant personal data such as history of employment and of drug or alcohol abuse. Over the course of many decades, however, parole authorities have not been able to use these data to improve parole release decisions.[78]

Peter Hoffmann compared the success and failure rates of prisoners released on parole and those who served their full terms (in prisoner jargon, they "jammed out" or "maxed out"). Of the 1,135 adult male offenders released in 1968 who had been convicted of robbery, burglary, or manslaughter, the parolees did better than those who served their full terms. Only half as many parolees as full-termers were arrested for a new offense. Many of the offenders who served their full terms, however, were false positives. Parole authorities held them in prison in the erroneous belief that they would be recidivists. Many of those who were paroled, meanwhile, were false negatives. They were deemed ready for release (rehabilitated) when in fact they did commit new crimes.[79]

Abolish Parole?

Disillusionment with parole reached such a point in the 1970s that several jurisdictions simply abolished it. The Determinate Sentencing Law enacted by California in 1976 abolished discretionary parole release. Release dates are mandatory once a prisoner has served the sentence imposed by the judge and good time has been deducted. A one-year period of parole supervision remains, however. The federal sentencing guidelines that took effect on November 1, 1987, also abolished parole and replaced it with presumptive sentences.[80]

Abolition of parole may or may not be a good idea. The basic question is whether you think discretion in parole release is useful or likely to be abused. Either way, abolition of parole is irrelevant to crime control.

Our position is as follows:

PROPOSITION 39
Changing or abolishing parole will not reduce serious crime.

REINTEGRATION AND
RESTORATIVE JUSTICE

A new approach to rehabilitation involves the concept of restorative justice. Our legal system has traditionally regarded the state as "the victim" of a crime. This is the basis for the basic distinction between *crimes*, as offenses against the public, and *torts*, as private harms. It is also the reason that we have a criminal justice system representing "the public." In a major paradigm shift, restorative justice regards "[t]he person who was violated [as] the primary victim, and the state [as] a secondary victim."[81]

Consequently, instead of an adversarial system focused on punishment, restorative justice emphasizes dialogue, negotiation, and the reestablishment of a positive relationship between victim and offender. In practice, restorative justice has involved restitution, in the form of financial compensation, community service, and mediation, usually in the form of face-to-face acknowledgment of guilt. The basic goal of restorative justice is to build and maintain a healthy community with positive social relations.[82] This concept grows out of the recognition that the traditional approaches to criminal justice—both punishment and rehabilitation—have not proven to be effective. It seeks the traditional rehabilitative goal of reintegrating the offender but through different means.

Much of the inspiration for restorative justice comes from John Braithwaite's provocative book *Crime, Shame and Reintegration*.[83] He primarily emphasizes the process of shaming as the key to controlling crime, but his theory applies to other forms of restorative justice as well. Citing the criminological literature on deterrence, he argues that informal sanctions "imposed by relatives, friends or a personally relevant collectivity have more effect on criminal behavior than sanctions imposed by a remote legal authority."[84] Shame deters not only the offender (specific deterrence) but others who will want to avoid being shamed (general deterrence).

Restorative Justice in Operation

How well does restorative justice work in practice? As with many of the so-called new intermediate punishments we discussed earlier, the restorative justice programs of financial restitution and community service are not entirely new. Evaluations of experimental programs have tended to find slightly lower recidivism rates than for offenders receiving restorative justice than for those given traditional sentences of prison or probation. The differences are not always consistent, however, and many questions remain regarding the implementation and outcomes of such programs.[85]

We have many reasons for being skeptical about restorative justice as a response to serious crime. First, although it may well be appropriate for less serious crimes, especially minor property offenses, is it appropriate—from the standpoint of justice—for serious crimes? Second, although it may be appropriate for first-time offenders, is it appropriate for fourth- or fifth-time offenders? Third, has it demonstrated its effectiveness with serious repeat offenders?

From a practical standpoint, a number of problems arise with the theory of restorative justice as described by Braithwaite. Common sense suggests that the informal sanctions of family, friends, or community are likely to be more effective in controlling behavior than the threats and actions of remote official agencies. But a major part of the crime problem in the United States today is the collapse of families, peer groups, and communities for many people. As Hagan's theory of social embeddedness suggests, some individuals are deeply embedded in lives that encourage lawbreaking rather than law abiding. In our poorest, most economically ravaged and drug-ridden neighborhoods, "community," in the positive sense of the term, has disappeared. The structure of families has collapsed for too many people. The peer group influence too often leads to drugs and crime. The concept of restorative justice may well be appropriate and effective for the young juvenile delinquent in a middle-class neighborhood but irrelevant for those aspects of our society that are the center of most serious crime.

In a more general sense, Braithwaite's theory is based on a nostalgic view of community in the United States. The informal mechanisms of social control that he prizes—the disapproval of family, friends, and neighbors—were in fact the primary means of crime control in seventeenth-century colonial New England. They worked because those communities were small and extremely homogenous (almost entirely white, English, and Protestant). As this country grew into a large and diverse nation, characterized not only by different racial, ethnic, religious, and cultural groups but also by largely anonymous social relations, the old mechanisms no longer worked. That is one of the main reasons that Americans created the modern criminal justice system in the early nineteenth century. There is no returning to this vanished society.[86]

This leads us to the following conclusion:

PROPOSITION 40

Forms of restorative justice may prove to be an appropriate response to minor crimes by first-time offenders but are not likely to be an effective means of reducing serious crime.

REHABILITATION: RUNNING ON EMPTY?

In the end, the evidence on rehabilitation does not look very good. We do not seem to have devised any "planned intervention" programs that substantially reduce recidivism rates. None of the much-publicized innovations seem to be more successful than the traditional forms of probation and parole. It is true that some things work: as Glaser and others argue, some programs work for some offenders. The problem, however, is that the liberals who advocate rehabilitation are no more effective in predicting future behavior than are the conservative advocates of incapacitation.

The recent innovations in corrections—intensive supervision, home confinement, electronic monitoring, boot camps—emphasize surveillance and control of offenders, often with little in the way of meaningful services. Insofar as they succeed in detecting misbehavior and sending offenders to prison, these programs should be considered incapacitative "lock 'em up" programs rather than rehabilitation programs. As Frank Williams and Marilyn McShane suggest, few if any really innovative ideas in corrections have been proposed. Instead of genuine innovations, reformers have been "running on empty."[87]

The new intermediate punishments, along with the spectacular increase in the number of offenders on probation and parole (triple the number fifteen years ago), adds an important perspective on the traditional liberal calls for making greater use of alternatives to incarceration. For years, groups such as the National Council on Crime and Delinquency (NCCD), the Sentencing Project, and others have argued that we imprison too many people and that we should use more alternative sentences. It is undeniable that we lock up an enormous number of people. But it is also true that we have also increased the number of people in community-based alternatives. These alternatives may very well be less expensive and more humane than prison, but we do not have any persuasive evidence that they are any more effective in reducing recidivism and as a result lowering the level of serious crime.

NOTES

1. Charles H. Logan and Gerald G. Gaes, "Meta-Analysis and the Rehabilitation of Punishment," *Justice Quarterly* 10 (June 1993): 245–263.

2. Lee B. Sechrest, Susan O. White, and Elizabeth Brown, *The Rehabilitation of Criminal Offenders: Problems and Prospects* (Washington, D.C.: National Academy of Sciences, 1979), pp. 18–19.

3. Michael Gottfredson and Travis Hirschi, "The True Value of Lambda Would Appear to be Zero: An Essay on Career Criminals, Criminal Careers, Selective Incapacitation, Cohort Studies, and Related Topics," *Criminology* 24 (1986): 213–234.

4. David C. Anderson, *Crime and the Politics of Hysteria* (New York: Times Books, 1995); The Sentencing Project, *The Lessons of Willie Horton: Thinking About Crime and Punishment for the 1990s*

(Washington, D.C.: The Sentencing Project, 1989).

5. Bureau of Justice Statistics, *Sourcebook of Criminal Justice Statistics—1991* (Washington, D.C.: Government Printing Office, 1992), p. 130.

6. Anderson, *Crime and the Politics of Hysteria*, pp. 270–271.

7. Robert Martinson, "What Works? Questions and Answers About Prison Reform," *Public Interest* 35 (Spring 1974): 22–54.

8. Robert Martinson, "Symposium on Sentencing: Part II," *Hofstra Law Review* 7(2) (1979): 243–258. The full report is published as Douglas Lipton, Robert Martinson, and Judith Wilks, *The Effectiveness of Correctional Treatment* (New York: Praeger, 1975).

9. Samuel Walker, *Popular Justice: A History of American Criminal Justice*, 2d ed.,

revised (New York: Oxford University Press, 1998).

10. Lipton et al., *The Effectiveness of Correctional Treatment*.

11. Sechrest et al., *The Rehabilitation of Criminal Offenders*, pp. 14, 31, 102.

12. Logan and Gaes, "Meta-Analysis and the Rehabilitation of Punishment."

13. Daniel Glaser, "What Works, and Why It Is Important: A Response to Logan and Gaes," *Justice Quarterly* 11 (December 1994): 711–723.

14. Logan and Gaes, "Meta-Analysis and the Rehabilitation of Punishment," p. 255.

15. Glaser, "What Works?" p. 721.

16. Ibid.; see also John Hagan, "The Social Embeddedness of Crime and Unemployment," *Criminology* 31 (November 1993): 465–491.

17. Ted Palmer, *The Re-emergence of Correctional Intervention* (Beverly Hills, CA: Sage, 1992).

18. Norval Morris and Michael Tonry, *Between Prison and Probation* (New York: Oxford University Press, 1990).

19. Raymond T. Nimmer, *Diversion: The Search for Alternative Forms of Prosecution* (Chicago: American Bar Foundation, 1974).

20. Ibid., pp. 11–18, 41–51.

21. President's Crime Commission, *The Challenge of Crime in a Free Society* (Washington, D.C.: Government Printing Office, 1967), p. 165.

22. Vera Institute of Justice, *The Manhattan Court Employment Project: Final Report* (New York: Vera Institute of Justice, 1972).

23. U.S. Department of Justice, *Diversion of Felony Arrests: An Experiment in Pretrial Intervention* (Washington, D.C.: Government Printing Office, 1981).

24. Thomas G. Blomberg, "Widening the Net: An Anomaly in the Evaluation of Diversion Programs," in Malcolm W. Klein and K. S. Teilman, eds., *Handbook of Criminal Justice Evaluation* (Beverly Hills, CA: Sage, 1980), pp. 572–592.

25. Eugene Doleschal, "The Dangers of Criminal Justice Reform," *Criminal Justice Abstracts* 14 (March 1982): 133–152. A different perspective on criminal justice reform is in Samuel Walker, *Taming the System: The Control of Discretion in American Criminal Justice, 1950–1990* (New York: Oxford University Press, 1993).

26. Blomberg, "Widening the Net," p. 592.

27. Joan Petersilia and Susan Turner, *Intensive Supervision Probation for High Risk Offenders: Findings from Three California Experiments* (Santa Monica, CA: Rand, 1990).

28. Jamie Gorelick, "Pretrial Diversion: The Threat of Expanding Social Control," *Harvard Civil Rights—Civil Liberties Law Review* 10 (1975): 180–214.

29. Bureau of Justice Statistics, *Correctional Populations in the United States, 1994* (Washington, D.C.: Government Printing Office, 1996), Table 1.1.

30. Bureau of Justice Statistics, *State Court Sentencing of Convicted Felons, 1992* (Washington, D.C.: Government Printing Office, 1996).

31. Todd R. Clear and Anthony A. Braga, "Community Corrections," in James Q. Wilson and Joan Petersilia, eds., *Crime* (San Francisco: ICS Press, 1995), p. 431.

32. Bureau of Justice Statistics, *Recidivism of Felons on Probation, 1986–1989* (Washington, D.C.: Government Printing Office, 1992).

33. Joan Petersilia, Susan Turner, James Kahan, and Joyce Peterson, *Granting Felons Probation: Public Risks and Alternatives* (Santa Monica, CA: Rand, 1985).

34. Gennaro F. Vito, "Felony Probation and Recidivism: Replication and Response," *Federal Probation* 50 (1986): 17–25.

35. Michael R. Geerken and Hennessey D. Hayes, "Probation and Parole: Public Risk and the Future of Incarceration Alternatives," *Criminology* 31 (November 1993): 549–564.

36. Clear and Braga, "Community Corrections," p. 431.

37. Petersilia and Turner, *Intensive Supervision Probation for High Risk Offenders*, p. 47; Petersilia, "Measuring the Performance of Community Corrections," p. 62.

38. John Hagan, "The Social Embeddedness of Crime and Unemployment," *Criminology* 31 (November 1993): 465–491.

39. Bureau of Justice Statistics, *Sourcebook of Criminal Justice Statistics—1995* (Washington, D.C.: Government Printing Office, 1996), p. 81.

40. Morris and Tonry, *Between Prison and Probation*.

41. Richard A. Ball, C. Ronald Huff, and J. Robert Lilly, *House Arrest and Correctional Policy* (Beverly Hills, CA: Sage, 1988).

42. Bureau of Justice Statistics, *Sourcebook of Criminal Justice Statistics—1995*, p. 95.

43. Bureau of Justice Statistics, *Correctional Populations in the United States, 1992*, p. 33.

44. J. Banks, A. A. Porter, R. L. Rardin, T. R. Silver, and V. E. Unger, *Evaluation of Intensive Special Probation Projects* (Washington, D.C.: Government Printing Office, 1977).

45. Todd Clear and Patricia Hardyman, "The New Intensive Supervision Movement," *Crime and Delinquency* 36 (January 1990): 42–60.

46. Petersilia and Turner, *Intensive Supervision Probation for High Risk Offenders*.

47. Ibid.

48. Todd Clear, S. Flynn, and C. Shapirto, "Intensive Supervision in Probation," in Belinda McCarthy, ed., *Intermediate Punishments* (Monsey, NY: Willow Tree Press, 1987), pp. 10–11.

49. Petersilia, "Measuring the Performance of Community Corrections," p. 67.

50. Clear and Hardyman, "The New Intensive Supervision Movement."

51. Joan Petersilia, "When Probation Becomes More Dreaded Than Prison," *Federal Probation* 54 (March 1990): 23–27.

52. Ibid.

53. Bureau of Justice Statistics, *Correctional Populations in the United States, 1992*, pp. 33, 112.

54. Marc Renzema and David T. Skelton, *Use of Electronic Monitoring in the United States: 1989 Update* (Washington, D.C.: Government Printing Office, 1990).

55. Bureau of Justice Statistics, *Correctional Populations in the United States, 1992*.

56. Bureau of Justice Statistics, *Performance Measures for the Criminal Justice System* (Washington, D.C.: Government Printing Office, 1993), pp. 67–68.

57. Bureau of Justice Statistics, *Sourcebook of Criminal Justice Statistics—1995*, p. 95.

58. Doris Layton MacKenzie, Robert Brame, David McDowall, and Claire Souryal, "Boot Camp Prisons and Recidivism in Eight States," *Criminology* 33 (August 1995): 351.

59. Ibid, p. 328.

60. Ibid.

61. Ibid., p. 340.

62. Ibid., pp. 352–353.

63. Merry Morash and Lila Rucker, "A Critical Look at the Idea of Boot Camp as a Correctional Reform," *Crime and Delinquency* 36 (April 1990): 204–222.

64. Laura A. Gransky, Thomas C. Castellano, and Ernest L. Cowles, "Is There a 'Second Generation' of Shock Incarceration Facilities? The Evolving Nature of Goals, Program Elements, and Drug Treatment Services in Boot Camp Programs," in John Ortiz Smykla and William Selke, eds., *Intermediate Sanctions: Sentencing in the 1990s* (Cincinnati: Anderson, 1995), pp. 89–111.

65. Bureau of Justice Statistics, *Correctional Populations in the United States, 1992*, p. 5.

66. Bureau of Justice Assistance, *National Assessment of Structured Sentencing* (Washington, D.C.: Government Printing Office, 1996), pp. 26–27.

67. David J. Rothman, *Conscience and Convenience: The Asylum and Its Alternatives in Progressive America* (Boston: Little, Brown, 1980); Jonathan Simon, *Poor Discipline: Parole and the Social Control of the Underclass, 1890–1990* (Chicago: University of Chicago Press, 1993).

68. Petersilia, "Measuring the Performance of Community Corrections."

69. Bureau of Justice Statistics, *National Corrections Reporting Program, 1992* (Wash-

ington, D.C.: Government Printing Office, 1994), p. 69.

70. Bureau of Justice Statistics, *Recidivism of Young Parolees* (Washington, D.C.: Government Printing Office, 1987).

71. Bureau of Justice Statistics, *Correctional Populations in the United States, 1992*, p. 104.

72. Simon, *Poor Discipline*, pp. 80–84.

73. Robert Martinson and Judith Wilks, "Save Parole Supervision," *Federal Probation* 41 (September 1977): 23–27.

74. Ibid.

75. Bureau of Justice Statistics, *Recidivism of Young Parolees*, Table 9.

76. Walker, *Popular Justice.*

77. Robert Martinson, "California Research at the Crossroads," *Crime and Delinquency* (April 1976): 180–191.

78. Don M. Gottfredson and Michael Tonry, eds., *Prediction and Classification: Criminal Justice Decision Making* (Chicago: University of Chicago Press, 1987).

79. Peter B. Hoffman, "Mandatory Release: A Measure of Type II Error," *Criminology* 11 (February 1974): 541–554.

80. Bureau of Justice Statistics, *A National Assessment of Structured Sentencing.*

81. Mark S. Umbreit, *Victim Meets Offender: The Impact of Restorative Justice and Mediation* (Monsey, NY: Willow Tree Press, 1994), p. 2.

82. The old and new paradigms of justice are contrasted in ibid., Table 1, pp. 3–4.

83. John Braithwaite, *Crime, Shame and Reintegration* (New York: Cambridge University Press, 1989).

84. Ibid., p. 69.

85. See the various contributions to Burt Galaway and Joe Hudson, *Criminal Justice, Restitution, and Reconciliation* (Monsey, NY: Willow Tree Press, 1990), especially Laurie Ervin and Anne Schneider, "Explaining the Effects of Restitution on Offenders: Results from a National Experiment in Juvenile Courts," pp. 183–206.

86. This is one of the central themes of Walker, *Popular Justice*, 2d ed.

87. Marilyn D. McShane and Frank P. Williams, "Running on Empty: Creativity and the Correctional Agenda," *Crime and Delinquency* 35 (October 1989): 562–576.

1 2

Reform the Law
and the System

Two traditional liberal proposals involve reforming the criminal justice system. One calls for decriminalizing certain kinds of behavior. The other suggests eliminating injustices in the system, particularly race discrimination. Let us take a look at these proposals and see whether they might affect serious crime.

DECRIMINALIZATION

In their 1970 book *The Honest Politician's Guide to Crime Control*, Norval Morris and Gordon Hawkins call decriminalization a "first principle." Specifically, they propose removing criminal penalties on (1) public drunkenness; (2) purchase, possession, and use of all drugs; (3) all forms of gambling; (4) disorderly conduct and vagrancy; (5) abortion; (6) private sexual activity between consenting adults; and (7) juvenile "status" offenses.[1]

It is important to clarify exactly what kinds of behavior are involved in the list offered by Morris and Hawkins. Public drunkenness is included but not drunk driving. The person drunk on the street may be a nuisance but poses no threat of harm to anyone else. The drunk driver does pose such a threat. Sexual activity between consenting adults is covered but not sex between an adult and a child. In short, the standard decriminalization proposal covers a limited range of activity and not a general repeal of all criminal laws governing drinking or sex.

Some of these proposals are also supported by libertarian conservatives. As we will discuss in detail in Chapter 13, a number of prominent conservatives now support the legalization of drugs. In short, just as many liberals have adopted traditional conservative crime control ideas, so have some conservatives embraced some traditional liberal ideas.

The Rationale for Decriminalization

The basic assumption underlying decriminalization is the long-standing belief among liberals that the criminal law in the United States covers too much behavior. This problem is referred to as the "overreach" of the criminal law. In his classic work *The Limits of the Criminal Sanction*, Herbert L. Packer argues, "The criminal sanction is indispensable, [but] we resort to it in far too indiscriminate a way."[2]

The overreach of the criminal law has several undesirable consequences.[3] First, it overburdens the justice system with relatively minor offenses, such as public drunkenness, leaving it with less resources for the really serious crimes of murder, rape, robbery, and burglary. Public drunkenness is a good example. A 1971 book published by the American Bar Foundation defines the problem as *Two Million Unnecessary Arrests*.[4] Actually, the number of arrests for drunkenness has been declining steadily, from 1.2 million in 1975 to 713,000 in 1994.[5] Nonetheless, 700,000 arrests consume a large amount of police and court resources.

A second problem is that no strong public consensus prevails about whether some behavior should be criminalized. Packer argues that "the criminal sanction should ordinarily be limited to conduct that is viewed, *without significant social dissent*, as immoral" (emphasis added).[6] The problem, however, is that there is much dissent on many issues. Americans have very mixed attitudes about gambling, for example; they feel that something is immoral about it, but they love to bet on sports nonetheless.

One of the results of conflicting public attitudes is selective and often arbitrary law enforcement. This violates the principle of equal protection of the law and leads to cynicism about law enforcement among the public and police officers. Packer argues that "respect for law generally is likely to suffer."[7]

A third problem is that making various forms of recreation illegal leads to the development of criminal syndicates that provide the goods and services people want. Thirty years ago the President's Crime Commission argued, "The core of organized crime activity is the supplying of illegal goods and services . . . to countless numbers of citizen customers."[8] Gambling was historically the principal source of revenue for organized crime, and the U.S. demand for illegal drugs sustains vast international networks and neighborhood drug gangs. In this sense, the law becomes criminogenic, creating forms of criminal behavior.

Fourth, the criminal syndicates that are created by making gambling and other activities illegal corrupt the justice system. The Knapp Commission investigation into police corruption in New York City in the early 1970s found that police officers were receiving a weekly "pad" of between $300 and $1,500 a month for protecting illegal gambling.[9] Twenty years later, the Mollen Commission found that the worst forms of police corruption and brutality in New York City were associated with drug trafficking.[10]

Fifth, many people believe that certain kinds of recreation—sex and the use of some substances—is a matter of private choice. The overwhelming majority of Americans believe that sex between two adults of the opposite sex should not be a crime. About half of all Americans today now believe that sex between two adults of the same sex should not be a crime. Over 80 percent of Americans believe that women have a right to terminate a pregnancy by abortion.[11]

Sixth, many criminal justice and public health experts believe that the problems associated with drinking, gambling, and sex are really social, psychological, and medical problems that should not be addressed through the criminal law. The President's Crime Commission concluded that the criminal justice system "is not in a position to meet [the chronic alcoholic's] underlying medical and social problems."[12] Arrest and prosecution do nothing to help the chronic alcoholic deal with his or her drinking problem, and in many cases they make matters worse. Medical and social services would be a far more effective response.[13]

The Terms of the Debate

Not everyone agrees with the traditional arguments in favor of decriminalization. The debate between advocates and opponents of decriminalization raises fundamental questions about the role of the criminal law, involving issues of moral standards and the practical effects of criminalization.

Everyone does agree with the principle that the criminal law expresses (or should express) the basic values of society and defines the boundaries of acceptable conduct. Robbery is a crime because we believe that taking something that belongs to another person is wrong. Murder is a crime because taking another person's life is wrong. As Patrick Devlin puts it, "The criminal law as we know it is based upon moral principle."[14]

The question is not *whether* the law should express the values of society but *which values* it should express. As Packer says, "Whose morality are we talking about?"[15] Is gambling morally wrong or a legitimate form of entertainment? Is homosexual behavior morally wrong or a matter of private choice? Is abortion morally wrong (murder, in the eyes of antiabortion activists) or a constitutionally protected private choice? Conservatives generally believe that these behaviors are morally wrong and therefore should be prohibited by the criminal law. Liberals generally believe that there is nothing immoral about these same behaviors and therefore they should not be made illegal. According to criminologist Gilbert Geis, certain forms of behavior are "not the law's business."[16]

Whether certain forms of behavior are wrong depends on how you define "harm." Advocates of decriminalization believe that gambling, for example, is a "victimless crime." Advocates of criminal prohibition believe that it produces real harms: that people can become addicted to gambling, that it can ruin their personal finances and harm their family, that it can lead to other crime as people try to pay off their gambling debts. Similarly, as we will discuss in Chapter 13, advocates of drug decriminalization believe that marijuana, for example, does not do the harm that it is alleged to do. Supporters of the current drug laws believe that marijuana does real physical, psychological, and social harm. Devlin sums up the prohibitionist position by arguing that "society is entitled by means of its laws to protect itself from dangers, whether from within or without."[17]

Decriminalization is also debated in terms of the practical consequences of making certain behavior illegal. As we mentioned earlier, advocates of decriminalization believe that criminal prohibition overburdens the justice system, leads to arbitrary enforcement, encourages corruption, and does not help people who have a medical or psychological problem. The advocates of criminalization would reply that the moral issues at stake outweigh the bad consequences. Even if the law does not completely deter drug abuse, society should still condemn this behavior through the criminal law.

THE IMPACT OF DECRIMINALIZATION

Now let us take a look at some of the specific items on the old decriminalization agenda.

Public Disorder Crimes

Public drunkenness, disorderly conduct, and vagrancy are essentially public nuisances rather than predatory crimes. They may offend our sensibilities, but they do not inflict tangible harm on someone the way robbery and burglary do.[18]

The crime control strategy underlying decriminalization of these offenses assumes an indirect effect. The assumption is that decriminalization will give the police more time to concentrate on serious crimes. As we indicated, 713,000 arrests were made for drunkenness in 1994, representing 5 percent of all arrests and almost as many as arrests for all violent index crimes (778,730).[19]

The basic assumption is flawed. As we learned in Chapter 5, adding more patrol officers will not prevent more crime, and adding more detectives will not raise clearance rates. Insofar as decriminalization of public drunkenness saves police time and resources, it might be desirable as a cost-saving measure. We have no reason to assume, however, that it will help reduce serious crime.

Not everyone agrees with our analysis. Public-order offenses such as drunkenness and urinating in public are a central part of the "zero-tolerance" policy adopted by then New York City police commissioner William Bratton. He and others claim that aggressively enforcing the law on these minor crimes has contributed directly to the reduction of murder and other serious crimes.[20] Critics, however, point out that crime has also fallen in cities that do not have the zero-tolerance policy and that the decline began before Bratton became police commissioner.

Arrest trends indicate that we have been deemphasizing public-order arrests for many years. Between 1975 and 1994, the number of arrests for drunkenness fell from 1.2 million to 700,000. Several factors accounted for this decline. First, some court decisions held that arresting someone because of a medical condition—as opposed to some behavior—was unconstitutional. In 1966, the U.S. Court of Appeals for the District of Columbia ruled in *Easter v. District of Columbia* that DeWitt Easter could not convicted for public intoxication.[21] Second, states have decriminalized public intoxication (in part due to court rulings). Third, police departments informally deemphasized public-order offenses and concentrated on serious crimes.

Abortion

Abortion was decriminalized by the famous 1973 Supreme Court decision *Roe v. Wade*, which declared existing criminal abortion laws unconstitutional.[22] We will not to debate the morality of abortion here. It is important, however, to note that this issue dramatizes better than any other the moral basis of the criminal law and the conflict between different moral perspectives in our society. If you believe the fetus is a human being, then it logically follows that abortion is murder. But if you believe that the fetus is not a human being, then it follows that the abortion decision is a private choice.

Whatever your views on abortion might be, it is difficult if not impossible to find a connection between it and serious crime. Legalizing or criminalizing abortion has no effect on robbery and burglary.

Sex Between Consenting Adults

States traditionally outlawed different kinds of sexual behavior, including activity between consenting adults such as adultery, cohabitation, homosexuality, and sodomy (which in some states includes "unnatural" sexual acts as well as acts between people of the same sex). By the mid-1980s, thirteen states still had laws making it illegal for unmarried people to live together, and thirteen had laws against "fornication" (sexual intercourse between people who are not married).[23] The 1910 Mann Act makes it a federal crime to take someone of the opposite sex across state lines for "immoral purposes." These laws are another good example of how the criminal law is used to define the moral boundaries of society.

In actual practice, the laws on sexual activity were rarely enforced, and as public attitudes about sex began to change in the 1960s, enforcement dropped even further. Many states abolished their laws in this area. About half the states, for example, no longer consider sex between adults of the same sex to be a crime.[24]

Whatever your views on adultery, cohabitation, or homosexuality, it is impossible to establish any connection between these activities and serious predatory crime. Legalizing or criminalizing cohabitation will have no effect on burglary or robbery.

One possible exception to this rule might be prostitution. In some instances, prostitution facilitates ancillary crimes: customers are robbed; prostitutes are beaten by their pimps. It is possible that a system of legalized and regulated prostitution would remove street walkers from the streets and reduce some of these crimes.

Gambling

The legal status of gambling in the United States has undergone a massive change in recent years. The old moralistic objections to gambling have collapsed as many states have created lotteries and authorized casino gambling.[25] Many Native American tribes have established betting casinos on tribal lands that are exempt from federal and state gambling laws. Despite the spread of legal gambling, however, many of the popular forms of illegal gambling—sports betting pools, the numbers game—continue to flourish.

Advocates of decriminalizing gambling see a number of possible benefits: saving scarce resources, ending arbitrary law enforcement, and undercutting the economic basis of organized crime, for instance. There is no expectation, however, that it would reduce predatory crime, which is the issue that concerns us.

Some opponents of legalized gambling believe that legalized gambling might actually lead to an increase in crime. They argue that gambling casinos attract a criminal subculture that involves more thefts, robberies, and other crimes. Several studies have examined this issue. The Illinois Criminal Justice Information Authority found that the advent of riverboat gambling had no impact on crime in Joliet, Illinois.[26] David Giacopassi and B. Grant Stitt found that casino gambling had a mixed impact on crime in Biloxi, Mississippi. Auto theft and larceny did rise, but no significant changes were noted for other crimes.[27] Finally, crime did increase in Atlantic City, New Jersey, after gambling was legalized there in 1976, but it was primarily "in-house" crime inside the casinos themselves. No increase occurred in the community generally.[28] In short, no consistent evidence indicates that legalized gambling leads to higher crime rates.

Summary

Many arguments exist for and against criminalizing the different kinds of behavior we have discussed. We can debate this issue on moral grounds, in terms of the practical consequences of criminal penalties, or both. It seems very clear, however, that we have no reason to expect any reduction in serious crime. This leads us to the following conclusion:

PROPOSITION 41
Decriminalizing drunkenness, abortion, sex between consenting adults, and gambling will have no impact on serious crime.

Legalizing Drugs?

Legalizing drugs may be an exception to this rule. Many experts believe that criminal prohibition of drugs is criminogenic: that drug users commit high rates of crime to support their habits and that drug gangs engage in gun battles to control their turf. Supporters of the current drug laws reply that legalization would lead to more rather than less crime. This is an extremely important issue. We will examine it in detail in Chapter 13 as part of our discussion of drug policy.

ELIMINATE INJUSTICE

A major liberal goal for improving criminal justice is to eliminate injustice from the system itself. The most important injustices involves discrimination based on race, sex, or social class.

The nature and extent of discrimination in the justice system is a matter of great controversy. African Americans comprise about 14 percent of the United States population but about half of all prisoners.[29] Coramae Richey Mann sees this as the result of systematic race discrimination.[30] Jerome Miller characterizes the justice system's approach to young African American men as one of "search and destroy."[31] There is particularly striking evidence of race discrimination in the war on drugs.[32] William Wilbanks, on the other hand, challenges the "myth of a racist criminal justice system."[33]

In *The Color of Justice*, Walker, Spohn, and DeLone argue that discrimination is contextual rather than systematic.[34] That is, some discrimination exists in most and perhaps all points of the justice system, but it is often subtle and confounded with other factors. As Marjorie Zatz points out, the cumulative effect of small amounts of discrimination at various points has an enormous effect on the overall results of the criminal process.[35]

Arrest as a Case Study

Field research conducted by Albert Reiss and Donald Black for the President's Crime Commission found no evidence of direct race discrimination in arrest. They did find an important indirect race effect in that disrespect for the police officer was a significant factor in arrest and that African American males were more likely to express disrespect.[36] The data from the Police Services Study (PSS), based on three metropolitan areas, indicate that "race does matter" in arrest decisions.[37] The Rand Corporation, meanwhile, found that African American men arrested in California were more likely than whites to have their cases dismissed. It also appeared that they were more likely to be arrested on weaker evidence. These points suggest some discrimination in arrest decisions.[38]

The most blatant evidence of race discrimination in the justice system, including arrest, involves drug offenses. The Sentencing Project reports that African Americans represent an estimated 13 percent of all drug users but 35 percent of persons arrested for drug offenses.[39] This disparity in drug arrests is not necessarily the result of arrest discrimination by individual officers on the street but of department-level enforcement strategies that concentrate drug enforcement efforts in racial minority neighborhoods.

In short, evidence exists to suggest race discrimination in arrests. Criminologists are primarily arguing over the nature and extent of it. Discrimination should be eliminated. For our purposes, the question is whether this would reduce crime.

One school of criminological thought holds that there is a connection between how people are treated by the justice system and their criminal behavior. *Labeling theory* argues that once a person is labeled, for example as "mentally ill" by the mental health system or a "criminal" or "delinquent" by the criminal justice system, that person has great difficulty escaping the label. Other officials respond to the person as he or she has been labeled. Thus, the kid who has been labeled a delinquent, for example, is more likely to be arrested and processed through the system than the kid who has done the same thing but has not been so labeled.[40]

This process contributes to crime in several ways. The individual acquires a longer official record, which produces more adverse consequences such as difficulty getting a job. He or she becomes more alienated from society and therefore more likely to violate its norms. Also, the person internalizes the label and begins to act accordingly.

Labeling theory has been severely criticized, however. It assumes that individuals are entirely passive, only responding to the reactions of others and not acting themselves. Also, it fails to explain how and why the individual came into contact with the law in the first instance. Finally, it does not account for the many people who do have some contact with the justice system but do not go on to more criminal activity.[41]

In sum, it is difficult to argue that much of our crime problem is the result of a labeling process. It follows, therefore, that eliminating discrimination is not going to reduce serious crime to any significant degree.

Summary

Discrimination clearly exists in the criminal justice system. No one seriously argues that it does not. The debate is over how much there is and its real sources. All forms of discrimination need to be eliminated. The basic principle of our legal system is equal justice under law. Unfortunately, eliminating discrimination is not going to help reduce the crime rate, which leads us to the following proposition:

> ### PROPOSITION 42
> Eliminating discrimination from the criminal justice system will result in a fairer system of justice but will not reduce crime.

CONCLUSION

Many things are wrong with the criminal law and the criminal justice system. We criminalize too much behavior, and discrimination in the system persists. Decriminalizing a lot of behavior would probably have some substantial benefit. But it will not reduce serious crime. By the same token, all forms of discrimination should be eliminated. Doing so, however, will not reduce the crime rate.

With respect to serious crime, the reform suggested by the system approach discussed in this chapter is a classic example of avoiding the problem by changing the subject. Liberals have had trouble coming up with effective crime policies and have frequently changed the subject to discuss other problems. None of the proposals considered in this chapter are likely to have any impact on crime.

NOTES

1. Norval Morris and Gordon Hawkins, *The Honest Politician's Guide to Crime Control* (Chicago: University of Chicago Press, 1970), p. 3.

2. Herbert L. Packer, *The Limits of the Criminal Sanction* (Stanford, CA: Stanford University Press, 1968), p. 364.

3. The best overview of this issue is still Packer, *The Limits of the Criminal Sanction*.

4. Raymond T. Nimmer, *Two Million Unnecessary Arrests* (Chicago: American Bar Foundation, 1971).

5. Federal Bureau of Investigation, *Crime in the United States, 1975* (Washington, D.C.: Government Printing Office, 1976),

p. 179; Federal Bureau of Investigation, *Crime in the United States, 1994* (Washington, D.C.: Government Printing Office, 1995), p. 217.

6. Packer, *The Limits of the Criminal Sanction*, p. 264.

7. Ibid., p. 287.

8. President's Commission on Law Enforcement and Administration of Justice, *The Challenge of Crime in a Free Society* (New York: Avon, 1968), p. 437.

9. Knapp Commission, *Report on Police Corruption* (New York: Braziller, 1973).

10. Commission to Investigate Allegations of Police Corruption and the Anti-Corruption Procedures of the Police Department, *Report* (New York: City of New York, 1994).

11. Bureau of Justice Statistics, *Sourcebook of Criminal Justice Statistics—1995* (Washington, D.C.: Government Printing Office, 1996), p. 228.

12. President's Commission on Law Enforcement and Administration of Justice, *Task Force Report: Drunkenness* (Washington, D.C.: Government Printing Office, 1967), p. 3.

13. Nimmer, *Two Million Unnecessary Arrests.*

14. Patrick Devlin, *The Enforcement of Morals* (London: Oxford University Press, 1965), p. 7.

15. Packer, *The Limits of the Criminal Sanction*, p. 263.

16. Gilbert Geis, *Not the Law's Business* (New York: Schocken, 1979).

17. Devlin, *The Enforcement of Morals*, p. 13.

18. President's Commission, *Task Force Report: Drunkenness.*

19. Federal Bureau of Investigation, *Crime in the United States, 1994*, p. 217.

20. George L. Kelling and Catherine Coles, *Fixing Broken Windows* (New York: Kessler, 1996).

21. *Easter v. District of Columbia*, 361 F.2d 50 (D.C. Cir. 1966).

22. *Roe v. Wade*, 410 U.S. 113 (1973).

23. Mitchell Bernard, Ellen Levine, Stefan Presser, and Marianne Stecich, *The Rights of Single People* (New York: Bantam, 1985), pp. 12–13.

24. Vincent J. Samar, *The Right to Privacy: Gays, Lesbians, and the Constitution* (Philadelphia: Temple University Press, 1991).

25. John D. Rosecrance, *Gambling Without Guilt: The Legitimation of an American Pasttime* (Pacific Grove, CA: Brooks/Cole, 1988).

26. Illinois Criminal Justice Information Authority, *Riverboat Gambling and Crime in Illinois* (Springfield: ICJIA, 1994).

27. David Giacopassi, and B. Grant Stitt, "Assessing the Impact of Casino Gambling on Crime in Mississippi," *American Journal of Criminal Justice* 18(1) (1994): 117–131.

28. Daniel Curran and Frank Scarpitti, "Crime in Atlantic City: Do Casinos Make a Difference?" *Deviant Behavior* 12(4) (1991): 431–450.

29. Bureau of Justice Statistics, *Sourcebook of Criminal Justice Statistics—1995* (Washington, D.C.: Government Printing Office, 1996), p. 562.

30. Coramae Richey Mann, *Unequal Justice* (Bloomington: University of Indiana, 1988).

31. Jerome G. Miller, *Search and Destroy: African-American Males in the Criminal Justice System* (New York: Cambridge University Press, 1996).

32. Marc Mauer and Tracy Huling, *Young Black Americans and the Criminal Justice System: Five Years Later* (Washington: The Sentencing Project, 1995).

33. William Wilbanks, *The Myth of a Racist Criminal Justice System* (Pacific Grove, CA: Brooks/Cole, 1987).

34. Samuel Walker, Cassia Spohn, and Miriam DeLone, *The Color of Justice* (Belmont, CA: Wadsworth, 1996).

35. Marjorie Zatz, "The Changing Forms of Racial/Ethnic Biases in Sentencing," *Journal of Research in Crime and Delinquency* 24 (February 1987): 69–92.

36. Donald Black, *The Manners and Customs of the Police* (New York: Academic Press, 1980).

37. Douglas A. Smith, Christy Visher, and Laura A. Davidson, "Equity and Discretionary Justice: The Influence of Race on

Police Arrest Decisions," *Journal of Criminal Law and Criminology* 75 (Spring 1984): 234–249.

38. Joan Petersilia, *Racial Disparities in the Criminal Justice System* (Santa Monica, CA: Rand, 1983).

39. Mauer and Huling, *Young Black Americans.*

40. Howard S. Becker, *Outsiders: Studies in the Sociology of Deviance* (New York: Macmillan, 1963).

41. Charles Wellford, "Labelling Theory and Criminology: An Assessment," *Social Problems* 22 (February 1975): 332–345.

PART V

The Drug Problem

One of the ground rules for this book is that we would focus on robbery and burglary. We are now going to violate that rule by examining drug policy. Why? The drug problem is at the center of crime policy today. Drugs are the driving force behind some of the most important changes in the criminal justice system over the past twenty years, especially the soaring prison population. Also, many people believe that drugs and the predatory crimes of robbery and burglary are closely connected. Reduce illegal drug use, they believe, and we will reduce serious crime. Let us take a look at the problem of drugs, the drug-crime connection, and the larger question of drug policy.

1 3

Sense and Nonsense About Drugs

THE DRUG PROBLEM

To talk seriously about crime policy, we have to talk about drugs and drug policy. Drugs have been the focal point of the crime problem in the United States for many years. Directly or indirectly, they were responsible for the dramatic rise in the murder rate in the 1980s, gang violence, the soaring prison population, the worsening crisis in race relations, and the steady erosion of individual rights in the Supreme Court.[1]

When we discuss drug policy, we can apply much of what we have learned so far. Conservative drug policies emphasize getting tough with drug offenders through more arrests and tougher punishments, whereas liberals prefer prevention, education, and treatment. Because the purpose of this book is to find policies that will lower serious crime, we will not be able to undertake a full discussion of drugs and drug abuse. This chapter focuses on drug policies that might reduce predatory crime.

Hysteria over Drugs

Public hysteria over drugs and drug-related crime inhibits sensible discussion of policy. It seems that this has always been the case. In the 1930s, a wave of national hysteria arose over "reefer madness," with wild stories about the alleged dangers of marijuana. A similar scare erupted in the 1980s over the so-called "crack babies."

Sensational news media stories appeared in 1988 about 375,000 crack babies born to addicted mothers. Reports claimed that these infants had severe physical and psychological damage, would never develop normally, and would be a permanent burden to society. One medical expert said, "It's as if the part of the brain that makes us human beings capable of discussion or reflection is wiped out."[2]

The truth turned out to be very different. The number of crack babies was grossly exaggerated. The original reports counted all babies who had been *exposed* to drugs during pregnancy, not just those who were genuinely addicted or even harmed. Some hospitals included mothers who had used marijuana. Later research found that the long-term damage even to addicted babies had been exaggerated. By age four, those who received adequate care did rather well. It is true that drugs can harm a fetus, but tobacco and alcohol may do as much damage. The most serious problem with low-income babies is the lack of adequate prenatal care, especially good nutrition.

Equally sensational stories are publicized about drug gangs that misrepresent the real nature of gangs in our society.[3] Scare stories about reefer madness, crack babies, or drug gangs prevent us from thinking clearly about drug policy.

MYTHS AND REALITIES
ABOUT DRUGS AND CRIME

To help sort our way through the debate over drug policy, we need to establish some basic facts about drugs and crime. As with most criminal justice issues, many myths about drugs and crime inhibit the development of sound and effective policies on this problem. Let us begin by exploring some of the facts about the extent of illegal drug use, drug use trends, and the relationship between drugs and crime.

The Extent of Illegal Drug Use

The first question is, How extensive is illegal drug use? Four different surveys provide some reasonably good estimates.[4] The National Household Survey, which collects self-reported data from 4,000 to 9,000 Americans, is the broadest survey of drug use. It has a number of limitations, however. Respondents may not fully report their illegal drug use, and as a household survey it misses many of the most serious drug abusers: the very poor, transients, and the homeless.

The 1995 National Household Survey offers both good and bad news. It confirms the fact that use of illegal substances is widespread: "Nearly half of young adults age 21–25 had tried illicit drugs at least once in their lifetime."[5] An estimated 6.1 percent of the people over the age of twelve (12.8 million people) were "current users," meaning that they had used an illegal drug in the past month.

Percentage reporting use

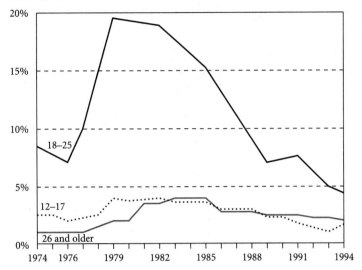

Note: The survey was conducted in 1974, 1976, 1977, 1979, 1982, 1985, 1988, 1990, 1991, 1992, 1993, and 1994.

FIGURE 13.1 Past year use of cocaine, by age of respondent, 1974–1994.

SOURCE: Office of National Drug Control Policy, *Fact Sheet: Drug Use Trends* (Washington, D.C.: Government Printing Office, 1996).

The good news from the National Household Survey is that drug use has declined significantly. The number of current users dropped by more than half, from 14.1 percent in 1979 to 6.1 percent in 1995. Cocaine use has fallen more than 70 percent (see Figure 13.1) and marijuana use more than 60 percent. This is a significant decrease and should be cause for celebration.

There is also some recent bad news. Illegal drug use among teenagers (age twelve to seventeen) has been increasing the past five years (Figure 13.2).[6] This is both a reversal of the trend since 1979 and contrary to the trends among older age groups. It is worth pointing out that the trends in drug use among teenagers resemble the homicide trends that we examined in our discussion of gun violence in Chapter 10: a decline in the general population but an increase among teenagers.

The Monitoring the Future survey (also known as the High School Senior Drug Abuse Survey) provides self-report data from 2,400 seniors in 130 public and private schools.[7] Although obviously not representative of the population as a whole, it does capture an important segment of the at-risk population. Its major weakness is that it misses kids who have dropped out of school—precisely those who are most likely to be the heaviest drug abusers. The most recent reports parallel the findings of the National Household Survey: a significant decline since the early 1980s followed by an increase beginning around 1991.[8]

Percentage reporting use

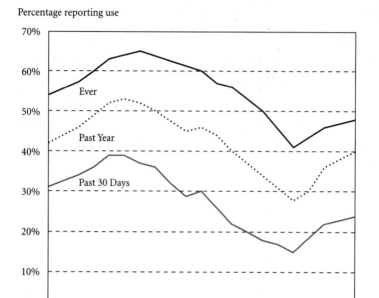

FIGURE 13.2 Drug use by high school seniors, 1975–1995.

SOURCE: Office of National Drug Control Policy, *Fact Sheet: Drug Use Trends* (Washington, D.C.: Government Printing Office, 1996).

A third survey, the Drug Abuse Warning Network (DAWN), tells a very different story. DAWN reports drug-related deaths and visits to emergency rooms from over 700 hospitals in twenty-one metropolitan areas and from eighty-seven medical examiners (or coroners) in twenty-seven metropolitan areas. This survey is obviously not an estimate of general drug use, but it does indicate trends in the most serious consequences of drug abuse.

DAWN presents a very grim picture. Cocaine-related emergency room visits quadrupled between 1985 and 1989. As a result of a reorganization of the DAWN survey, more representative national data are available for the 1988–1994 period. Cocaine reported "mentions" increased from 101,578 in 1988 to 142,878 in 1994. (One major limitation is that a mention in a medical report does not necessarily mean that the drug *caused* the medical emergency.) Heroin/morphine mentions increased by about the same percentage, whereas the rates for marijuana and methamphetamine both doubled.[9] These trends are clearly at odds with those from the National Household Survey.

Finally, the Drug Use Forecasting (DUF) program collects urine specimens and self-reported data on drug use from arrested persons. In 1995, DUF collected data on adults in twenty-three cities, along with juveniles in twelve of those sites. Although not a representative sample of the population, DUF does provide useful data on trends in drug availability in local communities. In San Diego, for example, 72 percent of all male arrestees tested positive for some illegal drug in 1995, compared with 54 percent in Omaha. Evidence of cocaine use was found in 51 percent of the males arrested in St. Louis but only 18 percent of those in San Jose.[10]

What do these four data sets tell us about the drug problem in the United States? Elliott Currie argues persuasively that we have two separate drug problems.[11] Among the vast majority of Americans, illegal drug use has declined substantially since the late 1970s. At the same time, however, the drug problem has worsened dramatically among the underclass. With the arrival of crack in the mid-1980s, entire neighborhoods were devastated by open drug markets, gangs, and gang-related violence. In important respects, U.S. society has become more deeply divided along social class and racial lines than ever before.[12]

The Drug-Crime Connection

A second important question involves the relationship between drugs and crime. Many people believe that drugs *cause* crime and that if we reduced illegal drug abuse, we would have much less crime. The myth persists of the "drug-crazed criminal" who robs and murders while high on drugs. This is similar to the old "reefer madness" view that women become sexually promiscuous because of marijuana.

Drugs and crime are related, but it is a very complex relationship.[13] Crime associated with drugs falls into three categories. First, there are *drug-defined crimes*, such as the possession and sale of illegal substances. Second, there are *drug-related* crimes, including violent behavior caused by the pharmacological effects of a drug or robberies committed to get money to buy drugs. Third, there are crimes *associated with a drug-using lifestyle*, in which individuals both use drugs and commit crime.[14]

Our concern in this book is with burglary and robbery. Very few of these crimes are directly drug related. Only 13 percent of jail inmates and 17 percent of prison inmates say they committed their offense to get money to buy drugs.[15] Drug-associated crime is an extremely complex subject. On the one hand, criminals are more likely to use drugs than are law-abiding people. The DUF data clearly indicate that people who are arrested use drugs at a much higher rate than the national average. Merely testing positive for drugs, however, does not mean that the crime was *caused* by drugs. This is similar to the problem we discussed in Chapter 6: Just because a driver tests positive for alcohol does not mean that his or her driving was impaired by drinking. Studies of high-rate offenders have found that many began their criminal activity before they began using drugs. For others, drug use preceded their criminal activity. Still others became involved in crime and drugs at about the same time. As a Justice Department report concludes, "For some individuals drug use is independent of their involvement in crime. These people may continue to commit crimes even if drugs were unavailable."[16]

At the same time, the National Household Survey data indicate that drug use does not lead to crime in any direct fashion. Few of the estimated 12 million people who use illegal drugs every year become addicts or career criminals. Most drug use is casual and recreational and does not lead to either addiction or serious criminal activity.

In short, crime is associated with drug use, but no direct causality exists. A fact sheet published by the Office of National Drug Control Policy concludes, "The drug/crime relationship is difficult to specify because . . . most crimes result from a variety of factors."[17] This interpretation has important implications for our policy choices. It means that even if we succeeded in eliminating all illegal drug use, we would achieve only a limited reduction in crime. Crimes related to drug trafficking would certainly be reduced, but the impact on crimes associated with deviant lifestyles, which include the vast majority of robberies and burglaries, would be very limited.

THE DRUG POLICY CHOICES

What should we do about drugs and crime? Peter Reuter classifies policy advocates into three groups: Hawks, Doves, and Owls (these categories are borrowed from the debate over the Vietnam War in the 1960s and 1970s).[18] Hawks emphasize law enforcement to eradicate drug abuse, believing that we simply need to get tougher than we have been. Enforcement strategies include both supply reduction, designed to reduce the availability of drugs, and demand reduction, designed to decrease peoples' desire to use drugs.[19] American drug policy is dominated by the Hawk approach, with most of the emphasis on supply reduction.

Owls prefer prevention and treatment of drug abuse, which are essentially demand reduction strategies. Current drug policy includes prevention and treatment, but they have always received less emphasis than supply reduction–oriented law enforcement approaches.

Doves believe that we should completely rethink our national drug policy. In general, they would prefer to define drug abuse as a public health problem. The National Council on Crime and Delinquency (NCCD) asserts that "it should be defined primarily as a health-related problem that should reside in the public health domain."[20] The radical Owl approach is to legalize drugs. A more moderate approach is referred to as "harm reduction," which generally means keeping the criminal penalties for drugs on the books, but not enforcing them as intensively. This is essentially the approach taken by many European countries, particularly the Netherlands.[21]

To a certain extent, the debate is over what causes the greatest harm: drugs or drug policy. Hawks believe that drugs are the problem. Doves believe that drug policy is the problem, causing more harm than good.

The Hawk/Dove/Owl categories do not conform to the conservative/liberal dichotomy we have used in this book. The Reagan and Bush administrations put tremendous emphasis on tough law enforcement, while First Lady Nancy Reagan simultaneously led a highly publicized "just say no" antidrug education campaign. The 1994 Violent Crime Bill endorsed by President Bill Clinton includes both tough law enforcement measures (100,000 more police) and money for prevention programs.

THE WAR ON DRUGS:
POLICY AND CONSEQUENCES

Since the 1914 Harrison Act, the Hawks have dominated American drug policy. That is, we have defined certain substances as illegal and attempted to suppress their use though criminal law enforcement. Over the past twenty years, our policy has become increasingly hawkish, as a succession of presidents have declared "war" on drugs, and arrests and imprisonment for drug possession and sale have soared.[22]

The war on drugs reached a new peak on September 5, 1989, when then-president George Bush created the Office of National Drug Control Policy (the head of which is often referred to as the "drug czar) and announced a set of new policies. Bush declared drugs "the gravest domestic threat facing our nation today."[23] His "war" essentially repackaged existing policies, including (1) intensive street-level drug enforcement; (2) joint federal, state, and local enforcement efforts; (3) cooperative arrangements with other countries to interdict the flow of drugs into the country and eradicate the cultivation of drugs in the field; (4) tougher sentencing policies for drug offenders; (5) a renewed attack on the use of "soft" drugs such as marijuana on the grounds that they are the "gateway" to the use of harder drugs; and (6) more antidrug public education.

Impact of the War on Drugs

The war on drugs has had an enormous impact on U.S. society, on the criminal justice system, and on racial minorities in particular. Federal expenditures for drug enforcement, for example, have soared, reaching $13.7 billion in 1995. The number of persons arrested for drug offenses doubled, from 601,000 in 1975 to 1.3 million in 1994. Persons convicted of drug offenses are the primary factor in the spectacular increase in the prison population. By 1994, 60 percent of all adults in federal prison had been convicted of drug offenses, compared with only 25 percent in 1980. Convictions for drug offenses were responsible for half of the increase in the prison population between 1980 and the mid-1990s.[24]

Many critics argue that racial minorities are the primary victims of the war on drugs. The National Criminal Justice Commission argues that "we are on the verge of a social catastrophe because of the sheer number of African-Americans behind bars."[25] Some would argue that the catastrophe is already here. Data compiled by the Sentencing Project (Figure 13.3) indicate that African Americans are treated more harshly at every stage of the criminal justice system. Yet, the National Household Survey states that they are only somewhat more likely to use illegal drugs. Hispanics are even less likely than whites to use drugs. In 1995, 6.0 percent of whites were current users, compared with 5.1 percent of Hispanics and 7.9 percent of African Americans.[26]

The National Criminal Justice Commission argues that street-level drug enforcement "focus[es] almost exclusively on low-level dealers in minority

Percentage African American

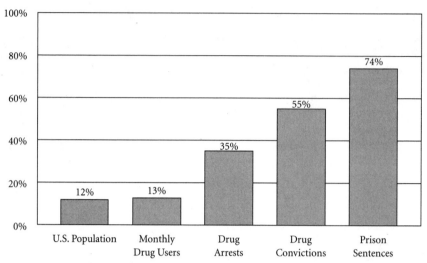

FIGURE 13.3 African Americans and the war on drugs (1992–1993 data).

SOURCE: Marc Mauer and Tracy Huling, *Young Black Americans and the Criminal Justice System: Five Years Later* (Washington, D.C.: The Sentencing Project, 1995).

neighborhoods."[27] The most blatant aspect of bias in the system, meanwhile, is the differential penalties for powdered and crack cocaine under the federal sentencing guidelines. Possession of five grams of crack nets a mandatory minimum sentence of five years, whereas possession of the same amount of powdered cocaine carries a maximum sentence of only one year. This has a grossly disparate racial impact, as crack is favored by African Americans and powdered cocaine is preferred by whites.[28] Yet, the Congress and the courts have refused to revise the guidelines.

Arrest and imprisonment are such common experiences in underclass neighborhoods that they have lost virtually all of their deterrent effect. As some critics have pointed out, drug use has declined among the general population, but the war on drugs has been waged primarily against poor and racial minority Americans.

In short, the war on drugs has undoubtedly had a tremendous impact on U.S. society and on racial minorities in particular. Whether it has succeeded in reducing illegal drug use or serious crime associated with drug use is another question.

Now let us take a look at some of the major components of the drug war.

Police "Crackdowns"

The streets are the front line in the war on drugs. As we learned in Chapter 5, simply adding more police patrol is not likely to reduce crime, including illegal drug activity. We have no reason to think that the 100,000 additional police officers promised by the 1994 Violent Crime Control Act, by themselves, will do anything to reduce drug abuse or drug-related crime.

The principal police strategy for reducing drug abuse is aggressive law enforcement. One variation is the "crackdown," an intensive, short-term, geographically focused effort.[29] One well-known crackdown was Operation Pressure Point (OPP) in New York City's Lower East Side. Directed at an open drug market, OPP flooded the area with police officers, produced a high volume of arrests, and sought to scare away drug buyers. Evaluations of Operation Pressure Point claimed some short-term benefits: an end to open drug dealing and a reduction in crime. Many important questions remain unanswered, however. The enforcement effort may have displaced drug dealing to other areas. Even within the targeted area, drug dealers adapted their procedures to insulate themselves from the police. The evaluations made no serious attempt to assess the outcomes of the arrests. Improper police tactics may have been used, particularly the harassment of potential buyers who drove in from suburban areas. There was also no serious discussion of the long-term cost-effectiveness of a mass arrest policy.[30]

The most telling criticism of OPP is that the drug problem in New York City worsened dramatically over the next few years with the arrival of crack. Open drug markets spread to many neighborhoods. Even the New York City police department tacitly admitted that the crackdown strategy was futile, and in the early 1990s it reduced both the number of officers assigned to the tactical narcotics teams (TNTs) and the number of drug arrests.[31] Many street-level police officers candidly admitted that they could make all the arrests they wanted, but new dealers and buyers would just take the place of those arrested. Other crackdowns such as Operation Hammer in Los Angeles had little impact on drugs or gang activity and were done mainly for the short-term publicity effect.[32]

The University of Maryland report to Congress on crime prevention programs concludes, "The evidence on drug crackdowns shows no consistent reductions in violent crime during or after the crackdown is in effect."[33] We agree.

PROPOSITION 43

Police crackdowns will not reduce drug use or serious crime associated with drugs.

This does not mean that all police antidrug efforts do not work. Some community policing or problem-oriented policing programs have shown some signs of success. The SMART (Specialized Multi-Agency Response Team) program in Oakland, California, reduced drug-related activity without displacing it to neighboring areas.[34] The difference may be that SMART's multi-agency approach, which mobilizes many agencies to attack a range of neighborhood problems, particularly housing, addresses underlying community problems better than mere arrests of drug users and dealers. The Maryland report *Preventing Crime* found that some community policing projects did not work but that others with a clear crime-specific focus did show some promise.[35] These kinds of programs merit further research and analysis.

Interdiction and Eradication

Two major supply reduction efforts by the federal government include *interdiction*, stopping the flow of drugs entering the country, and *eradication*, reducing the production of drug plants in the field. The conservative policy advocates William J. Bennett, John J. DiIulio, and John P. Walters argue that interdiction of drugs should be a "top national security priority" for the United States.[36] In fact, the federal government has made a huge and steadily increasing effort at interdiction. In 1995 federal agencies alone seized over 1.2 million pounds of drugs, including 2,527 pounds of heroin, 221,549 pounds of cocaine, and a million pounds of marijuana.[37] Meanwhile, federal authorities were eradicating over 100 million marijuana plants a year by the late 1980s.[38]

Major drug seizures by both federal and local officials are always accompanied by enormous publicity. Law enforcement officials tout these events as evidence that they are aggressively stopping the flow of illegal drugs. The truth is that interdiction efforts have been a failure. Many experts believe that the combined efforts of federal, state, and local law enforcement succeed in seizing only about 10 to 15 percent of the total supply.

The failure of interdiction is easy to understand. The borders of the United States are too great (about 20,000 miles), the possible methods of smuggling drugs too many, and the number of people engaged in the trade too numerous. Increased enforcement, moreover, produces a variety of adaptations: new points of entry, new methods of smuggling, shifts in drug use as prices change, and so on.[39] Insofar as tougher enforcement raises the risks of drug trafficking, it drives the trade into the hands of those who are better organized, more heavily armed, and willing to take the risks—in short, the cartels that dominate the international cocaine market.

Total worldwide production of drugs increased significantly between 1987 and 1991 alone. Production of marijuana rose from 13,000 to 23,000 metric tons, while coca leaf production increased from 291,000 to 337,000 metric tons.[40] The combined enforcement efforts of federal, state, and local agencies succeed in seizing only a portion of this total. As a Rand report concludes, "Increased drug interdiction efforts are not likely to greatly affect the availability of cocaine in the United States."[41]

PROPOSITION 44
Drug interdiction and eradication efforts are doomed to fail.

Tougher Sentencing

Tough sentencing policies for persons convicted of drug offenses has been another major strategy of the war on drugs. This represents the strategies of incapacitation and deterrence that we studied in Chapters 6 and 7. There is no need to cover that material again here.

Our conclusion was that neither strategy is effective in reducing crime. With respect to drugs, incapacitation is undermined by the replacement effect. Persons who are imprisoned for drug offenses are replaced by someone else who is willing to take the risks. The lack of legitimate opportunities (jobs, prospects for upward mobility) creates a substantial pool of potential new offenders.

It is important to note that drug use and crime associated with drugs has remained highest among the underclass, the very group that has been the primary target of the war on drugs. Arrest and imprisonment have obviously not had deterrent or incapacitative effects.

> **PROPOSITION 45**
>
> **Tougher sentencing is not likely to reduce illegal drug use
> or crime associated with drugs.**

THE LIMITS OF THE CRIMINAL LAW

Many critics of current drug policy argue that a war-on-drugs approach is doomed to fail. History provides valuable perspective on this issue by offering a number of examples of attempts to control products or services through the criminal law. Let us take a look at some of the more notable ones.

- *Prohibition.* Between 1920 and 1933, the manufacture and sale of alcoholic beverages were illegal under the Eighteenth Amendment to the U.S. Constitution. Stories from Prohibition have entered the national folklore: speakeasies, Al Capone, gangland shootouts, and so on. Prohibition did reduce drinking and probably contributed to the decline in deaths from cirrhosis of the liver (from 13.3 per 100,000 in 1910 to 7.2 per 100,000 in 1930). Citing these figures, some historians argue that Prohibition was a success.[42] Other historians, however, argue that Prohibition clearly did not end drinking and inflicted enormous collateral damage on the country.[43] By turning millions of casual drinkers into criminals, it undermined respect for the law. It created a vast illegal market that was filled by organized criminal syndicates. These syndicates corrupted police and politicians. Prohibition enforcement was accompanied by widespread abuses, particularly illegal searches and seizures.

- *Social gambling.* Gambling policy in the United States has undergone a revolution in recent years, with the spread of state lotteries and casinos. Until recently, it was a heavily restricted activity, confined to a small number of racetracks, Las Vegas, and church-based bingo games. Nonetheless, millions of Americans routinely engaged in illegal betting—on athletic events, through the "numbers" game, and so on. The laws restricting gambling had many of the same collateral effects as Prohibition. Gambling has long been the primary source of revenue for organized crime and was the main cause of police corruption.[44]

- *Gun control.* As we learned in Chapter 10, we have many laws barring certain people from owning guns, especially criminals. Yet, active criminals have no trouble obtaining weapons, through friends, the black market, or theft.

- *The old criminal abortion laws.* Before the 1973 *Roe v. Wade* decision, abortion was a criminal offense in every state (several states did liberalize their laws between 1967 and 1973). Yet, these laws did not eliminate abortions; in fact, as many as a million illegal abortions may have been performed a year. The harmful consequences included deaths and permanent injury to women from unsanitary back-alley abortions.

- *Sodomy, fornication, adultery, and prostitution laws.* Various forms of sexual activity have traditionally been illegal in the United States: sex between members of the same sex (sodomy), sex between unmarried people of different sex (fornication), sex between a married person and someone other than his or her spouse (adultery), and sex for pay (prostitution). To put it mildly, these laws, which remain on the books in many states, have failed to stop people from engaging in these forms of sexual behavior. All of these behaviors have occurred since the beginning of recorded history.

The Lessons of History

These examples suggest the following conclusions about the limits of the criminal law. First, if a large number of people want a product or service, someone will try to supply it. Second, efforts to suppress that supply will be undermined by massive evasion. Third, the enforcement effort itself will cause harm in the form of secondary crime, corruption, abuse of individual rights, and loss of respect for the law. Fourth, intensifying the enforcement effort encourages adaptations, either substitution of products (as in the case of some drugs) or transfer of the service to people more willing to take the increased risks.

In short, criminal law enforcement is inherently weak in the face of a strong public demand for a product or service. Shortly, we will look at some policies designed to reduce the demand for drugs.

When Enforcement Does Work

It is not true that all efforts to prevent bad behavior fail. The criminal law defines the basic standards of society. As children, we learn that stealing things and hitting people are wrong. To the extent that the criminal law shapes the values and habits of most people, it does work. The problem, of course, is that this process of socialization fails for a certain number of people.

The case of smoking offers an interesting example of an apparently successful attempt at curbing harmful behavior. Smoking among adults has declined significantly in recent years. Between 1965 and 1993, the percentage of American men who smoked fell from 52 to 26 percent. Among women it declined from 34 to 22 percent.[45] This is partly the result of formal restrictions on smoking in many buildings and public areas, along with a massive public education effort (including warning labels on cigarette packages).

It is important to recognize, however, that we have not completely eliminated smoking, and we have not tried to. The new restrictions only attempt to regulate and restrict smoking. In many respects, they have reinforced changing public attitudes about health. It is reasonable to speculate that a complete prohibition on smoking (similar to the one on alcohol in the 1920s) would produce a backlash that might only reinforce pro-smoking attitudes. We might speculate on what would happen if tobacco were outlawed. Would prohibition succeed? Would the results be like those during Prohibition in the 1920s and like the current prohibition of drugs? Or would they be different?

It is also worth noting that smoking has recently increased among white teenagers, particularly females. In other words, the national antismoking effort has not affected one major at-risk group, indicating that there are some limits as to what restrictions and education can accomplish. We will have more to say about this subject as we now turn to the question of drug education programs.

DEMAND REDUCTION: DRUG EDUCATION

The Owl drug policy favored by most liberals includes demand reduction through education and treatment. Let us take a look at drug education programs.

"Just Say No"

The most widely used demand reduction programs involve public education efforts designed to persuade people not to use drugs. The most famous was Nancy Reagan's "just say no" campaign in the 1980s. The first priority of a drug control policy proposed by conservatives William Bennett J. Bennett, John J. DiIulio, and John P. Walters is "Teach the young that drug use is wrong."[46] The relevant question, however, is whether drug education efforts actually work. Programs employ a variety of educational strategies.[47]

The most common strategy is *information dissemination*. This approach seeks to change behavior simply by providing information. A sex education program, for example, would discuss the basic facts about reproduction. A health education program would explain cholesterol.

Another strategy is *fear arousal*, which attempts to change behavior by frightening people. A safe-sex education program would emphasize the danger of getting AIDS from unprotected sex. In the "scared straight" program adult prisoners told juvenile offenders about the horrors of imprisonment.[48]

The *moral appeal* strategy emphasizes the idea that certain behavior is wrong—that sex outside marriage is a sin or that gambling is immoral, for example.

A final strategy is known as *affective education*. This approach attempts to develop personal and social skills that will help people resist certain behavior.

A sex education program, for instance, would try to teach teenagers how to say no to someone who is pressuring them to have sex.

Nancy Reagan's "just say no" campaign combined fear arousal and moral appeal. The famous "this is your brain, this is your brain on drugs" ad campaign developed by the Partnership for a Drug-Free America also used fear arousal.

We have good reasons for questioning the effectiveness of antidrug educational programs. The problems are similar to the ones we discussed in Chapter 6 regarding deterrence theory: the message has to reach the intended audience, members of that audience have to perceive a real risk, and these people have to make rational decisions to change their behavior.

First, many antidrug messages probably do not even reach their target audience. For example, the National Campaign for a Drug Free America runs expensive full-page ads in the *Wall Street Journal*. But how many teenagers or low-income people—those most at risk for illegal drug use—read the *Journal?* Second, many members of the target audience do not think that a real risk exists. Teenagers especially tend to believe that they are invulnerable—that they will not be caught by the police, that they are not too drunk to drive, that drugs will not hurt them, and so on. Also, as with deterrence theory, the risk has to be perceived in a cost-benefit context, as being worse than the alternative. But many people trapped in very poor neighborhoods do not perceive any realistic long-term hopes for economic advancement. Consequently, the short-term benefits of immediate gratification weigh much more heavily for them.

Some of the education program messengers, meanwhile, are not credible. Was Nancy Reagan, for example, an influential role model for low-income teenagers in the 1980s? Another problem is that some fear arousal programs backfire by glamorizing the forbidden behavior. They may heighten the allure of drinking, smoking, sex, and drugs by portraying them as adult-only activities. In fact, the famous "this is your brain on drugs" concept became the subject of many parodies that undermined the purpose of the original campaign.[49]

Third, we cannot assume that the members of the target audience are going to act rationally—that they will hear the message and make a conscious decision to change their behavior accordingly. Teenagers, as we mentioned, are notoriously focused on short-term gratification rather than long-term consequences. An education program is only one small factor influencing behavior and is likely to be very weak in the face of peer group influence.

DARE: Success of Failure?

The most popular antidrug education program in recent years has been DARE (Drug Abuse Resistance Education). Created by the Los Angeles Police Department (LAPD) and the Los Angeles school system in 1983, the program consists of seventeen 45- to 60-minute classes, taught by sworn police officers, for fifth and sixth grade students. It relies primarily on affective education, attempting to provide the "skills for recognizing and resisting social pressures to experiment with tobacco, alcohol, and drugs" and "developing skills in risk assessment and decision making."[50]

DARE is extremely popular with parents, politicians, and the police. DARE bumper stickers can be seen everywhere. By 1997, the program was operating in 70 percent of all school districts, at a total cost of an estimated $750 million a year. Evaluations of the program, however, have cast doubt on its effectiveness. These assessments have attempted to measure students' knowledge about drugs, attitudes toward drug use, social skills in resisting pressure to use drugs, and actual drug usage. A meta-analysis of eighteen evaluations by the Research Triangle Institute (RTI) of North Carolina concludes that the program's effect on drug use is "slight, and except for tobacco use, not statistically significant."[51] Studies that have followed DARE and non-DARE students for up to five years after the program have consistently found that "DARE does not have long-term effects on drug use."[52] It is worth pointing out, too, that the recent increase in teenage drug use has occurred in spite of the massive DARE effort directed at precisely that audience.

Several reasons are possible for the lack of impact on drug use. The RTI meta-analysis suggests that the teaching method, relying primarily on lectures, are inherently less effective than participative methods used in other kinds of programs. Some critics have suggested that police officers may not be well trained for this activity and may not be effective role models. A more fundamental question is whether, even in the best of circumstances, a seventeen-hour in-school program can even be powerful enough to overcome the other influences over a teenager's life—family (including a dysfunctional family), peer group, neighborhood, and so on. It is likely that the program works only where it supplements existing positive influences such as a strong family and peer group environment.

Publication of the RTI meta-analysis and other individual evaluations of DARE touched off a storm of controversy. Parents, police officials, government officials, along with DARE leaders, strongly objected to the unfavorable findings. In fact, serious allegations have been made of attempts to suppress publication of the results and even to harass critics of DARE.[53] This response recalls the attempt to suppress Martinson's unfavorable review of correctional treatment programs in the early 1970s, which we discussed in Chapter 11.

The evidence on DARE leads us to the following conclusion:

PROPOSITION 46

No evidence indicates that drug education, including DARE, significantly reduces illegal drug use.

But *Some* Education Programs Do Work

Not all education programs are worthless—some are effective. But it is important to examine why they work for certain audiences.

AIDS education programs are a good example. Good evidence exists indicating that safe-sex education programs have changed behavior. In New York, the average number of unsafe sexual encounters dropped from eleven to only one per year between 1980 and 1991. As a result, the incidence of new AIDS cases among adult gay men also dropped.[54] Unfortunately, unsafe activity has continued among people in the underclass, including both unprotected sex and the use of unclean needles. As a result, AIDS has spread from male drug addicts to their female sexual partners and on to other men. Surveys of members of the underclass have found an incredible indifference to the known risks of using unclean needles and engaging in unprotected sex.[55]

Why the difference between the two groups? The adult gay community is a relatively successful group in U.S. society, with relatively high levels of education and professional careers. That segment of the gay community is also very cohesive, with a strong self-identity, networks of community institutions, and strong peer group support. Needle-drug users are at the other end of the social scale: they are unemployed, with little if any education, substantial criminal records, and no community identity or institutions. It is reasonable to conclude that successful, educated people are more likely to respond to information dissemination programs: to receive the information, process it, and make a rational decisions to change their behavior. This process reflects a sense of empowerment and capacity to control one's own life. That sense of power and control is precisely what people at the bottom of society do not have.

Despite the early success of safe sex education programs, disturbing recent evidence indicates that they are not having the same degree of success with a younger generation of gay men. The reasons for this are not yet clear, but the situation does highlight the fact that people's behavior is influenced by a complex mix of personal and social factors. We cannot assume that education programs, by themselves, will have a dominant influence over behavior.[56]

Another example is the antismoking crusade, which we have already discussed. As we mentioned earlier, smoking has increased among teenagers recently, despite a significant decline among adults. Why the difference? We can argue that adults, especially successful, middle-class, and professional adults, are more likely to make rational choices about their behavior. Teenagers are far more likely to make reckless decisions, to consider themselves invulnerable, and to fail to think about either the immediate or the long-term consequences of their actions.

The response of different groups to education programs is closely related to the problems associated with deterrence theory, which we have already considered. Just as some people are more likely to be deterred by the threat of criminal sanction than others, so educational programs will be more effective with some groups than others. People with a stake in society are likely to respond very differently than people at the very bottom who feel they have nothing to lose.

DRUG TREATMENT

Along with education, drug treatment represents the prevention and demand reduction approach favored by most liberals. Treatment raises all of the issues related to rehabilitation that we discussed in Chapter 11. It is a planned intervention designed to change someone's behavior.

One of the major issues related to drug treatment is the availability of treatment programs. Critics of current drug policy argue that programs are not adequately funded and that many people who want treatment cannot receive it. Their proposal calls for funding to provide "treatment on demand." An estimated 944,208 people were attending alcohol and drug treatment programs across the country in 1993; 236,023 were enrolled for drug treatment only, and another 382,233 for combined alcohol and drug treatment.[57] It has also been estimated that about three or four times as many people need drug treatment as are currently receiving it.[58]

Varieties of Treatment

As is the case with drug education, several different kinds of drug treatment programs are available.[59]

Methadone maintenance provides methadone as a substitute for heroin. A supervised medical treatment maintains the addiction at a steady level to prevent deeper dependency, eliminates the addict's need to turn to crime, and presumably reduces his or her association with drug addicts and criminals (and their peer influence). A supervised program of withdrawal can also be included. Because it involves providing an addictive drug, methadone maintenance is the most controversial of the three major forms of treatment.

Therapeutic communities are residential programs using intensive individual or group counseling techniques. Their primary goal is to temporarily remove the external influences that contribute to drug dependency and through counseling to restructure the client's personality. Some of the more famous therapeutic communities include Synanon and Phoenix House. This is the most expensive of the three major types of programs.

Outpatient drug-free programs provide counseling and other services to clients who remain in the community. Services include individual and group counseling on drug abuse and counseling or training with respect to employment, family problems, or other problems. Because they are the least expensive and least controversial type of program, outpatient programs are the most common.

Drug users can get into treatment in a variety of different ways. They can enter a program voluntarily. Many famous celebrities, for example, go to the Betty Ford Clinic, an example of a therapeutic community. Others are compelled to enter treatment through the criminal justice system. Drug abuse counseling is often a condition of a diversion program, probation, or parole. Most of the new intensive probation supervision (IPS) and boot camp programs (see Chapter 11) include drug and alcohol counseling. Opponents of drug legalization argue that the coercive aspect of the criminal law is necessary to get most people into treatment.

Does Treatment Work?

The evidence on the effectiveness of treatment programs is very mixed. One review concludes that "all" the major types of programs "have been shown to be successful."[60] Another survey concludes optimistically that "research provides convincing evidence for the effectiveness of treatment for drug abuse."[61]

Evaluations of drug treatment programs generally show that clients who successfully complete the programs are less likely to use illegal drugs and to commit crimes than before treatment. An evaluation of one Philadelphia methadone maintenance program found that clients averaged nine "crime days" per month before treatment but only three after treatment; their average number of days per month employed went from three to eleven. Of 202 men who completed the Phoenix House therapeutic community program, 72 percent were arrested in the three years before entering the program, whereas 41 percent were arrested in the three years afterward. A Drug Abuse Reporting Program (DARP) outpatient treatment program reduced the arrest rate of clients from 87 percent beforehand to 22 percent after three years.[62]

Upon closer inspection, however, these claims offer a lot less than they appear to. First, few if any programs claim to reduce completely illegal drug use or criminal activity. Especially disturbing are the high dropout rates in virtually all programs. Program evaluations that include only those who complete the program are artificially inflating their success rate.

Even more serious, treatment programs report high rates of relapse into drug use. In criminal justice jargon, they recidivate. The same report that says treatment is effective also states that "relapse to drug use is the rule."[63] It is not exactly a ringing endorsement to say that failure is "the rule." Treatment programs seem to work for those clients who have made a personal commitment to get off drugs. Interviews with ex-addicts repeatedly reveal that they decided that the drug life was too much hassle, that they could not put up with it any more. In other words, treatment works for those who have decided to make it work. But treatment programs do not seem to be able to produce that change in personal commitment.[64]

The relapse problem arises with programs designed to treat alcoholism or smoking, reduce weight, or rehabilitate criminals. Millions of people try to give up smoking or lose weight every year. Most of them fail. In fact, most fail many times. We all know people who have made several efforts to quit smoking or lose weight. In some cases, however, they succeed. They finally quit smoking or lost the twenty pounds they always wanted to lose.

The challenge for effective treatment is to match the right program with the right client.[65] To a great extent, the "right" client is the person who has already made a commitment to change his or her life. But as one treatment expert puts it, "Little progress has been made in classifying drug users to identify what kinds of users will benefit most from particular kinds of programs."[66] If this sounds familiar, it is because it is another version of the prediction problem we have encountered several times before. As we have seen, bail decisions, selective incapacitation, probation, and parole all depend on identifying just the right people and only those people. Overpredicting produces false positives; underpredicting leads to false negatives. And as we have seen, the data and diagnostic tools are not available to us to make the precise predictions we want.

This leads us to the following proposition:

> ## PROPOSITION 47
> **Drug treatment serves the needs of individuals who have decided to end their drug use. But treatment, as a primary strategy, will not reduce the national drug problem.**

LEGALIZE DRUGS?

By the 1980s, many thoughtful observers had concluded that the war on drugs was a disaster. With the arrival of crack, the drug problem had actually gotten worse, at least in the underclass, despite increasing arrests and soaring imprisonment rates. The war was having a devastating effect on racial minority communities. Jerome G. Miller argues that it represents a "search and destroy" policy directed at young African American men.[67]

These criticisms led to a radical new proposal to legalize drugs. Legalization is no longer something advocated by hippies left over from the 1960s. The advocates include prominent conservatives, such as the Nobel Prize–winning economist Milton Friedman and writer William F. Buckley. They are joined by civil libertarians, who agree with these conservatives on almost no other criminal justice issue.[68] The American Civil Liberties Union (ACLU) adopted a policy in 1994 calling for the "full and complete decriminalization of the use, possession, manufacture and distribution of drugs."[69]

The new debate over legalization was sparked by Ethan Nadelmann's 1989 article in *Science* magazine, "Drug Prohibition in the United States."[70] His case for legalization includes the following points: criminal prohibition has not eliminated or even reduced drug use; we spend billions of dollars a year in this seemingly futile effort; the war on drugs produces numerous harmful side effects, including corruption and damage to poor and minority neighborhoods, prohibition of potentially beneficial medical uses of marijuana, and so on. The "logic of legalization," he argues, consists of two main points: that "most illegal drugs are not as dangerous as is commonly believed" and that abuse of the most dangerous drugs will not rise significantly under legalization.[71]

Only a small segment of the public supports legalization of drugs at this time. Different public opinion surveys have found that between 10 and 24 percent of the public support full legalization of marijuana (which is the softest of all drugs).[72] Yet, nearly half approve of legalizing the medical use of marijuana. And in the 1996 elections, voters in California and Arizona approved referenda providing some legal use of medically prescribed marijuana. (The legal status of these new laws vis-à-vis federal law remains in doubt as this chapter is being written.)

Varieties of Legalization

The debate over legalization has been confused because the term means different things to different people. It is often used interchangeably with *decriminalization*. Both terms embrace a variety of specific proposals. The basic point of both is the removal of criminal penalties for the possession and sale of at least some currently illegal drugs. Beyond that, however, much disagreement prevails over four issues: (1) Are all drugs to be legalized, or only some? (2) Are possession *and* sale to be legalized, or only possession? (3) Will legalization apply to adults *and* juveniles, or just adults? (4) Will some kind of regulation replace criminal penalties, and if so, what kind?[73]

As Nadelmann points out, "There is no one legalization option."[74] Figure 13.4 presents a matrix of the various drug policy options. Legalization *maximalists* take the extreme position, advocating legalization of both sale and possession of all drugs for juveniles as well as adults. Legalization *moderates* want to remove criminal penalties for the possession of many drugs, the sale of some drugs, but for adults only. Legalization *minimalists*, meanwhile, would eliminate penalties only for adult possession of marijuana and perhaps other less dangerous drugs. Finally, *agnostics* have not taken a final position on legalization but are convinced that current policy has failed and that we need a national debate on a new approach to drugs.[75]

Within this general framework are a number of different policy options. One approach is to give states the right to set their own drug policy, allowing them to experiment as they see fit. This would abandon a national policy. Under a proposal drafted by Daniel K. Benjamin and Roger Leroy Miller, any conflict between federal and state laws would be resolved in favor of state law.[76] Another alternative would be to legalize particular drugs for medical use only. California and Arizona took a step in this direction in 1996. A more comprehensive option would have the government issue "user's licenses" to individuals who pass a required test.[77]

Except for radical libertarians, most legalization proposals would maintain some government regulation over drugs. The issue of regulation, however, is widely misunderstood. A wide range of "legal" products today are regulated (for example, tobacco and alcohol). Similarly, you cannot just buy a cow and sell milk from your front porch. These regulations are ultimately backed up by criminal penalties. It is illegal to sell cigarettes or beer to minors. Thus, legalization does not necessarily mean the complete elimination of all forms of government control or the threat of criminal punishment. But it does represent a shift in the basic direction of drug policy.

Drug	Possessed by		Sale by		Sale to	
	Adults	Juveniles	Adults	Juveniles	Adults	Juveniles
Heroin						
Cocaine Granular						
Cocaine Crack						
Marijuana						
LSD						
PCP						

FIGURE 13.4 Drug legalization options

The Impact of Legalization

What would happen if we legalized drugs? Obviously, the answer depends on which form of legalization we are talking about. The effect of radical legalization would be very different from the moderate or conservative alternatives.

Whichever policy were adopted, these questions arise: (1) Would drug use increase or decrease? (2) Would predatory crime such as robbery and burglary increase or decrease? (3) How much money would in fact be saved? (4) What would happen to the drug–related criminal syndicates? (5) What would be the overall impact on the criminal justice system? (6) Would there be fewer violations of individual rights? (7) Finally, what would be the overall effect on the quality of life in the United States?

A Specific Proposal

To focus our discussion of these questions, let us examine a specific legalization proposal drafted by Richard B. Karel that appears in a collection of essays on the legalization debate.[78]

Karel proposes legalizing drugs only for adults and making distinctions among various drugs based on their toxicity and potential harm. He would completely legalize coca leaves, which could be sold in supermarkets "as tea is now sold." Granular cocaine would be illegal, but people could obtain cocaine gum similar to the nicotine gum currently available. Access would be rationed through an ATM-type system. You would have a card and you could "withdraw" so much per day or week. Crack cocaine would be completely illegal. Smokable and edible forms of opium would also be available through an ATM system. Heroin would be available to addicts, through either medical prescription or the ATM system, but PCP would remain illegal. Psychedelic drugs would be legally available to people who could demonstrate "knowledge as to their effects" through a written test and interview. The government would regulate the market by controlling distribution and ensuring product purity, much as the government now regulates alcohol and tobacco.

Karel's proposal falls somewhere in the moderate-to-conservative range of legalization alternatives. The most dangerous drugs—crack and PCP—would still be illegal. All drug use by and sale to juveniles would be illegal.

What would be the result? First, there would be an immediate and significant reduction in the number of arrests and persons sent to prison. This would reduce the workload of the justice system and save a certain amount of money, particularly in terms of imprisonment costs. The dollar savings would be a lot less than many legalization advocates believe, however. With cocaine still illegal for adults and all drugs illegal for juveniles, we would still maintain most of the present law enforcement apparatus. And we should not forget that police do a lot of other things besides investigate drug crimes. Criminal syndicates would probably not disappear, because they would still try to serve the demand for cocaine and other drugs that were still illegal. In short, many of the gains promised by legalization advocates—the dollar savings, the disappearance of the drug profits and the criminal syndicates—would not materialize.

Karel's proposal also makes some assumptions about drug users that are debatable. His scenario assumes that they are basically rational people, deciding to go to the clinic to get their ration of gum cocaine or methadone, much the way middle-class yuppies decide whether to buy domestic or imported beer. This scenario does not come to grips with the irrational and self-destructive nature of drug abuse. Among teenagers, drug and alcohol abuse are acts of rebellion. Among the underclass, heroin and cocaine abuse is a way of retreating from a brutal world with no apparent opportunities.

Would Karel's proposal reduce crime? In one limited sense, yes. By definition, it eliminates certain drug-defined crimes involving possession and sale. It is not likely to reduce drug-associated crimes, such as robbery and burglary, however. As we already noted, most of this criminal behavior is part of a deviant lifestyle that is the product of many different factors. Relatively little predatory crime is directly caused by drugs, and legalization will not end that criminal behavior. Because crack would still be illegal, drug gangs would still engage in the same violent struggle for control of the market.

Let us move beyond Karel's proposal and discuss the legalization of all drugs. Would drug use increase? Much controversy exists over this question. Even Ethan Nadelmann, one of the leading legalization advocates, concedes, "It is thus impossible to predict whether or not legalization would lead to much greater levels of drug abuse."[79]

Opponents of legalization argue that a tremendous increase in drug use would result. They believe that existing criminal penalties curb drug use, both by the threat of arrest and punishment and because the criminal law represents a statement about society's values.[80] Some evidence, however, suggests that drug use would not increase. The National Household Survey clearly indicates that millions of Americans use illegal drugs every year without becoming heavy users, addicts, or criminals. They do not because the process of socialization operates somewhat effectively. They may engage in some minor deviance—casual drug use, vandalism, even some petty theft—but they do not cross over the line into addiction or criminality. Moreover, drug abuse is not rampant in those European countries that have relatively tolerant drug policies. These countries do not have the same level of crime the United States has, and their example may not be relevant in this context.

The danger, however, is that the mechanisms of socialization might be overwhelmed by legalization. In a suburban high school, for example, drug use could become so prevalent that peer pressure encourages pervasive cocaine use. As drug use increases, academic performance could decline, leading to a complete change in the culture of the school.

To a great extent, this is exactly what has already happened in many schools and neighborhoods. Drug use is so pervasive that it is extremely difficult for young people to resist the pressures to join. Drug-related crime contributes to the dreadful quality of neighborhood life. This is one of the main reasons that African American leaders are some of the most vocal opponents of legalization. People such as Representative Charles Rangel, whose district includes Harlem, see a covert form of racism in the legalization idea.[81] They argue that it would abandon their communities to drugs.

The legalization issue is not completely polarized along racial lines. Mayor Kurt Schmoke of Baltimore, also an African American, is one of the leading advocates of an alternative to our current drug policy. In fact, his firsthand experience as a prosecutor convinced him of the futility of the war on drugs.[82] He and others argue that the war on drugs has already failed to protect poor neighborhoods. The calamity Rangel describes—of open drug trafficking and abuse, of rampant crime and violence—is already here.

One of the strongest arguments against the war on drugs is that it converts many otherwise law-abiding people into criminals. The Rand Corporation interviewed people arrested for drug offenses in Washington, D.C., and found that two-thirds held regular jobs. Drug dealing was essentially a part-time job. Their regular jobs paid an average of $11,000 to $14,000 a year, while they said they made an average of $24,000, tax-free, from their drug dealing. The illegal drug markets represented a very tempting way to supplement their annual income. Looking at it another way, their $7 an hour jobs were not adequate to support a decent lifestyle.[83] Legalizing drugs would eliminate this temptation to engage in criminal activity and save thousands of people from arrest and imprisonment and the subsequent problems associated with having a criminal record.

The full impact of legalization remains entirely a matter of speculation. This leads us to the following conclusion:

> ## PROPOSITION 48
> **Legalization is a high-risk gamble that needs further discussion.**

CONCLUSION

In the end, what can we recommend in the way of a sensible drug policy? The first step should be to face squarely the fact that we do not have any convincing evidence of a program or policy that has been proven effective in reducing drug abuse and crime associated with drugs. Politicians continually restate the same old policies ("longer prison terms," "more treatment") without any evidence regarding their effectiveness.

The starting point should be to recognize that we really do not have the answers at the moment. The major contribution of the advocates of legalization has been to force a wide-ranging discussion of our current drug policy. As Ronald Bayer argues, the advocates of legalization have "revitalized the public debate over the fundamental structure of American drug policy."[84] This is a major contribution. The Drug Policy Foundation's 1992 *National Drug Reform Strategy* calls for the creation of a national commission "to seriously examine alternatives to prohibition."[85]

The purpose of this book is to find policies that will reduce serious crime. As we have found, the drug-crime relationship is extremely complex. It does appear that most of the serious crime associated with drug use is not directly caused by drugs. Thus, even if we found a solution to the drug problem, we would probably still be faced with the crime problem.

NOTES

1. Elliott Currie, *Reckoning: Drugs, the Cities, and the American Future* (New York: Hill & Wang, 1992); Steven R. Donziger, ed., *The Real War on Crime: The Report of the National Criminal Justice Commission* (New York: HarperPerennial, 1996).

2. Dale Gieringer, "How Many Crack Babies?" in Arnold Trebach and Kevin B. Zeese, eds., *Drug Prohibition and the Conscience of Nations* (Washington, D.C.: Drug Policy Foundation, 1990), pp. 71–75.

3. The best analysis of the subject is Malcolm W. Klein, *The American Street Gang: Its Nature, Prevalence, and Control* (New York: Oxford University Press, 1995).

4. Office of National Drug Control Policy, *Fact Sheet: Drug Use Trends* (Washington, D.C.: Government Printing Office, 1996); Bureau of Justice Statistics, *Drugs, Crime, and the Justice System* (Washington, D.C.: Government Printing Office, 1992).

5. Department of Health and Human Services, *Preliminary Estimates from the 1995 National Household Survey on Drug Abuse*, Advance Report 18 (Washington, D.C.: Department of Health and Human Services, 1996), p. 12.

6. Ibid., p. 13.

7. National Institute of Drug Abuse, *Drug Use Among American High School Seniors, College Students, and Young Adults, 1975–1990* (Washington, D.C.: Government Printing Office, 1991).

8. Office of National Drug Control Policy, *Fact Sheet: Drug Use Trends*, p. 2.

9. Ibid., p. 4; Department of Health and Human Services, Advance Report 17, *Preliminary Estimates From the Drug Abuse Warning Network* (Washington, D.C.: Department of Health and Human Services, 1996).

10. National Institute of Justice, *1995 Drug Use Forecasting* (Washington, D.C.: Government Printing Office, 1996).

11. Currie, *Reckoning*.

12. Andrew Hacker, *Two Nations: Black, White, Separate, Hostile, and Unequal* (New York: Scribner's 1992).

13. David N. Nurco, Timothy W. Kinlock, and Thomas E. Hanlon, "The Drugs-Crime Connection," in James A. Inciardi, ed., *Handbook of Drug Control in the United States* (New York: Greenwood, 1990), pp. 71–90.

14. This typology is taken from Office of National Drug Control Policy, *Fact Sheet: Drug-Related Crime* (Washington, D.C.: Government Printing Office, 1994).

15. The data in this paragraph are summarized in ibid.

16. Bureau of Justice Statistics, *Drugs, Crime, and the Justice System*, p. 2.

17. Ibid., p. 3.

18. A good discussion of the different positions on drug policy is Peter Reuter, "Hawks Ascendant: The Punitive Trend of American Drug Policy," *Daedalus* 121 (Summer 1992): 15–52.

19. Mark H. Moore, "Controlling Criminogenic Commodities: Drugs, Guns, and Alcohol," in James Q. Wilson, ed., *Crime and Public Policy* (San Francisco: ICS Press, 1983), Chapter 8.

20. Marsha Rosenbaum, *Just Say What? An Alternative View on Solving America's Drug Problem* (San Francisco: National Council on Crime and Delinquency, 1989), p. 17.

21. Ed Leuw, "Drugs and Drug Policy in the Netherlands," in Michael Tonry, ed., *Crime and Justice: A Review of Research*, vol. 14 (Chicago: University of Chicago Press, 1991), pp. 229–276.

22. Jerome G. Miller, *Search and Destroy: African American Males in the Criminal Justice System* (New York: Cambridge University Press, 1996); Donziger, ed., *The Real War on Crime*.

23. *New York Times* (September 6, 1989).

24. Edna McConnell Clark Foundation, *Seeking Justice: Crime and Punishment in America* (New York: Edna McConnell Clark Foundation, 1995), p. 21.

25. Donziger, ed., *The Real War on Crime*, p. 99.

26. Department of Health and Human Services, *National Household Survey on Drug Abuse: Population Estimates 1995* (Washington, D.C.: Government Printing Office, 1996).

27. Donziger, ed., *The Real War on Crime*, p. 115.

28. Michael Tonry, *Malign Neglect: Race, Crime, and Punishment in America* (New York: Oxford University Press, 1995), pp. 188–189; Bureau of Justice Statistics, *Sentencing in the Federal Courts: Does Race Matter?* (Washington, D.C.: Government Printing Office, 1993).

29. Lawrence W. Sherman, "Police Crackdowns: Initial and Residual Deterrence," in Michael Tonry and Norval Morris, eds., *Crime and Justice: A Review of Research*, vol. 12 (Chicago: University of Chicago Press, 1990), pp. 1–48.

30. Lynn Zimmer, "Proactive Policing Against Street-Level Drug Trafficking," *American Journal of Police* 9(1) (1990): 43–74.

31. "How Much Ban from TNT?" *Law Enforcement News* (December 31, 1992).

32. Paul Hoffman, "The Feds, Lies, and Videotape," *Southern California Law Review* 66 (May 1993): 1453–1532.

33. Lawrence W. Sherman, Denise Gottfredson, Doris MacKenzie, John Eck, Peter Reuter, and Shawn Bushaway, *Preventing Crime: What Works, What Doesn't, What's Promising* (College Park: University of Maryland, 1997), pp. 8–28.

34. Lorraine Greene, *Policing Places with Drug Problems* (Thousand Oaks, CA: Sage, 1996).

35. Sherman et al., *Preventing Crime*, pp. 8–39.

36. William J. Bennett, John J. DiIulio, and John P. Walters, *Body Count: Moral Poverty . . . And How to Win America's War Against Crime* (New York: Simon & Schuster, 1996), p. 189.

37. Bureau of Justice Statistics, *Sourcebook of Criminal Justice Statistics—1995* (Washington, D.C.: Government Printing Office, 1996), p. 437.

38. Bureau of Justice Statistics, *Drugs, Crime, and the Justice System*, p. 150.

39. Ibid., Chapter 2.

40. Ibid., p. 36.

41. Peter Reuter, Gordon Crawford, and Jonathan Cave, *Sealing the Borders: The Effects of Increased Military Participation in Drug Interdiction* (Santa Monica, CA: Rand, 1988), p. xi.

42. Mark H. Moore, "Actually Prohibition Was a Success," in Rod L. Evans and Irwin M. Berent, eds., *Drug Legalization* (LaSalle, IL: Open Court, 1992), pp. 95–97.

43. Samuel Walker, *Popular Justice: A History of American Criminal Justice*, 2d ed. (New York: Oxford University Press, 1998), pp. 158–159.

44. The Knapp Commission, *The Knapp Commission Report on Police Corruption* (New York: Braziller, 1973).

45. Bureau of the Census, *Statistical Abstract of the United States, 1995* (Washington, D.C.: Government Printing Office, 1996), p. 144.

46. Bennett et al., *Body Count*, p. 187.

47. Gilbert J. Botvin, "Substance Abuse Prevention: Theory, Practice, and Effectiveness," in Michael Tonry and James Q. Wilson, eds., *Crime and Justice: An Annual Review of Research*, vol. 13 (Chicago: University of Chicago Press, 1990), pp. 474–477.

48. James O. Finckenauer, *Scared Straight and the Panacea Phenomenon* (Englewood Cliffs, NJ: Prentice Hall, 1982).

49. Jesse Greene, "Flirting with Suicide," *New York Times* (September 15, 1996), p. 41.

50. Bureau of Justice Assistance, *An Introduction to DARE*, 2d ed. (Washington, D.C.: Government Printing Office, 1991).

51. Susan T. Emmett, Nancy Tobler, Christopher Ringwalt, and Robert L.

Flewelling, "How Effective Is Drug Abuse Resistance Education? A Meta-Analysis of Project DARE Outcome Evaluations," *American Journal of Public Health* 84 (September 1994): 1394–1401.

52. Richard R. Clayton, Carl G. Leukefeld, Nancy Grant Harrington, and Anne Cattarello, "DARE (Drug Abuse Resistance Education): Very Popular but Not Very Effective," in Clyde B. McCoy, Lisa R. Metsch, and James A. Inciardi, eds., *Intervening with Drug-Involved Youth* (Thousand Oaks, CA: Sage, 1996), p. 104.

53. Stephen Glass, "Don't You D.A.R.E.," *The New Republic* (March 3, 1997): 18–28.

54. Green, "Flirting with Suicide."

55. Currie, *Reckoning*, pp. 247–251.

56. Greene, "Flirting with Suicide."

57. Bureau of Justice Statistics, *Sourcebook of Criminal Justice Statistics—1995*, p. 582.

58. Bureau of Justice Statistics, *Drugs, Crime, and the Justice System*, p. 109.

59. George De Leon, "Treatment Strategies," in Inciardi, ed., *Handbook of Drug Control in the United States*, pp. 115–138; Bureau of Justice Statistics, *Drugs, Crime, and the Justice System*, pp. 107–111.

60. M. Douglas Anglin and Yih-Ing Hser, "Treatment of Drug Abuse," in Tonry and Wilson, eds., *Drugs and Crime* (Chicago: University of Chicago Press, 1990), p. 393.

61. De Leon, "Treatment Strategies," p. 120.

62. Ibid.

63. Ibid., p. 127.

64. Currie, *Reckoning*, pp. 154–155.

65. Ibid., pp. 132–133.

66. Anglin and Hser, "Treatment of Drug Abuse," p. 395.

67. Miller, *Search and Destroy.*

68. A history of the debate over decriminalization/legalization of drugs is in Ronald Bayer, "Introduction: The Great Drug Policy Debate—What Means This Thing Called Decriminalization?" in Ronald Bayer and Gerald M. Oppenheimer, eds., *Confronting Drug Policy: Illicit Drugs in a Free Society* (New York: Cambridge University Press, 1993), pp. 1–23.

69. American Civil Liberties Union, Board of Directors, "Minutes, April 9, 1994," ACLU Briefing Paper 19, *Against Drug Prohibition* (New York: ACLU, n.d.).

70. Ethan A. Nadelmann, "Drug Prohibition in the United States: Costs, Consequences, and Alternatives," *Science* 245 (September 1, 1989): 939–947.

71. Ibid., p. 943.

72. Bureau of Justice Statistics, *Sourcebook of Criminal Justice Statistics—1995*, pp. 181, 199.

73. See the questions posed by James A. Inciardi, "The Case Against Legalization," in Inciardi, ed., *The Drug Legalization Debate* (Newbury Park, CA: Sage, 1991), pp. 45–79.

74. Nadelmann, "Drug Prohibition in the United States," p. 939.

75. Drug Policy Foundation, *National Drug Reform Strategy* (Washington, D.C.: Drug Policy Foundation, 1992).

76. Cited in Arnold Trebach, "Thinking Through Models of Drug Legalization," in *The Drug Policy Newsletter* 23 (July/August 1994): 12.

77. These options are discussed by Trebach in ibid.

78. Richard B. Karel, "A Model Legalization Proposal," in Inciardi, ed., *The Drug Legalization Debate*, pp. 80–102.

79. Nadelmann, "Drug Prohibition in the United States," p. 944.

80. James Q. Wilson, "Against the Legalization of Drugs," *Commentary* 89 (February 1990): 21–28.

81. See the thoughtful discussion in William Kornblum, "Drug Legalization and the Minority Poor," in Bayer and Oppenheimer, eds., *Confronting Drug Policy*, pp. 115–135.

82. Kurt L. Schmoke, "Drugs: A Problem of Health and Economics," in David Boaz, ed., *The Crisis in Drug Prohibition* (Washington, D.C.: Cato Institute, 1990), pp. 9–12.

83. Peter Reuter, Robert MacCoun, and Patrick Murphy, *Money from Crime: A*

Study of the Economics of Drug Dealing in Washington, DC (Santa Monica, CA: Rand, 1990).

84. Bayer, "The Great Drug Policy Debate," p. 20.

85. Drug Policy Foundation, *National Drug Reform Strategy*.

PART VI

Conclusions

1 4

The Paradox of Crime
and Crime Policy

As we near the end of the century, we face an extraordinary paradox with respect to crime policy. Since the early 1990s, the crime rate has been falling dramatically. The number of murders in New York City in 1996, for example, was the lowest in thirty years. This is a tremendous success story, one that we should all celebrate.

And yet, this success has occurred in spite of the fact that few if any programs have proven effective in reducing serious crime. The basic argument of this book has been than nothing really works. Remember our first proposition: "Most current crime control policies are nonsense." But if that is true, how do we explain the dramatic decline in serious crime? Obviously, *something* is happening in American society. But what is it? What has caused crime rates, and violent crime rates in particular, to drop?

THE GREAT AMERICAN PATERNITY FIGHT

We are about to witness one of the greatest paternity fights in history. Everyone wants to take credit for the reduction in crime. President Bill Clinton claimed in 1997 that his administration's policies, particularly the 1994 Violent Crime Control Act, were responsible. Former New York City police commissioner William Bratton and his followers argue that the NYCPD's "zero-tolerance" policy toward minor quality-of-life offenses has sent a strong message that also helps reduce more serious crime. Community policing advocates believe that their programs prevent crime. Conservatives across the country, meanwhile, argue that our massive imprisonment policy has successfully incapacitated repeat offenders. Death penalty advocates feel that the return of executions has deterred violent offenders. Supporters of DARE and other drug education programs believe that they have successfully discouraged illegal drug use.

There is an old cliché that says failure is an orphan but success has many parents. So it is with crime policy. Everyone wants to claim credit for our recent success. Our task is to sort our way through all of these claims, which are politically motivated on both sides, and try to develop a sensible explanation for the current crime trends.

A WORD OF CAUTION

A word of caution is in order here. As this is being written, in mid-1997, it appears that the reduction in crime is a genuine national trend. The drop in crime has been going on now for almost five years, so we cannot dismiss it as a temporary aberration or the result of some one-year statistical artifact.

By the time you read this, however, the situation may have changed. In Chapter 1 we cited the dire warnings of James Alan Fox about the so-called "ticking time bomb."[1] As he points out, the murder rate among teenagers soared from the late 1980s onward, even while it was stable or dropping among older age groups. The census data indicate that a second baby boom is soon to reach the high-crime years (fourteen to twenty-four years old). Fox argues that if the high murder rates among teenagers persist as this large group enters the teenage years, we could face an explosion of violent crime.

In short, the good news of the mid-1990s might not continue. Fox has properly combined two reliable sets of data and made a reasonable projection of future crime trends. The unknown factor in this equation, however, is whether the high teenage murder rate will continue into the future. If it does, we face some very bad prospects. If it does not, the good news about crime is likely to continue.

A QUICK REVIEW OF
WHAT WE HAVE LEARNED

In response to the many claims of credit for reducing crime, let us review quickly some of what we have learned in this book.

Let us begin with policing, because that is the front line of the criminal justice system. The president of the United States claims that the funding for 100,000 additional police officers provided by the 1994 Violent Crime Control Act has played a major role in reducing crime. Yet, we learned in Chapter

5 that simply adding more police does not prevent crime. There are additional problems. All 100,000 of the promised new positions have not been funded. Not every city has added a significant number of new officers. And, finally, we do not know what all the new officers are in fact doing out there on the street. We should be very skeptical about the claims made for the impact of the 100,000 officers.

Former police commissioner William Bratton, criminologist George Kelling, and others argue that the zero-tolerance policy adopted by Bratton in the NYCPD is responsible for reducing serious crime.[2] Several things are wrong with this argument, however. First, despite the claims of zero-tolerance advocates, the connection between minor offenses and murder is tenuous at best. Second, the reduction in crime began before Bratton was even appointed commissioner of the NYCPD. Third, a similar reduction in crime has occurred in Los Angeles where, according to media reports, the police department is demoralized and making fewer arrests than in the past. In short, we should be skeptical about the claims for zero-tolerance policing in New York City.

With respect to drug education programs, the DARE program is extremely popular with parents, police, and politicians. Yet, as we learned in Chapter 13, evaluations of DARE have consistently failed to find any significant impact on illegal drug use.

Advocates of incapacitation believe that crime has fallen because so many repeat offenders are locked up in prison. Yet, as we learned in Chapter 7, there is no solid persuasive evidence that incapacitation works as a crime reduction strategy. Even Zimring and Hawkins's study of imprisonment in California, which found some apparent incapacitative effect (but at a high social cost), could not clearly distinguish the precise causal relationship between imprisonment trends and crime rates.[3] Moreover, when you look at trends in incarceration rates, you find that the imprisonment binge began twenty years ago. If incapacitation works, the effects should have begun to appear at least by the early 1980s, not the mid-1990s.

In short, many claims are made for effective crime reduction programs, but the evidence to support these claims is weak at best.

This conclusion, however, leaves the basic paradox unresolved. If crime control programs do not work, then why is crime down? The answer is that it may be difficult to specify a direct cause, at least in a way that would satisfy most social scientists. The fact is that human behavior changes in fundamental ways over the long term. Historians believe that serious crime and disorder in all industrial societies fell from the mid-nineteenth century until the post–World War II period.[4] Why? Police and prisons probably had little to do with it. A more general "civilizing" effect of the new urban society seems to have taken hold: pervasive patterns of work and daily life that disciplined behavior. Historians also agree that crime and disorder in all societies turned upward after World War II. Why? The answers are not clear, but it certainly was not any single cause, such as television (to name one popular villain).

It may be that we are at the onset of another broad change in behavior. Not only is crime down, but reports indicate that teenage pregnancy has also fallen in the mid-1990s. This decline has occurred despite the evident failure of several decades of sex education programs previously. It is possible that the downward trend in serious crime began in the early 1980s but was interrupted by the advent of crack (see our discussion of murder trends in Washington, D.C., in Chapter 1, for example). The general point is that we may not be able to explain these long-term changes in behavior. The more specific point is that we should not accept unwarranted claims of credit for these changes by the advocates of particular programs.

CRIME PREVENTION:
THE MARYLAND REPORT

The most comprehensive survey of the effectiveness of crime prevention programs is a 1997 report to Congress, *Preventing Crime*, by faculty from the University of Maryland.[5] As its subtitle indicates, it sought to identify what works, what does not, and what is promising. The primary purpose was to help Congress better understand the effectiveness of the nearly $4 billion a year that the U.S. Department of Justice spends on crime prevention. This figure is only one small part of the more than $100 billion (1992 data) that the country spends at all levels of government on criminal justice.

Because of its comprehensive scope and sophisticated method of analysis, *Preventing Crime* is simply the best treatment of crime policy available, and it should be the starting point for all future discussions of the subject. The section on the nature of scientific inquiry and the problems of applying social science to social policy should be required reading for all serious students of criminal justice.

What does the report say? *Preventing Crime* identifies seven "institutional settings" in which crime prevention programs operate: communities, families, schools, labor markets, places (in the sense of "specific premises"), police, and criminal justice. The latter includes a wide array of criminal justice system programs, including punishment-oriented programs such as imprisonment. The authors of the report properly note that the distinction between "prevention" and "punishment" is an artificial one. These terms represent different means to the same end: the reduction in crime. Each of these institutional settings is the subject of a long chapter devoted to the relevant literature.

What did the Maryland team learn? Their systematic review of the literature found that some things work, a lot of programs do not, and, most important, there is a lot we do not know. Many crime prevention programs have not been studied at all, or have been studied imperfectly, or have been studied in ways that do not address larger questions of context (such that the impact of the program in question cannot be precisely determined). Many of the report's conclusions are similar to those in this book.

One clear pattern emerges from the *Preventing Crime* report, although the authors shy away from its political implications. Repeatedly, they conclude that the programs that do seem to work are most effective with the people and communities that need these programs the least. Consistently, their evidence points to solutions that lie outside the criminal justice system.

Chapter 3 of *Preventing Crime* addresses community-oriented crime prevention programs. "In study after study," the authors conclude, "evidence emerges that crime prevention programs are more likely to take root, and more likely to work, in communities that need them the least."[6] They add that "communities with the greatest crime problems are also the hardest to reach through innovative program efforts." The heart of the crime problem lies in the "underlying structural conditions" in high-crime areas.

Chapter 4 on family-oriented crime prevention programs points in the same direction. The Maryland team concludes that although some programs show promise, they ask, "Whether these programs, by themselves, can overcome the effects of surrounding a family with a high-crime community is unclear."[7] A similar conclusion is reached in Chapter 5 with regard to school-focused crime prevention programs. Some programs show promise of effectiveness, but "too many schools are overwhelmed by a criminogenic community context."[8] Common sense suggests that, as with communities, crime prevention programs are most likely to succeed with families and schools that are already basically stable and healthy. But the same interventions are much less likely to succeed in contexts that are swamped by crime and its related problems.

Chapter 6 on labor markets provides a context for the conclusions in other chapters and, at the same time, reveals the major weakness of the entire report. The authors argue that "of all the dimensions of neighborhood life, this one [jobs, work] may have the most pervasive influence on crime."[9] This is hardly startling news. You do not need to be a criminologist to understand that having work and prospects for the future (as opposed to having neither) makes all the difference in your life and the life of your neighborhood. It is the lack of work, in the sense of the pervasive lack of employment opportunities (including jobs with prospects for advancements, not just dead-end jobs at the local fast-food restaurant), that defines our high-crime neighborhoods. Sociologist William Julius Wilson develops this argument in his recent book, *When Work Disappears*.[10]

Moreover, it is this lack of work that defines the "structural conditions" that limit the impact of the few successful community, family, and school-oriented programs that the report reviews. We will return to this important point shortly.

With respect to places, in the sense of specific locales, the report finds that it has been possible to reduce crime in certain limited locations, most notably airports and transit systems. But the authors are skeptical about our ability to reduce crime in larger geographic areas.[11]

Chapter 9 of *Preventing Crime* covers many of the same criminal justice programs examined in this book (although in a far more comprehensive fashion). It also finds "little evidence that increased incarceration has reduced crime" but is far more optimistic about the effectiveness of corrections-based drug treatment programs, prison-based rehabilitation programs, and the institutionalization of some juvenile offenders.[12]

The report's discussion of policing reveals the fundamental flaw in the overall report. It argues, as we did in Chapter 5, that simply adding more police will accomplish little but that clearly focused crime prevention programs appear to have genuine potential.[13] It does warn that too heavy-handed an approach (in the sense of overly aggressive policing, or abuse of citizens) can backfire, however, by undermining confidence in the police and respect for law.

Citing the evidence of success for some focused police programs, the authors proceed to argue that once such programs achieve a certain "threshold level of public order and safety," other programs oriented toward families, community, schools, and labor markets might become more effective. The problem with this conclusion is that it ignores the clear message of other sections of the report. The authors make policing the linchpin for all other crime prevention efforts. On the one hand, this asks too much of the police. They may be able to accomplish some good things, but it is unreasonable to expect them to save our society—and to save our poorest neighborhoods in particular.

Most important, in placing so much hope in the police, the authors of *Preventing Crime* ignore their earlier conclusions. After reviewing community, family, and school-based crime prevention programs, they repeatedly argue that even the successful programs are overwhelmed by the "structural conditions" of the neighborhoods in which they operate. They are very clear in their conclusion that programs are more likely to work in communities that need them least. It is equally reasonable to conclude what the authors refuse to: that police programs are more likely to be successful in the neighborhoods that need them least (that is, those with relatively less crime). Police crime prevention programs in neighborhoods that need them most are likely to be overwhelmed by the same "underlying structural conditions."

The report's refusal to address seriously these "underlying structural conditions" is clearly evident in the chapter on labor markets. Although the authors argue persuasively that work is the most important single factor regarding crime, they refuse to discuss policies designed to increase the availability of work. They cover various programs designed to fix people up to get jobs but not job creation programs.

There is a reason for this failure. To address the larger question of economic opportunity is to move the discussion of crime prevention out of the realm of criminal justice and into the world of social and economic policy. It would also point in the direction of some radical alternatives to current economic policy. The authors of *Preventing Crime* choose to focus on more limited issues.

But what if their conclusions in the sections on communities, families, and schools are right? What if the key to crime prevention really is the "underlying structural conditions"? What if William Julius Wilson is right in his closely related analysis that programs designed to help people and neighborhoods are doomed to fail "when work disappears"?

CONCLUSION

The purpose of this book has been to identify sensible policies to reduce serious crime. We found that most current crime policies and proposed alternatives are not effective. We found that both conservatives and liberals are guilty of peddling nonsense with respect to crime policy. This does not mean that we cannot do anything at all about crime. The implicit message of *Preventing Crime* seems to be that the real solution to the crime problem lies outside the criminal justice system. If that is true, the task undertaken in this book has not been worthless.

Experts in criminal justice have a professional obligation to search for the truth and to speak the truth, even though most people would prefer not to hear it. The truth about crime policy seems to be that most criminal justice–related policies will not make any significant reduction in crime. If we have helped discover that truth in this book, we have fulfilled our professional responsibilities.

NOTES

1. James Alan Fox, *Trends in Juvenile Violence* (Washington, D.C.: Government Printing Office, 1996).

2. George Kelling and Catherine M. Coles, *Fixing Broken Windows* (New York: Kessler, 1996).

3. Franklin E. Zimring and Gordon Hawkins, *Incapacitation: Penal Confinement and the Restraint of Crime* (New York: Oxford University Press, 1995).

4. Samuel Walker, *Popular Justice: A History of American Criminal Justice*, 2d ed. (New York: Oxford University Press, 1998).

5. Lawrence W. Sherman, Denise Gottfredson, Doris MacKenzie, John Eck, Peter Reuter, and Shawn Bushaway, *Preventing Crime: What Works, What Doesn't, What's Promising: A Report to the United States Congress* (1997). As this book was being written, the report was available through the World Wide Web at www.ncjrs.org. By the time you read this, other published versions may be available. Also, because of the problems associated with downloading and printing, the page references cited here may be different than other available copies.

6. Ibid., pp. 3–10.

7. Ibid.

8. Ibid., pp. 3–11.

9. Ibid., pp. 3–12.

10. William Julius Wilson, *When Work Disappears* (New York: Knopf, 1996).

11. Sherman et al., *Preventing Crime*, pp. 3–13.

12. Ibid., pp. 3–15.

13. Ibid., pp. 3–14.

Index